Poetry and Myth in Ancient Pastoral

PRINCETON SERIES OF COLLECTED ESSAYS

This series was initiated in response to requests from students and teachers who want the best essays of leading scholars available in a convenient format. Each book in this series serves scholarship by gathering in one place previously published articles representing the valuable contribution of a noted authority to his field. The format allows for the addition of a preface or introduction and an index to enhance the collection's usefulness. Photoreproduction of the essays keeps costs to a minimum and thus makes possible publication in a relatively inexpensive form.

POETRY AND MYTH
IN ANCIENT PASTORAL

Essays on Theocritus and Virgil

BY

CHARLES SEGAL

Princeton University Press
Princeton, New Jersey

To Michael Putnam
and
To the memory of Cedric Whitman
(*Maenalus et gelidi fleuerunt saxa Lycaei*)

Contents

Acknowledgments

Except for the Introduction, all of the essays in this volume have been previously published.

I wish to thank the following editors, journals, and publishers for gracious permission to reprint these essays:

1. " 'Since Daphnis Dies': The Meaning of Theocritus' First *Idyll*," *Museum Helveticum* 31 (1974), 1-22. Reprinted by permission of *Museum Helveticum*.

2. "Death by Water: A Narrative Pattern in Theocritus (*Idylls* 1, 13, 22, 23)," *Hermes* 102 (1974), 20-38. Reprinted by permission of *Hermes* and Franz Steiner Verlag, GMBH.

3. "Adonis and Aphrodite: Theocritus, *Idyll* 3.48," *L'Antiquité classique* 37 (1969), 82-88. Reprinted by permission of *L'Antiquité classique*.

4. "Simaetha and the Iynx (Theocritus, *Idyll* 2)," *Quaderni Urbinati di Cultura Classica* 15 (1973), 32-43. Reprinted by permission of *Quaderni Urbinati di Cultura Classica*.

5. "Theocritean Criticism and the Interpretation of the Fourth *Idyll*," *Ramus* 1 (1972), 1-25. Reprinted by permission of *Ramus*.

6. "Theocritus' Seventh *Idyll* and Lycidas," *Wiener Studien*, Neue Folge 8 (1974), 20-76. Reprinted by permission of *Wiener Studien* and Hermann Böhlaus Nachf. GMBH, Vienna.

7. "Simichidas' Modesty: Theocritus, *Idyll* 7.44," *American Journal of Philology* 95 (1974), 128-136. Reprinted by permission of the *American Journal of Philology*, and The Johns Hopkins University Press.

8. "Thematic Coherence in Theocritus' Bucolic *Idylls*," *Wiener Studien* N. F. 11 (1977), 35-68. Reprinted by permission of *Wiener Studien* and Hermann Böhlaus Nachf. GMBH, Vienna.

9. "Landscape into Myth: Theocritus' Bucolic Poetry," *Ramus* 4 (1975), 115-139 (*Ancient Pastoral, Ramus Essays on Greek and Roman Pastoral Poetry* [Melbourne, Australia 1975], 33-57). Reprinted by permission of *Ramus*.

10. "Vergil's *Caelatum Opus*: An Interpretation of the Third *Eclogue*," *American Journal of Philology* 88 (1967), 279-308. Reprinted by permission of the *American Journal of Philology*, and The Johns Hopkins University Press.

11. "Pastoral Realism and the Golden Age: Correspondence and Contrast between Virgil's Third and Fourth *Eclogues*" *Philologus* 121 (1977), 158-163. Reprinted by permission of *Philologus* and the Akademie der Wissenschaften der D.D.R., Berlin.

12. "*Tamen Cantabitis, Arcades*: Exile and Arcadia in *Eclogues* 1 and 9," *Arion* 4, no. 2 (1965), 237-266. Reprinted by permission of the Trustees of Boston University from *Arion: A Journal of the Humanities and the Classics*.

13. "Virgil's Sixth *Eclogue* and the Problem of Evil," *Transactions of the Amer-ican Philological Association* 100 (1969), 407-435. Reprinted by permis-sion of *Transactions of the American Philological Association.*
14. "Two Fauns and a Naiad? (Virgil, *Ecl.* 6, 13-26)," *American Journal of Philology* 92 (1971), 56-61. Reprinted by permission of the *American Journal of Philology*, and The Johns Hopkins University Press.
15. "Caves, Pan, and Silenus: Virgil's Sixth *Eclogue* and the Pastoral *Epigrams* of Theocritus," *Živa Antika*, 26 (1976), 53-56. Reprinted by permission of *Živa Antika*.

In addition to specific acknowledgments in separate essays, I would like to thank my colleague at Brown University, Professor Michael C.J. Putnam, for years of warm friendship and sharing of ideas on Virgil and other poets. To him and to the memory of a teacher and friend dear to us both I dedicate this book in affection and gratitude.

I also thank the staff of Princeton University Press for their courtesy, efficiency, and encouragement in producing this volume. Brown University generously helped with the preparation of the index, which was compiled by Craig Manning. One happy result of turning back to Theocritus and Virgil and reflecting on work previously written about them is the realization of how much more there remains always to say. I hope that making these essays more widely available may help to continue the dialogue among readers of these beautiful and inexhaustible poems.

Providence, Rhode Island
January 1981

Abbreviations

AC, Ant. Class.	*L'Antiquité Classique*
AJP	*American Journal of Philology*
Anth. Pal., A.P.	*Anthologia Palatina, Palatine Anthology*
C & M	*Classica et Mediaevalia*
CJ	*Classical Journal*
CP	*Classical Philology*
CQ	*Classical Quarterly*
CR	*Classical Review*
CW	*Classical Weekly, Classical World*
D	Ernestus Diehl, ed., *Anthologia Lyrica Graeca* (Leipzig, 1925)
DK	Hermann Diels and Walther Kranz, eds., *Fragmente der Vorsokratiker*⁶ (Berlin, 1952)
E	J.M. Edmonds, ed., *The Fragments of Attic Comedy* (Leiden, 1957-61)
FGrHist	Felix Jacoby, ed., *Die Fragmente der griechischen Historiker* (Leiden, 1954ff.)
G & R	*Greece and Rome*
GIF	*Giornale Italiano di Filologia*
GRBS	*Greek, Roman and Byzantine Studies*
HSCP	*Harvard Studies in Classical Philology*
JHS	*Journal of Hellenic Studies*
K	Theodor Kock, ed., *Comicorum Atticorum Fragmenta* (Leipzig, 1880-88)
LEC	*Les Études Classiques*
LP	Edgar Lobel et Denys Page, *Poetarum Lesbiorum Fragmenta* (Oxford, 1955)
LSJ	Liddell-Scott-Jones-McKenzie, eds., *A Greek English Lexicon*⁹ (Oxford, 1940), with Supplement (1968)
MH	*Museum Helveticum*
MLN	*Modern Language Notes*
NGG	*Nachrichten der Gesellschaft der Wissenschaften zu Göttingen, phil.-hist. Klasse*
NJbb	*Neue Jahrbücher für das klassische Altertum*
P, Page	Denys Page, ed., *Poetae Melici Graeci* (Oxford, 1962)
PCPhS	*Proceedings of the Cambridge Philological Society*
PP	*La Parola del Passato*
Quad. Urb., QUCC	*Quaderni Urbinati di Cultura Classica*
RE, R.-E.	Pauly-Wissowa-Kroll, eds., *Realencyclopädie der classischen Altertumswissenschaft* (Stuttgart, 1894ff.)
REA	*Revue des Études Anciennes*

REG	*Revue des Études Grecques*
RFIC	*Rivista di Filologia e di Istruzione Classica*
RhM	*Rheinisches Museum für Philologie*
RPh, Rev. Phil.	*Revue de Philologie*
SB Leipzig	*Bericht über die Verhandlungen der Sächsische Akademie der Wissenschaften zu Leipzig*, phil.-hist. Klasse
SIFC	*Studi Italiani di Filologia Classica*
TAPA	*Transactions and Proceedings of the American Philological Association*
UCPCP	*University of California Publications in Classical Philology*
WS	*Wiener Studien*
YCS	*Yale Classical Studies*

Poetry and Myth in Ancient Pastoral

"Hast any philosophy in thee, Shepherd?"
SHAKESPEARE, *As You Like It*

INTRODUCTION

Poets and Goatherds, Forests and Consuls: Art, Imagination, and Realism in Ancient Pastoral Poetry

I

DESPITE MULTIPLE PERMUTATIONS AND VARIATIONS, pastoral poetry has proven remarkably durable and consistent in its long journey from ancient Greece and Rome to the culture of modern Europe and America. The bucolic poetry of Tasso, Milton, or even Mallarmé is far closer to its classical models than is, say, Shakespearean tragedy to Sophocles or the nineteenth-century novel to Apuleius or Heliodorus. In pastoral, perhaps more than in any other literary genre, the modern reader is impelled back to the ancient originals and is immeasurably helped by comparison with the ancient writers.[1]

The reason for pastoral's fidelity to origins is probably to be sought in the form itself rather than in historical accidents like Boileau's exhortation to "follow Theocritus and Virgil," "Que leurs tendres écrits, par les Grâces dictés, / Ne quittent point vos mains, jour et nuit feuilletés." As critics from Empson to Poggioli have suggested, pastoral is itself a distillation of the process of poetic creation. The emotions of friendship, loss and death, the intense reaction to beauty joined with innocence and purity, the atmosphere of freedom and leisure to convey such feelings amid peace, calm, and receptive companionship all lie at the heart of pastoral and at the same time are also basic to the creation of poetry.

Part of the delight that pastoral gives is its evocation of the entirety of its tradition in a kind of timeless present. This may be a result of pastoral's tendency to exclude the temporal dimension or its late development as a highly conventional self-conscious literary form. Its

---

[1] This point is admirably made by Thomas G. Rosenmeyer, *The Green Cabinet* (Berkeley and Los Angeles, 1969). In this Introduction I shall not generally repeat documentation and bibliography to be found in the footnotes of the essays below, nor will I attempt a complete bibliographical survey of work done on ancient pastoral in the last fifteen years. For the *Eclogues* see the excellent survey by A. G. McKay, "Recent Work on Vergil (1964-1973)," *CW* 68 (1974-75), 10-19, his regular review of Virgilian scholarship in *Vergilius*, and Viktor Pöschl's recent survey in *Anzeiger für die Altertumswissenschaft* 32 (1979), 1-20. The commentary of Robert Coleman, *Vergil, Eclogues* (Cambridge, 1977) also contains a useful introduction and bibliography.

conventional nature also allows it to absorb a wide range of previous literary works and blurs the distinction between creation and imitation. As a form of original creation, pastoral underlines the fact that all literature exists with reference to other works of literature and not as an unmediated representation of "reality." For the same reasons pastoral particularly needs to be placed in its poetic tradition. Indeed, it demands that the reader locate it at once within that tradition. What Northrop Frye says of Milton's *Lycidas* is equally true of Theocritus' *Idylls* and Virgil's *Eclogues*:

> An avowedly conventional poem like *Lycidas* urgently demands the kind of criticism that will absorb it into the study of literature as a whole, and this activity is expected to begin at once, with the first cultivated reader. Here we have a situation more like that of mathematics or science, where the work of genius is assimilated to the whole subject so quickly that one hardly notices the difference between creative and critical activity.[2]

The difficulty of reading such poems and the reward of such readings lie in their vision of an almost tangible world of art where all poetry, regardless of language, period, or style, is one. The homogeneity of the pastoral landscape and the generality of the pastoral characters, whether in Theocritus or Milton, in Tasso or Pope, contribute to this sense of the simultaneous and visible coexistence of all the parts of the tradition, the latest developments with the first beginnings.

Pastoral's obvious artificiality and artifice make explicit the frame that every work of art draws around experience. The peaceful garden and songful forest can serve as an emblem for the privileged removal of art—equally in suspension from "reality" and therefore equally ambiguous—where emotion may be recollected, relived, or vicariously experienced in an artificial tranquillity. The transference of these experiences from actuality to imagination is accomplished openly and visibly in the pastoral form, with its clarity of conventions, its more or less sharply crystallized code of language, symbols, and behavior, the particularity of its strongly delineated and delimited world and characters.

The realistic side of pastoral, its concern with the daily, prosaic events of country life ("idyll," after all, means "little picture"), only sets off the power of art that transforms and transfigures the daily round. Enframed and irradiated by the poetic form, the herdsman's toil, the diurnal and seasonal rhythms of nature, the pungent, concrete details of the rustic world acquire a new freshness and beauty. The

[2] Northrop Frye, *Anatomy of Criticism* (Princeton, 1957), p. 100.

ordinary life of the everyday is touched with the luminous aura of myth. The mysterious entrance of Lycidas into the agrarian regularity of *Idyll* 7 is perhaps the clearest instance of pastoral's tension between the ordinary and the poetic, reality and imagination (see essay no. 6, infra). But that tension and the vibrations it evokes resonate throughout the "pastoral" tradition of Western culture. A 1907 painting entitled *Polyphemus* by Maurice Denis (in the Pushkin Museum, Moscow) shows the mythical protagonist of *Idylls* 6 and 11 in his Theocritean role, piping to a remote Galatea who swims inaccessibly out among the waves. Seated on a rock, his back toward us, facing the sea, Polyphemus could be just an ordinary bearded amateur of the flute taking a holiday by the ocean. His Galatea is obscure in the distant water, while human bathers, in the familiar gestures and attitudes of the seashore, recline or walk past. We cannot be sure whether "Polyphemus" and "Galatea" are human or mythical. The entire scene, harking back forcefully to the Sixth and Eleventh *Idylls* (6.6-9, 11.13-18), utilizes a characteristic pastoral blurring of real and imaginary. This modern version of pastoral enacts the magic of the artistic or poetic vision, its power to reveal to us the rare, elusive beauty that may lie just the other side of prosaic routine. It makes transparent the veil between the two. Conversely, it also calls attention to the ordinariness of the raw material of daily life or reality that, by the intervention of the framing device of picture or poem, suddenly, perhaps arbitrarily, becomes the privileged realm of art.

In pastoral the thematic variations are relatively few, the range of metaphor and trope limited, the possibilities of experience reduced from infinity to manageable finitude.[3] This is the ground on which the young poet can learn the difficult art of "putting the complex into the simple" (Empson) or the mature poet can reflect on the poetic processes of selection, limitation, and condensation. As Poggioli puts it, "The famous advice that Boileau once gave to Racine: 'Faire difficilement des vers faciles,' seems to apply better to the pastoral than to any other literary form."[4] Thus poets from Theocritus to Mallarmé have used the pastoral as the field for exploring the essence of poetry. For the same reasons perhaps poets tend not to remain in the pastoral oases they have created. Virgil, Milton, and Tasso went on to write martial epic, Pope mock-epic. Whether or not Theocritus wrote pastorals evenly throughout his life, they are not the sole product of his Muse: he also wrote mimes, epyllia, love poems, and epigrams.

[3] See Rosenmeyer, *The Green Cabinet*, chaps. 3 and 12.

[4] Renato Poggioli, "The Poetics of the Pastoral," in *The Oaten Flute: Essays on Pastoral Poetry and the Pastoral Ideal* (Cambridge, Mass., 1975), p. 157.

The pastoral experience tends to be "a temporary retirement to the periphery of life."[5] For this reason too it develops only relatively late in ancient Greece, where literature is intimately linked to social life and poetry expresses the values and ideals of a culture that gave a privileged place to strenuous civic participation in politics, war, athletics, and art as a communal form. Pastoral poetry develops only as the cultivation of art and of the self apart from the community becomes an important end, only as friendship and the realm of the private (combined in Epicurus' garden) become ideals valued for their own sake, apart from duty, notions of virtue (*aretē*), social cohesion, politics, or war. Although "pastoral" elements occur in Greek literature from Homer and Hesiod through Euripides, Aristophanes, and Plato, the peculiar combination of attitudes, concerns, and poetic expression that results in a bucolic genre separate from other literary forms occurs only in the Hellenistic period and, so far as we can tell, first in Theocritus. But the story of its development need not be repeated here.

Pastoral not only stands in tension with the activist, communal values of classical Greek literature but also arises in tension with the social, economic, and even literary values of the dominant urban culture that saw its birth. The poet's real or imagined abandonment of the city for the song-filled glades of the forest or the still slopes of the mountains signifies more than taking a vacation or having a picnic. Yet that civic realm is always there as the implied opposite pole of the bucolic experience. This most easeful of literary forms paradoxically has tension and antithesis as an inherent part of its mental world.

Pastoral's deliberate simplification of life, therefore, is far from simple. It expresses the paradox inherent in all art, that an imaginative and imaginary distancing from reality is simultaneously a means of intensifying and clarifying reality. The various forms of this paradox are a recurrent subject of the essays in this volume. They reflect the tendency of recent criticism to reject the view of pastoral as a nostalgic dream of indolence. I should agree with Alpers' recent statement that pastoral is "a way of facing reality, and not . . . a 'dream' or a 'trance' which historical reality disrupts."[6] Interpreters have gradually moved from emphasis on the mimetic realism of a genre whose principal trait is simplicity to acknowledging the complexity of works informed

---

[5] Ibid., "The Oaten Flute," p. 11.

[6] Paul Alpers, *The Singer of the Eclogues: A Study of Virgilian Pastoral* (Berkeley and Los Angeles, 1979), p. 143. Alpers would probably agree with the Elizabethan view of the seriousness of pastoral poetry in its concern with "the problem of the values inherent in the good life": see Hallett Smith, *Elizabethan Poetry* (1952; repr. Ann Arbor, 1968), pp. viii and 41-43.

by the subtleties of late Hellenistic poetics. In ancient pastoral both sides exist. The resultant tension between the simple and the complex, between nature and artifice, is an essential part of the meaning of these works and should not be prematurely resolved on one side or the other.

In antiquity, at least, pastoral developed at moments of political and social crisis. Is it coincidental that the remarkable efflorescence of studies of the *Eclogues* and the strongest new directions in approaches to ancient pastoral in the United States came when we were involved in a costly, unpopular, and divisive war?

Over the last ten or fifteen years American interpreters of pastoral have been more attuned to its subsurface tensions than to its quietism, to the pulls between reality and imagination in Theocritus (Lawall) and between art and life, individual and society, interiority and community in the *Eclogues* (Putnam); to the disruptiveness rather than the levity of pastoral loves (Otis, Leach); to the complexities rather than the simplicities of the form (Van Sickle). To this view the interpretations I present here subscribe, for the most part, but not without recognizing the lighter side also.

If nothing else, the criticism of the past fifteen years should make clear that concentration on the historical circumstances and literary sources, followed by a polite nod to the adept versification and pretty sounds, will not do. Such an approach, the dominant one in classical studies in this area until the mid-sixties, does not get us even remotely near the center of these poems.

As the title of this Introduction implies, both Theocritus and Virgil exploit discrepancies between widely different places, occupations, social levels. Theocritus brings the elevated style of Homer, Hesiod, and Pindar into rustic talk of nannies and billy-goats, staves, rennet, different kinds of grasses and thorns. To these contrasts Virgil adds those between poetry and history, song and politics, shepherds and soldiers, sylvan tamarisks and Roman generals. It is curious that so complex and difficult an art of conjoining dissimilars should ever have been regarded as primarily realistic in its aims and simple (or simplifying) in its spirit. The consummate poetic skill that creates a seamless elegance of surface distracts us from noticing the imaginative leaps across very distant realms. When one thinks of the ways in which both Theocritus and Virgil incorporate pieces of earlier poets, parts of other literary traditions, songs of varied poetic personae, one is tempted to apply Lévi-Strauss's notion of *bricolage*. These poets of melodious surface flow are also bold collagists of heterogeneous fragments.

The ancient critics classified bucolic as a subspecies of epic, partly

because it uses the dactylic hexameter, partly because its existence
depends on implicit or overt play with the grandeur of heroic epic
and the communal values of martial epic.[7] Centuries of literary tra-
dition have given "bucolic" and "pastoral" a certain respectability and
dignity. But *boukolos* in Greek and *pastor* in Latin denote the lowly
figure of the herdsman, smelly, uneducated, often a slave, the fit
companion of the beasts with whom he spends most of his time.
Bucolic poems have an aristocratic, elitist air; but "bucolic" to a con-
temporary of Theocritus was more likely to evoke the rude toil of
slave labor than graceful hexameters: we may compare Plato's passing
reference to a "cowherd-slave," *boukolos doulos* (*Ion* 540c). Both Theoc-
ritus and Virgil are explicit about the servile status of some of their
characters (e.g., *Id.* 5.5-10; *Ecl.* 1.27-32).[8] Far from the city, the *boukolos*
(or *pastor*) is deprived of the amenities, to say nothing of the graces,
of urban life. Hence the discrepancy between the noble associations
of the verse-form and the humble rusticity of the characters is far
sharper for the ancient audience than we often realize.

When Theocritus in the Seventh *Idyll* gives the malodorous Lycidas
the attributes of Homeric divinity and the Hesiodic Muses' gift of
hauntingly beautiful song, he is himself developing a pastoral myth
of origins. He places us imaginatively *in illo tempore*, in a fabled time
of remote beginnings (in Mircea Eliade's sense), where the contra-
dictions of epic and bucolic, lofty inspiration and humble country toil,
god and goatherd, mythical lyricism and realistic vignette are brought
into a creative fusion that perhaps mirrors the beginnings of the genre
itself. This poem can be viewed as a brilliant mythic recreation of the
origins of pastoral, a symbolic reconstitution of the opposites that
intersect at its beginnings, as well as an accomplished exemplar of its
perfections.

The self-conscious juxtaposition of the grand themes of the mythic
tradition with the lowly life of herdsmen is one of the dominant
features of these poems and a recurrent concern in the essays below.
How does a Hellenistic poet use older mythical patterns? Does any-
thing of the vitality and richness of myth in archaic and classical Greek
poetry survive in this "artificial" medium of a more quietistic, inward-
looking time? And, if so, what form does mythical representation take
in a post-mythic age, an age marked by ironical self-awareness, a

[7] See John Van Sickle, "Epic and Bucolic," *QUCC* 19 (1975), 3-30, and "Theocritus
and the Development of the Conception of the Bucolic Genre," *Ramus* 5 (1976), 19.

[8] On *boukolos* and derivatives see now K. J. Dover, *Theocritus, Select Poems* (Basingstoke
and London, 1971), pp. liv-lv; on the servile status of Tityrus in *Ecl.* 1 see Eleanor
Winsor Leach, *Vergil's Eclogues: Landscapes of Experience* (Ithaca, N.Y., 1974), pp. 119-
23.

playful belief in art for art's sake, and scholar-poets whose erudition insulates them against the "naive" beliefs and assumptions of the audiences of Homer or Sophocles? These are some of the questions that the Theocritean studies in the first part of this collection address.

When the young Virgil was trying out his wings as the first Latin pastoral poet, Theocritus and subsequent imitators like Bion and Moschus were already part of a crystallized literary tradition more than two centuries old. Literary artifice and artificiality in essaying this genre are therefore far more marked for the Latin poet than for the Greek. The fact that Theocritus is already "tradition" for Virgil makes the polarities of Virgil's pastoral poetry quite different from those in Theocritus.

Virgil allows a far sharper contrast between poetry and contemporary events. Theocritus' bucolic is truly at the periphery of political and even communal life. Even if Theocritus wrote some of his bucolic *Idylls* in the Ptolemaic capital of Alexandria, little of that city's life or concerns finds its way into these works (for those subjects Theocritus used the urban realism of a mime like *Id.* 15). The few allusions to political events in Theocritean pastoral are so unobtrusively woven into the fabric of these works that we are hardly certain that they are there at all. *Idyll* 7 *may* contain a passing reference to Ptolemy Philadelphus; *Idyll* 4 *may* hint at recent wars in southern Italy.[9] In both cases the allusions are so veiled and so fully integrated into the poetic frame that their very existence is controversial. With centuries of a well-developed poetic tradition behind him, Theocritus can assume a coherent art-world of song, poetry, and literary concerns; this autonomous realm of poetry need only refer to itself. Virgil must create the art-world of his *Eclogues*, and it is far more precarious.

No Roman poet of the late Republic could escape the impact of the political events shaking and transforming the Mediterranean. Politics are no longer at the periphery but at the very center of these works. The mythical world that Theocritus' literary antecedents had shaped over centuries—Homer and Hesiod, monodic and choral lyric, tragedy—however much it had been assimilated by the Roman intelligentsia, belonged to an alien culture. Theocritus' pastoral could keep history at arm's length; Virgil's could not. The dynamics of Virgilian pastoral, then, rest not so much on a contrast of fantasy and reality in the private realms of love and art as on the question of art's very existence in a turbulent and violent world. This juxtaposition of poetry and war is sharpest in *Eclogues* 1 and 9, but it informs all of the *Eclogues* and is responsible, in part, for their poignant balance between lyricism

[9] For Ptolemy see below, no. 7, note 24; for *Id.* 4 see A. Barigazzi, *RFIC* 102 (1974), 310-11.

and sadness, creation and loss, sensitive responsiveness to nature's beauty and a tragic sense of the human condition.

II

The Virgilian portion of this volume views the *Eclogues*, then, as serious poems about war and art, passion and civilization, the relation of poetry to history, irrational violence, and the problem of order and disorder in human life. The books of Putnam, Leach, and now Alpers, all published later than the longer essays on the *Eclogues*, have added important arguments for this view. Brooks Otis' brief treatment of the *Eclogues* in his *Virgil: A Study of Civilized Poetry* (1964) made an important step toward this serious view of the poems. It helped counter Bruno Snell's influential interpretation of Virgil's pastoral world as a dreamy inward realm of wish-fulfillment and fantasy, a wholly "spiritual landscape" of imagined settings and unreal rustics in contrast to the hard-edged lucidity and earthy realism of Theocritus.[10] But Otis' own exaggeration of the positive side of the Eclogue-Book as a gradual movement from violence to a proto-Augustan order led him to understate the darker tones and more pessimistic moods of the work.[11] Still, in stressing the sharpness of the clash between lyricism and historical reality and in emphasizing Virgil's break with neoteric poetry in a development that led organically toward the *Georgics* and the *Aeneid* (here following the direction of Klingner), Otis made an important and influential contribution. The work of the past fifteen years has now given us a better perspective for discerning the balance between the optimistic and the somber sides of these poems and a fuller awareness of their concern with art and poetics alongside war, love, violence, and disorder.

Advances in our understanding of Theocritus' bucolic *Idylls* have necessarily also brought changes in our view of Virgil. The simplistic contrast of a realistic Theocritus with a symbolical Virgil implicit in Snell's view has long needed refinement on both sides. Several of the papers reprinted below attempt such a reexamination (see nos. 5, 9, 10, 12). Viewed within his own literary tradition rather than retrospectively as a source for the *Eclogues*, Theocritus is in many ways as symbolic as Virgil. Conversely, when viewed against the contemporary

[10] This view is still represented in Gordon Williams, *Tradition and Originality in Latin Poetry* (Oxford, 1968), pp. 306ff. See the critical survey in Leach, *Vergil's Eclogues*, pp. 20-21.

[11] For the limitations of Otis' view see C. P. Segal, "The Achievement of Virgil," *Arion* 4 (1965), 131-33; John Van Sickle, *The Design of Virgil's Bucolics* (Rome, 1978), pp. 30-35.

background of social, political, and moral disruption incorporated into the bucolic frame, Virgil appears as far more realistic than Theocritus.[12] The terms are too vague to be other than dangerously misleading. As the studies of *Idylls* 1, 4, and 7 below suggest, Virgil's concern with a poetics of pastoral and his technique of symbolic integration owe a great deal to Theocritus. The two poets profit from being read as parallel rather than in contrast to one another.

In *Idylls* 1 and 7 particularly, Theocritus reflects on the process by which his art creates its own privileged locus of peace, leisure, and beauty. He too goes back to the primordial beginnings of pastoral song in the stories of Daphnis and Comatas in *Idylls* 1 and 7. Virgil's myth of origins, however, bursts the bounds of the pastoral frame. The cosmic regeneration in the Fourth *Eclogue* is a version of the familiar myth of the divine child whose new life and innocence bring hope and joy back to a fallen age and a despairing race of men. For all of its heavy reliance on mythical patterns, Theocritus' bucolic has nothing of this scope. Here, as to some extent also in *Eclogues* 5 and 6, Virgil was able to combine the pastoral impulse toward the stillness and simplicity in which we can hear the music of nature with a cosmic return to childhood innocence and vitality. Virgil's genius for the imaginative synthesis of many traditions is perhaps most distinctive in *Eclogue* 4, where he goes back before Theocritus to Hesiod, while using the still recent Latin poetry of Catullus. Here as throughout the *Eclogues* Virgilian pastoral makes the most of its position between two cultures and two languages. This fact may have something to do with the cosmopolitan air of the *Eclogues* (in contrast to the far greater localism of the *Idylls*) and their resultant central position in the European literary tradition that Theocritus never enjoyed.

III

Pastoral poetry runs the risk of verging too close to the sentimental on the one hand and the artificial on the other. If it fails it may become, as Samuel Johnson complained, "easy, vulgar, and therefore disgusting." If it succeeds it offers a lyrical reflection on our need for hope, fantasy, imagination, the belief in innocence, purity, and the restorative power of art that exist, if at all in our self-conscious and skeptical age, only in the most sheltered part of our lives, protected if not buried by a firm carapace of irony.

Though full of feeling and sentiment, Theocritus and Virgil are

[12] See, for example, Brooks Otis, *Virgil: A Study in Civilized Poetry* (Oxford, 1963), p. 135; Segal, "The Achievement of Virgil," 133. For the problem of "realism" and "idealism" in discussions of Theocritus and Virgil see also Leach, *Vergil's Eclogues*, pp. 71ff.

rarely sentimental. This is not only because of the ironical distancing of love by humor and of innocence by self-conscious literary artifice and convention but also because of the demanding rigor of the form, the high level of assimilated learning, and the background of a mythical tradition that gives personal experience and subjective feeling the toughness of a larger, impersonal point of view. As I try to show in the study of *Idyll* 3, for example (no. 3 below), the archetypal myths of death and renewal place the amorous speaker's concerns in a perspective that both enlarges and gently parodies them. The nymph-inhabited seascapes of *Idylls* 6, 7, and 11 perform a similar function: they open onto a suggestive realm of imaginative experience, but also distance that experience through literary echoes. Virgil gains similar effects through his echoes of Theocritean lovers in *Eclogues* 8 and 10. What Greek myth does for Theocritus, Theocritean poetry itself does for Virgil. Behind the pathos of both poets' dying shepherd-lovers or herdsmen-singers, as Berg suggests, may lie the religious and emotional seriousness of an age-old Mediterranean theme, the death and resurrection of a shepherd-king and poet whose sufferings reflect and implicate the entire natural order.[13] The evidence for a ritual origin of pastoral is not strong; but both poets may be nonetheless utilizing the mythical overtones of these stories to create their own myth of pastoral song. In this myth song (poetry, art) has the regenerative power to recapture a lost sympathy between man and nature, a lost harmony between intellect and feeling, a paradisal garden where the tree of life stands and love and innocence can coexist.[14]

In both Theocritus and Virgil irony and humor hold a fine balance between seriousness and levity, the great and the small; but the irony is never corrosive. It generally has the spirit of play, which, as Huizinga and others have shown, is among the most serious functions of human civilization. These works are not mere melodious musings on empty trifles but a form that holds the essence of poetry, irreducible to conceptual formulation or abstract logic, inseparable from the rhythms, sounds, images, and sensuous texture of the verse itself. The underlying pastoral *mythos*—a return to origins, to childhood, to simplicity, and to clarity of feeling—is fully exemplified in the pastoral style and

[13] William Berg, *Early Virgil* (London, 1974), pp. 12-22. There is perhaps some survival of this sacred dimension of the pastoral in Elizabethan pastoralists' use of the biblical story of Cain and Abel and of Christ as the Good Shepherd: see Hallett Smith, *Elizabethan Poetry*, p. 3, which cites Michael Drayton's "To the Reader of his Pastorals," "In the Angels Song to Shepheards at our Saviours Nativitie Pastorall Poesie seemes consecrated."

[14] Frye, *Anatomy of Criticism*, pp. 152-53. See also Leach, *Vergil's Eclogues*, pp. 31-32, 35, and chap. 2 passim on the themes of the Golden Age in Republican and Augustan literature and art.

gives these poems their multilayered relevance for art, the social order, love, friendship and community, man's relation to nature and his environment. Interpreters tend to choose one of these areas as the base of their critical analysis; but it is important to recognize (as I tried to do in my study of *Idyll* 4, no. 5) that all the levels are present simultaneously and each implies the others. The very artificiality and conventionality of the pastoral form, the generality of the setting, the lack of highly specific characterization of the actors allow for and even promote the multivalent reference.

Anglo-American classicists have been rather slow to develop a criticism sympathetic and adequate to these delicate and polysemous works. To Lawall belongs the credit for the first book-length attempt in English to study the tension between imagination and reality that lies at the heart of Theocritean pastoral. Although a few German and Swiss scholars had approached the *Idylls* (and particularly *Idyll* 7) in such terms in the fifties and sixties, especially Kühn, Ott, and Puelma, the fields of Theocritean criticism a dozen years ago looked uninvitingly bare. Even now they are not exactly flourishing, but the situation is far better. Rosenmeyer's *Green Cabinet* has brought some much-needed definition of the genre and clarification of the modes and limits of Theocritean poetry, although his insistence on the realism, clarity, and simplicity of the genre needs to be balanced by a fuller appreciation of artistic complexity and mythic and symbolic patterns. Anna Rist's new translation has intelligent and sensitive introductions that incorporate some of the recent views of the poems. Walker's introductory volume *Theocritus* (in the Twayne Series) has an excellent brief discussion of the pastoral *Idylls*, stressing the importance of love and art in "creative sublimation," the power of myth and poetry, and the unity of conception throughout the bucolic corpus.[15] In his new book on the *Eclogues* Alpers is able to incorporate a fuller appreciation of Theocritean poetics into his study of Virgil, and it is gratifying to observe that some of the studies reprinted here have helped in that direction.[16]

The *Eclogues* have fared better than the *Idylls* in recent criticism partly because they have always held a more conspicuous place in the mainstream of European literature. Even in Virgilian scholarship it is a sobering thought that whereas the last decade has seen at least five major books on the *Eclogues* by American scholars, H. J. Rose's *The Eclogues of Virgil* (1942) held the field for the preceding quarter-century.

[15] Anna Rist, *The Poems of Theocritus* (Chapel Hill, N.C., 1978) and see my review in *Toronto University Quarterly* 48 (1979), 394-97; Steven Walker, *Theocritus* (Boston, 1980), especially chap. 2.

[16] E.g., Alpers, *The Singer of the Eclogues*, pp. 206-207, 210, 214.

The striking increase in both the quality and quantity of interpretive studies of ancient pastoral is nothing less than revolutionary.[17] The New Criticism of the fifties provided classicists with the tools and the impulse to reexamine these complex works as literature rather than as historical or biographical documents. Putnam's full-scale literary commentary on the *Eclogues* brings these techniques to bear on the thematic issues of poetry, freedom, and the individual. The increasing appreciation of literary convention and greater sophistication in dealing with imitation, irony, ambiguity, allusiveness, and verbal echoes have also been important. The search for limited political allegories has gradually given way to a recognition of multidimensional symbols. Despite limitations, Snell's essay on Virgil's Arcadia as a "spiritual landscape" and Panofsky's "*Et in Arcadia Ego*," along with Poggioli's "The Oaten Flute," provided a broad cultural perspective and larger horizons against which both Theocritean and Virgilian pastoral might be viewed.[18] The concern with Arcadia as a symbolic realm of art, painfully and precariously created, is one of the valuable contributions of Van Sickle's *The Design of Virgil's Bucolics*, while the affinities of the *Eclogues* with contemporary landscape-painting against the background of the turbulence of the Roman revolution concern Leach in *Vergil's Eclogues: Landscapes of Experience*. Above all, the issue of poetics in both Greek and Roman pastoral, the conditions of and the obstacles to artistic creation, emerge as a major theme of nearly all recent writings on pastoral, the present volume included. Berg's *Early Virgil* stresses the importance of Hellenistic poetics for the *Eclogues*, and Van Sickle has argued for poetry itself as their primary concern.[19] The reaction against the historicist views of interpreters like Franz Skutsch, H. J. Rose, or even Brooks Otis has possibly gone too far in the opposite direction, and we may anticipate an eventual reaction (indeed there are already signs of one in the recent renewal of controversy about the chronology of the *Eclogues*). It is to be hoped, however, that the next wave of pastoral specialists will not lose sight of the questions of literary interpretation raised in the last fifteen years.

IV

The fifteen papers collected in this volume were published between 1965 and 1977. They reflect some of the revaluation of ancient pas-

---

[17] For a useful survey of approaches to the *Eclogues* and the pastoral tradition in the period ca. 1955-1970 see Leach, *Vergil's Eclogues*, pp. 32ff.

[18] Poggioli's essays are now conveniently collected in *The Oaten Flute* (above, note 4).

[19] To these studies of poetics should also be added E. A. Schmidt, *Poetische Reflexion: Vergils Bukolik* (Munich, 1972).

toral during this period and approach the poems through the issues described in the first part of this Introduction. All of them share a concern with the tensions between art and experience, the far and the near, fantasy and reality, or poetry and history. All of them stress the complexity rather than the simplicity of the form, the element of contrast and polarity, the dynamic rather than the static qualities, and the shifting between surface and depth, realistic detail and symbolic overtone. The Theocritean essays emphasize the continuing vitality of archaic mythical patterns. Virgil seems to have appreciated this mythical dimension of Theocritus and was able to utilize it for his wider political concerns, most explicitly in *Eclogues* 4 and 5, while also refashioning the apolitical art-world of Theocritean pastoral into a medium that could contain his harsher polarities of art and violence.

With one or two exceptions, the essays on Virgil are earlier than those on Theocritus. I came to Theocritus, however, not so much via Virgil as through the study of the Greek literary and mythical tradition. This is certainly not the only route, but it is, I believe, the better way. Theocritus explains more in Virgil than Virgil explains in Theocritus. It is harder to get a handle on Theocritus. His smooth, objective-looking exterior, as I suggest below in number 5, offers fewer explicit clues to his intentions. Partly as a result of a long tradition of refined hexameter narrative, his personal voice tends to be absorbed into the voices of his characters. The emotional tonality of Virgilian pastoral—the pathos, wistfulness, grief, or hopefulness—comes across in more intimate relation to the speaking voice of the poet as the aura of feeling emanating from the sensibility of an individual whom we might come to know. As Leach, Van Sickle, and Alpers have recently emphasized, we should not, of course, confuse the voice of Virgil's dramatic characters with the voice of the poet himself.

In Theocritus the emotions are no less intense or involving, but their source in the mental life of the poet is far more concealed. The surface of Theocritus' poems is less penetrable as the expression of an intimate, personal voice. It is more fully controlled by poetic models, mythic patterns, and intellectual design than by the rhythm of feeling. Virgil, of course, lacks neither design nor poetic models, but his poetry follows a more emotional pulse and a discontinuous lyricism that often works in subtle counterpoint to the overt intellectual design. Interpreters have variously defined this emotional tonality of Virgil: "integration" (W.F.J. Knight), "subjective," "empathetic-sympathetic," "psychological" (Otis), "imaginative amalgam of Greek and Roman" (Gordon Williams). It remains one of the most essential and one of the most elusive qualities of Virgil's poetry.

In Theocritus such moments of emotional intensity tend to be

pulled back into the smoothness of the rhetoric and the playful irony
of juxtaposing great and small. In Virgil they break forth into an
independent existence as strong points of feeling that we are allowed
to hold and savor. We may compare Theocritus *Idyll* 4.38-40 with
Virgil, *Eclogue* 2.57-61:

ὦ χαρίεσσ' Ἀμαρυλλί, μόνας σέθεν οὐδὲ θανοίσας
λασεύμεσθ'· ὅσον αἶγες ἐμὶν φίλαι, ὅσσον ἀπέσβης.
αἰαῖ τῶ σκληρῶ μάλα δαίμονος ὅς με λελόγχει.

O graceful Amaryllis, you and only you we will not forget, not even
in your death. As my goats are dear to me, so (dear) were you
extinguished. Alas for the fate (*daimōn*), so very hard, that has fallen
to my lot.

heu heu, quid uolui misero mihi? floribus Austrum
perditus et liquidis immisi fontibus apros.
quem fugis, a! demens? habitarunt di quoque siluas
Dardaniusque Paris.

Alas, what did I wish for myself, miserable? Lost, I let loose the
South Wind upon the flowers, boars upon the clear springs. Whom
are you fleeing, alas, in your madness? The gods too dwelt in for-
ests, and Dardanian Paris.

Theocritus has behind him centuries of reflection on the lot of a "hard
fate" or *daimon* and plays off the rustic situation against the tragic
lament, the herdsman's "love" for nanny-goats against a hopeless love
for a dead girl. The discrepancy of styles keeps the experience dis-
tanced, the emotional tone light, vague, unreal. Virgil's Alexis has no
such restraining frame. Though ironical distance is not absent, it is
contained in the entire situation rather than the specific utterance.
Virgil thus invites us to enter more fully into the localized affect of
the speaker's "I" (*quid uolui misero mihi?*) and allows this flow of feeling
a greater role in organizing the poem and leading us on through it.
For this reason, perhaps, Theocritean bucolic is more amenable to
analysis of underlying narrative structure, Virgilian to the close study
of diction, connotation, mood.

   The first five essays, then, approach Theocritus through narrative
and mythical patterns. *Idyll* 1, I suggest in number 1, should be ap-
proached through the objective, universalizing properties of Greek
myth rather than through a realistic psychology of the characters.
One answer to the thorny problem of the reasons for Daphnis' death,
I suggest, lies in the contrast between the two singer-herdsmen, Thyr-
sis and Daphnis, the one connected with the waters of life, the other
with the waters of death. Daphnis, the mysteries of whose end are not
fully resolved in the *Idyll*, embodies a view of art as attempting to

assert its autonomy, proudly but tragically, against the rhythms of nature's processes of birth, procreation, and death. In Thyrsis, however, art appears as harmonious with nature, celebrating a joyful responsiveness to and fusion with the energies that unite men with all living things. For him the energies of poetic creation are continuous with the life-energies of sexuality, procreation, and growth; for Daphnis art expresses the otherness, the alienation, of human consciousness and feeling from the rest of nature, the separation that exists between the reflective distancing capacity of art and civilization and the uncomplicated fulfillment of instinctual drives.

The engraved cup in the first part of the poem contains these tensions in another form, holding episodes of frustrated love, toil, and symbols of poetic creation in a frame of exuberant natural growth. The contrasts between static description and mythical narration, between gods and rustics, between different views of art and the configuration of love, poetry, nature, and death in a complex unity make this one of the richest of the bucolic *Idylls*. These antitheses recur in other forms in both Theocritus and Virgil, as the papers below on *Idyll* 7 and on Virgil's First, Third, and Ninth *Eclogues* show (nos. 6, 10, 12). In adapting parts of Daphnis' story in *Eclogues* 3, 5, and 10, Virgil evokes these large questions of the relation between art, passion, death, and nature and draws richly upon the meanings that Theocritus had established for this constellation of motifs (see no. 10 below).

The second paper, "Death by Water," extends the analysis of the mythic pattern of *Idyll* 1 to several other poems in the Theocritean corpus. Entrance to a mysterious watery place marks a journey beyond the familiar limits of life and knowledge to a point where life and death cross. Theocritus uses these mythical motifs to bring together the mysteries of love, artistic creativity, and death. One point of this essay is the continuity that runs from the strictly bucolic *Idylls* to the other poems (*Id.* 13 and 22). While the pastoral *Idylls* have a certain coherence as a thematic and stylistic unity, they also have many links with the nonbucolic poems. Hence the inclusion of the urban *Idyll* 2 (no. 4), where the themes of love, the large frame of nature, and the oscillation between self-deception and honesty in emotional life overlap with the concerns of the bucolic poems. The contrast between the vast open heavens and the interior realm of Simaetha's passions at the end of *Idyll* 2, briefly remarked in the last footnote of number 4, is a good example of the difference between the Virgilian "subjective" presentation of emotions and Theocritus' greater reliance on an objective world of myth and of nature. In the bucolic *Idyll* 3, studied in the third essay, these themes form the center of the humorous discrepancy between grandiose myths of nature-divinities and the foolish, deluded rustic speaker.

Essay 5 approaches its detailed study of *Idyll* 4 through a general comparison of Theocritus' bucolic poetry and Virgil's. I am particularly concerned with qualifying the dichotomy between a "realistic" Theocritus and a "symbolist" Virgil. Even this most "realistic" of the bucolic *Idylls* is far from one-dimensional mimetic realism. What makes Theocritus' pastoral fascinating and difficult is the total incorporation of the symbolic levels of meaning into the surface structure. Unlike Virgil, Theocritus never indicates explicitly at what level of seriousness his poems should be read. Lawall's emphasis on sexual energy and Van Sickle's on modes of poetry in their respective interpretations of *Idyll* 4 are not mutually exclusive: the *Idyll* draws implicit parallels between sex, artistic creativity, and harmony with nature in the pastoral cosmos. Thus it contains many of the issues of *Idyll* 1 but condensed and rephrased into an ironic, low-keyed atmosphere of prosaic rusticity rather than projected upon an expansive mythical world of Olympian deities or obviously symbolic emblems (the cup of *Id.* 1).

Idyll 7 has always been recognized as the most important of the pastoral *Idylls* both for its length and its central concern with poetry and pastoral myth. It deservedly receives detailed study in two essays, nos. 6 and 7. Abandoning the notion of a "bucolic masquerade" that conceals a circle of Alexandrian poets, I view *Idyll* 7 in terms of a series of expanding contrasts between its two main characters, Simichidas and Lycidas. Simichidas, like Thyrsis of *Idyll* 1, reflects an art based in the tangible gifts and rhythms of nature; Lycidas is in touch with its mystery and otherness, with the elusiveness of imagination, and the proximity of the human world to the divine through art and love. At another level the farm to which the urban Simichidas is traveling, presided over by its agrarian deity of tamed nature, Demeter, also contrasts with the mountains of Lycidas, connected with the god Pan. Lycidas tells a myth of the origins of pastoral in the story of "divine Comatas," mysteriously kept alive by bees' honey, and the loves of Daphnis, whereas the narrator, Simichidas, alludes to myths of epic heroism full of violence, aggression, and destructiveness (149-153).

The Harvest Festival (*thalysia*) at the end, from which the poem took its ancient title, juxtaposes images of fixity and agrarian settledness with the mythical Odyssean world of mysterious voyages to the unknown. Thus it harks back to the mystery of Lycidas' entrance into Simichidas' urban world. This intersection of city by country, of realistic normality by myth and the supernatural, is itself emblematic of Theocritus' pastoral poetics. The figure of Lycidas is, among other things, the miracle of Theocritus' own infusion of myth and lyricism into the daily life of the countryside in creating the pastoral genre.

He enters the world of Simichidas as the latter is "on the road," suspended between city and the agrarian regularity of the farm. Surrounded by the attributes of Homeric and Hesiodic divinity, Lycidas is himself the elusive mystery of pastoral myth and pastoral poetry entering, casually it would seem, the prosaic surface of the rustic world.

The shorter study of *Idyll* 7, "Simichidas' Modesty" (no. 7), focuses on a different aspect of Theocritus' art, the elegant humor and urbanity of personal relations in an implied community of poets and lovers of poetry—an aspect of pastoral justly emphasized by Rosenmeyer and recently by Alpers. The precision, graceful allusiveness, and cultivated irony of Theocritus' language invite us to read between the lines and reconstruct a genuinely dramatic interchange between the two characters, amusingly human in the depiction of vanity and playful understanding of another's foibles. Theocritus is a master at this art of the brilliant, rapid sketch, quickly giving us the essentials of a fully realized mood and a full human presence.

The Theocritean series closes with the two general essays on the bucolic corpus as a whole. These are also the latest of the Theocritean studies in order of composition. As they imply a detailed knowledge of the individual poems, I place them at this point; but the reader who knows the corpus well could profitably read them as an introduction to the specific interpretations.

In the first of these, no. 8, I argue for the stylistic and thematic unity of the seven bucolic *Idylls* without having recourse to Lawall's notion of a "poetry book." It is, of course, not impossible that Theocritus published the bucolic poems together, but the manuscript evidence provides only very weak support for such a collection in his lifetime.[20] The poems themselves, however, suggest that he was aware of the interrelations within his bucolic corpus. I suggest three levels of the bucolic style: the high mythic seriousness of *Idylls* 1 and 7, which provide the pastoral genre with a myth of origins; the nonmythical rustic "realism" of 4 and 5; and in between the mixture of rusticity and myth in 3, 6, and 11, which use mythical motifs with deliberate and humorous incongruity. This general framework (which is not meant to be stiffened into a Procrustean bed) enables us better to understand the shifting levels of intent within the bucolic works. It also enables us to get closer to Theocritus' technique of poetic invention, particularly his use of variation on a limited number of topics and motifs. Tracing individual themes through a cross section of the

[20] Arguments for a Theocritean pastoral book have again been set forth by Van Sickle, *Ramus* 5.33 with note 81, p. 42 (above, note 7); and the evidence *contra* is briefly surveyed again by Dover, *Theocritus*, pp. xvii-xviii. For a balanced view (favoring an original sequence 1, 3-7, 11) see Walker, *Theocritus*, pp. 78-84.

Idylls (e.g., song, friendship, nature, love, truth, sea, mountains), we can see how their value and meaning change in accordance with the tone or level of style in each *Idyll*.

In essay 9 I return to the issues of realism and imagination touched on in number 5. Developing the preceding essay's notion of a coherent bucolic world set out at different levels of elevation, I try to show how deeply the landscape of the bucolic *Idylls* is imbued with meanings drawn from the mythical tradition. The settings shift from a surface of more-or-less realistic rusticity to an imaginary realm of art and song. I stress again the continuity of Theocritus' poetry with the mythic tradition of earlier Greek literature, the connections between the bucolic and the nonbucolic *Idylls*, and the importance of *Idylls* 1 and 7 for creating the mythical foundation of his poetics of pastoral. This essay probably provides the fullest synthesis of my approach to Theocritus. As it is rather condensed, I recommend reading it after the others and in conjunction with nos. 1, 6, and 8.

V

The Virgilian portion of this volume consists of the three longish pieces on *Eclogues* 3, 1 and 9, and 6 (nos. 10, 12, 13), along with three shorter studies of specific problems. I have already described my general approach to Virgil sufficiently above. These essays stress the moral and poetic seriousness of the *Eclogues*, their imaginative transformation of Theocritus, and the close interrelation among the individual poems in the unified design of the Eclogue-Book.

The study of *Eclogue* 3 (no. 10) shows how Virgil gives Theocritus' cup of *Idyll* 1 a very different symbolic value in his own poetry. Whereas Theocritus had a rich literary and mythical tradition to draw upon (see no. 1 above), Virgil had to create his symbols more or less self-consciously. By blending together a number of different Theocritean contexts ranging from the earthy realism of *Idylls* 4 and 5 to the symbolic artifact of *Idyll* 1, Virgil is not merely showing his dependence on an earlier poet or flaunting his skill at adaptation but revealing his art of creating a new form of poetry that can absorb and metamorphose a wide range of previous elements into a new and original synthesis. This richly diversified poem can provide its own myth of origins for the creation of the pastoral locus in the speech of Palaemon in the center, a technique highly reminiscent of Theocritus; but it can also incorporate Hellenistic learning and contemporary Roman poets and politicians. This essay should be compared with the study of *Idyll* 4 (no. 5) for the different relation between realistic detail and symbolic meaning in the two pastoral poets. In retrospect I would of course be less tentative about the symbolical significance of the cup of *Idyll* 1 (see essay no. 1).

Eclogue 3, among other things, also leads into the grand themes of the three central poems, 4, 5, 6, after the more strictly pastoral beginning of the collection. Essay 10 studies some neglected verbal echoes between *Eclogues* 3 and 4 to show how Virgil deliberately contrasts the lower with the higher reaches of his pastoral song and implicitly stakes out the greater solemnity of his pastoral poetry. Like Theocritus (see nos. 8 and 9 above), he delineates the levels of style in his corpus; and like Theocritus he calls attention to the broad mythical vision that his art can encompass, moving from contentious herdsmen to a myth of cosmic rebirth and renewal. But Virgil's collection has a focus and direction as a poetry book that was lacking in Theocritus. Moving back and forth within his collection through verbal echoes and cross references in a way that Theocritus could not, he not only links poems and suggests progressions and parallelisms but also develops overtones of meaning through the juxtaposition and interrelation of the individual poems.

Essay no. 12, a comparative study of *Eclogues* 1 and 9, focuses on the question of the optimism or pessimism of these poems and lays heavy emphasis on Virgil's transformations of Theocritus in bringing the harsh present realities of war and land-confiscations into his bucolic world. In looking back at work done fifteen years ago I would obviously change a great deal, but the close comparison of so careful and imaginative an imitator as Virgil with his model is always valuable. I would prefer now to lay more emphasis on the continually and subtly shifting balance between "optimism" and "pessimism" rather than choosing one or the other side. I would maintain my emphasis on the unresolved, suspended tone of the end of *Ecl.* 1, but would now lay greater stress on similar suspensions in *Ecl.* 9 as well.[21] I would severely qualify my remarks on "peaceful description" and "sense of rustic continuity" in *Ecl.* 9.9, *ueteres, iam fracta cacumina, fagos* (p. 280), which points back to the song under the beech tree in *Ecl.* 1.1 and to the *densas, umbrosa cacumina, fagos*, of 2.3, probably marking a rather ominous progression within the Eclogue-Book. A greater appreciation of the coherence of the Book would also lead me now to connect 9.60-61, *hic, ubi densas / agricolae stringunt frondes, hic, Moeri, canamus*, more closely with 1.56, *hinc alta sub rupe canet frondator ad auras*, and to stress the continued precariousness and hesitancy of pastoral song in this disrupted setting (see p. 285).[22] (Incidentally on p. 291, line 6, "Moeris'

[21] Along with Alpers, *The Singer of the Eclogues*, pp. 97-103 and M.C.J. Putnam, *Virgil's Pastoral Art: Studies in the Eclogues* (Princeton, 1970), p. 332.

[22] For some of these echoes see now Putnam, *Virgil's Pastoral Art*, p. 316; Alpers, *The Singer of the Eclogues*, p. 137; Van Sickle, *Virgil's Bucolics*, p. 51, note 21.

song of 23-25" contains a typographical error: the reference should
be to lines 27-29.)[23]

The section on the end of *Ecl.* 9 still seems to me adequate to the
mood of uncertainty and unrest in this poem. The discussion of *Ecl.*
10 at the end recognizes the importance of exile from Arcadia, the
painful contrast of exile and song, the isolation of the poet's "love"
for Gallus in an ambiguous setting. Again, I should now lay more
stress on the lack of resolution in the final impression than on the
"hopeful and positive" note, a modification made some years later in
the next paper (no. 13).

Hindsight would also modify a number of points of comparison
between Theocritus and Virgil in *Ecl.* 9. Thanks to no. 6, written
nearly ten years later, I would take a different view of some aspects
of Simichidas' journey and its own peculiar conjunction of myth and
realism. Hence in my remarks on the end of *Id.* 7, p. 286, I should
discriminate more fully between agrarian and pastoral elements.
These form a dynamic antithesis essential for the understanding of
Id. 7, although the general contrast between Theocritus' settled, fertile
farm and the violated natural world and agrarian disruption in *Ecl.*
9 remains valid. My discussion of the silence of winds, sea, and sky,
Ecl. 9.56-58 and Theocr. *Id.* 7.56-60, 2.38-39, and 165-66 (p. 284)
could have made fuller use of the contrast between enclosure and
open, exterior space in both the Second and Seventh *Idylls*. In dis-
cussing the nightfalls of the *Eclogues* here (p. 284), I am sorry that I
did not cite 8.14-16, surely one of the loveliest passages in the collec-
tion:

> frigida uix caelo noctis decesserat umbra,
> cum ros in tenera pecori gratissimus herba:
> incumbens tereti Damon sic coepit oliuae.

> Night's cold shadow had now departed from the sky, the time when
> the dew on the tender grass is most pleasing to the flock. Resting
> on the smooth olive thus Damon began.

These lines too are not mere static ecphrasis, but must be viewed in
their dramatic and ironic relation to other risings and settings of the
sun within the poem (e.g., 8.17-18, 30, 88). In any case the nightfalls
of the *Eclogues* are one of the most significant articulating motifs of
the Book and deserve a full study in their own right.

Number 13, a full-length study of the difficult Sixth *Eclogue*,
achieves perhaps a better balance between the lighter and darker
tones. Within the structure of the Eclogue-Book the regained inno-

---

[23] For the interrelation of the songs of Moeris and Lycidas and a more "pessimistic"
interpretation see Leach, *Vergil's Eclogues*, pp. 205-11.

cence of *Ecl.* 4 contrasts painfully with the pervasive sense of its loss in *Ecl.* 6, a movement at the very center of the collection that is a serious obstacle to the notion of an overall progression from negative to positive. *Eclogue* 6 carries Virgil's tension between poetry and war, art and violence, retrospectively back into the mythical world of Hellenistic poetry. The framing device of Silenus' song creates a suggestive duality between Dionysiac-Orphic energy and Apollonian control, the emotional and the intellectual impulse in poetic creation. Standing between divine, human, and animal, Silenus and his song symbolize, among other things, a view of art as spanning the contrasts between form and feeling in ourselves and our creations. He is an Orphic singer who can hold a balance between earthy passion and the magical control that poetry exercises over the natural world. The dialectic between passion and order, matter and form, pervades the poem, reaching from the Orphic Silenus at the beginning through the vision of Gallus as a poet crowned by both Apolline Muses and rustic Linus and on to the implicit fusion of Silenus' song with Apollo's at the end. This *Eclogue* is one of Virgil's most ambitious efforts in poetic integration. Its synthesis of Greek and Roman, real contemporaries and mythical beings, the pastoral frame and diverse literary genres, is one of his boldest essays in the union of collage-like heterogeneity and smooth unity of style and poetic surface.

The figure of Gallus, like Pollio in *Ecl.* 3 and 4, has more than autobiographical meaning. Here he gains further symbolic value not just as a personal friend of Virgil but as a dramatic character who stands between poetry and passion, fantasy and reality. The crowning of Gallus by the Muse and Linus in *Ecl.* 6, however, must also be viewed in close relation with the themes of exile, frustrated love, war, and death that surround him in *Ecl.* 10. Thus I qualify here the more positive view of *Ecl.* 10 put forth in no. 12 above. This movement within the collection from brilliant *Dichterweihe* in *Ecl.* 6 to the motifs of death, loss, and exile in *Ecl.* 10 anticipates the more overtly tragic mood of parts of the *Georgics* and the *Aeneid.* The saddened and distraught poet Gallus, lamented (even if somewhat playfully) in an elegiac threnody drawn from the lament over Theocritus' archetypal bucolic poet in *Idyll* 1, anticipates Orpheus in the Fourth *Georgic*; and being *captus amore* by song will resonate more ominously in the *Aeneid* (cf. *Ecl.* 6.10 and *Aen.* 1.748-50).[24]

The amalgam of fantasy and reality in *Ecl.* 6 is also the main subject

[24] For some recent studies of the continuity between the *Eclogues* and the *Aeneid* see Putnam, *Virgil's Pastoral Art*, pp. 17-19; Leach, *Vergil's Eclogues*, pp. 211-15; Van Sickle, *Virgil's Bucolics*, pp. 230-32; Alpers, *The Singer of the Eclogues*, pp. 245-49; also my "Orpheus and the Fourth *Georgic*: Vergil on Nature and Civilization," *AJP* 87 (1966), 321-25.

of the last two studies of this collection (nos. 14 and 15). These two papers return to Silenus and show how Virgil's poetic imagination not only incorporates this figure of Hellenistic myth and art but also absorbs and fully appropriates the diverse strands of earlier poetic traditions. Chromis, for example, one of the "lads" who extorts Silenus' song, is a herdsman-singer (presumably) from Libya in Theocritus' First *Idyll* (26). Here, along with his companion Mnasyllus, he is suspended between myth and reality. Virgil leaves the division between his human or mythical status deliberately blurred, but gives just enough of a hint to suggest that these two *pueri* are fauns or young satyrs, not herdsmen. This element of unreality contributes to our sense of the magical power of poetry that is one of the themes of the Sixth *Eclogue*. While Virgil's bucolic world can incorporate this magic along with the mysterious sympathy between man and nature and the inconsequential sport of rustic demigods, it also sets them off against the harshness of the Roman present, always there just on the other side. Virgilian pastoral is ever poised in delicate awareness of its own fragility.

The pastoral *Epigrams* of Theocritus, the subject of the last paper, remind us that the theme of the magical power of rustic song was still alive in the Hellenistic world for Virgil to draw upon. He uses this motif, however, with a new awareness of the artificiality of its literary frame. *Eclogue* 6 is perhaps the most Theocritean of Virgil's pastorals. Its rustic divinities, inset myths, self-conscious literary frame, and sharp discontinuities invite comparison with the form of *Idyll* 3 and *Idyll* 7 (particularly the song of Lycidas). Yet it is in such imitation— if that is an adequate term—that one best appreciates the distinctive character of Virgilian poetry. The urban realities of history and politics that drive Meliboeus and Moeris from their fields and Gallus from an Arcadia of gentle loves and consoling song are present here in the opening *recusatio* to Varus, which acknowledges "grim wars," *tristia bella*, and martial encomia beside the pastoral poet's "slender reed" (*Ecl.* 6.5-8). These last two essays take us back to the contrasts and similarities between Theocritus and Virgil, to the important ways in which they illuminate one another, and to their different modes of tapping and revivifying ancient sources of myth in giving to the world a new genre of poetry.

«Since Daphnis Dies»: The Meaning of Theocritus' First Idyll

By Charles Segal, Providence, R.I.

I

The first Idyll of Theocritus is an extraordinarily closely knit and carefully constructed poem. Most of its second half consists of Thyrsis' song about 'the sorrows of Daphnis' (τὰ Δάφνιδος ἄλγεα, 19), a cowherd-singer (cf. 128–129) who is 'wasting away' because of an unexplained struggle with love. Attempts to find reasons for Daphnis' death have, on the whole, suffered from considering Daphnis apart from the rest of the poem[1]. The present paper seeks to place Daphnis' death in the perspective of the poem's total structure and thereby to offer an interpretation of the Idyll as a whole. In so doing, it draws heavily on the symbolism attaching to the elements of the pastoral world depicted in the Idyll, especially the symbolism of water.

The exact nature of Daphnis' death is itself a perplexing problem. Theocritus is brief and elusive (138–141):

> χὢ μὲν τόσσ' εἰπὼν ἀπεπαύσατο · τὸν δ' Ἀφροδίτα
> ἤθελ' ἀνορθῶσαι · τά γε μὰν λίνα πάντα λελοίπει
> ἐκ Μοιρᾶν, χὢ Δάφνις ἔβα ῥόον. ἔκλυσε δίνα
> τὸν Μοίσαις φίλον ἄνδρα, τὸν οὐ Νύμφαισιν ἀπεχθῆ.

'Him Aphrodite wished to raise up, but all the thread had run out from the Fates (Moirai), and Daphnis came to a stream. The eddy washed over the man dear to the Muses, one not hated of the Nymphs.'

The scholiasts thought that the 'stream' of 140 is Acheron[2], but there is no evidence that Theocritus ever refers to Acheron in such terms[3], nor should it 'wash

---

[1] The most important recent studies are as follows: G. Lawall, *Theocritus' Coan Pastorals. A Poetry Book* (Cambridge, Mass. 1967) ch. 1; R. M. Ogilvie, *The Song of Thyrsis*, JHS 82 (1962) 106–110; U. Ott, *Die Kunst des Gegensatzes in Theokrits Hirtengedichten*, Spudasmata 22 (Hildesheim 1969) 85–137; E. A. Schmidt, *Die Leiden des verliebten Daphnis*, Hermes 96 (1968) 539–552; F. J. Williams, *Theocritus, Idyll i 81–91*, JHS 89 (1969) 121–123. The recent study of the Daphnis myth by G. Wojaczek, *Daphnis. Untersuchungen zur griechischen Bukolik*, Beitr. z. klass. Philol. 34 (Meisenheim am Glan 1969) 33–38 is unhelpful since the author believes that Daphnis is a Dionysiac-Orphic initiate (p. 36) and Thyrsis' song «eine mystische Unterweisung» (p. 38).

[2] So the scholiast ad loc.; most recently Lawall (preceding note) 25–26, with note 6. So also Fritzsche-Hiller, *Theokrits Gedichte*[3] (Leipzig 1881) ad loc. and, reluctantly, H. W. Prescott, *A Study of the Daphnis-Myth*, Harv. Stud. Cl. Phil. 10 (1899) 138 with n. 2. For a recent survey see Ott (above n. 1) 129 with n. 371.

[3] For these objections to interpreting the 'stream' as Acheron, see Ogilvie (above n. 1) 109; A. S. F. Gow, *Theocritus*[2] (Cambridge 1952) ad I 140.

over' its victim. Others have suggested that Daphnis is metamorphosed into a spring[4], a view which has even less support from the text or from what is known of the myth of Daphnis. Of the traditional, apparently Sicilian myth of Daphnis, a herdsman punished with blindness for his infidelity to a Nymph to whom he pledged his love, there are, at best, only hints (see 88–91 and infra)[5]. A number of recent interpreters, however, maintain that Theocritus is following the traditional legend[6].

The most likely interpretation is that the 'stream' of 140 is a real stream and not a metaphor for death. On this view Daphnis dies by drowning[7]. Yet his death is no ordinary event. The water which washes over him is akin to the mysterious water which adorns other dangerous places in the Theocritean corpus, notably in Idylls XIII, XXII, and in the spurious XXIII[8]. The poet gives Daphnis a deliberately mysterious, archetypal death by water in order to enhance the range and suggestiveness of his tale. Such a fate is of a piece with the remote and mythical atmosphere of the tale as a whole: the appearance of gods, the Nymphs in the background, the conversation with Aphrodite.

At the same time water is an important unifying symbol throughout the poem. Inviting, refreshing, joyful at the beginning (1–8), the haunt of Nymphs of Sicily's rivers and streams in the song of Daphnis (68–69. 118), ominous and mysterious at Daphnis' death (140), and then finally benign and evocative of a fanciful Olympian mythology near the very end (150), water symbolizes opposing elements in Theocritus' pastoral world and in his art. The association of water and poetry goes back to the proem of Hesiod's Theogony, a passage which Theocritus perhaps has in mind in the opening of his Idyll (1–8)[9]. It is implicit also in the connection

---

[4] See especially E. Schwartz, *Theokrits Daphnis*, NGG (1904) 291, who interestingly connects the idea with Daphnis' 'wasting away' through love. Also R. J. Cholmeley, *The Idylls of Theocritus* (London 1919) 384; Williams (above n. 1) 122 n. 6.

[5] For the legend and the ancient sources see Gow's prefatory remarks to *Id.* I; also Cholmeley (preceding note) 383–374; Prescott (above n. 2) passim. The other allusions to Daphnis in the Theocritean corpus do not help much. In *Id.* VII 73–77, Daphnis loves one Xenea and is lamented by the mountains and oaks near the Himera, but no reason for his death is given. In ps.-Theocr. VIII 92–93 Daphnis wins a singing contest and marries the Nymph Nais. In *Epigram* III he is stalked by Pan and Priapus as he sleeps. *Id.* VII 73–77 is not inconsistent with the traditional myth nor with *Id.* I, but it neither proves nor disproves that Theocritus is following the traditional myth in *Id.* I.

[6] So Ogilvie (above n. 1), answered in part by Schmidt (above n. 1), especially 542. See also Prescott (above n. 2) 140, who accepts the traditional version with reservations; and see the same author's article, Ἔβα ῥόον (Theocritus Id. I, 139. 140), CQ 7 (1913) 176–187, especially 187, who stresses the parallel with the tale of Hylas.

[7] So Ogilvie (above n. 1) 109 and Ott (above n. 1) 129 with n. 371, with discussion of earlier scholarship. See also Williams (above n. 1) 123 n. 13.

[8] I develop these parallels in a separate study, *Death by Water: A Narrative Pattern in Theocritus*, forthcoming in Hermes.

[9] Hes. *Theog.* 39. 83–84. 97. The importance of the Hesiodic and also the Callimachean «Dichterweihe» for the Thalysia (*Id.* VII) has been shown by B. A. Van Groningen, *Quelques problèmes de la poésie bucolique grecque*, Mnemosyne, Ser. IV 12 (1959) 31–32 and M. Puelma, *Die Dichterbegegnung in Theokrits 'Thalysien'*, Mus. Helv. 17 (1960) 156–157 and extended more recently by G. Luck, *Zur Deutung von Theokrits Thalysien*, Mus. Helv. 23 (1966)

of the 'springs of the Seasons' (150) with the cup, the elaborately adorned artifact and prize of song which itself as a work of art symbolizes poetry and especially pastoral poetry.

II

Idyll I falls into three parts, each of which has its own distinctive geography. First comes the meeting between the two rustics at the beginning, with its quiet, beautiful, but not entirely secure pastoral *locus* (1–23). To this bucolic frame we return at the very end of the poem (143–152). Second stand the scenes on the cup. These belong to a more realistic workaday world (29–56), a pastoral version of the Homeric Shield of Achilles. This *locus* bears the imprint of human cultivation and habitation: there is a well-planted vineyard (46) and a rubble wall (47). Here nature is fenced in, demarcated for human use and not left to its spontaneous whisperings and gurglings, as in Thyrsis' world (cf. 1–8). Even the sheer rock by the sea serves human work: it is the place from which the muscular old fisherman casts his net (39–40). There is a certain aggressiveness between nature and man here. Foxes prowl around the intent boy of the third scene, looking for a chance to get at the grapes or his lunch. Musing and wrapt absorption may here bring their penalty. The concentrated weaving of the 'beautiful' ($\varkappa\alpha\lambda\acute{\alpha}\nu$, 52) cage for the grasshopper is a palpable symbol of poetry[10]. Yet even this scene is, in a way, connected with the theme of food-getting through the presence of the hungry and designing foxes. The making of the cage too implies fencing in, control, the containment of nature for human purposes.

Third and last is the setting of Daphnis' death. Its real geography shades off into the realm of myth and imagination. There are real Sicilian rivers and mountains, to be sure (68–69): «These points describe an area in western Sicily of about 60 kilometers from north to south», as one commentator notes[11]. But Pan, Priapus, Hermes, Aphrodite and the Nymphs are at home here and pass to and fro easily in converse with mortals. Jackals and lions, not very likely inhabitants of Theocritus' Sicily, dwell in Daphnis' mountains and lament his death (71–72. 115)[12].

Each of these three *loci* is, in a sense, unreal and artificial; but there are gradations of unreality[13]. The realm of Daphnis, despite its actual place names, stands at the furthest remove from reality. The workaday world of the cup is the closest. In between stands the shepherd world of Thyrsis and the Goatherd. For them

---

186–189 and by G. Serrao, *Problemi di poesia alessandrina I: Studi su Teocrito* (Rome 1971) 13–68, especially 29. 33. 37.

[10] So too the *tettix* in 148 may be an allusion to Callimachean theories: cf. *Aetia* I, fr. 1, 29ff. Pf. See also A. Dihle, *The Poem on the Cicada*, Harv. Stud. Cl. Phil. 71 (1966) 112 with n. 17. The word $\dot{\epsilon}\varphi\alpha\varrho\mu\acute{o}\sigma\delta\omega\nu$ in line 53 also suggests craftsmanlike activity appropriate to art.

[11] Ott (above n. 1) 120–121.

[12] See Ott (above n. 1) 121–122.

[13] In *Id.* VII also Theocritus exploits a narrative frame which stands on a different plane of reality from the episode which it encloses within it: see Luck (above n. 9) 187 and Puelma (above n. 9) 145.

nature is free, generous, unmarked by boundaries or tillage. Rustic gods haunt
their glades. Yet work is not entirely absent: Thyrsis still has to attend to the
pasturing of his companion's goats (14).

A complex pattern of parallel motifs and verbal repetitions relates these three
locales to one another[14]. Furthermore, the closing dialogue between the two rustics
holds all three settings present simultaneously for a final, synoptic moment.

The character of each *locus* also appears through the kind of water it contains.
The water of the rustics' world is gentle, beautiful, songful, in close sympathy
with art and leisure (1–8. 150). It is felt to be the haunt of the forest divinities,
the Nymphs (12 and 22). In the scenes on the cup water appears only indirectly
and secondarily: the sea is implied in the description of the fisherman casting his
net (39–40), but only the rock itself is actually mentioned. This *locus* belongs
primarily to earth and dry land rather than to water. As the poem once more
moves farther from reality in the song of Daphnis' death, water too becomes less
realistic, more magical. The nymphs, who appeared only briefly and obliquely in
the pastoral *locus* of the beginning (12. 22) are now much in evidence (68–69.
117–118). The water of this realm is 'sacred water', ἱερὸν ὕδωρ (69), or 'lovely
water', καλὸν ... ὕδωρ (118). It becomes, finally, the deadly, mysterious eddy which
closes over the cowherd (139–140).

'Sacred water' partakes of the ambiguity of this mythicized natural world. As
the haunt of Nymphs, it is life-giving and points back to the refreshing springs
by which Thyrsis and the Goatherd sing (12. 22). But to the herdsman embattled
against Aphrodite it shows its destructive side. To that ambiguity of water corre-
sponds an ambiguity within this mythical world as a whole. Aphrodite's 'secret
laughter' and 'heavy anger' (95–96) may be playful, as Zuntz has convincingly
argued[15]. Yet to cross the powers of love is dangerous; and Daphnis, for all the
goddess' wish to 'raise him up' (139), does, in fact, perish. This tension between
life and death is also hinted at in Daphnis' own scornful reference to Adonis[16].
Indeed, the hunting motif of 110 suggests the circumstances of Adonis' death.
Since Theocritus was interested in the myth of Adonis' death and resurrection
(Idyll XV), there may be a further irony in Daphnis' quarrel with Aphrodite. He
taunts her with her paramour in terms which evoke the myth of Adonis' death
and resurrection. Yet the herdsman who scorns the love-goddess cannot participate
in the cycle of death and renewal. She cannot 'raise him up'. The 'sacred water'
shows only its destructive power.

To the three geographical realms of the poem correspond three levels of art.
The least 'real' is the most emotionally intense and involving. The song of Daphnis'
sufferings is pervaded by a rhetoric and pathos that set a lofty and artificial tone,

---

[14] See below n. 18.
[15] G. Zuntz, *Theocritus I. 95f.*, CQ, N.S. 10 (1960) 37–40, whom most recent critics accept.
For the earlier literature see Ott (above n. 1) 124–125 with n. 358.
[16] Ott (above n. 1) 116–117 points out the contrast between Anchises and Adonis here.

far from 'realistic' representation (cf. 66–69. 80–86. 132–136). The procession of gods and pastoral figures, the dialogue between Daphnis and Aphrodite, the apostrophe to the Nymphs all serve to keep the narrative on a plane of remote, self-conscious mythicality. Of this atmosphere Daphnis' mysterious death by water is an integral part.

There is obviously a strong contrast between the fresh setting of the bucolic *locus amoenus* in the first part of the Idyll (1–23) and the mythical world of Daphnis at the end. This contrast, in turn, creates an ironic interplay between the serious and the playful, between gaiety and sorrow. The rustic gods, Priapus and the Nymphs, who occur in the bucolic frame in close association with water (12. 21–22, and cf. Pan in 3), recur, more dolefully, in the lament for Daphnis, where they again stand in close association with water (66–69. 81–83). The song of Daphnis, in fact, ends with Nymphs as it began with Nymphs (66 and 141). The symmetry is reinforced by the recurrence of the important word, 'stream' ($\acute{\varrho}\acute{o}ov$) in 68 and 140; and we may also recall the related $\varkappa\alpha\tau\alpha\varrho\varrho\epsilon\tilde{\iota}$ of the opening (5). Springs, though remote and mythical, recur in the bucolic frame that ends the Idyll (150), thus reminding us once more of the happier aqueous setting which enframes Daphnis' death. The rivers and springs which earlier invited the rustics to song (cf. 2. 8. 22) are now incorporated into the sorrows of Daphnis: they are a part of the strange, fleeting landscape of his tormented love (cf. 83). He himself bids farewell to 'Arethusa and the rivers that pour (their) lovely water down the Thybris' (117–118). If one were to seek a specific stream for Daphnis' death, as some interpreters have done, one would be tempted to look for it in the vicinity of these rivers[17]. What is significant, however, is precisely the fact that the 'stream' where Daphnis perishes is nameless. It is thus set apart from the 'great stream' ($\mu\acute{\epsilon}\gamma\alpha\nu$ $\acute{\varrho}\acute{o}ov$) of the Anapus or the 'sacred water' of the Acis in 68–69. Its reality stands on an entirely different plane; it is not of the sort to be verified on the map.

The contrast between Daphnis and the rest of the rustic world develops on several different levels[18]. It is clearest if we compare the scene on the cup. The playful 'love' there (eros, 37) becomes the frustrated and doomed 'love' of Daphnis (*eros:* 78. 85. 93. 97. 104. 130). The teasing 'laughter' (36) of the flirtatious woman on the cup becomes the hidden, mocking 'laughter' of the love-goddess herself (95–96). To one embroiled in the complexities of love (cf. $\delta\acute{\upsilon}\sigma\epsilon\varrho\omega\varsigma$, 85) the 'sweet' goddess can be 'bitter' (cf. 93 and 95), and her laughter can have a sinister or at best an ambiguous quality (96)[19].

---

[17] So in fact Ogilvie (above n. 1) 109. His suggestion of a plunge «from the mountain into water» (p. 110) has little support either from *Id.* I or from Callim. *Epigram* XXII which he adduces.

[18] Both Lawall (above n. 1) 30–31 and Ott (above n. 1) 132–137 have sensitive observations on these contrasts, but neither develops the antitheses as far as the material permits nor relates them to the settings and the symbolism of the poem as fully as I seek to do here.

[19] See above n. 15

The goatherd's plea for a song from Thyrsis ends with a playful and conventional reference to Hades: 'Come, my friend, for you won't keep your song for Hades who brings forgetfulness' (πόταγ', ὠγαθέ· τὰν γὰρ ἀοιδάν | οὔ τί πα εἰς ᾽Αίδαν γε τὸν ἐκλελάθοντα φυλαξεῖς, 62–63). In Daphnis' lament, however, Hades is far more ominous (cf. 103. 130), and in both of these passages it is connected with Eros. In Daphnis' world of tragic emotions, death and love go together, as they have for tragic lovers of all times. On the cup the labors of love are only mock-serious: love is treated here with the humorous exaggeration attaching to the amours of country bumpkins, as the ponderous rhythms of 38 make clear: δηθὰ κυλοιδιόωντες ἐτώσια μοχθίζοντι.

The motif of 'sweetness' forms an even stronger link between the bucolic frame, the cup, and the story of Daphnis[20]. The rustics enjoy the 'sweet' sounds of springs, rustling trees, and song (1–2. 7). The cup has been 'washed with sweet wax' (27). Thyrsis introduces the Daphnis song with a reference back to this sweet singing (65); and the Goatherd's praise in the closing frame sounds the motif for one final time, even more sensually and exuberantly than before, in the comparisons to honey and figs (146–148). But within the episode of Daphnis sweetness occurs only in the ambiguous laughter of Aphrodite (95). Instead, the cowherd 'fulfils bitter love' (ἄννε πικρὸν ἔρωτα, 93). Here too love and death are closely associated through the symmetry of the line and the repeated verb 'fulfilled' (93): ἄννε πικρὸν ἔρωτα, καὶ ἐς τέλος ἄννε μοίρας. In the bucolic frame the Goatherd had warned of the possible 'bitterness' of Pan (16–17). But rustics can avoid the dangerous aspects of their god as Daphnis cannot avoid the dangers of 'bitter Eros'.

The rustics' respect for Pan (16) contrasts with Daphnis' confident insulting of Aphrodite (100ff.). In the rustic world of the opening section Pan is a quietly accepted presence with whom the experienced herdsman reckons as a normal part of rustic life (cf. 3. 16–18). But when Pan recurs in Daphnis' complaint, it is in more strident and emotional tones: ὦ Πὰν Πάν (123)[21]. The impassioned address and listing of his haunts in 123–126 also recalls the indignant tone of the narrator's apostrophe to the Nymphs at the very beginning of the Daphnis song (66–69). That emotionality, however, is now transferred from the narrator to the sufferer himself. Whereas the narrator, Thyrsis, addressed the absent Nymphs in terms of rivers and the 'lovely vales of Tempe' (67–69)[22], Daphnis addresses the absent Pan in terms of the remote and rugged mountains of Arcadia, Lycaeus and Maena-

---

[20] Lawall (above n. 1) 18 observes that «sweetness» forms «a symbolic pattern throughout *Idyll* 1», but does not explore it in detail.

[21] Ott (above n. 1) observes the recurrence of Pan in 15–18 and 123–130, but says only: «Im Daphnislied, V. 123–130, tritt der Syrinxspieler Pan – auf mythischer Ebene und in pathetischerem Stil – noch einmal auf.» For Wojaczek (above n. 1) 37 Daphnis' address to Pan is «ein Höhepunkt des Liedes», but he makes the invocation subserve his Orphic-Dionysiac thesis.

[22] Thyrsis, however, also mentions the Pindus (67) and 'the peak of Aetna' (69), though without emphasizing the mountainous landscape as Daphnis does in 124–126.

lus (124–126)[23]. It is as if Daphnis is blind to the gentler features of his world and little cognizant of its gentler divinities, despite their good will toward him (141).

Love and death, laughter, bitterness and sweetness thus occur in all three sections of the poem. This contraposto of emotional tones concentrates heavily on water. The mysterious 'eddy' washes over Daphnis (ἔκλυσε δίνα 140). But the cup, where love and laughter are facile and happy, is 'washed with sweet wax' (κεκλυσμένον ἁδέι κηρῷ, 27). The contrasts of sweetness and water here fuse. The verb κλύζειν is not common. Theocritus uses it in these two passages and nowhere else.

In one sense the scenes on the cup and the story of Daphnis stand on the same level: both are enclosed within an artificial frame and both are incorporated into the larger rustic world within which Thyrsis and the Goatherd pasture their flock, meet, and sing. Through this frame Theocritus self-consciously juxtaposes ecphrastic art and narrative art. The one is static, distanced, ironical, unemotional[24]. The other is full of movement, emotionally tense, pathetic. The contrast between the two kinds of narrative and between the two landscapes corresponds also to the contrast between the two aspects of the motif of water: the refreshing, inviting water of the bucolic frame and the destructive, mysterious water of Daphnis' deadly 'stream'; the fatal 'washing over' of Daphnis (140) and the figurative 'washing' of the cup with 'sweet wax' (27).

On the cup the natural world is joyful. The twisting ivy 'rejoices' in its yellow fruit (ἀγαλλομένα, 31). The boy carved on it 'takes joy' (γαθεῖ, 54) in his plaiting. In the Daphnis episode nature's vital processes are inverted 'since Daphnis dies' (132–135). The word 'dies' (θνάσκει, 135) follows immediately upon the description of these inversions of normal growth. It echoes the only other direct, non-metaphorical reference to death, the beasts' lament over Daphnis 'dead' (θανόντα) in 71–72. Beginning and end of the song are thus, once more, drawn together. Nature's sympathy for the dying poet frames the tale, but there is an added pathos in the contrast between the drier, more objectively (though still rhetorically) conveyed sympathy of 71–72 and the victim's own cry, with all its hyperboles, in 132–136. The difference is analogous to that between 66–69 and 123–126 discussed above. It is a difference similar also to that between the rustics' third-person talk of Pan in 16–18 and Daphnis repeated invocation, 'O Pan, Pan ...' in 123–126.

---

[23] The old controversy about the existence of an Arcadian bucolic poetry (maintained by Reitzenstein) does not concern us here: see P. Legrand, *Etude sur Théocrite*, Bibl. des Ecoles françaises d'Athènes et de Rome 79 (Paris 1898) 207ff.

[24] C. Gallavotti, *Le coppe istoriate di Teocrito e di Virgilio*, Parola del Passato 21 (1966) 421, is right to insist on the «animated quality of the scenes on the cup and their spirit of observation». Yet the fact remains that, relative to the story of Daphnis, which has a beginning, a middle, and an end, the scenes on the cup are static. This point is well appreciated by Lawall (above n. 1) 27. 30 and by Ott (above n. 1) 133–135 with further literature on p. 135 n. 394.

Feeling becomes more intense as we draw closer to the dying man and enter into his emotional life. The rhetorical exaggerations of 132–135 depict for a lingering moment that last glimmer of poetic power and still living consciousness which struggle against this fate and protest its bitterness. We draw near to Daphnis and participate sympathetically in his fate, however, only to draw apart again to a more distanced relationship. The refrain, 'Cease, Muses, come cease the bucolic song' (137), follows immediately upon Daphnis' hyperboles and in its stylized repetition removes us once more from Daphnis' turbid emotionality. The half-line, 'So speaking Daphnis ended' (χὣ μὲν τόσσ' εἰπὼν ἀπεπαύσατο, 138), marks the conclusion both of Daphnis' speech and Daphnis' life. The verb ἀπεπαύσατο of 138 has a restrained pathos very different from the wild, unreal pathos of Daphnis' rhetoric[25]. Its calm, fading note and its unadorned factuality, helped by the evocation of Homeric style in this formal closure, seal the reality of his death and closes the tension between emotionality and objectivity.

The inversions of nature's growth in 132–136 form the climax as well as the conclusion of Daphnis' lament. The verb 'dies' (135) and the inversion of nature prepare for the actual death of Daphnis and place it in a larger perspective, a cosmic alternation of life and death. Aphrodite's wish to 'raise up' the dying cow-herd continues the antithesis between life and death, and the destructive water completes it, for it recalls the joyful waters earlier (cf. 1–8. 22. 27), especially as the Nymphs are mentioned immediately (140; cf. 12. 22).

The closing words of Thyrsis, framing the song of Daphnis, now extend to the realm of art that contrast between death and the life-giving forces of nature. Thyrsis makes a libation to the Muses (σπείσω, 144). This joyful liquid image follows the deadly water of 140. Sucess balances failure. The Muses who could not help Daphnis, dear to them though he was (140–141), will, presumably, be propitious to this other rustic singer.

This passage reflects still other contrasts between Thyrsis and Daphnis. 'Fare-well' (χαίρετ'), Thyrsis addresses the Muses, 'and I will sing to you later too (καὶ ἐς ὕστερον) still more sweetly' (145). 'Farewell' (χαίρεϑ'), Daphnis called to the wild beasts, 'for I, Daphnis the cowherd, would exist for you no longer (οὐκέτ') in the woods' (116). The sharp contrast between the two statements opposes continuity and finality, hope and despair. For Daphnis there is no 'later' (145), only 'no longer' (116). Thyrsis will 'sing again' (145), whereas Daphnis has 'stopped' (ἀπεπαύσατο, 138) forever. The motif of sweetness then recurs (ἅδιον, 145), in contrast to Daphnis' 'bitter' love (93). In the Goatherd's reply sweetness returns, as we have noted (148), but it is now conjoined with 'fulness'. The two occurrences of 'sweet' (ἅδιον and ἁδεῖαν, 145. 148) enframe the word 'full' (πλῆρες repeated) at the beginning of both lines 146 and 147: sweet – full, full – sweet is the pat-

---

[25] In *Id.* VII 90 ἀπεπαύσατο is used merely to mark the end of a song, without the pathetic ambiguity of *Id.* I 138. For the defence of the reading ἀπεπαύσατο (instead of ἀνεπαύσατο in some Mss.) see Gow ad loc.

tern. The prayer for 'fulness' adds to the contrast of sweet and bitter a contrast between the emptiness of Daphnis 'wasting away' (τάκεσϑαι, 66. 82. 88. 91) and the joyful 'fulness' of honey and figs. Since these images describe the mouth, i.e. the song, of Thyrsis, the contrasts also embrace the realm of art: they suggest an antithesis between the joyfulness of the singer who belongs to the bucolic frame and the sad plaints of Daphnis within the song. This singer's only utterances are taunting or doleful. The happy exuberance of Thyrsis is like that of the cup (cf. ἀγαλλομένα, 31). His art may embrace sorrow and frustration, but in itself it is sweet and joyful. Its very inclusiveness is, like the gaily encompassing ivy of 31, a source of joy. Thyrsis is not touched by the sorrow of his song. One might compare also the intentness of the boy who 'takes such joy in his plaiting' that he is untouched by the loss of his grapes and his lunch (53–54).

As the dialogue of the two rustics at the end leads back to the bucolic frame of the beginning (142–145 and 4–11), so the motif of the cup recurs, again with liquid imagery (149–150): 'How fine it smells. You would say it was washed in the springs of the Seasons'. The Seasons (Horai) are divinities associated with the life-giving processes of nature. In Idyll XV they lead the risen Adonis from the grave (XV 102–105). Only here, apparently, are they associated with springs of water. Theocritus may have intended a fusion between the Nymphs and the Seasons, both connected with nature's vitality. In any case these springs of 150 connect the cup with the bucolic frame where, as we have seen, springs have a prominent place (1–8. 21–22). Over against these life-giving springs stand the springs where Daphnis' abandoned girl sought him ('by all the springs', πάσας ἀνὰ κράνας, 83) and, of course, the water where he dies. The repeated verb, κλύζειν, as already noted, sharpens the contrast (27 and 140).

It may be amusing to have a goatherd so appreciative of lovely scent (149). Elsewhere Theocritus is not above explicitness as to the odoriferous side of this rustic calling (cf. V 52 and VII 16)[26]. But the Goatherd of Idyll I is in touch with many levels of nature's beauty and vitality. It is his he-goat, aroused, who closes the poem (151–152). Earlier Priapus, reproaching Daphnis for the neglect of his girl, compares him to a goatherd who 'wastes away in his eyes' with envy for his lascivious goats (87–88). Daphnis' neglect of love here parallels his removal from the life-energies of the world which surrounds him. The rutting billy at the end unites that antithesis with the other sections of the poem, the cup and the rustic dialogue.

The contrast implied in 150–152 operates on two planes simultaneously, a higher and a lower, or a poetical and a more prosaic. On the higher and more poetical plane, the mythological 'springs of the Seasons' contrast with the deadly waters of Daphnis' stream. On the lower plane the contrast is earthier and more rustic: the vitality of the eager goats contrasts with the death of the love-lorn herdsman. This separation into a higher and lower level is, in one sense, artificial, for Theo-

[26] On the «realism» of Id. VII 16 see Serrao (above n. 9) 14–15.

critus means us to see the mythological element of the Seasons' springs and the naturalistic element of the goats as binary aspects of the same thing, opposite, simultaneous perspectives upon the same terrain. Hence Thyrsis' first gesture as possessor of the cup is to pour a libation of milk to the Muses (143–144). The libation is itself connected with the fruitfulness of his companion's herds and thus with the rhythms and bounty of the natural world. At the same time, he has to milk the goat before he can perform the libation (143–144):

> καὶ τὺ δίδου τὰν αἶγα τό τε σκύφος, ὥς κεν ἀμέλξας
> σπείσω ταῖς Μοίσαις.

The practical necessities of the situation resume the realism of the rustic frame of the beginning (cf. ἀμέλγειν in 6 and 25 ∼ 143. 151).

Goats enable Thyrsis to make his libation to the Muses, but for Daphnis they reflect another dimension of Aphrodite's victory. The simple, instinctive loves of rutting goats outlast and mock the emotional complexities of a human lover who is δύσερως (85)[27]. In struggling against Aphrodite (for whatever reason), Daphnis alienates himself from a crucial aspect of that very world from which he, as a rustic singer, draws his strength. He is dear to the Nymphs, who are rustic deities associated with the vitality of nature and the life-giving qualities of water. Even the Muses who love him (141) have a place in the rustic setting amid talk of lambs and sacrificial beasts (9–11). Rejecting love, cut off from his ties to the life-giving powers of nature and the life-giving waters of its springs, Daphnis cannot be resurrected (139). It is the he-goat who will 'rise up', the last word in the poem (ἀναστῇ, 152). The Idyll closes on an earthy note, a basic sexual vitality which, however, closely parallels the more metaphorical, 'higher' image of that vitality in the springs of the Seasons.

The two levels, high and low, poetical and 'realistic', unite harmoniously in the image of a libation of goats' milk for the Muses, poured from a cup that belongs to the rustic world (αἰπολικὸν θάημα, 56), but is yet adorned with elaborately carved scenes. Keeping in mind the antitheses between Daphnis and the other herdsmen, we may contrast the gaiety of this 'wonder for shepherds' of which the Goatherd speaks (56) with Daphnis' tomb of Arcas which is 'admired even by the blessed gods' (τὸ καὶ μακάρεσσιν ἀγητόν, 126). The one speaks of shepherds, the other of gods; the one of a cup, the other of a tomb. Daphnis' horizons are larger, reaching from his native Sicily to far-away Arcadia, from the rustic world to gods and learned mythologies. Yet his subjects are grimmer, his tone sadder.

Water is a unifying symbol of whatever is alive and vital in this pastoral world. It is a symbol both of the life-giving aspects of nature and of the vital energies on

---

[27] Both Schmidt (above n. 1) 549 ff. and Williams (above n. 1) 122–123 have argued that δύσερως means suffering from the difficulties and especially from an excess of love and therefore militates against the «Hippolytus» theory of Daphnis' death.

which the poet draws. Springs of water invite the rustics to song (1–8. 22)[28], and an elaborate work of art is, figuratively, washed in the springs of the goddesses who guide nature's movements through the year (150). Yet the powers of nature can be dangerous: Pan can be 'bitter' (17), and water can bring death as well as life. It is men who determine on which side of these powers they will stand. Daphnis insults Aphrodite as 'hateful to mortals', ϑνατοῖσιν ἀπεχϑής (101). But he may be taking too one-sided a view. At his death he is called 'not hateful to the Nymphs' (τὸν οὐ Νύμφαισιν ἀπεχϑῆ, 141). He has forced upon the deities of the natural world an enmity which is not necessarily theirs. Aphrodite herself would 'raise him up' (139). Her laughter is playful, her 'wrath' (ϑυμός, 96) only pretence. But Daphnis takes both very seriously and colors them with his own embittered emotionality[29].

III

Approaching the poem in these terms may help us to understand the vexed question of why Daphnis dies. Interpreters have adduced evidence from Theocritus' text to support the view that he is following the traditional, Sicilian version: Daphnis has vowed fidelity to a Nymph, is unfaithful to her, and is consequently punished with blindness or, possibly, death[30]. The κώρα of Priapus' speech (82) could be the girl with whom Daphnis is unfaithful. His 'wasting away in the eyes' (τάκε(τ)αι ὀφϑαλμώς, 88 and 91) could allude to his blindness. The Nymph of his oath might be one of the 'maidens' at whose laughter, according to Priapus, Daphnis 'wastes away in his eyes' (90–91)[31]. Yet, to dwell on this last passage for a moment, it is hard to see why Theocritus speaks of 'maidens': Nymphs are not usually *parthenoi*, nor, according to the legend, did Daphnis love more than one.

It is certainly possible that the details mentioned above *may* be an allusion to the traditional myth. One fact about them, however, is curious. They all occur in Priapus' speech and not elsewhere in the song about Daphnis. Possibly Priapus' interpretation of Daphnis' plight reflects that divinity's characteristic preoccupations, but not necessarily the truth, since that interpretation receives no clear objective confirmation elsewhere in the poem. Outside of Priapus' speech, nothing

---

[28] Cf. Callim. *Hymn to Apollo* 111–112 and A. Kambylis, *Die Dichterweihe und ihre Symbolik*, Bibl. d. klass. Altertumswiss. 2 (Heidelberg 1965) 23–30. 44.

[29] Of the Nymphs here Wilamowitz, *Daphnis*, Reden und Vorträge I⁴ (Berlin 1925) 268, remarked, «... sie repräsentieren die elementare Natur, und diese hat für die Entsagung kein Verständnis, die ja der Natur zuwiderläuft.» Lawall (above n. 1) 25–26 maintains the opposite, that Daphnis remains in harmony with nature and does so through his chastity: «By retaining his chastity, he remains faithful to nature, wild animals, woods, and streams» (p. 25).

[30] For the legend, see above n. 5.

[31] So Ogilvie and Williams (above n. 1). Legrand (above n. 23) 145–148 advances a rather fanciful explanation of Daphnis' suffering: he does not requite a maiden's love, she asks Aphrodite for help, and the goddess makes Daphnis waste away with a hopeless passion. As an argument against Daphnis' chastity, however, he observes, as have others, the fact that Aphrodite is still sympathetic to him (p. 147).

else in the song of Thyrsis is inconsistent with the view, accepted by many inter-
preters, that Daphnis dies because he resists love in order to remain chaste, like
Hippolytus. Yet it must be admitted that nothing firmly supports that view
either[32]. If Daphnis is dying because of his resistance to love rather than because
of an excessive indulgence in it or excessive desire, Priapus would hardly be the
god to understand that[33].

If Theocritus is aware of the traditional version and is referring to it, obliquely
and teasingly, in the passages cited above, he has nevertheless so transformed it
within his own narrative as to make its familiar content virtually unrecognizable.
Even Ogilvie, the staunchest recent defender of the view that Theocritus follows
the traditional myth, has to confess that the poet «has veiled the whole story in
a cloak of allusive obscurity»[34].

Such a distortion of the myth in a poet as learned and sophisticated as Theo-
critus cannot but be intentional. The effect of departing from the received legend
while subtly hinting at it, as Priapus' speech seems to do, forces the reader to
explore further. The very *mystery* of Daphnis' end may be the most essential
element in the poem. Whether Daphnis dies for chastity or is paying the price
of his amorous infidelity, the essential fact remains that within the narrative
which the poem itself provides, Daphnis feels himself at odds with Aphrodite.
The fact that she remains well-disposed toward him (139) does not alter *his* sense
of bitterness toward her[35]. He has some sort of difficulty with love ($\delta\acute{v}\sigma\varepsilon\varrho\omega\varsigma$, 85)
and is wrestled to a fall by Eros (98), whom he himself hoped to throw (97) and
hurt even in Hades (103)[36]. As a result of this struggle with Eros he is 'wasting
away', and his weakened state involves a waning and inversion of nature's vitality
(cf. 87–88. 132–136). The language of resurrection and erection in 139 and 152
and the allusion to Adonis in 109 also suggest that Theocritus means us to bring
Daphnis' death into relation with the cycles of death and resurrection in vegeta-
tion myths, though such a possibility does not entitle us to interpret Daphnis
himself simply as a vegetation god as nature-mythicists of the nineteenth century
did[37].

As in Idyll III, Theocritus is playing upon a mythical archetype in a complex

---

[32] Ogilvie (above n. 1) 106–107 and Schmidt (above n. 1) 540–541, who survey the scholarship
on this point, trace the view of Daphnis' chastity back to Gebauer in 1856.

[33] Williams (above n. 1) 122 points out the «jeering» and «offensive» tone of Priapus in 81–91.
See also the good remarks of J.-H. Kühn, *Die Thalysien Theokrits (id. 7)*, Hermes 86
(1958) 58 on Priapus' inability to understand Daphnis.

[34] Ogilvie (above n. 1) 108. See also Prescott (above n. 2) 140.

[35] This point is overlooked by those who, like Legrand (above n. 23) 147, stress Aphrodite's
good will toward Daphnis as evidence against his being a chaste, Hippolytus-like figure.

[36] Schmidt (above n. 1) 549–550 thus lays insufficient stress on the conflict between Aphrodite
and Daphnis and does not really account for the bitterness of Daphnis' reply to the goddess
or for his wish to be a *kakon algos* to Eros even in Hades (103).

[37] e.g. K. F. Hermann, *Disputatio de Daphnide Theocriti* (Göttingen 1853) 19–20. See also
Prescott, CQ (above n. 6) 178.

and allusive way[38]. The waters of death close over the living singer (cf. 128–129) whose tensions between Nymph and maiden are left unresolved, whereas the waters of life bathe the cup (150), whose gaily entwining ivy (31) encloses playful love, work, growth, childhood, maturity, and old age, in a calm balance and tranquillity. In more condensed form, the antithesis is between the 'stream' of death which closes over Daphnis and the 'springs of the Seasons' which wash the cup, object of enduring beauty and the prize of happy singers.

The Idyll's self-conscious juxtaposition of different levels of fiction and of the different modes of language appropriate to each level (rustic conversation – cup – rustic song – rustic conversation) suggest that the poem is as much about art as it is about love. As the 'washing' of the cup (27) and its 'springs' (150) contrast with the 'washing' of Daphnis and his 'stream' (140), so the happy rustic singer, Thyrsis, contrasts with the tragic rustic singer, Daphnis. Daphnis' pipe has 'breath like honey' (μελίπνουν, 128) and so, in the Goatherd's wish, Thyrsis' mouth should be 'full of honey' (πλῆρές τοι μέλιτος, 146)[39]. But within the poem Daphnis himself does not sing. Since he is 'dear to the Muses' (141), he is, presumably, a singer of considerable talent, as Theocritus suggests elsewhere too[40]. But the only time there is mention of his art, it is in pathetic farewell: Daphnis consigns his honey-voiced pipe to Pan, for he is being dragged down to Hades by Eros (128 to 130):

> ἔνθ᾽, ὦναξ, καὶ τάνδε φέρευ πακτοῖο μελίπνουν
> ἐκ κηρῶ σύριγγα καλὸν περὶ χεῖλος ἑλικτάν·
> ἦ γὰρ ἐγὼν ὑπ᾽ Ἔρωτος ἐς Ἅιδαν ἕλκομαι ἤδη.

His art stands under the shadow of the fate engulfing him. It too is overshadowed by death. Hence his 'wasting away in his eyes' when he sees the maidens and cannot dance with them may be due not so much to erotic desire, as Priapus seems to think (90–91), as to the frustration of his artist's desire to pipe and sing. Thyrsis, on the other hand, in happy relation with his world and its divinities, blooms in his singing and wins the prize, itself a symbol of art's joyful and fruitful comprehensiveness. The 'real' singer, Thyrsis, stands in close and harmonious relation to the exuberance of nature's rhythms. The mythical singer, Daphnis, stands apart from them. Dragged to Hades by Eros (130), he must abandon his pipe. His fate enacts a tragic union of art and death.

As an interpreter of the primal experiences of love and death, the poet-singer-rustic stands in a special relation to the mysterious vital energies of nature. This relation is presented as opposing, but complementary extremes in the antithesis

---

[38] See my essay, *Adonis and Aphrodite: Theocritus, Idyll III 48*, Ant. Class. 38 (1969) 82–88.
[39] Note also the repeated motif of wax in 27 and 129, where there is another contrast of happiness and sadness.
[40] *Id.* V 80–81, 'the bard Daphnis', loved by the Muses. See also ps.-Theocr., *Id.* VIII 92–93 and Diod. 4, 84, 3, who makes Daphnis the inventor of bucolic song. See also Prescott (above n. 2) 132.

between Daphnis and Thyrsis. Yet this polarity is, in turn, only a part of the larger antithetical structure of the Idyll. On the one side stands the death of the bucolic singer whom Aphrodite cannot 'raise up'. On the other stands the 'rising up' of the happy singer's he-goats in a beautiful pastoral *locus*, an expression par excellence of untrammeled access to creative energy in its most basic form. As a singer, Daphnis is loved both by the Muses and the Nymphs (141), and there is a pathos and irony in the fact that he dies in the element which both symbolizes life and is associated throughout the poem with the divinities who love him (22. 66–69)[41].

Water throughout the poem mediates between art and nature and between life and death. The water of Daphnis' geographically wider world is dangerous, whereas the water associated with art, both in the rustics' pastoral locale and in the springs of the Seasons, is life-giving and benign. Sweetness, springs of water, and symbols of art (song and cup) span the arc of the whole poem. The Idyll opens with Thyrsis' comparison of his companion's song to the whispering of the pine 'by the springs' (1–3). The Goatherd develops the comparison, moving from the implicit, paratactic comparison of 1–3 to explicit and hypotactic comparison: 'Sweeter your song, O shepherd, than that water which flows down from the rock high above' (7–8):

> ἅδιον, ὦ ποιμήν, τὸ τεὸν μέλος ἢ τὸ καταχές
> τῆν' ἀπὸ τᾶς πέτρας καταλείβεται ὑψόθεν ὕδωρ.

All this sweetness and liquid imagery return in the Goatherd's compliments at the end (146–149). Yet the positive symbolism of water has become far more complex, not only in the reference to the mythological 'springs of the Seasons' in the Goatherd's next line (150), but also in the fact that the symbolical association of water and art have been deepened by the intervening elements, the cup 'washed' in sweet wax and Daphnis 'washed over' by the deadly stream. Song (art, poetry) is seen to stand in a more complex relation to those springs from which it draws its life and its images of beauty.

The rustics' comparison of song to whispering trees and flowing water in the opening lines makes nature itself songful: it sings, as it were, in responsion to the sweetness of the rustics' music. But over against this sympathetic relation between nature and song and between the happy rustics and their natural world stands the discordant relation of Daphnis. Not only does water cause his death; not only does he invert nature's rhythms of growth in his closing lines (132–136); but also, in the very last of those lines – and therefore in his last utterance in the poem – he envisages the defeat of song. This defeat is part of the topsy-turviness of his embittered view of nature: 'And from the mountains owls would chatter to the nightingales' (κἠξ ὀρέων τοὶ σκῶπες ἀηδόσι γαρύσαιντο, 136). The owls do

---

[41] On the ambiguity of Daphnis' relation with the Nymphs see above n. 29. The litotes of 141 may also hint at this ambiguous relation.

not merely 'vie with nigthingales', the more common *topos*, but, it would seem, disturb their music[42]. The more raucous sounds of the rustic world drown out its sweeter notes. These owls come 'from the mountains', the realm inhabited by the pastoral divinities, the Nymphs (67–69), Hermes (77, ἀπ' ὤρεος), and Pan (123, κατ' ὤρεα; also 124–126). Thyrsis too comes from Mount Aetna (65). Daphnis' image of owls and mountains in 136 not only negates the songfulness of the rustic world[43], but also reverses the harmony between song and landscape established by the two herdsmen in their opening lines. They are in accord with nature's songs (1–3) and even boast of improving on them (7–8). Significantly, Daphnis' defeat of song stands in close association with his words of death and violence: the phrase 'since Daphnis dies' and an image of hunting immediately precede (Δάφνις ἐπεὶ θνάσκει, καὶ τὰς κύνας ὤλαφος ἕλκοι, 135). Aside from the brief allusion to Pan's hunting in 16, the only other reference to hunting in the poem comes in Daphnis' challenge to Aphrodite (110). There, as here, it shatters the peace of the bucolic setting and there too it is associated with death and disaster in love: the death of Adonis as he hunts the boar.

Daphnis' association of death and song also contrasts with Thyrsis and the Goatherd. They had also juxtaposed song and death, but in a playful way which, in fact, stressed enjoyment of the present and championed continuity over discontinuity[44]. In exhorting Thyrsis to sing, the Goatherd had teased, 'You won't keep your song in Hades who brings forgetfulness' (τὰν γὰρ ἀοιδάν | οὔ τί πᾳ εἰς Ἀίδαν γε τὸν ἐκλελάθοντα φυλαξεῖς, 62–63). These two passages, 62–63 and 135–136, stand at the beginning and end of the sufferings of Daphnis respectively and, like the enframing water, help focus the antitheses between Daphnis and the other parts of the Idyll.

Some of these antitheses may be set forth in the following diagram:

Thyrsis and Goatherd	*Daphnis*
Water and song in joyful setting (nature in harmony with man) sweetness	Death and song (136. 111) (inversion of nature, 132–136) bitterness
Art and water in joyful setting (150)	Water and death (139–140)
Fulness (146–147)	Wasting away (66. 82. 88. 91)
Sexual energy and exuberance (152)	Failure of the 'raising up' of Daphnis (139) Envy of rutting goats (87–88)
Nymphs' presence in a watery setting which fosters song (1–8. 21–22) (waters of life, song, vitality)	Nymphs' withdrawal to their 'streams' at Daphnis' death (66–69. 141) (waters of death)

[42] See Gow ad loc. for the problem of interpretation here.

[43] Compare also Daphnis' taunting reference to Mt. Ida in 105 and his description of mountains as the habitat of bears in 115. In *Id.* VII 87–88 and 92–93 being 'on the mountains' is part of a peaceful bucolic life of song and closeness to the Muses. Lycidas also elaborates his song 'on the mountain', VII 51. See Puelma (above n. 9) 154 n. 31.

[44] Cf. 116 and 144, discussed above.

IV

As a *boukolos*, Daphnis shares the same world as Thyrsis and the Goatherd. But unlike Thyrsis and his companion, Daphnis never himself mentions either the Muses or the Nymphs. He invokes the rivers, as he invokes Pan, only to bid farewell (117–118. 123–129). In Thyrsis' song both wild and domestic creatures mourn Daphnis' plight (71–75), the latter at his feet (74–75). Yet in Daphnis' own utterances, only wild and unproductive animals are addressed: wolves, jackals, bears in their mountain caves (115–116). Though Thyrsis makes the mountains inhabited by Nymphs (67) and by Hermes (77), Daphnis places there not just Pan (123), but also the bears (115), the rude-voiced owls (136), and the sad myths of Callisto and Arcas (125–126). These passages, taken together with Daphnis' inversion of nature in 131–136, depict a certain removal from what is life-giving and gentle in his world, what the goats, the Nymphs, Aphrodite all share.

Daphnis' 'bitterness' (cf. 93) calls out the potential 'bitterness' of Pan (cf. 16) and destroys the 'sweetness' of the rustic world which enframes his suffering (cf. 1–2. 7–8. 65. 95. 145–148). The phrase καὶ ἁ πίτυς of the poem's very first line recurs, in the identical metrical position, in Daphnis' doleful inversion of nature in 134 καὶ ἁ πίτυς ὄχνας ἐνείκαι. In his upside-down perspective the songful pine of the happy rustics must now bear an alien fruit. The springs where rustics sing (1–2. 21–22) become, through Daphnis, the place of a foresaken maiden's wanderings (πάσας ἀνὰ κράνας, 83). The mountains visited by gods and Nymphs (67. 77. 105) are for him the place from which owls come to defeat the songful nightingale (136). The lovely trees which Thyrsis and the Goatherd admire for shade and sound become an item in Daphnis' taunt of Aphrodite (106ff. and cf. δρύες in 23 and 106). 'Pasturing' itself figures here in scornful tones (νομεύει, 109; cf. νομευσῶ, 14). Whereas Thyrsis and the Goatherd found the natural sounds of their setting an invitation to song and an occasion for compliments (1–8), Daphnis uses these sounds mockingly. In a lovely line he describes the pleasing buzz of bees around their hives (αἱ δὲ καλὸν βομβεῦντι ποτὶ σμάνεσσι μέλισσαι, 107), a common motif in the bucolic *locus amoenus*[45]. But the resonant beauty of the line is at variance with Daphnis' embittered tone. His irony destroys the very beauty which his words create. The tone is totally different from the rustics' simple, unironical, grateful acceptance of their world and their ingenuous belief in and respect for its gods (cf. 16–18). Their matter-of-fact caution in their talk of Pan in these lines (16–18) differs also from the emotionality and rhetoric of Daphnis' death-burdened invocation to Pan (123–130), where, in fact, a tomb enters into his sweep over Pan's Arcadia (αἰπύ τε σᾶμα, 125).

Daphnis' taunting of Aphrodite is his boldest challenge to the spirit of life and sexual energy from which he is alienated. This challenge itself threatens to burst the limits of the pastoral world. Daphnis invokes epic battle scenes in heroic language (112–113):

---

[45] See V 46; VII 81 and 142; XXII 42. Also [VIII] 45–46, *A.P.* 9, 564 (Nikias).

αὖτις ὅπως στασῇ Διομήδεος ἆσσον ἰοῖσα,
καὶ λέγε «τὸν βούταν νικῶ Δάφνιν, ἀλλὰ μάχευ μοι».

Both stylistically and thematically these two verses sound a note discordant with pastoral peace and pastoral song. Epic language (cf. ἆσσον ἰοῖσα, 112)[46] and the call of battle (ἀλλὰ μάχευ μοι, 113) reveal a spirit at variance with the happy limits of style and setting accepted by Thyrsis and the Goatherd. The *hybris* of this challenge to Aphrodite finds expression in a corresponding *hybris* of style (112)[47]. In both cases this is also the *hybris* of art (or one view of art) against nature.

The 'springs of the Seasons' and the rutting goats of the end assert the victory of nature's powers, self-contained and indifferent, over the fevered emotionality of the mortal who defies them. Yet these lines also affirm a more positive vitality, accessible to those less recalcitrant, less violent singers who know the ways of goats, but can also speak of mythological life-giving springs. Daphnis may die, but other, happier dwellers in this rustic world remain to inherit the whispering pines by the spring and the rill dripping down from its high rock. Their songs can incorporate the 'sorrows of Daphnis' (19); but they themselves go beyond this suffering, death-bent pathos in a more inclusive and more affirmative vision of the relation between art and nature, fiction and reality. So the cup, also a symbol of art, contains scenes of frustration, toil, imminent damage to crops and food; yet in its totality it remains joyful (31) and retains associations with sweetness (27) and life-giving water (150).

This contrast between the death of the embittered individual and the continuity and creative life of art may also be reflected in the juxtaposition of Μοιρᾶν and Μοίσαις in identical metrical positions in the last two lines of Thyrsis' song (140–141). 'Fates' and 'Muses', death and poetry are thus counterposed. A coincidence of this nature is unlikely in a poet as conscious of repetition and sound as Theocritus, and the antithesis seems too deeply related to the main themes of the Idyll to be accidental. In the only other place in the Idyll where *moira* occurs, 'Muses' also follow immediately in the next line, this time in the refrain (93–94). The Muses to whom Thyrsis and the Goatherd offer sacrifices and libations (9–11. 143–145) foster life and profit from the herd's increase; but they can be only helpless bystanders of Daphnis' death (141).

Daphnis' isolation, as Lawall has rightly remarked, has an heroic stamp. Like an Homeric hero, he challenges the gods and with his death he calls into question the entire order of the natural world: 'Let *everything* (πάντα) be upside down since Daphnis dies' (134–135). At his death 'all' the rustic herdsmen ask after him (πάντες, 81), and Priapus speaks of the girl, forlorn on his account, wandering among 'all the springs, all the groves' (πάσας ἀνὰ κράνας, πάντ' ἄλσεα, 83). 'Do you

---

[46] Cf. *Il.* 15, 105 and 22, 92.

[47] Note too Daphnis' recondite and unhappy myths in his invocation to Pan in 125–126. Such a tone is very different from the rustic level on which Thyrsis and the Goatherd speak of Pan in 15–18.

think that my every sun (πάνϑ' ἄλιον, 102) has set?' Daphnis mockingly charges Aphrodite. Adonis, he says, 'hunts all wild beasts' (ϑηρία πάντα, 110). His death brings a tragic dimension into a realm which tends to pull away from such sufferings into either rustic realism or mythical fantasy. Hence it is a momentous event in the pastoral world. It shows the pastoral poet seeking to connect his art with the prior traditions of Greek tragic and heroic poetry. Even this fanciful and artificial framework deals, after its fashion, with the facts of suffering, loss, isolation. Daphnis' sufferings, nevertheless, are framed by the talk of rustic herdsmen, enclosed within a song with a stylized refrain, and juxtaposed with the self-conscious *ekphrasis* on the cup. Thus they are also kept at a certain distance. Daphnis is not merely a sufferer, but also a singer, the archetypal pastoral singer. According to Diodorus (4, 84, 3) he was called simply Boukolos and invented bucolic song. All the inhabitants of the pastoral world, therefore – animals, rustics, deities, even Pan himself – are implicated in his death and asked to share his grief.

If through the enframing theme of the cup Theocritus is exploring the capacity of his art to encompass, with pathos and sympathy, the lighter losses of life and to touch disappointment with a gentle and humorous irony, through the Daphnis song he explores these disappointments in greater depth and in a darker tonality. Daphnis' death is a statement of an eternal and tragic conflict, not only between will and instinct, but also between art and nature[48]. The calm beauty of the pastoral frame can encompass both sides: harmony with nature and discord; playful and tragic love; happy and tormented rustics; realistically beautiful springs and the ominous, archetypal stream of death.

Through his careful handling of structure, allusion, and pathos Theocritus has enabled the transformed myth of Daphnis to say even more to us. Art – poetry, song, the carving on the cup – is both in touch with the vital energies of goats, winding ivy, melodious springs and at the same time is removed from them in a tragic assertion of autonomy. Metaphorically speaking, it draws its strength from the 'springs of the Seasons', and yet it may also defy the gods of love and meet death in the element associated with creativity and refreshment. Hence Theocritus uses the ancient Homeric and Hesiodic metaphor equating the sweetness of song and the sweetness of running water (7–8). But the 'bitterness' of unfulfilled love (93) brings a union of song and death (128–130. 135–136). The 'sacred water' of kindly Nymphs (cf. 69. 141) becomes ultimately the water of death (140). The ambiguity of water corresponds to an ambiguity in art itself: art's participation in a life-giving and beautiful natural world on the one hand (cf. 1–8. 21–22) and its union with death as an aspect of its *hybris* in rejecting the 'natural' on the other hand.

In one sense Theocritus' Daphnis is descended from the mythical heroes who

---

[48] The statement by Kühn (above n. 33) 58 is, therefore, only partially valid when he speaks of «Daphnis, der von Liebesleidenschaft erfüllt ist, aber seiner Strebung den Trotz des Willens entgegensetzt» and of «der Zwiespalt zwischen Geistwillen und Triebnatur».

assert the independence of their emotional or spiritual life over against the busy, happy natural rhythms surrounding them, an independence which can only be tragic. The line runs from Homer's Achilles to Sophocles' Antigone and Electra, from Euripides' Hippolytus and Pentheus to Virgil's Orpheus[49]. Such heroism, like all heroism, is not at home in pastoral, and so Daphnis' motives remain obscure. His death, therefore, partakes more of the pathetic than of the tragic.

Unlike the heroic personages mentioned above, Daphnis does not die for any larger commitment or any clearly defined spiritual purpose. Inviting as this hypothesis is, there is not a word in the poem that tells us clearly that he dies for the sake of preserving chastity. That he dies out of a quarrel with Aphrodite and Eros is clear, but the basis of that quarrel is not revealed. We cannot assert with certainty that, like Virgil's Orpheus in the Fourth Georgic, he resists physical love in the name of some higher devotion to sentiment or to art. We are not even sure that he dies, δύσερως (85), out of an excess or out of a deficiency of desire. It is rather the poignancy of his obscure death and the contrast of that death with the rest of his pastoral world that are important. The very mystery of his end heightens this poignancy. He is simply a rustic singer doomed to die. That is how he appears to us, a figure laden with the lugubrious burden of a destiny which is given, unexplained, a fixed, unchangeable fact. It is like the mysterious fate of figures in the mythical background of the Iliad and the Odyssey: Bellerophon in Iliad VI or Niobe in Iliad XXIV or the daughters of Pandareus in Odyssey XX. And in the very fixity and factuality of his fate, Daphnis is also an unchanging symbol for an aspect of art. Hence the poem emphasizes less his personality per se than the world of mythicized, sympathetic or mysterious nature and divinity which surrounds him and survives him.

As Daphnis is a symbol of only one aspect of art, so the world he creates about him reflects only one aspect of reality. Its mournful, elegiac coloring and the negative, destructive force of its water belong to that side of art which does violence to nature and stands apart from it in its own autonomy and pride. On the other side stand the happier singers and the easy, melodious, exuberant generosity of their pastoral environment (1–28. 146–152). Viewing the 'sorrows of Daphnis' as a self-contained narrative cannot clarify the mystery of his death, no matter how hard we scrutinize the text of 66–141 as an isolated unit. Neither Daphnis nor the world he occupies *can* stand by itself. That is in part the meaning of Thyrsis' song. Each is part of a dialectic, of which the happier rustics, the cup, the frisky goats, the whispering pines, the singing waters form the other side.

Without the awareness of this polarity within Theocritus' art not only Idyll I, but other Idylls as well remain unintelligible. The Seventh Idyll, which Gow found «an enigmatic masterpiece», its problem «unsolved»[50], becomes fully meaningful only in terms of the antitheses between its two main figures, their setting,

---

[49] Lawall (above n. 1) 20 and passim.
[50] Gow, CQ 34 (1940) 50. Cf. Kühn (above, n. 33) 64 with n. 2.

character, style[51]. The contrast between Thyrsis and Daphnis, cup and inset song, expresses an aspect of the same dialectic that binds together Lycidas and Simichidas in VII, Corydon and Battus in IV, Lacon and Comatas in V, Milo and Bucaeus in X: a dialectic between sentiment and factuality, between hopeless passion and the continuities of work, between dreamlike aspiration and practical acceptance, between imagination and reality. These tensions in the fictions and the characters of the Idylls represent tensions both within the inner world of the poet and within the outer world of the human condition as the poet grasps it and can render his vision accessible to others.

Seen in this perspective, Daphnis is not an isolated personality in Theocritus. His affinities lie with figures like the sentimental goatherd of III, Battus of IV, Bucaeus of X. These characters are wrapped up entirely in their own emotions and distort reality in their tendency to color events with their own projected personalities and passions. Daphnis shares in their melancholy and their penchant for invoking death. In his case, however, this death-bent sentimentality reaches tragic dimensions and takes on universal proportions. Daphnis the singer exemplifies a view of art which weaves its stuff almost entirely out of the emotional world of the artist and thus runs the risk of losing touch with reality. The antidote to it is the practical realism and resiliency of a Thyrsis (I), or a Corydon (IV), or a Milo (X), who see life with a down-to-earth precision and celebrate the 'real' beauty before them rather than search for a beauty not given in the world as it is.

This aspiration toward the impossible, toward 'what is absent', τὰ ἀπεόντα, in the terms of Idyll X (8), is an element in the melancholy of Daphnis. On the one hand this unhappiness with the world as it is may be a divine discontent which leads the poet to harken to a music within him finer than that which whispering pines or plashing springs can create. On the other hand it can also constitute a removal from reality in a negative sense, an inwardness which feeds upon and destroys the healthy capacity to enjoy life as we find it.

Even before the artificial and sophisticated Alexandrian literary circles which Theocritus knew, the poet in Greek society had ceased to occupy the clearly defined social and public position of a Tyrtaeus, a Solon, an Aeschylus. The poet's world becomes more inward, self-conscious, self-reflective. Thus he inevitably becomes aware of his ambiguous relation to reality. Indeed, from Euripides on, he is persistently engaged in the task of questioning just what 'reality' is.

For all his apparent earthiness and simplicity, Theocritus is heir to this tradi-

---

[51] See especially Kühn (above n. 33) passim. For a recent critical survey of the scholarship on *Id.* VII see Serrao (above n. 9) 13–68. Serrao himself accepts some elements of this dialectical interpretation (see especially pp. 41 ff. and 59 ff.). On the whole, however, he treats the two songs in terms of complementarity rather than polarity and in terms of moral rather than aesthetic considerations. Though he excellently observes the complex blending of realistic detail and idealization in the characters of the poem (pp. 26–28), he tends at the end to oversimplify Theocritus' tension between reality and imagination and to fall back on the traditional view of bucolic escapism (pp. 66–68 with n. 113).

tion of poetic self-examination and exploration of the roots of his art. The first Idyll, as we have seen, develops a series of ramifying divisions between the celebration of life and the dark longing for death, between loves that are open and exuberant and loves that are obscure and doomed. The artist mediates between these two realms, between outer and inner, between joyous participation in the present and exploration of the hidden and unknown realms that most men cannot or dare not enter, between continuity in a public world and an 'irresponsibility' that scorns companions and demands a fierce independence. A modern artist and thinker who has pondered art's ambivalence between life and death may shed some light on Theocritus:

«Nowhere so clearly as here does one see how virtue and morality are the task of life, a categorical imperative, a command on the part of life, whereas all aestheticism is of a pessimistic and orgiastic nature, that is, belongs to death. It is only all too certain that all art has this inclination, tends to the abyss. But art, despite the interconnection of death and beauty, is yet wonderfully bound to life and contains its own antidotes. Love of life and welcoming of life (Lebensfreundlichkeit, Lebensgutwilligkeit) form one of the artist's basic instincts ... The artist, it seems to me, is truly and literally the (ironic!) mediator between the worlds of Death and Life.» (Thomas Mann, «Über die Ehe».)

Here, to be sure, we are venturing beyond Theocritus' text, yet not so far as might at first seem, for Theocritus has recast an ancient myth of a doomed poet into a form which expresses universal antitheses in the nature of art. These antitheses are no less gripping and no more resolvable in our day than they were in the third century B.C., for they are fundamental to the condition of a being who, over and above his physical needs, possesses consciousness, yearnings, imagination and thus has the ambiguous capacity to make himself unhappy for no good reason. The perception of such discrepancies between reality and imagination, outer and inner worlds, may permit a comic or even grotesque view of the human condition, as expressed in the Goatherd of III or the Cyclops of VI or XI. But these discrepancies also have tragic implications, and these Theocritus develops in the tale of Daphnis in Idyll I.

Through the polarities between Daphnis and Thyrsis, as through those between the pairs of the other Idylls, Theocritus also expresses his recognition that the creative power of his art flows from a tension of opposites, from the ability of the poet to acknowledge a profound cleavage within the nature of reality[52]. The poet spans the abyss between the two worlds as with a fine wire, and, like Pope's spider, «lives along the line».

---

[52] For this aspect of Theocritus' art see Lawall (above n. 1) 13. 101. 105–108; Kühn (above n. 33) 57–61 and 66–69. Yet one must be careful not to focus the issue too narrowly or to limit it solely to questions of expression of personality. See my review of Lawall, CJ 63 (1968) 227–228 and my remarks in *Theocritean Criticism and the Interpretation of the Fourth Idyll*, Ramus I 1 (1971) 1–25. See also Luck's criticism of Kühn (above n. 9) 187 and J. Van Sickle, *Poetica teocritea*, Quad. Urbin. 9 (1970) 71ff.

In Idyll I, accordingly, Daphnis is not a whole figure, a complete personality whose motives can be analyzed in depth. As a figure in a narrative he has, to be sure, his individual pathos which wins our involvement in the sad and elusive beauty of his story. But, like the contrasting waters of the poem, he is also a symbolical element within a larger frame. And in this larger frame the sadness of his mysterious end finds its appropriate foil and response in Thyrsis' joyful libations and the Goatherd's lively flock.

These goats and springs frame Daphnis' sufferings at either end of the poem just as elms, oaks, Priapus and sacred springs framed the first reference to 'the sorrows of Daphnis' (19) at the beginning (21–23). Each side needs the other to anchor it to the wholeness of reality. And each stands in a perpetual oscillation with the other. Between the two poles vibrates the wide field of possible attitudes to life, to art, and to nature, from the acceptant to the aggressive, from rustic contentment to heroic restlessness, from self-effacing modesty (note that the Goatherd is nameless)[53] to self-assertive individualism, from the bucolic to the epic style. All of the antitheses together are implicit in each one of them individually, and they all overlap. Thus they are all contained symbolically in the contrast between Thyrsis' springs on the one hand and the mysterious eddy which closes over Daphnis on the other. In their complex totality and interrelatedness only symbol can hold them all simultaneously. In this sense too Theocritus' poem, with its inset of cup and song and its heavily articulated enframing motifs, provides its own key to the meaning of Daphnis' death.

---

[53] For a different view of the Goatherd's anonymity see Ott (above n. 1) 136–137.

DEATH BY WATER: A NARRATIVE PATTERN IN THEOCRITUS
(IDYLLS 1, 13, 22, 23)

I.

In four poems of the Theocritean corpus a major character meets disaster either in water or in close association with water. At the end of Idyll 1 Daphnis 'goes to the stream' and dies. In 13 Hylas is drawn into a Nymph-haunted pool. In 22 Amycus fights his ill-fated match with Polydeuces beside clear, flowing water. In the pseudo-Theocritean 23 the arrogant boy drowns in an artificial pool.

This common motif is especially interesting for the three genuine Theocritean pieces, for it reveals a single poetic sensibility spanning both the bucolic *Idylls* and the so-called *epyllia*. The tracing of this and related motifs allows the four poems to shed light on one another and also gives us a renewed feeling for the unity of Theocritus' work.

In the three genuine *Idylls* (1, 13, 22) water forms part of the *locus amoenus*, the lovely setting, melodiously and gracefully described, which is one of the most familiar features of the *Idylls*. The term 'Idyll' itself (εἰδύλλιον) probably did not mean, as some have thought, 'little picture'; but description of nature plays an important role[1], and the *locus amoenus* is an essential part

---

[1] On *eidyllion* and the descriptive element in Theocritus see H. FRITZSCHE and E. HILLER, edd., Theokrits Gedichte³, Leipzig 1881, 4; A. KÖRTE, Hellenistic Poetry, tr. HAMMER and HADAS, New York 1929, 285; and most recently E. STAIGER, Theokrit, Die echten Gedichte, Zürich 1970, 18—19.

of this scenic, graphic element. Yet Theocritus' descriptions do not exemplify Hellenistic *ekphrasis* merely for its own sake. They are also expressive of the themes and tones of the individual poems. In the *Idylls* in question, they have an ambiguous and sinister side to which in turn corresponds an ambiguous quality in this 'idyllic' world as a whole.

From the earliest times water is a sacred element. Theocritus twice speaks of 'sacred water', ἱερὸν ὕδωρ (1, 69, 7, 136)[2]. Inhabited by gods and demigods, springs and rivers are literally 'sacred'. Water's sacredness also derives from its associations with the powers of nature that give and consequently may withhold life. Long before Theocritus poets appropriated this sacredness for their own purposes, either as an element in a symbolic landscape or as a metaphor for the joy, beauty, and mystery of poetic creation or as a symbol of an elusive happiness[3]. In the *Odyssey* a sacred spring or river is the setting for meetings which bring the hero closer to his goal or to the identity which he is seeking to regain (cf. Od. ε 441—453; ζ 85—87; ρ 206ff.; υ 158ff.). In Euripides modesty (*aidos*) is like a river which waters the *locus* symbolizing the hero's chastity (Hipp. 73—78)[4]. Hesiod had already associated the Muses with springs of water (Theogony 3 and 8). Like Homer (cf. Il. A 249), he had compared the power of song (or speech) to a sweet 'flowing' (Theog. 39, 84, 97) or to a 'sweet dew' (Theog. 83). Pindar richly developed this symbolic association of water and poetry[5]. By Theocritus' time the association is familiar and readily intelligible to the cultivated reader[6] and is strengthened by the connection between springs and oracular powers[7].

Theocritus is following in this venerable tradition when, in Idyll 7, he uses sacred springs as the setting for an important meeting of singers (6ff. and

---

[2] Cf. also the ἀβλαβὲς ὕδωρ of 24, 98, of the purifying force of water. Note Virgil's *fontis sacros* (E. 1, 52 and cf. E. 2, 59).

[3] The persistence of the imagery of the *locus* will appear from a remark by F. L. Lucas quoted in B. Blanshard, The Life of the Spirit in a Machine Age, Neilson Lecture, Smith College, Northampton, Mass. 1967, 13: »If I sought a symbol for happiness, it would perhaps be a mountain spring gently, but unfailingly, overflowing its basin with living water. There seems to be nothing in life more vital than to keep always this surplus of energy. One should always overflow«.

[4] See my essay: The Tragedy of the Hippolytus: The Waters of Ocean and the Untouched Meadow, HSCP 70, 1965, 117—169.

[5] See, e. g., Pae. 6, 7—9; N. 4, 1—5; N 7, 12 and 62; I. 6, 62—64; see further C. Segal, Pindar's Seventh *Nemean*, TAPA 98, 1967, 465—467 with note 73.

[6] E. g. Plato, Phaedrus 230b and 278b, Callim., Hymn to Apollo (2), 111—112. See in general A. Kambylis, Die Dichterweihe und ihre Symbolik, Bibl. d. klass. Altertumswiss. 2, Heidelberg 1965, 23—30 and 44; M. Puelma, Die Dichterbegegnung in Theokrits "Thalysien", MH 17, 1960, 156—157 with note 44; most recently A. La Penna in Studi filologici e storici in onore di V. De Falco, Naples 1971, 232.

[7] See especially Simonides frag. 26 D. = 72 Page; Plut., De Pyth. Or. 17, 402 C—D; generally Kambylis (preceding note) 27—30.

136 ff.). As LAWALL suggests, these springs serve »to mediate between the public world and the narrator's private experience of his meeting with Lycidas [8]«. In a lovely spot refreshed by clear, flowing water, one may meet the deities who bestow the marvelous gift of song. Callimachus, in the proem to his *Aetia*, had given influential new life to this motif of the Hesiodic 'Dichterweihe'[9]. The springs at the beginning of Idyll 1 and the Nymphs' 'sacred water' in Idyll 7, 136—137, both reflect the magical qualities, the serenity and the exuberant richness, of the *locus* where the 'Dichterweihe' occurs.

In all these cases water functions as a numinous substance whose presence marks man's entrance into a world beyond his normal ken and normal powers, a world which may be the realm of artistic or prophetic inspiration or sexual vitality or death. The water motif of Idyll 1 brings us at once into this mysterious realm. There, as we shall see, water is not only the element in which Daphnis meets his death; it is also akin to the life-giving water of the Hesiodic tradition, for the opening of the *Idyll* gives a complex and sophisticated formulation to the archaic association of water and poetic creativity[10].

This ambiguity of water parallels the ambiguity of the *locus amoenus* which it adorns and refreshes. Such *loci* are frequently the haunt of deities who may be either friendly or destructive or both by turns[11]. In Theocritus' fourth Epigram water has an important place in a *locus amoenus* which shelters a potent image of Priapus. In Idyll 1 the lovely locale where the two rustics pasture their flocks is also the resting place of 'bitter Pan' whom they 'fear' (Id. 1, 15—19).

Here too Theocritus is drawing upon very ancient strata in Greek culture. A beautiful setting with paradoxically dangerous overtones goes back to the very beginnings of Greek literature. One thinks of the harbor of the Laestrygonians or Circe's island in the *Odyssey* or the flowering meadow at the beginning of the Homeric *Hymn to Demeter*. It doubtless has even remoter origins in folktales wherein dangerous magic may lurk in the inviting pleasance of

[8] G. LAWALL, Theocritus' Coan Pastorals, A Poetry Book, Cambridge, Mass. 1967, 78.

[9] The importance of the Hesiodic and Callimachean "Dichterweihe" for Idyll 7 has been much discussed: see PUELMA (above, note 6) 156—157 with notes 37—38, 44; G. LUCK, Zur Deutung von Theokrits Thalysien, MH 23, 1966, 186—189; most recently G. SERRAO, Problemi di poesia alessandrina, I, Studi su Teocrito, Rome 1971, 13—68, especially 32 ff.; see also B. A. VAN GRONINGEN, Quelques problèmes de la poésie bucolique grecque, Mnemosyne, Ser. IV, 12, 1959, 31—32.

[10] One need hardly emphasize the "art for art's sake" tendency in Hellenistic poetry: see Bruno SNELL, Poetry and Society, Bloomington, Ind. 1961, 102 ff.

[11] See, for example, Leonidas of Tarentum, A. P. 6, 334. 9, 326. Plan. 230; Asclepiades, A. P. 9, 64, 1—2; Callim. Bath of Pallas 71—74. See also KAMBYLIS (above, note 6) 59—61 with note 121; P. LEGRAND, Étude sur Théocrite, Bibl. des Écoles françaises d'Athènes et de Rome, 79, Paris 1898, 210 with note 3. Note also the bucolic setting for the bacchantic violence of Theocr. 26 (3—5).

witch or ogre. This magical atmosphere is suitable both for the pastoral, where Nymphs and Satyrs and Pan are close neighbors of the herdsmen (cf. Epigrams 3 and 4), and for the Hellenistic epyllion, in which supernatural agencies often have a prominent role.

The elegant surface and the episodic character of these genres of Hellenistic poetry are able to utilize the strangeness and ambiguity of such settings, for the plot is often less firmly bound to a tight logical concatenation of events and easily admits unexpected leaps in the action. The intrusion of supernatural powers permits the display of recondite mythological lore. The sudden turns thereby given to the action encourage the development of shock-effects and pathos within a restricted compass. The Hellenistic poet who most keenly perceived and exploited the possibilities of combining elegant surface description and mysterious divine forces was a Roman: Ovid[12].

Theocritus' use of archaic ritual elements and ancient symbols is an important aspect of his art and one which deserves more recognition and study than it has received. In using such material he creates an effective and sometimes ironic tension between the sophistication of his form and the primitive resonances of his material. The fertility myths of Idyll 3, the whipping of Pan in 7, or the Adonis song in 15 are familiar examples[13]; but, as will appear, there are traces of this device in all the poems here discussed.

This tension, in turn, is related to the search in Hellenistic poetry for new effects of pathos. Contact with the uncanny, the mysterious, the primitive provides a special kind of emotional *frisson* and allows for the creation of lurid effects and violent emotional situations beyond the pale of reason or logic. Such is the effect of the magical incantations of Idyll 2 or Circe's purifications in the fourth book of Apollonius' Argonautica (4, 659—752), where water is also a part of the weird setting (4, 663. 670—671).

II.

Thyrsis' song of »the sufferings of Daphnis« ends as follows (1, 139—141):

τά γε μὰν λίνα πάντα λελοίπει
ἐκ Μοιρᾶν, χὠ Δάφνις ἔβα ῥόον. ἔκλυσε δίνα
τὸν Μοίσαις φίλον ἄνδρα, τὸν οὐ Νύμφαισιν ἀπεχθῆ.

All the thread from the Fates ran out, and Daphnis went
to the stream.
The rippling water washed over a man loved of the Muses,
one not hated of the Nymphs.

---

[12] See my *Landscape in Ovid's Metamorphoses*, Hermes Einzelschriften 23, Wiesbaden 1969, chap. I.

[13] See my: Adonis and Aphrodite: Theocritus, Idyll III, 48, AC 38, 1969, 82—88.

Commentators have long puzzled over the details of Daphnis' end. Both ancient and modern interpreters have suggested that the unnamed 'stream' of 140 is Acheron[14]. But, as Gow has duly noted, 'went to the stream' is an odd euphemism, if such it is, for 'died.' Acheron does not usually 'wash over' its victim. Elsewhere in Theocritus Acheron is either mentioned by name as a synonym for Hades (15, 86 and 141), or else the deceased stands by it (16, 31) or passes over it (17, 47). Others have suggested Daphnis turns into a spring or pool[15]. This view strains the Greek even more than the former interpretation. It also requires us to assume that Theocritus is following the version of the legend in which Daphnis has offended a water Nymph, a point on which the poem is silent[16].

Daphnis, then, dies by drowning[17]. The phrase ἔκλυσε δίνα (140), in emphatic asyndeton, carefully individualizes the watery nature of his death. The noun conveys the visual image of the circling ripples of water closing over the place which the cowherd has entered. Apollonius uses a similar expression of a Nymph pulling Hylas into her spring (1, 1239): μέση δ' ἐνὶ κάββαλε δίνη[18]. Theocritus himself uses δίνα elsewhere of the eddies of a river (22, 50). In Idyll 2, 30, the only other place where the word occurs in Theocritus, it describes the whirling movements of the magical 'iunx'. Even in this passage the word implies vivid physical movement, and hence the alleged metaphorical meaning of 'stream' in 1, 140 is all the less probable. That graphic and particularized glimpse of the 'eddy' would be misplaced if 'went to the stream' were a mere euphemism for 'died'.

The parallels with Idylls 13 and 22, especially with the former, here help us. They suggest that the poet is drawing upon an archetypal form of mysterious death. The actual manner of the death is less important than the mysterious atmosphere which surrounds it. The herdsman vanishes into a sort of 'whirlpool', never to be seen again. This 'eddy' adds to the suggestiveness of a

---

[14] See the scholia ad loc.; A. S. F. Gow, Theocritus[2], Cambridge 1952, ad 1, 140. For a recent survey of the scholarship see U. OTT, Die Kunst des Gegensatzes in Theokrits Hirtengedichten, Spudasmata 22, Hildesheim 1965, 129 with note 371.

[15] For instance, Ed. SCHWARTZ, Theokrits Daphnis, NGG 1904, 291.

[16] For the legend see Diodorus 4, 84; Aelian, V. H. 10, 18; Parthenius 29. See Gow's introductory note to Idyll 1 in his Commentary. Several recent scholars have argued for the traditional legend, notably R. M. OGILVIE, The Song of Thyrsis, JHS 82, 1962, 106—110, and F. J. WILLIAMS, Theocritus, Idyll I 81—91, JHS 89, 1969, 121—123. See, contra OGILVIE, E. A. SCHMIDT, Die Leiden des verliebten Daphnis, Hermes 96, 1968, 539—552. I plan to examine the question in more detail in a paper entitled *'Since Daphnis Dies': The Meaning of Theocritus' First IDYLL*, forthcoming in MH.

[17] So OGILVIE and WILLIAMS (preceding note).

[18] In Arg. 1, 1327 Apollonius uses δίνη of ripples of water closing over the demigod Glaucus, and here the verb κλύζειν occurs in the next line (1328).

strange death by water. It is a pastoral version of the end which claims Odysseus' companions and almost Odysseus himself: deadly, whirling water in a fairytale setting (cf. Odyssey μ 235—243. 430—444)[19].

Against this destructive side of pastoral water stand the melodious springs of the pastoral frame at the beginning (1—8). Springs occur again at the end of the poem: the cup is as fragrant as if it had been »washed in the springs of the Seasons« (150). The "sweetness" of Thyrsis' song (145—148, cf. 1—3, 7) contrasts with the 'bitterness' of Daphnis' love (93), as images of fulness (πλῆρες ... πλῆρες, 146—147) contrast with Daphnis' 'wasting away' (τάκεσθαι, 66. 82. 88. 91), and as the aroused billy-goat contrasts with Aphrodite's inability to 'raise up' the dying cowherd (152 and 139).

Water, then, helps to focus a large antithesis between life and death, between joyful rustic and a dying rustic, between pastoral figures content with their world (1—8) and a pastoral figure who would turn his world upside down (132—136). Through the art-world of the cup and the archaic associations of water with poetic creativity, these contrasts also express different views of pastoral art: joyful, acceptant, exuberant on the one hand; pathetic, sorrowful, defiant of the 'natural' in a tragic assertion of autonomy and heroic independence on the other[20].

The two enframed, set pieces of the *Idyll*, the cup described by the Goatherd (27—56) and the 'sorrows of Daphnis' sung by Thyrsis (66—141), present antithetical but possibly complementary ways of grasping reality through art[21]. On the cup joy predominates. The entwining ivy »rejoices (ἀγαλλομένα) in its yellow fruit« (31) and the boy, in one scene, »takes joy (γαθεῖ) in his plaiting« (54). These are scenes of realistic, workaday figures. Their sufferings and frustrations the poet views with a gentle irony. Neither the flirtation (33—38) nor the intent boy's loss of lunch and grapes is very serious.

Thyrsis' song creates a more mysterious world of mythological figures. Here Nymphs and gods converse with pastoral folk. Daphnis' struggle with love proves fatal. Aphrodite's laughter in 95—96, though not malicious[22], is more ominous than the laughter of the woman on the cup (36). Water symbolism again expresses the sharpest contrast. The cup is »washed with sweet wax« (κεκλυσμένον ἁδέι κηρῷ 27), whereas the mysterious eddy "washes over" Daphnis (ἔκλυσε δίνα, 140). The verb κλύζειν occurs only in these two passages in Theocritus.

---

[19] Contrast also the saving water or the Phaeacian river and its life-giving δίνη: Od. ε 116; cf. also ε 441—453, ζ 85—87. See G. R. LEVY, The Gate of Horn, London 1948, 268 with note 2.

[20] This point will be further developed in my paper on Idyll 1 (see above, note 16).

[21] For the contrasts between the two scenes, with a different emphasis, see LAWALL above, p. 22 note 8) 30—31, OTT (above p. 24 note 14) 132—136.

[22] See G. ZUNTZ, Theocritus I. 95 f., CQ n. s. 10, 1960, 37—40. Also OTT (above, p. 24 note 14) 124—125 with note 358.

This contrast, in turn, connects the two-sidedness of water with a double voice in art: the earthy, joyful realism of the Goatherd and the loftier, more remote, more pathetic and stylized mythology of Thyrsis. Hence after Daphnis' watery death liquid imagery recurs, now in close association both with song and with natural vitality. Thyrsis ends with a libation to the Muses, to be poured from the Goatherd's cup, now Thyrsis' prize (142—145). The Goatherd replies with comparisons to honey and figs, speaks of the «springs of the Seasons«, and refers to the sexual energies of his billy-goat (146—152). All the contrasts of the poem are concentrated in this closing passage: sweet *versus* bitter; life *versus* death; destructive *versus* benign waters; awakened, in-stinctive sexuality *versus* emotional complexity and Aphrodite's failure (139).

The positive side of the antitheses at the end not only enframes the sadness of the tale of Daphnis, but also harks back to the beautiful water of the opening dialogue, a correspondence reinforced by the motifs of sweetness (1—3. 7. 145—148) and milking (6. 25. 143. 151). There, however, both rustics spoke of water and associated water with poetry (1—8). Here only the Goatherd mentions springs (150), now the mythological springs of goddesses who usher in the movements of nature and guide her rhythms. Yet Thyrsis too is con-nected with the positive and joyful side of this imagery through his libations to the Muses (143—145).

The motif of water undergoes a development and a gradual elevation in the course of the poem. It moves from the naturalistic, though still melodious and divinely inhabited (22) springs of the beginning to the mythological »springs of the Seasons« in 150 and the libations to the Muses in 144[23]. This elevation takes place appropriately after Thyrsis' creation of the mythical realm of Daphnis, with its divinities and its mysterious water of 140. The dying singer, Daphnis, leaves his 'honey-voiced' (μελίπνουν) pipes to Pan (128—130). The living, 'real' singer is praised in terms of honey (μέλιτος, 146). Daphnis dies. Thyrsis lives on (contrast the ways Hades is talked of in 63 and 130); and the joyful, life-giving waters of his art both include and triumph over the deadly water which drowns Daphnis.

Water thus expresses the fundamental contrast between life and death and thus links together in a single unified design the pastoral frame (1—8. 150), the cup (27), the geography of the song (68—69), and Daphnis' death (140). Life-giving, Olympian waters have the last place (150) and with them the earthy, vital instincts of pastoral in a more realistic vein (151—152). The pathos of Daphnis' death by water remains powerful and haunting, but it is enframed by something more joyful, more enduring.

---

[23] For the device of an enclosed narrative and frame on different levels of reality see PUELMA (above, p. 21 note 6) 145 and LUCK (above, p. 22 note 9) 187, à propos of Idyll 7.

III.

This use of water in a tale involving love and death has its closest parallel in the Hylas poem, Idyll 13. Setting out to fetch water for his companions' dinner, Hylas »noticed a spring in a low-lying place« (τάχα δὲ κράναν ἐνόησεν / ἡμένῳ ἐν χώρῳ 39—40). The place abounds in lush vegetation, attractively described (40—42). After this bit of *ekphrasis*, water returns. »In the middle of the water« (ὕδατι δ᾽ ἐν μέσσῳ, 43) Nymphs are dancing. These Nymphs are divinities of a bountiful nature, figures of grace and joy. Yet they are also »goddesses terrible for country folk« (δειναὶ θεαὶ ἀγροιώταις, 44)[24]. One recalls the sinister side of Pan in the First Idyll (16—17). The Nymphs are introduced in predominantly heavy, spondaic rhythms (42—44)[25]. The one who, in a much admired phrase, »has the look of springtime in her eyes« (ἔαρ θ᾽ ὁρόωσα, 45), bears the name of night, Nycheia, an ominous touch, as we shall soon see[26]. Accordingly the pool of these Nymphs adorns a *locus amoenus*, but also holds a strange fate for the lad who innocently wanders into it. The ambiguity of this pool closely approximates that of Ovid's Nymph, Salmacis, in the fourth book of the *Metamorphoses*[27].

The episode occurs at night (cf. δειελινοί, 33). These Nymphs do not sleep (ἀκοίμητοι, 44), another sinister note. We have already observed the nocturnal element in the name of the most lovely of them, Nycheia. The sailing which abandons Hylas irremediably to his fate takes place at midnight (μεσονύκτιον, 69).

It is strange that the vegetation of this *locus amoenus* is described in such detail (40—42) when it cannot be seen. Several critics have noted the anomaly[28]. On the one hand, as Gow suggests, »... One who follows the lines of Theocritus' picture with too curious an eye will find them blurred[29].« But on the other hand the darkness contributes to the atmosphere of unfamiliarity

---

[24] The parallels with Homer's Circe and Calypso are noted by Gow, ad loc., and by D. J. MASTRONARDE, Theocritus' Idyll 13: Love and the Hero, TAPA 99, 1968, 278 with note 9.

[25] See MASTRONARDE (preceding note) 285—286.

[26] For the sinister touch see MASTRONARDE (above, note 24) 285—287; for the nocturnal setting see also G. SERRAO, Ila in Apollonio e in Teocrito, Helikon 5, 1965, 562 ff. = Problemi (above, p. 22 note 9) 146 ff.

[27] See Met. 4, 297—388. Compare the similar motif in the stories of Narcissus (3, 407—414) and Arethusa (5, 587—591). See my *Landscape in Ovid's Metamorphoses* (above, p. 23 note 12) 25—26 and 46—49.

[28] So MASTRONARDE (above, note 24) 288, note 33; A. KÖHNKEN, Apollonios Rhodios und Theokrit, Hympomnemata 12, Göttingen 1965, 46 and 81; SERRAO (above, note 26) 553 = Problemi 129, who notes that while the darkness in Apollonius is an indispensable part of the narrative, in Theocritus it is »in contrasto con la descrizione del paesaggio e non necessaria allo svolgersi dell' azione.«

[29] A. S. F. Gow, The Thirteenth Idyll of Theocritus, CQ 32, 1938, 16, à propos of 13, 69.

and danger. The incongruity alerts us to the fact that the *ekphrasis* has something awry in it. The beauty of this pleasance is at variance with the circumstances in which it is encountered and the fate which it forebodes[30].

The ambiguity of water continues throughout Hylas' adventure. He falls into 'the black water' (μέλαν ὕδωρ, 49). The darkness of this water contrasts with the brightness of the blazing star slipping into the sea in the simile which describes his fall (50—51). The Nymphs' reception of Hylas has a similar double aspect. They »hold the boy on their knees and with gentle words console him as he weeps« (53—54). Their 'consoling' is expressed in the verb παρεψύχοντο. This verb can suggest the refreshing coolness of water (cf. 5, 33)[31], but it can also describe the chill of violent emotions (2, 106. 16, 11), and of death (16, 31). Hence it can hint at the coldness of death which such a subaqueous love might mean for a mortal.

This mysterious union of love and death, black water and bright star, reflects the mysterious double nature of Hylas' fate. He is lost to his human companions, but he is also »numbered among the blessed ones« (72). Hence his reception by the Nymphs carries overtones of death on the one hand (hinted at also in the 'feeble voice' which 'goes out from the water' in 59—60), but intimations of immortality on the other.

The simile which describes Hylas' fall into the pool deepens these tensions (13, 50—52):

> ... ἀθρόος, ὡς ὅτε πυρσὸς ἀπ' οὐρανοῦ ἤριπεν ἀστήρ
> ἀθρόος ἐν πόντῳ, ναύταις δέ τις εἶπεν ἑταίροις,
> "Κουφότερ', ὦ παῖδες, ποιεῖσθ' ὅπλα· πλευστικὸς οὖρος."

> ... as when a blazing star falls all at once from the sky
> into the heavens, and some sailor says to his companions,
> »Make the gear loose, lads: it's a sailing wind.«

Critics have treated this simile severely[32], but it has an important, if subtle, function. Its second part evokes the situation in the mortal world from which Hylas is cut off. His companions are sailors and they in fact embark abruptly at the end of the poem (68—70). The imaginary sailor's cry in the simile is a »startlingly practical utterance«[33] which jarringly conjoins the heroic and the fairytale narratives. This incorporation of the "real" human world into the description of Hylas' mysterious fate ironically sharpens the contrast between

---

[30] See H. TRÄNKLE, Das Graslager der Argonauten bei Theokrit und Apollonios, Hermes 91, 1963, 505: »Aus seiner Hirtenpoesie also hat Theokrit diesen freundlichen Zug in die heroische Welt übertragen, nicht ohne ihn umzustilisieren und epischer zu gestalten.« See also MASTRONARDE (above, p. 27 note 24) 284.

[31] The scholiast on 54 refers the word only to the coolness of springs.

[32] Gow ad 52; KÖHNKEN (above, p. 27 note 28) 81; MASTRONARDE (above, p. 27 note 24) 280—281.

[33] MASTRONARDE (above, p. 27 note 24) 280—281.

the narrative frame (the sailing and the expedition) and the strange event enclosed by that frame, a device which, as we have seen, Idyll 1 utilizes even more expressively.

In 13 the contrast between the human and the supernatural realms forms part of a larger contrast between the active, heroic sphere of the Argonauts and Heracles on the one hand and the static, remote world of the Nymphs on the other. Here too we may compare the contrast in Idyll 1 between the bucolic setting of the two rustics and the epic ambitions and emotionality of Daphnis. That tension is more ironical in Idyll 13, however, since the entire poem purports to be on the heroic, elevated level, whereas Idyll 1 begins more modestly, and in its song-within-a-song structure articulates an open and clear contrast between a more humble and a more elevated tone.

The irony of Idyll 13 revolves about the unheroic character of Hylas' fate. Loved by the nymphs, he is reduced to an almost childlike passivity. The Nymphs »hold him on their knees and console him with gentle words as he cries« (53—54):

Νύμφαι μὲν σφετέροις ἐπὶ γούνασι κοῦρον ἔχοισαι
δακρυόεντ᾽ ἀγανοῖσι παρεψύχοντ᾽ ἐπέεσσιν.

It is revealing to contrast the treatment of the erotic element here with Apollonius (Argonautica 1, 1229—1239)[34]. Apollonius places the erotic elements much more in the foreground. He isolates a single Nymph who »through love made Hylas her husband« (1, 1324—1325, Ὕλαν φιλότητι θεὰ ποιήσατο νύμφη/ὃν πόσιν). Both poets describe the confusion and emotional turbulence of their respective Nymphs:

Id. 13, 48:   πασάων γὰρ ἔρως ἀπαλὰς φρένας ἐξεφόβησεν

Argon. 1, 1232—1233:   τῆς δὲ φρένας ἐπτοίησεν
Κύπρις, ἀμηχανίῃ δὲ μόλις συναγείρατο θυμόν.

Apollonius has made the erotic attraction more violent by joining the amechanie motif to the 'fluttering' of the Nymphs' phrenes[35]. Theocritus' addition of the adjective ἀπαλάς to phrenas is gentler, more pathetic. It stresses the Nymphs' susceptibility to love, to be sure, but this love is a collective phenomenon (πᾶσαι, πασάων, 47—48), a fact which, while it heightens the rhetorical effect, lessens the erotic realism. In Apollonius this 'flutter' of the heart follows directly upon a description of the Nymph's vision of the lovely boy in the moonlight (1, 1229—1232). This sequence relates the emotional impulse immediately to the physical sensation which has stimulated it. In

---

[34] Most recent discussion in SERRAO (above, p. 27 note 26); see the bibliography also in MASTRONARDE (above, p. 27 note 24) 273—274, note 1 and the discussion in B. OTIS, Virgil, Oxford 1963, 398—405. There is a growing consensus on Apollonius' priority.

[35] With the amechanie motif here cf. Id. 1, 85.

Theocritus, however, this direct, sensual relationship is much attenuated. Hylas is only 'the fair-haired one' (36) and, even at the crucial moment, merely 'the Argive lad' (49). His beauty was described thirty verses before, and that briefly (6).

Theocritus' more condensed and choppy narrative emphasizes the *locus amoenus* and the Nymphs more than the boy himself. The erotic motif enters abruptly, without the careful sensuous preparation which Apollonius has given it (Argon. 1, 1229—1232). There is much less 'psychology' in Theocritus' narrative. His Nymphs are more akin to elemental forces who break suddenly and without explanation into human life. They are »goddesses fearful to country folk« (44).

The sequel too is correspondingly mysterious and discontinuous in Theocritus. Hylas »fell all together into the black water« (κατήριπε δ' ἐς μέλαν ὕδωρ / ἀθρόος, 49—50), like a star falling into the sea. The entrance into this watery world is an abrupt, mysterious, sudden plunge. The adjective ἀθρόος conveys the idea not only of suddenness[36], but of simultaneous collapse of all the limbs, total surrender, loss of control[37]. The verb κατήριπε too implies a helpless fall, as of an inert mass, *vis consili expers*. There is no suggestion of resistance by Hylas or of effort on the part of the Nymphs beyond their »clinging to his hand« three lines before (47). In Apollonius, on the contrary, the Nymph "draws" the boy in (ἔσπασε) and »throws him down in the middle of the eddy« (μέση δ' ἐνὶ κάββαλε δίνη, 1, 1239).

This physical effort on the part of Apollonius' Nymph is given its full complement of erotic force: »At once she put her left arm around his neck, reaching out to kiss his tender mouth, and with her right hand she pulled his arm« (1, 1236—1239):

> . . . αὐτίκα δ' ἥγε
> λαιὸν μὲν καθύπερθεν ἐπ' αὐχένος ἄνθετο πῆχυν,
> κύσσαι ἐπιθύουσα τέρεν στόμα, δεξιτερῇ δὲ
> ἀγκῶν' ἔσπασε χειρί· μέση δ' ἐνὶ κάββαλε δίνη.

Details so visual and so precise (note the placing of right and left hands) are absent in Theocritus. The result is due not merely to condensation, but to a different conception of the event. Theocritus lets it stand out in all its primitive, mythic power, unpsychologized and unexplained, a part of the mysterious world in which it transpires.

Not only does Theocritus relegate the erotic elements to the background and refuse to individualize the love of a single Nymph, but he also blurs the nature of Hylas' union with his kidnappers. Whereas Apollonius says explicitly that 'through love' (φιλότητι, 1, 1324) the Nymph made Hylas 'her hus-

---

[36] See Gow, ad loc. Also Id. 25, 252.
[37] Cf. Ap. Rhod. 1, 428 and 1007.

band' (ὃν πόσιν, I, 1325), Theocritus says only that Hylas »is numbered among the blessed ones« (72). His union with the Nymphs is as much maternal as erotic. Eros may flutter their hearts (48), but when they possess the object of their desires they treat him as a mother treats a child: »Holding him on their knees, they consoled the tearful lad with gentle words« (I, 53—54).

Over against Hylas' strange passivity and the Nymphs' quasi-maternal love stands the vehement male heroism of Heracles and his almost paternal love[38]. »As a father teaches a son, he taught Hylas everything that he himself had learned and became thereby noble and glorious« (8—9):

κaί νιν πάντ᾽ ἐδίδασκε, πaτὴρ ὡσεὶ φίλον υἱόν,
ὅσσa μaθὼν ἀγaθὸς κaὶ ἀοίδιμος aὐτὸς ἔγεντο.

The poem develops a sharp contrast between these aspirations of Heracles for the lad he loves and the boy's actual fate. He is petted and protected by solicitous females in their watery world, while Heracles shouts at the top of his mighty lungs (58) and wanders with bow and club (56—57) over the whole island (64—67).

The maternal, enclosing love of the Nymphs for Hylas has one thing in common with Heracles' love. In both cases the beloved is sheltered and held in total passivity. Earlier in the poem, after the lines on Heracles' paternal care for Hylas' education (8—9), Theocritus describes how Heracles would never let him out of sight (10—15). In its own way, Heracles' love is as protective as that of the Nymphs. Thus one of the terms which describes Heracles' solicitude is a two-line vignette of young birds returning to the nest »when the mother (μaτρός) rustles her feathers« on the perch (13—14). This simile helps build up the image of childlike dependence in the boy's relation to his lovers which will appear obliquely in the Nymphs' consolation (53—54).

The framework surrounding the Hylas episode, then, articulates a double contrast. First there is a contrast between the practical realities of the human world (ships, sailors, dinner) and the magic of the Nymphs' realm. Second there is a contrast between an active, heroic, homosexual love which involves distant journeys and dangerous exploits on the one hand and on the other hand a strange, non-human passive, though heterosexual, love in a removed, watery setting.

Both of these contrasts, in turn, form part of the irony with which the poem treats heroic world and traditional epic heroism[39]. Not only does the autonomy of strong-willed personalities dissolve into passivity and fruitless

---

[38] The contrast between Heracles and Hyllas is enhanced by the difference between Hylas' non-heroic πολυχaνδέa κρωσσόν (46) and the club which always 'fills' (ἐχάνδaνε, 57) Heracles' hand. Gow, CQ 32. 1938, 11 finds the use of the verb in 57 'unexampled', a point which makes the clash with 46 even more striking.

[39] See MASTRONARDE (above, p. 27, note 24) 275; OTIS (above, p. 29, note 34) 401.

shouting (contrast Odysseus' more resourceful and successful search for his lost companions in the Circe episode of Odyssey χ)[40], but even mature erotic relationships arc undercut by hints of infantile dependence and uterine symbolism.

These contrasts are focussed through the motif of water. Hylas has set out »to bring water for dinner« (ὕδωρ ἐπιδόρπιον οἴσων, 36) when he comes upon the spring (39), and it is from the strange 'black water' (49) that his feeble voice, near the end, barely emerges (60). The contrast between the violent shouts of Heracles (58) and Hylas' 'thin voice' out of the water (59—60) emphasizes the youth's mysterious distance from the human world. He is near, and yet he seems far off: παρεὼν δὲ μάλα σχεδὸν εἴδετο πόρρω (60). This paradoxical distance-in-nearness belongs to the mysterious atmosphere of the Nymphs' world. Having crossed the boundary of ordinary experience into this strange realm, the hero is ever so close to the human world and yet irrevocably cut off from it.

The 'thin voice' and the ambiguity of distance and nearness can simultaneously be read as another aspect of the womblike quality of Hylas' watery abode. Only a small barrier separates him from the human world, but it is impassable. Pulled by gentle, maternal women, falling abruptly and mysteriously, descending to their watery world, and then consoled as he cries, on their knees, Hylas enacts a fantasy of returning to the womb and being born again. Such a fantasy is appropriate to the character which he is given in the poem, sheltered and watched at every point (see 10—14). Perhaps, Theocritus suggests, this is the natural form of erotic consummation for a figure like Hylas.

Hylas' plunge into his mysterious water has the opposite outcome from Daphnis' in the First Idyll. Hence Daphnis speaks of the sun setting for him (1, 102), whereas Hylas' fall, though the water itself is 'black', is likened to a shooting star (13, 50—51). In both myths water mediates between life and death, between the vital and the destructive aspects of the mysterious powers which surround the characters of the *Idylls*. Daphnis, though »not hated by the Nymphs«, seems to neglect these female powers and never addresses them in his lament. Hylas is himself taken up by them and plunges into their dark realm to emerge an immortal (13, 72). The resurrection withheld from Daphnis (1, 139) seems to be conferred upon Hylas. For Hylas, passive and free of Daphnis' tragic, self-assertive independence, the Nymphs' water proves ultimately a benign, womblike haven from which he is regenerated to new life. Yet the mystery of nature's powers still remains in the background, and the protagonist accepts their encompassing embrace only reluctantly. He continues

---

[40] See my »Circean Temptations: Homer, Virgil, Ovid«, TAPA 99, 1968, 425 ff.

to weep (54), and his voice, though feeble, seeks to answer Heracles' call (59). The detail of the »feeble voice from the water« (59—60) touches a pathos akin to that of the Daphnis story. The human individual is swallowed up into a vast and incomprehensible power.

In both the Daphnis and the Hylas episodes humanity defines itself through this encounter with the non-human. Daphnis resists and dies. Hylas acquiesces and gains a place among »the blessed ones« (72). Yet he pays a price: he loses his heroic identity and his contact with the heroic, male world of Heracles and the Argonauts. Daphnis' death expresses a tragic humanity which has its roots in the humanism of the poets and dramatists of the archaic and classical periods from Homer to Euripides[41]. Hylas loses something of that human individuality for the sake of which Daphnis fought against Aphrodite and Eros.

From this bucolic heroism there results a tension in both *Idylls* between bucolic and epic elements. In 13, however, that tension has a lighter and more mocking irony. This irony derives in large part from the ambiguity of the pastoral *locus* and the suspended position of the protagonists within it. Hylas moves from an heroic to a bucolic setting, from Argonauts to Nymphs. As one critic remarks, »The pretty boy is finally in the pastoral world where he belongs[42]«. Yet, thanks to the mystery of the watery setting, he is not exactly *in* this bucolic world. He is, to be precise, *under* it, entrapped in it, part of, but removed from the lovely flowers described in 40—42. His 'thin voice' emerging from the water bears pathetic witness to his separation. Hence the mysterious water reinforces the indefiniteness and fluidity of Hylas' identity. Just as love in his case veers ambiguously between male and female roles and between eroticism and maternal dependence, so his place in both the bucolic and heroic worlds is ambiguous. He is not ready for the eros of these Nymphs and does not really become a part of the pastoral world, but remains in a kind of limbo in the 'black water' of their pool.

It is natural for apotheosis to appear under the symbolism of rebirth. Idyll 13, however, develops that symbolism in such a way that the heroic aspect of the apotheosis appears as almost ludicrous beside the associations of infantile helplessness in the scene of Hylas among the Nymphs (53—54). The motif of apotheosis gives the tale of Hylas an ostensibly happy ending, but it enters the narrative so abruptly and irrationally that it scarcely neutralizes the negative elements in the rest of the adventure. The irrationally of such a divinization can be accepted as a supernatural or a fairytale motif when it is

---

[41] See LAWALL (above, p. 22, note 8) 20 ff.

[42] MASTRONARDE (above, p. 27, note 24) 287. He makes another unjustified assumption on p. 275: Hylas »will (*by implication*) graduate to the active role of male lover of females« (my emphasis).

related as a bare event, an unexplained mythical fact, without background and without character, as it appears, for example, in Callimachus, Epigram 22 Pf. (24):

'Ἀστακίδην τὸν Κρῆτα τὸν αἰπόλον ἥρπασε Νύμφη
ἐξ ὄρεος, καὶ νῦν ἱερὸς 'Ἀστακίδης.
οὐκέτι Δικταίῃσιν ὑπὸ δρυσίν, οὐκέτι Δάφνιν
ποιμένες, 'Ἀστακίδην δ' αἰὲν ἀεισόμεθα[43]

Against the heroic background of Theocritus' poem, however, the suddenness of this event cannot quite be accepted at face value, for it stands out incongruously in the heroic setting, and it contrasts harshly with the very different kind of apotheosis earned by Hylas' foil, Heracles. The very arbitrariness of conferring immortality on this the most passive and helpless of the Argonauts suggests a *reductio ad absurdum* of the whole heroic machinery.

Theocritus' irony is not above this kind of self-mockery. In a poem of very different genre he obtains a similar effect, making fun of the very tradition which he is supposedly elaborating and adorning. In Idyll 15 Praxinoe's naiveté and down-to-earth colloquialism humorously undercut the grandiose Ptolemaic paraphernalia of apotheosis which the setting seems to be celebrating (15, 46—47):

πολλά τοι, ὦ Πτολεμαῖε, πεποίηται καλὰ ἔργα
ἐξ ὧ ἐν ἀθανάτοις ὁ τεκών.

Many the good works that have been done, o Ptolemy, since your father has been among the immortals ...

The following lines on the dangers of Egyptian streets (15, 47—50) increase the distance between the perspective of the character speaking and the realm of the "immortals" in which the Ptolemies move.

IV.

The water symbolism of Idyll 22 occupies only a small part of the whole poem and is consequently less complex than that of Idyll 1 or 13. The situation begins like that of the Hylas Idyll[44]. Castor and Polydeuces come ashore on an unfamiliar island, are separated from their companions (22, 32—35), and see a mysterious forest, παντοίην ... ἄγριον ὕλην (36). Like Hylas, they find a

---

[43] For the folktale motif present in both Theocritus and the Callimachean epigram, of the Nymph carrying off a young man see H. W. PRESCOTT, CQ 7, 1913, 187.

[44] For the parallels see Gow, ad loc.; TRÄNKLE (above, p. 28, note 30) 504; OTIS (above. p. 29, note 34) 399, who speaks of »a designed correspondence«.

spring (37, cf. 13, 39). The water is clear and inviting, with bright pebbles visible in its depths (22, 37—40):

> εὗρον δ' ἀέναον κρήνην ὑπὸ λισσάδι πέτρῃ
> ὕδατι πεπληθυῖαν ἀκηράτῳ· αἱ δ' ὑπένερθε
> λάλλαι κρυστάλλῳ ἠδ' ἀργύρῳ ἰνδάλλοντο
> ἐκ βυθοῦ.

As in Idyll 1, 7—8, it is near a steep rock (22, 37); and, as in Idyll 13, 40—42, trees and flowers grow in abundance (22, 40—43).

This charming *ekphrasis* of natural beauty is balanced by an *ekphrasis* of ugliness: the uncouth figure of massive Amycus (45—57). The two *ekphraseis* are of almost the same length (37—43 and 45—52). The contrast between the beauty of the setting and the ugliness of its inhabitant is intentional and effective. It is sharpened, and again in terms of water, by the comparison of the bulging muscles of Amycus to huge boulders carried away by the violent eddies of a river in spate (22, 49—50):

> . . . ἠύτε πέτροι ὀλοίτροχοι οὔστε κυλίνδων
> χειμάρρους ποταμὸς μεγάλαις περιέξεσε δίναις.

As the threatening Amycus contrasts with the peace and beauty of the place which he inhabits, so this roaring, turbid water contrasts with the calm, limpid spring which first attracts the Dioscuri (37—40).

In this poem Amycus takes the place of the dangerous Nymphs of Idyll 13 or the sinister elements in the pastoral background of Idyll 1 (16—18. 140). The Nymphs of 13 are »goddesses fearful to country folk« (δειναὶ θεαὶ ἀγροιώταις, 13, 44); Amycus is »fearful to behold« (δεινὸς ἰδεῖν, 12, 45). In both cases the encounter by water is dangerous. The quarrel with Amycus begins over water (τοῦδε πιεῖν ὕδατος, 62), and he proves to be as 'wild' or 'uncivilized' as the woodland he inhabits (ἄγριος εἶ, 58; cf. ἄγριον ὕλην, 36).

In Idyll 22 Theocritus adapts motifs from the purely bucolic Idylls, but gives them a new twist. Hence Amycus' countrymen come together »under shady sycamores«, ὑπὸ σκιερὰς πλατανίστους (22, 76), like the herdsmen of Idyll 1 or 7[45]. The meeting here, however, is not to exchange or judge rustic songs, but to fight. The battle, which develops in high epic language and even ends with a reminiscence of Homer, i. e. Polyphemus' invocation of Poseidon (22, 133—134), is sharply at variance with the bucolic setting of pool and shade[46].

---

[45] Cf. Id. 1, 1; 7, 9 and 88—89; 12, 8; 18, 46. The motif occurs also in pastoral epigrams: cf. A. P. 9, 313 and Plan. 228 (Anyte).

[46] The parallel between Polyphemus and Amycus suggests another neutralization of the destructive force of water. Polyphemus calls on Poseidon to bring the dangerous power of the sea to bear against Odysseus; Amycus swears by Poseidon that he will do no further harm to strangers.

In one important respect Amycus differs from the sinister figures of Idylls 1 or 13. He may be »terrible to look upon« (45), but he is not a 'terrible goddess' like the Nymphs of 13. The divine power is, this time, on the side of the new-comers: it is they who are the demigods, Amycus who is the mortal. Hence the significance of the encounter by water reverses itself. It brings disaster and nearly death (22, 130) to the inhabitant of the forest world rather than to the interloper.

V.

The pseudo-Theocritean *Erastes* or 'Lover' (Idyll 23) cannot claim the literary merit of the three poems discussed above, though Gow is perhaps unduly severe[47]. It presents a scene of conventional, stylized pathos colored by a melancholy sensuality characteristic of late Hellenistic poetry. The lover laments the unrequited love he feels for a boy, threatens to hang himself in the courtyard of the boy's house, and then rather abruptly carries out the threat. The boy finds the corpse, is not very deeply affected, and proceeds to the gymnasium to bathe. There the statue of the god Eros falls into the water and kills him. In his dying breath the boy repents and urges the mockers of Eros to love, »for the god knows how to exact just punishment« (64).

There is no *locus amoenus* in this poem, nor is the water especially mysterious: it is simply the pool of the local gymnasium. Yet there is a certain aura of mystery, and this derives primarily from the presence of the god's statue and its terrible 'leaping' (ἅλατο, 60) upon the boy. The boy »came to the god whom he insulted« (58), and the statue moves suddenly from its stone base (58—60):

> λαϊνέας δέ
> ἵπτατ' ἀπὸ κρηπῖδος ἐς ὕδατα· τῷ δ' ἐφύπερθεν
> ἅλατο καὶ τώγαλμα, κακὸν δ' ἔκτεινεν ἔφαβον.

This event is the equivalent of the encounter with mysterious water in the other poems. Not unskillfully the poet combines water with the uncanny event, similar to that in the stories of Pygmalion or Don Juan, of the statue gaining a fearful supernatural life (note the verbs of 59—60). What the poem lacks, however, is that delicate, suggestive evocation of a mysterious, mythical realm which the genuine *Idylls* can create. A bourgeois setting and an accompanying bourgeois sentimentality crowd out the mythical element.

---

[47] See Gow's Preface to Id. 23 in his Commentary: »The narrative is bald, frigid, and improbable; the sentiment is sloppy, and embodied in an address to the boy who, *ex hypothesi*, cannot hear it. These faults are not relieved by any particular elegance in the style and the poem is the least attractive of the whole Theocritean corpus«.

For an interesting defense of the literary quality of the Idyll see F. O. COPLEY, TAPA 71, 1940, 52—61.

The death of 23 is a literal one, and there is no room for the play of imagination in the fate of the protagonist, as there is in Idylls 1 or 13. The effects of the wound are described: »The stream was reddened« (νᾶμα δ' ἐφοινίχθη, 61). The rest of line 61, however, is perhaps borrowed from the Hylas poem: »The voice of the boy floated (over the water)« (παιδὸς δ' ἐπενάχετο φωνά). Compare 13, 59—60:

$$\text{ἀραιὰ δ' ἵκετο φωνά}$$
$$\text{ἐξ ὕδατος, παρεὼν δὲ μάλα σχεδὸν εἴδετο πόρρω.}$$

The differences, however, are as great as the similarities. The phrase of 23, 61 lacks the mysterious pathos which the supernatural setting confers on the passage of 13. Whereas there is a moving and suggestive restraint in reducing Hylas to but a 'thin voice', this voice of 23 pronounces an insipid piece of moralism about divine vengeance and kindness to lovers. The author of 23 has retained certain external features of the water motif, but reduced them to subserve a simplistic scheme of divine retribution. He has completely lost the element of an inward struggle with love that so deepened the pathos of Daphnis in Idyll 1. The death of 23 is framed in far narrower, more trivial terms.

The genuine *Idylls* of Theocritus are able to convey something of the mystery of divine presences working in and through the elements of the bucolic world which itself still remains open to myth and magic. His later imitator has borrowed the narrative pattern, but greatly restricted its scope and its affective power. Theocritus has a feeling for the ambiguous vitality of nature and its deities: Pan, the Nymphs, Aphrodite, Priapus[48]. The imitator has secularized and trivialized what in Theocritus is still sacred and mysterious. An event full of wide and imaginative implications becomes in the imitator a minor local story characterized by a complacent and dubious moralizing. He has replaced Theocritus' living divinities with a statue and the mysterious flowing 'sacred water' with a pool in a man-made building. The change from living, Nymph-haunted spring to artificial pool might itself serve as a symbol of poetic degeneration. But the very falling off teaches us to appreciate better the suggestive power of Theocritus' art.

In Idylls 1 and 13 Theocritus successfully exploits the archetypal associations of his watery *locus*. It is just this ability to draw upon the ancient power of myth and symbol that his imitator in 23 cannot manage. With restraint and a few rapid strokes Theocritus is able to evoke an atmosphere of numinous power in these nameless streams or springs. Like Daphnis' stream in Idyll 1, these settings resist precise localization because through them the poet is striving to say things which are sayable only in symbolical language. All these

[48] Compare also the mysterious *loci amoeni* haunted by Pan and Priapus in Theocritus, Epigrams 3 and 4.

springs and streams are symbols of entrance to hidden realms, places where the paths of life and death cross and where their secrets seem to lie closer to the surface. The mortal wanderer there may find death, like Daphnis, or immortality, like Hylas, but he does not return.

Brown University   CHARLES SEGAL

ADONIS AND APHRODITE

THEOCRITUS, *Idyll* III, 48

In Theocritus' Third *Idyll* the amorous goatherd ends his love-plaint with a list of mythical lovers which includes Aphrodite and Adonis :

τὰν δὲ καλὰν Κυθέρειαν ἐν ὤρεσι μῆλα νομεύων
οὐχ οὕτως ῎Ωδωνις ἐπὶ πλέον ἄγαγε λύσσας
ὥστ' οὐδὲ φθίμενόν νιν ἄ τ ε ϱ μ α ζ ο ῖ ο τ ί θ η τ ι ;

And did not Adonis, as he fed his sheep upon the hills, drive the fair Cytherea to such frenzy that even in death *she puts him not from her breast* (III, 46-48, A. S. F. Gow's translation).

On the phrase emphasized above Gow comments, « The noun is hardly less surprising than the preposition, for its associations are maternal rather than erotic » [1]. As an instance of this erotic use of μαστός (Attic μαζός) Gow cites Euripides, *Andromache*, 629 (when Menelaus saw Helen's breast — *mastos* — he threw away his sword). In an appendix (II, 592) Gow adds Catullus 61, 105, *a tuis teneris...| secubare papillis ;* but this passage does not help, for Latin *papillae* do not have the primarily maternal associations of Greek *mazos* (*mastos*). Indeed the *Andromache* passage is an exception to Euripides' customary use of this word with reference to the maternal breast [2]. Gow might have cited a closer parallel : pseudo-Theocritus, *Idyll* XXVII, 49-50 [3] :

---

[1] A.S.F. Gow, *Theocritus*, Cambridge, 1950 II, 74. See also A.T.A. FRITZSCHE, *Theocriti Idyllia*, ed. 2, Leipzig, 1870, *ad. loc.*

[2] *E. g.* EURIPIDES, *Alc.*, 639 ; *Andromache*, 224 ; *Bacch.*, 700 f ; *Cycl.*, 55 ; *El.*, 1207 ; *Hecuba*, 142, 424, 560 ; *Ion*, 319, 762, 962, 1372, 1492 ; *Iph. Aul.*, 1152 ; *Orest.*, 527, 841 ; *Phoen.*, 31, 306, 987, 1434, 1527, 1568, 1603 ; *Tro.*, 570, 759.

[3] *Idyll*, XXVII, the *Oarystys* or *Intimate Conversation,* is almost certainly a later imitation of Theocritus. Philippe Legrand, the Budé editor of the *Bucoliques Grecques*, Paris, 1953, places it toward the end of the Alexandrian age (II, 103). But this

τί ῥέζεις, σατυρίσκε ; τί δ' ἔνδοθεν ἄψαο μαζῶν ;
— μᾶλα τεὰ πράτιστα τάδε χνοάσοντα διδάξω.

Yet, as Gow notes, the maternal reference of μαζός is by far the more common, both in earlier Greek poetry and in Theocritus' own contemporary, Callimachus [4], especially in the singular. What is more important, it occurs earlier within Theocritus' Third *Idyll* (again in the singular), with its maternal meaning unmistakable (15-16) :

νῦν ἔγνων τὸν "Ερωτα · βαρὺς θεός · ἦ ῥα λεαίνας
μαζὸν ἐθήλαζεν, δρυμῷ τέ νιν ἔτραφε μάτηρ ...

Theocritus uses words carefully, and one may wonder whether his use of μαζός in III, 48 may not be intentional. I suggest that this rather strangely phrased expression may have a ritual explanation and, more specifically, that it may refer to the myth and cult of Adonis. The Fifteenth *Idyll*, entitled in the manuscripts Συρακόσιαι ἢ 'Αδωνιάζουσαι, confirms Theocritus' interest in this cult. He ends this vignette of the Alexandrian middle class with a dirge sung to accompany the ritual burial of the god [5].

In support of this approach, we may note, first, the context of the Adonis passage of *Idyll* Three. Here Adonis and Aphrodite are immediately followed by Endymion and Iasion. Endymion may be a purely « literary» reference [6], chosen perhaps because of a certain romantic coloring, like Atalante in the preceding lines (40-43). Iasion, however, is a figure of very old origin and

---

realistic and unsentimental work has some touches of fine poetry, as in the contrast between the girl's half-acquiescent concern, nicely conveyed in the broken rhythm, and Daphnis' confidently lyrical reply (57-58) :

— μίμνε, τάλαν· τάχα τίς τοι ἐπέρχεται· ἦχον ἀκούω.
— ἀλλήλαις λαλέουσι τεὸν γάμον αἱ κυπάρισσοι.

[4] E. g. HOMER, *Il.*, 22. 80 and 83 ; *Odyssey* 11, 448 ; 19, 483 ; AESCHYLUS, *Cho.*, 531, 545, 897 ; SOPH., *El.*, 776 ; CALLIMACHUS, *Hymns* 1, 48 ; 4, 274 ; 6, 95 ; *Epigrams* 50 (51). *Mastos* may, however, have a purely neutral reference to the breast simply as part of the body : SOPH., *Trach.*,925 ; HERODOTUS, 2, 85 ; 3, 133 ; 4, 202.

[5] For a detailed analysis of this song and the ritual of Adonis see W. ATALLAH, *Adonis dans la littérature et l'art grecs*, Paris, 1966, pp. 105-35, with his bibliographical references.

[6] See SAPPHO, frag. 199 L.-P. ; *Anth. Pal.* 5, 165 ; schol. on AP. RHOD., 4, 57-58.

almost certainly the survival of a fertility god. Homer tells briefly, but vividly, of his union with Demeter « in a thrice-plowed field » when the goddess « yielded to her passion » [7]. Hesiod relates that this union took place « in the rich land of Crete » and produced Plutus [8]. Hellanicus adds the interesting point that « after the flood Iasion was the only one found to possess seeds » [9]. Diodorus [10] provides a wealth of detail, some doubtless later embroidery or allegorical interpretation (for example, he explains the birth of Plutus as « in reality the gift of grain »). Still, it is revealing that Diodorus makes Iasion the first to initiate strangers into the mysteries, has him marry the goddess Cybele, and father Corybas, the eponymous founder of the Corybantes. Theocritus does not, of course, tell Iasion's story at length. But he obviously knows its primitive and sacrosanct nature since he addresses Demeter and refers to the mysteries which he will not reveal to the « profane » (50-51) :

$$\zeta\alpha\lambda\tilde{\omega} \ \delta\acute{\epsilon}, \ \varphi\acute{\iota}\lambda\alpha \ \gamma\acute{\upsilon}\nu\alpha\iota, \ \text{'}I\alpha\sigma\acute{\iota}\omega\nu\alpha,$$
$$\mathring{o}\varsigma \ \tau\acute{o}\sigma\sigma\omega\nu \ \grave{\epsilon}\varkappa\acute{\upsilon}\varrho\eta\sigma\epsilon\nu \ \mathring{o}\sigma' \ o\mathring{\upsilon} \ \pi\epsilon\upsilon\sigma\epsilon\tilde{\iota}\sigma\theta\epsilon \ \beta\acute{\epsilon}\beta\alpha\lambda\omicron\iota.$$

Like Iasion, Adonis is a transmuted form of a youthful vegetation god, simultaneously the son and lover of the Great Goddess (Aphrodite, Astarte, Isis-Hathor). The scholiast on Theocritus III, 48 makes the vegetation-character of the myth clear :

> They say about Adonis that at his death he spent six months in the arms of Aphrodite, as well as six also in those of Persephone. This tale is in truth as follows : Adonis, that is, the sown grain, spends six months in the earth from the time of sowing ; and for six months Aphrodite — that is, the temperate air — has him. And then men receive him.

This explanation belongs, of course, to the allegorizing tendency of later Greek rationalism. In the more primitive form of the myth, Adonis, as vegetation god, fructifies the Great Goddess and helps in the bringing forth of crops. As in all such myths, the god dies annually, is mourned by the Goddess and her devotees, and is reborn as the Goddess' son-consort once more. *Idyll*

---

[7] *Odyssey*, 5, 125 ff.

[8] *Theogony*, 969-71.

[9] JACOBY, *FGrHist*, 4F, 135 = Schol. on *Od.*, 5, 125.

[10] 5, 48-49.

XV, 136-44 refers to Adonis death and resurrection in the cycle of each year [11].

A version of the myth told by Apollodorus is important for connecting the Goddess with Adonis' infancy and birth. Aphrodite becomes enamored of the new-born child, « whom for the sake of his beauty, while he was still an infant, Aphrodite hid in a chest unknown to the gods and entrusted him to Persephone. But when Persephone beheld him, she would not give him back » (3, 14, 4 in Frazer's translation). The reason for Aphrodite's action is left obscure. But it may well reflect an older, more primitive stage of the myth wherein Aphrodite is the mother. For the role of the mother in concealing a divine child in a chest or elsewhere (or being concealed with him) one may compare the legends of Moses, Perseus, Oedipus, Cypselus, Iamus, Ion and Romulus. The maternal and sexual relation between the Young God and Great Mother are, then, originally part of a single complex whole. But such a combination, offensive to Greek taste, is avoided by the interposition of a mortal mother, Myrrha or Smyrna.

The breasts of the Great Goddess are universally emphasized in figural representations, for obviously they embody the positive values of birth, nurture, abundance over which she presides. This symbol of the Great Goddess' bounty, then, plays a large role in that part of the myth which celebrates the death of the god, the waning of life, the barren part of the earth's cycle. Erich Neumann remarks on this theme, « The widely distributed 'Astarte type' of the Great Goddess, pressing or showing her breasts, has the same significance where the breasts are beaten in token of mourning, e. g. for Adonis it means that they are accused as the vital principle that has failed to defeat death » [12]. One may note here that Theocritus includes the baring of breasts in his account of the Adonis-ritual [13].

Representations of this archetypal Mediterranean goddess show a close similarity between the nursing goddess and the mourning goddess. In Minoan representations the Great Goddess appears as the Mater Dolorosa and as the Earth Goddess at the same

---

[11] ATALLAH (above, note 5), especially pp. 119 ff.

[12] ERICH NEUMANN, *The Great Mother*, ed. 2, Engl. transl. R. Manheim, « Bollingen Series », vol. 42, New York, 1963, p. 128.

[13] *Idyll* XV, 135-36.

time [14]. Neumann illustrates two bronze groups from pre-Roman
Sardinia in which the Goddess holds the Young God to her breast,
and in one of these it is the dead god whom she is holding [15].
One may compare with these figures the many representations
of the Goddess nursing the Young God, whom she holds in exactly
the same position as the Dead God of the Sardinian group [16].
This pose is most familiar from the Egyptian statues of Horus
being suckled by Hathor-Isis. Neumann describes such figures
of Horus (or Adonis) as « the Mother Goddess holding her living
and her dead son, at once child and man » [17].

Theocritus, like other Alexandrians and especially the author
of the *Aitia*, was much interested in matters of cult and myth. He
lived in a city where civilizations met and religious syncretism
was highly advanced. He was thoroughly familiar with the Adonis
cult, as his Fifteenth *Idyll* shows. He had doubtless seen the ubi-
quitous Egyptian representations of Isis with the Young God,
Horus, at the breast. Theocritus' line, then, points back to the
deepest layers of the myth : the telescoping of the three irrevo-
cable stages of life — birth, sexual consummation, and death —
into one and the presentation of the ambiguous dyad—male and
female, husband and wife, son and mother. His phrasing in line
48 catches this archetype — the Goddess simultaneously mother
and lover, lamenting her youthful son/consort — in an allusive,
yet tightly knit, almost sculptural manner.

Theocritus' description is a more condensed and complex ren-
dering of a scene which recurs in a later poem, the *Epitaphios
Adonidos* attributed to Bion (70-73) :

> λέκτρον ἔχοι, Κυθέρεια, τὸ σὸν νῦν νεκρὸς Ἄδωνις.
> καὶ νέκυς ὢν καλός ἐστι, καλὸς νέκυς, οἷα καθεύδων.
> κάτθεό νιν μαλακοῖς ἐνὶ φάρεσιν οἷς ἐνίαυεν
> ὡς μετὰ τεῦς ἀνὰ νύκτα τὸν ἱερὸν ὕπνον ἐμόχθει [18].

Bion makes no mention of Aphrodite's breast, nor does his
language contain anything of the strained quality of Theocritus

---

[14] E. O. JAMES, *The Cult of the Mother Goddess*, London, 1959, pp. 134-35

[15] NEUMANN (above, note 12), plates 46 and 47.

[16] *Ibid.*, plates 37, 38, 44, 45, 94, 95, 147.

[17] *Ibid.*, p. 131.

[18] LEGRAND (above, note 3), II, 197, note 3, rightly calls attention to the erotic
sense of *hypnos* (« ce n'est pas de *dormir* ni de *sommeil* qu'il s'agit »).

III, 48. Yet it casts some light on this passage, for it provides a hint of what an Alexandrian poet might make of such a myth.

Both Theocritus and Bion exploit to the full the antithesis between the joys of love and the sadness of death. In Bion, the dead Adonis rests on the couch of the love-goddess ; but it is now his bier. Both poets, however, interpret the myth in terms of the pathos of wasted youth and tarnished bliss. Both reveal the romanticizing taste of a sophisticated age, whereas in the original meaning of the myth, alive still in Theocritus' day, the dead Adonis is held to the breasts which once nourished him, and the reference is not to the sadness of an ended romance, but to the elemental cycles of the natural world. The goddess who is the all-giving source of life laments her ephemeral creation and the brief joy she may have of him.

Both poets are aware of these strata of the myth and take special pleasure in incorporating into their sophisticated, self-deprecatory grace of verse the primitive seriousness behind their tale. But in Theocritus' Third *Idyll* more of that primitive seriousness shows through ; and the discrepancy thus created is part of the basic program of the poem.

Idyll III is a deliberately light and trifling poem. The humorous point of the goatherd's song lies in the inappropriateness of the myths which he cites. Not only is the use of such recondite mythology « out of place in the mouth of a rustic goatherd », as Lawall has recently emphasized [19] ; but the myths themselves are hardly felicitously chosen, as both Gow and Lawall have pointed out [20]. Lawall summarizes the effect of this mythology as follows :

> This is wholly in keeping with the poem's basic incongruity of theme and setting, and the mythological song admirably fits the goatherd's personality. He is completely unable to see things as they are... The sentimental goatherd is totally out of touch with reality [21].

The serious and complex meaning of the Adonis myth reflected in the phrasing of line 48 forms part of the poem's juxtaposition of the sombre and the ridiculous. The simple and foolish goatherd, in his naively blundering way, touches upon things far beyond his ken. He brings within the limited enclosure of his

[19] G. LAWALL, *Theocritus' Coan Pastorals*, Cambridge, Mass., 1967, p. 40.

[20] LAWALL, *loc. cit.* ; Gow (above, note 1), II, 74.

[21] LAWALL, p. 40-41.

conventional and trivial amorous problems the gigantic arche-
types and the tragic universality of primal fertility myths. He
compares his little affair with Amaryllis to an ancient *hieros gamos*
with Demeter recounted in ῀Iomer and Hesiod. And he even
stresses the solemnity of this material by referring to the mysteries
and the « profane » (βέβαλοι, 51). The abrupt contrast between
line 51, ending on « profane », and the next phrase, ἀλγέω τὰν
κεφαλάν, « I have a headache », leaves no doubt about the
breadth of the humor.

It is no mean achievement of Theocritus' refined art that his
elegant, distanced humor can incorporate such material. He is,
of course, able to draw upon the rich Hellenic tradition of freedom
and wit in religious matters. His technique ultimately owes much
to Aristophanes, from whom he is in other respects worlds apart [22].

Line 48, with its implicit contrast between φθίμενον and μα-
ζοῖο, between the dead Young God and the undying principle
of life and renewal, is thus the culminating and most daring point
in the poem's creation of a deliberately ponderous edifice of out-
sized solemnity. That edifice is suddenly toppled in the staccato,
paratactic simplicity of the goatherd's return to himself in the
last three lines :

'Αλγέω τὰν κεφαλάν, τὶν δ' οὐ μέλει. οὐκέτ' ἀείδω,
κεισεῦμαι δὲ πεσών, καὶ τοὶ λύκοι ὧδέ μ' ἔδονται.
ὡς μέλι τοι γλυκὺ τοῦτο κατὰ βρόχθοιο γένοιτο.

With a calculated shock, then, Theocritus transports us back
to the world of Amaryllis and the grazing nanny- and butting
billy-goats with which he began (1-5). The resonant liquids and
the proverbial ring of the poem's final line take us far from Asiatic
cult and archetypal Mediterranean myths and place us once
more back on the solid ground of this goatherd's homely, but
ultimately untroubled pastorality.

Brown University, Providence, R.I.   Charles SEGAL.
   U.S.A.

[22] Compare, for example, Aristophanes' use of Orphic, Eleusinian, and other ri-
tual material in the *Frogs*, and see my essay on this subject, *HSCP* 65 (1961), 207-42.
See also Bruno Snell's remarks on this literary freedom in religious matters in « The
Olympian Gods », *The Discovery of the Mind*, tr. T. Rosenmeyer, Cambridge, Mass.,
1953, p. 41.

Simaetha and the Iynx (Theocritus, Idyll II)

by Charles Segal

For the ancients, who live close to the realm of myth and mythical personification, words and acts may have associations not immediately obvious to us because they form part of a pattern of thought which we no longer share. Especially in matters of ritual or magic the poet may exploit age-old associations and draw upon a sensibility and suggestibility in his audience which we have to make a special effort to recover. A recent analysis of the mythology of the iynx by Marcel Detienne allows us to appreciate one such neglected train of associations in Theocritus' second *Idyll*[1]. First we must observe the prominence given the iynx in the structure of the poem, and then we may consider what significance the iynx may have not only for the incantation of Simaetha in the first part, but for the *Idyll* as a whole.

" Iynx, draw you that man to my house ": ten times in Theocritus' second *Idyll* the desperate Simaetha repeats this line as she performs the rites which are to restore her lover, Delphis, to her. The first and last occurrences have an important structural function: the line begins and ends Simaetha's magical operations, " expressing the ever-recurring thought and keeping the object of the incantation before the mind. Thus it forms an artistic separation between the invocation and the incantation "[2]. After the introduction of the iynx-motif in line 17, there are nine turns of the magical wheel as Simaetha plies her enchantments.

---

[1] Marcel Detienne, *Les jardins d'Adonis: La mythologie des aromates en Grece*, Paris 1972, 159-72. For the iynx see also A.S.F. Gow, *Journ. Hell. Stud.* 54, 1934, 1-13, and his commentary, *Theocritus*, Cambridge 1952, *ad* II 17; E. Tavenner, *Trans. Proc. Am. Philol. Assoc.* 64, 1933, 109-27.

[2] M. C. Sutphen, ' Magic in Theokritos and Vergil ', *Studies in Honor of Basil L. Gildersleeve*, Baltimore 1902. 321.

The sixteen-line speech preceding the magic, addressed half to herself and half to her maid, Thestylis, portrays the pathos of her love-sickness. Her incantation then dramatizes the present effects of that sickness. Her lover has not come for twelve days (4). Eros and Aphrodite have turned his thoughts elsewhere (6-7). Simaetha calls upon the moon (9-10), and asks the dread goddess Hecate to make her enchantments " in no way weaker than those of Circe, Medea, or yellow-haired Perimede " (15-16). Then she addresses the iynx for the first time (17). Her last incantation echoes the first (compare 18-21 and 58-62) [3]; and that echo, combined with the last recurrence of the iynx refrain in 63, formally rounds off and closes this section of the poem. Theocritus then returns to the dramatic situation already drawn in 1-16, the girl alone and close to tears (νῦν δὴ μώνα ἐοῖσα πόθεν τὸν ἔρωτα δακρύσω; 64). With this resumption of a more realistic and direct depiction of Simaetha's plight, we move backwards in time as she narrates the origin of her love : ἐκ τίνος ἄρξωμαι; τίς μοι κακὸν ἄγαγε τοῦτο; (65). Thus for both halves of the poem the iynx stands in immediate juxtaposition with Simaetha's subjection to her passion.

Detienne has shown that the iynx is not merely a love charm, but is also the focal point of an antithesis between marriage and seduction, legitimate and illegitimate union. The myths connected with the iynx and the mythical personage of Iynx herself center upon the destruction of or the interference with a stable, enduring union in matrimony. " Iynx " was another name for Mintha, the concubine of Hades who tries to disturb the union of Hades and Persephone [4]. It is also the name of an enchantress, daughter of Echo or Peitho, who attempts to seduce Zeus, either for herself or for Io. As a result, she is transformed by Hera into the bird known as the iynx, the wryneck [5]. This bird's peculiarities of movement suggested to the Greeks sensuality and debauchery [6]. Ixion, who seeks to seduce Hera, is punished by

---

[3] See *ibid.* 315; G. Lawall, ' Simaetha's Incantation: Structure and Imagery ', *Trans. Proc. Am. Philol. Assoc.* 92, 1961, 284.

[4] Detienne (above, note 1), 159-60; *FGrHist* 19 F4 and cf. 33 F2.

[5] See the scholiast *ad* Theocr. II 17; Detienne, 163.

[6] Detienne, 160-1 and p. 163 with note 2; Tavenner (above, note 1), 117 and also 110-11.

being attached to a revolving wheel: he becomes a sort of living iynx [7]. According to Pindar his union with the cloud fashioned by Zeus is " without charis ", ἄνευ Χαρίτων, an unhallowed mating whose fruits are as perverse and monstrous as the act itself, for the offspring is the Centaur, γόνον ὑπερφίαλον, which receives no honor among men or gods.

In the stories of the enchantress Iynx and the iynx-like Ixion, the central figure threatens the union of Zeus and Hera which, as Detienne observes, " constitue le modèle mythique et rituel des relations matrimoniales de type monogamique " [8]. In all of these myths, in fact, marriage stands over against seduction or rape, just as the permanent, legitimate union of Zeus and Hera or (ultimately) Hades and Persephone stands over against the momentary, sensual union of concubine, seductress, violator.

A hydria from Populonia, illustrated both by Detienne and by Gow [9], adds a further detail. It shows Aphrodite and Adonis, the couple whose union is the archetype of short-lived, unhappy, unproductive, purely sensual love. They engage in amorous dalliance while before them hovers the winged figure of Himeros, Desire, holding a iynx-charm in his hands. Next to him sits an attractive woman, plausibly identified as Peitho, the power of erotic persuasion, who plays with what is perhaps a iynx-bird, the wryneck [10]. Here both the charm and the bird are joined in a context of an unstable, purely sensual, and doomed union.

The figurative use of the word ἴυγξ, meaning " desire " or " longing " [11], also stands in contexts of sudden, violent love which offers no continuity. In the *Oenomaus* Sophocles uses the word of the sudden flare-up of desire inspired by lovers' glances:

---

[7] Pind. *Pyth.* II 33-44, especially 40, τετράκναμον ... δεσμόν; cf. *Pyth.* IV 214, ἴυγγα τετράκναμον. See Detienne, 165-70.

[8] Detienne, 170.

[9] Detienne, 163-4 with accompanying plate; Gow, *Theocritus*, plate IV A, with the brief discussion *ad Id.* II 17.

[10] There is no absolute certainty that the bird on the hydria is a iynx. For the problem of identification of iynxes (both bird and charm) see Tavenner (above, note 1), 118-26.

[11] See Pind. *Nem.* IV 35; Aeschyl. *Pers.* 989; Aristoph. *Lys.* 1110. Further references in Gow, *Journ. Hell. Stud.* 54, p. 3 with note 6; Tavenner (above, note 1), 111.

ἴυγγα θηρητηρίαν ἔρωτος[12]. Lycophron and Heliodorus use the word with a similar significance and in similar erotic contexts[13].

" Iynx " can also refer to the aphrodisiac cry or scent of mating animals. Here it conveys the insistent, repetitive circularity of unsatisfied desire. Aelian discusses at length one instance of such a iynx, the example of the land tortoise, χερσαία χελώνη. The male of this species, " the most lustful of all creatures ", uses a iynx, a mysterious and potent herb, to charm the unwilling and cooler female[14]. Aelian specifically compares this iynx with that of Theocritus, *Idyll* II, and says that the tortoise's iynx is far stronger. What is especially relevant to our argument is the fact that the tortoise " fulfils his desire and then goes away ". He abandons his mate, now unable to move because of the weight of her shell and because she has been pressed into the sand, to become a prey to carnivores. Here the iynx is not only a potent erotic charm, but is also specifically a charm which results in the seduction *and cruel abandonment* of the beloved. Its effects, in other words, belong in the same category of unhappy, unstable unions as in the myths of Iynx the enchantress and the iynx-like Ixion.

In the fourth *Pythian* Ode Pindar describes the origin of the iynx as a love-charm[15]. Aphrodite, he says, first brought it among men for Jason, in order that he " might take away Medea's shame toward her parents and that a yearning for Hellas might whirl her, burning in mind, with the lash of Persuasion ":

> ὄφρα Μηδείας τοκέων ἀφέλοιτ' αἰδῶ, ποθεινὰ δ' Ἑλλὰς αὐτὰν
> ἐν φρασὶ καιομέναν δονέοι μάστιγι Πειθοῦς.

---

[12] Frag. 433 Nauck = 474 Pearson, and see Pearson's commentary *ad loc.*
[13] Lycophron 310; Heliodorus 8,5 (p. 258,3 Colonna).
[14] Aelian, *Nat. An.* XV 19. See Detienne, 164-5 and Tavenner, 111. The other passages from Aelian discussed by Detienne (IX 13 and V 40) are less to the point since Aelian seems there to be using " iynx " in its common metaphorical sense of " love charm ". In XV 19, however, Aelian dwells on the word with special emphasis and draws an explicit comparison with Theocritus II.
[15] *Pyth.* IV 214-9. For the details of Pindar's iynx charm see Tavenner (above, note 1), 116-7.

Once more the iynx is associated with seduction (note *peitho*) and with a maiden's loss of her " shame ", αἰδώς, a word whose connection with feminine chastity is familiar from Herodotus' story of Gyges (ἅμα δὲ κιθῶνι ἐκδυομένῳ συνεκδύεται καὶ τὴν αἰδῶ γυνή, Hdt. I 8, 3). Pindar's language here bears some affinities to that of *Idyll* II, particularly in the metaphors of " burning " and " whirling " (καιομέναν δονέοι). Theocritus' Simaetha repeatedly uses metaphors of fire to describe her state [16]. She prays also that Delphis may be " whirled " to her (δινεῖθ᾽, δινοῖτο, 30, 31). Madness, too, which Pindar associates with his iynx (μαινάδ᾽ ὄρνιν, *Pyth.* IV 216), has its place in Simaetha's incantation (48-51) and later in Delphis' speech (136). Like Pindar's Medea, Simaetha too has suffered the loss of the shame which goes with maidenhood (40-41): ὅς με τάλαιναν | ἀντὶ γυναικὸς ἔθηκε κακὰν καὶ ἀπάρθενον ἦμεν.

Simaetha's very first reference to the iynx in line 17 is immediately preceded by an allusion to Medea (16). To Medea she adds Circe and the rather mysterious Perimede (15-16):

φάρμακα ταῦτ᾽ ἔρδοισα χερείονα μήτε τι Κίρκας
μήτε τι Μηδείας μήτε ξανθᾶς Περιμήδας.

Of Perimede too little is certain to be helpful [17]. But Medea and Circe are not only enchantresses practised in potent *pharmaka*; they are also women whose relations with men are those of seduction and concubinage rather than marriage, unions unstable and ultimately doomed: Medea and Jason, Circe and Odysseus, Circe and Glaucus, etc. [18].

---

[16] The figurative use of fire in the *Idyll* occurs in lines 29, 40, 82, 131, 133-4; and actual fire occurs in lines 18-26 and 28. Cf. also 85 and 141, where heat is involved (the scholiast *ad* 85 glosses καπυρός by διάπυρος, πυρώδης).

[17] For Perimede see Gow, *Theocritus*, *ad* II 15 f.

[18] The connection of Glaucus and Circe is probably Ovid's own invention: see *P. Ovidius Naso Metamorphosen*[5], edd. Haupt-Korn-Ehwald-Albrecht, Dublin-Zürich 1966, *ad Met.* XIII 898 ff.; yet the episode of her passion is totally in keeping with Circe's character in the literary tradition: see C. Segal, ' Circean Temptations: Homer, Virgil, Ovid ', *Trans. Proc. Am. Philol. Assoc.* 99, 1968, 419-42. Cf. also the tale of Circe and Picus in Virg. *Aen.* VII 189-91 and Ovid, *Met.* XIV 320 ff.

In evoking these figures just when she sets in motion the magic
that is supposed to win back her own beloved, Simaetha is un-
knowingly confirming her own position among unhappy lovers,
victims or agents of seduction and inconstancy.   The pathos bears
some analogy with *Idyll* III where, in a far lighter vein, the Goat-
herd cites mythical examples which are not only grotesquely inap-
propriate, but in fact are also exemplary of ill-starred love [19].

The mythological associations of the iynx intimate a truth
to which Simaetha is blind, and her blindness enhances the pathos.
She hopes for a happy, stable union, but the instrument to which
she pins her hopes points only to seduction and ephemeral pas-
sion, to lust and madness, to the realm of the brief and transient
pleasure to which she has succumbed and for which she must now
pay the price.   Rather than lift her above her present condition
to durable and happy love, the iynx, by its very nature, can only
plunge her more deeply into the realm of changeful and deceptive
love, violence, and seduction.

These implications of the iynx become explicit near the end
of the poem.   Simaetha describes her first meeting with Delphis
and his first gesture on seeing her.   He fixed his eyes on the ground
(112).   Simaetha's only comment is the   word ὥστοργος, which
stands immediately next to the phrase, " fixing his eyes on the
ground ".   Gow explains the word as " incapable of lasting af-
fection, though not of sorrow " [20].   Legrand sees in *astorgos*
even less favorable connotations, an image of " un élégant de la
jeunesse dorée " [21].   The juxtaposition of ἄστοργος and ἐπὶ χθονὸς
ὄμματα πάξας in line 112 suggests, but does not fully confirm the
possibility that Simaetha realizes that her lover's downcast eyes

---

[19] On this device in *Id.* III see G. Lawall, *Theocritus' Coan Pastorals: A Poetry
Book*, Cambridge, Mass. 1967, 40-1; C. Segal, ' Adonis and Aphrodite: Theocritus,
Idyll III, 48 ', *Ant. Class.* 38, 1969, 82-8.   There are other links between *Idylls* II
and III, especially in the echo between II 82 and III 42 and possibly in the lioness,
whose puzzling presence in *Id.* II 68 might thus be explained by its association
with violent love in III 15-16.   For a different explanation see L. B. Lawler, *Trans.
Proc. Am. Philol. Assoc.* 78, 1947, 88-98 and Gow, *Theocritus, ad* II 68.

[20] Gow, *Theocritus, ad loc.*

[21] Ph. Legrand, *Étude sur Théocrite*, Bibl. des Écoles françaises d'Athènes et de
Rome 79, Paris 1898, 348.

are but feigned modesty [22]. When she goes on to cite his actual words in the next lines (114 ff.), her tone is objective, innocent. There is little to suggest that she herself has really understood how fully Delphis' style betrays his character. The reader, however, from his aesthetic distance, easily catches the meaning of Delphis' exaggerations and inflated commonplaces. They suggest the artificiality of contemporary love-poetry, and they are redolent of the seducer's insincerity [23]. The effect of this depiction of character through style did not escape the scholiast, who sets down Delphis' language and gestures as that of a man practiced in the ways of love, ἀνδρὸς ... τεχνικοῦ καὶ συνετοῦ τὰ ἐρωτικά. Theocritus' language, he observes, has caught a character of this type: τοιοῦτον δή τινα καὶ τὸν Δέλφιν δείκνυσιν ὁ ποιητικὸς ἡμῖν λόγος.

---

[22] Gow, *Theocritus*, *ad* II 112; R. J. Cholmeley, *The Idylls of Theocritus*, London 1919, *ad loc.* cites Musaeus 160. Fritzsche-Hiller, *Theokrits Gedichte³*, Leipzig 1881, *ad loc.* rightly refutes the view that the phrase refers to Delphis' modesty, and adds, " Auch mag Delphis wissen, dass ihm eine solche Haltung gut steht. Mir scheint dieser Zug nicht schlecht erfunden " (p. 171).

[23] Note especially Delphis' allusion to Dionysus and Heracles in 120-1, the door-motif of 127-8, the conceit of fire in 130-4. With this last we may compare *Anth. Pal.* V 209 and 210 (Asclepiades), on which see Gow and Page, *Hellenistic Epigrams*, Cambridge 1965, *ad* 829 and 982, and the Alexandrian Erotic Fragment, ed. B. P. Grenfell, Oxford 1896, line 9. There is perhaps a pathetic touch here in the contrast between Simaetha's αἴθω in the desperation of her enchantment (line 24) and Delphis' αἴθει in his ' literary ' conceit of line 134. For the use of complex and involved syntax to convey an impression of insincerity see Lichas' speech in Soph. *Trach.* 262-73, with the comments of U. Parlavantza-Friedrich, *Täuschungsszenen in den Tragödien des Sophokles*, Berlin 1969, 27-8, on the " Kompliziertheit der kausalen Zusammenhängen ". On the whole passage see Legrand (above, note 21), 118: " ... Notre bourreau de coeurs manie l'hyperbole avec désinvolture et renchérit sur de vieilles métaphores... En les lui attribuant, Théocrite entendait démontrer par contraste combien le jargon sentimental diffère du langage de la passion vraie ". In this contrast between Simaetha and Delphis Theocritus has represented through style and without sentimentality a basic and universal pathos. We may compare Rilke's remarks on the Letters of a Portuguese Nun: " ... This relationship definitely brings to light how much all that was achieved, borne, accomplished on the one side, the woman's, contrasts with the man's absolute inadequacy in love. She receives, so to speak, ... the diploma of ability to love, while he has an elementary grammar of this discipline in his pocket from which a few words have of necessity gone into him with which he occasionally forms sentences, beautiful and rapturous, as the familiar sentences on the first pages of language primers ": *Letters of R. M. Rilke* 1910-1926, tr. J. B. Greene and M. D. Herter Norton, New York 1948, 47.

As Simaetha's introduction of Delphis contained but one word of judgment and recognition, *astorgos* in 112, so her only comment when she leaves off quoting his speech is the single word ταχυπειθής, " too quick to believe ". This one stark and simple sign of recognition stands out in vivid contrast to the intricate syntax and high-sounding allusions of Delphis. Her earlier suspicion that Delphis loves another is now confirmed from an outside source (44, 150). Similarly her hesitant fear that Eros and Aphrodite might hold his heart elsewhere (6-7) is proved true by the report that Delphis always pours unmixed wine to Eros (151-2) [24], that is, is a skilled *erotikos* and not to be trusted. Here too the pathos of this new knowledge is increased by the contrast both with Simaetha's objective portrayal of their first meeting in the preceding lines (112-38) and the extreme simplicity of ἔστι δ' ἀλαθής in 154 [25]. There is a subtle, but dramatic movement from the objective account of Delphis as seducer in 112-38 to Simaetha's recognition of Delphis' character, including his subjection to Eros in 151-2, and then to the austere factuality of her acceptance of the reality in 154: " So the woman spoke, and she is truth-speaking ". Behind this development lies the deeper truth of seduction and unstable love contained in the associations of the iynx.

Delphis' last words are especially important for completing the implications of the iynx. They are a eulogy of Eros, Eros as the power of seduction, the principle of intensity and brevity in love, the flame which rages hotly, but burns itself out as quickly as it came (133-4):

αὔτως ἡμίφλεκτον · Ἔρως δ' ἄρα καὶ Λιπαραίῳ
πολλάκις Ἀφαίστοιο σέλας φλογερώτερον αἴθει ·

Delphis' Eros is the elemental Eros familiar from early Greek lyric

---

[24] On the meaning of this rather difficult expression see the discussion and examples in Gow, *Theocritus, ad* II 152. He translates, rather freely, " Ever he called for wine unmixed and his toast was Love ".

[25] On Simaetha's restraint see Lawall (above, note 19), 33; Legrand (above, note 21), 117-8: " Une épithète, deux tout au plus, expriment dans ses discours cette espèce de vague attendrissement où se complaisent parfois les coeurs mentis ".

poetry and tragedy [26], an amoral force heedless of social and moral order, constancy, or tenderness, cruelly shattering lives. It is hardly the " sweet Eros " which he lightly invoked when he triumphantly announced his presence (118): ναὶ τὸν γλυκὺν ἦνθον Ἔρωτα. The violence and recklessness of the Eros to which Delphis is devoted are perhaps also implied in his libations of " unmixed wine " to the god (151-2).

The very last lines of Delphis which Simaetha cites not only mention " madness " (κακαῖς μανίαις 136), but in fact dwell upon seduction and the disruption of marriage. " Eros with his evil madnesses affrights the maiden from her chamber and the new bride, leaving the still warm coverlets of her husband " (136-8):

σὺν δὲ κακαῖς μανίαις καὶ παρθένον ἐκ θαλάμοιο
καὶ νύμφαν ἐφόβησ' ἔτι δέμνια θερμὰ λιποῖσαν
ἀνέρος.

The word ἐφόβησε and the versification emphasize the amoral violence of this seductive eros. Theocritus sharply enjambs the word " husband " (ἀνέρος) and thus ends the speech at an abrupt first foot diaeresis, the harshest and most striking such enjambement in the poem. The long separation between νύμφαν and ἀνέρος thereby effected reveals Delphis as a destroyer, not a creator, of the lasting ties of love.

An anonymous Hellenistic epigram from the *Greek Anthology* closes the circle between Delphis' eros of seduction and the iynx. Delphis' words in 136-8 resemble the poetical dedication of a iynx by one Nico in *Anth. Pal.* V 205. This iynx, elaborately described, " can draw a man who is across the sea and boys [or girls?] from their chambers " [27]: ἴυγξ ἡ Νικοῦς, ἡ καὶ διαπόντιον ἕλκειν | ἄνδρα καὶ ἐκ θαλάμων παῖδας ἐπισταμένη. The epigram

---

[26] E.g. Alcman 59a (Page), Ibycus 287, Anacreon 398, 413; Alcaeus Z3 (327) (Lobel-Page), Sappho 47 and 130; Eur. *Hipp.* 1274 ff. The *topos* is, of course, no less common in Hellenistic literature: *Anth. Pal.* V 176-80, 215; XII 82-4 (all Meleager).

[27] Gow and Page (above, note 23), *ad* 3798 use Theocr. II 136 to maintain that παῖδας = " girls ". It is not, however, necessary that the epigrammatist had in mind the same balance of male and female as Theocritus.

does not speak explicitly of seduction, but it is implied in the phrase, ἐκ θαλάμων παῖδας, with which we may compare Delphis' παρθένον ἐκ θαλάμοιο. The poet of the *Anthology* may have had Theocritus' verses in mind. If so, he has taken the step logically suggested by Theocritus' poem and linked Delphis' tell-tale words with the symbol of seduction, the iynx. It does not greatly matter whether the παῖδες of the epigram are " girls " (Gow and Page) or " boys " (W. R. Paton) or even both. The important thing is the clear link which the epigram establishes between the magical iynx-charm and the kind of eros which Delphis embodies.

The final words of Delphis in 136-8 concretize the implications of the iynx as a symbol of unstable, illegitimate, non-durable love. Slowly and relentlessly the awareness dawns on Simaetha. The pathos remains intense as she veers between uncertainty (158), determination to win back her lover (159), vengefulness (160-2), and resignation (164).

Theocritus' dramatic, objective style does not entirely resolve these tensions and contradictions of her emotional situation. Yet her matter-of-fact report of Delphis' speech has clarified one aspect of her hopeless situation: Delphis' last words reveal him as the archetypal seducer, an embodiment of an impermanent and irresponsible eros. He is the masculine side of what is implied in the mythology of the iynx.

The fact that Simaetha tries to win back her seducer with the iynx, symbol of unstable and changeful union, only underlines the hopelessness and the pathos of her position. Seduced, she can have recourse only to magic, a force as irrational as her desire itself. And she can only reexperience the symbols of her seduction: *peitho, mania*, the wild " fires ", all of which belong to those impermanent unions presided over by the iynx. Simaetha resorts to the iynx to counter this realm of seduction; but the associations of the iynx, so ably revealed by Detienne, suggest that it can in fact only reinforce the inconstancy from which stem her sufferings. In seeking to counter seduction with the symbol of seduction, she is using the iynx inappropriately. Yet from a wider perspective her invocation of the iynx is totally appropriate, for her whole condition has been determined by seduction. She stands under the sign of the iynx — madness, lost maidenhood, abandonment, the unbreakable circle of desire. The elements are already present in the earliest literary handling of the iynx, Pindar's fourth *Pythian*.

The iynx dominates the first half of the *Idyll*. Here Simaetha is totally given over to the irrationality of magic and of love and to the violence with which the iynx is associated. Much of the pathos lies in her loss of contact with a reality which she can no longer grasp. Hence there is a pathetic contrast between the rapid whirling movements of the iynx and her hope that she will " bind fast " (καταδήσομαι, 3, 10, 159) the fleeting, inconstant seducer. The iynx, sign of circular, hopeless desire, can only return her to the wheel of her own unfulfilled passions, what Pindar, describing the first iynx, called its " unloosable circle " [28].

Yet while the associations of the iynx reinforce the pathos and hopelessness of Simaetha's condition, the poem depicts a movement, albeit unsteady, away from the magic and madness of the iynx [29] to a more human perspective and a more rational clarity. Simaetha may not be able to escape the circularity of her passion, but she can at least endure (164): ἐγὼ δ' οἰσῶ τὸ ἐμὸν πόθον ὥσπερ ὑπέσταν. Hence her next two lines, which are the last lines of the poem, seem to lead out of her enclosed, emotion-defined world of hopeless passion, out of the " house " to which the iynx would draw Delphis [30], to a circling of another kind, the broad, serene movements of " the stars, attendants on the car of tranquil Night " (166) [31]. Instead of " chthonic Hecate " (12) Simaetha now calls

---

[28] *Pyth.* IV 215: ἐν ἀλύτῳ ζεύξαισα κύκλῳ.

[29] The " maenad bird " of *Pyth.* IV 216 may be dimly behind the " madness " of Simaetha in 48-51, but the associations of love and madness are commonplace.

[30] Simaetha's house has an important function in the poem. It represents the fixed point of her passivity and helplessness. Her happiness or misery depends on others coming to or going from her in this house, which she herself does not leave, save for the fateful occasion of the festival of Artemis (70-77). After that point, she is closed within the house. She may send out an emissary (96-8) and call Delphis in (101-2), but all the action centers upon others " coming " to her: see 4, 7, 31, 50, 66, 118, 128, 132, 145.

[31] Contrast Simaetha's reference to the disturbed sea at 38-40. That image of a violent and turbulent natural phenomenon sets off the serenity of a personified and mythicized nature in 165-6. Cf. also 147-8. On the circling of the iynx and Simaetha's passion see Lawall (above, note 19), 32: " This intense and repeated circular motion reveals the inner turbulence of the speaker and vivifies the whole dark atmosphere of the magical rites and the terrifying apparition of dread Hecate ".

upon a goddess of the heavens; instead of the dark night which her sinister magic requires (60), she looks to a starlit night personified in plastic, mythological terms. Her farewell to Selene may even suggest the coming of dawn (cf. 60, ἇς ἔτι καὶ νύξ), and with the dawn lucidity, calm, mastery of passion [32]. In any case the darkness of night recedes into the background: Selene is " bright-throned " (165), and there are stars. Night's wide, luminous circling in a world of extended space answers the artificial, narrow, dark circling of the iynx.

Brown University
Providence, R. I.

---

[32] For a similar resigned mastery of passion, but in the poet's *propria persona*, see *Id.* XXX 27-32. The movement from passion to calm, from ἔρως to ἀσυχία, is taken by a number of interpreters as a major theme in Theocritus, especially in *Id.* VII and XI: see Gregorio Serrao, *Problemi di poesia alessandrina* I: *Studi su Teocrito*, Rome 1971, 61 ff.; E. B. Holtsmark, ' Poetry as Self-Enlightenment: Theocritus 11 ', *Trans. Proc. Am. Philol. Assoc.* 97, 1966, 253-59; Anne Brooke, ' Theocritus 11: A Study in Pastoral ', *Arethusa* 4, 1971, 73-81. Contrast Virgil's adaptation of *Id.* II at the end of *Ecl.* VIII. Here the girl does not escape her enclosed world of passions. Virgil leaves her ambiguously still in the realm of hope and dream: *credimus? an qui amant ipsi sibi somnia fingunt?* (*Ecl.* VIII 108).

THEOCRITEAN CRITICISM AND THE INTERPRETATION
OF THE FOURTH IDYLL

Charles Segal

If the critical re-evaluation of classical authors in recent years has brought nothing else, it has given us a humbling awareness of how difficult it is to arrive at a fully satisfactory reading of ancient pastoral poetry. The poet of the *Eclogues,* seen less and less as merely a painter of dreamy landscapes or a contriver of political allegories, has emerged increasingly as a self-conscious artist whose conventional, but highly symbolic and allusive language embraces questions of man's relation to art and imagination, to passion and work, to the potential for order and violence in his own being.[1] Is it valid to look at Theocritus in similar terms? Is there more in the *Idylls* than keenly etched portraits of shepherds among verdant hills singing of love in dulcet hexameters and in an atmosphere of easeful sensuousness? Or should we merely enjoy the surface felicities and depart sated and content, like Horace's well-fed guest? The rhythms and resonances of Theocritus will continue to give pleasure as long as Greek is read. Yet recent work in both ancient and later pastoral suggests that the *Idylls* will sustain and reward a critical reading which looks beneath this charming surface.

Theocritus, of course, is not Virgil. His poetry remains closer to the earth, more concerned with the rhythms of nature. The poignant Virgilian tension between war and rustic ease, between threatening *urbs* and defenseless *rus* is largely absent. The surface of Theocritus' poetry is more coherent and more self-contained than Virgil's. More fluid and more generous in the depiction of setting and narrative, it makes fewer immediate demands on the reader. Objective and ironical, Theocritus also offers fewer clues to his own attitudes or intentions and thus presents fewer critical handles for interpretation. Theocritus is, in a sense, the Homer of pastoral.[2] Narrative movement and setting are so pleasing and so gracefully conveyed that the primary, literal meaning remains always in the foreground and only at fleeting moments permits a glimpse of something else. Those moments are precious, however, for they reveal another essential dimension of Theocritus' art. He is not a poet of Homeric simplicity and directness, but an artist working in a sophisticated age, an age in which the highest art delights in putting on the trappings of simplicity.[3] For Theocritus, as a recent critic suggests, *ars latet arte sua.*[4]

The interpretation of a poet as subtle as Theocritus requires special tact in our critical terminology. "Symbolism" especially is a many-faceted term. All literature, all art use symbols, but with different degrees of self-consciousness and consistency. The arms of Achilles in the *Iliad* and of Aeneas in the *Aeneid* are both symbolic, but in the Roman poet the symbolic value is closer to the

surface and more fully integrated into a conscious design. The same difference
holds, to some extent, between the cups of Theocritus and Virgil in *Idyll* I and
Eclogue III.[5]   Theocritus' cup also has symbolic value, but the poet overlays this
more or less conscious symbolism with an appearance of "Homeric" naivete and
the one-dimensional directness reminiscent of Homer's shield of Achilles.
"Symbolism" in such a case becomes a vague, but convenient term (in default of
a better) to describe the heightened expressiveness of a certain kind of poetry: a
poetry which, without breaking the frame of its fictional situation or the unity
of its style and tone, reaches beyond itself to explore matters of large scope. The
whole poem is a symbolic ordering of experience through art. One cannot easily
say where direct narrative ends and symbolism begins. The two are inextricable.
Hence the poem is thoroughly satisfying read purely as an "imitation" of a scene
or an event; but this does not mean that one may not go further: the scene or
event so represented can be a means of representing other, more general ideas,
conflicts, tensions which the poet cannot otherwise reach.

The time-honored antithesis between the realism of Theocritus and the
soulfulness or emotional coloring of Virgil has foisted on the Greek pastoralist a
reputation for simplicity which reflects only the narrative surface. True, one
must beware of pressing the *Idylls* into the mold of the *Eclogues.* But one must
also face the possibility that Virgil discovered and accentuated the expressive
possibilities of pastoral already present in Theocritus. Theocritus may have been
Virgil's predecessor not only in the form, but also in the spirit of pastoral.
Theocritus, in other words, would have already established for pastoral its
double perspective, its tension between reality and imagination, its pregnant
atmosphere of the suspended moment in which more seems always to be
suggested than can be explicitly stated. Theocritean pastoral, even more than
Virgilian, reminds us again and again of the art of song and music, which it even
seeks to reproduce through the bucolic refrain. Here it edges toward a realm in
which "meaning" most nearly eludes verbal definition.

Theocritus' *Idylls* present still another difficulty. The *Eclogues,* despite the
poet's playful assertions to the contrary, carry a tone of seriousness, even
urgency. *Paulo maiora canamus*: this is an Augustan *vates* speaking. Apollo may
pluck his ear with Callimachean admonitions, but matters of some import are
clearly in the air. In the case of Theocritus, we are never so sure. The *Idylls* can
be read at several different levels of seriousness simultaneously, whereas the
unmistakable seriousness of the *Eclogues* forces itself upon the reader. This
divergence in Theocritus' "levels of intent" (to use Kenneth Quinn's convenient
phrase[6]) raises real problems. It means, for one thing, that a given poem may
give rise to a wider variety of critical views, all of which may be to some degree
right. Those who are determined to see "profounder meanings" in Theocritus
will not be convinced that their vision is a mirage; those who deny all such
interpretations will not be easily persuaded of their blindness. Both sides are
likely to have a grip on equally valid aspects of their poet. This state of affairs, as
we shall see, is partly represented by the difference between the attitudes of

Lawall and Rosenmeyer in their recent books on Theocritus.[7]   Given such a situation, empiricism may be preferable to theory. There have been few critical analyses of the shorter pastorals of Theocritus as integral poems. The Fourth *Idyll* is an especially useful case, for, if recent critics are correct, it contains a singularly harmonious and natural accord between surface meaning, symbolism, and structure.

I.

Superficially *Idyll* IV looks like a realistic genre-piece, "un quart d'heure de la vie de deux rustres," as Legrand suggested.[8]   A goatherd and a cowherd, Battus and Corydon respectively, meet; they discuss the flock and its absent owner, Aegon, and they exchange some not always friendly remarks and then bits of song involving Aegon and other local personages: here a pipe, festive play, and love have a prominent role. Corydon proffers encouraging advice, but at this point some adventuresome calves threaten the olive shoots. Battus, gaping after a heifer, gets a thorn in his foot, Corydon extracts it, and the poem closes with a brief exchange on the extraordinary virility of an old man, presumably the absent Aegon's father.

Gow's remarks in his very valuable commentary are typical of the usual view of the bucolic *Idylls*. The conversations of *Idylls* IV and V, he observes "approach more nearly to the possible speech of rustics than anything else in [Theocritus]." He stresses the "liveliness and verisimilitude" of the exchanges and finds a "reduction of the poetical element" which places this *Idyll* along with the Fifth, "poetically on a lower plain than [Theocritus'] other bucolic Idylls."[9]

Implicit in Gow's comment is the assumption that the "poetical element" is somehow separable from the whole. Lawall suggests a different view of what is "poetical" in the *Idyll*. He finds the "poetical element" in an integral structure of ideas, symbols, and images rather than in individual felicities of mellifluous phrasing or charm of setting and dialogue. For Lawall the Fourth *Idyll* is "a study in human and animal loves." He exploits the hints in words like ποθεῦντι ("longing,"12) the symptoms of loss of appetite in 14-16, the implications of the wound of the thorn, Battus' interest in the heifer (52-3), and the vigor of the old man at the end to interpret the poem in terms of a contrast between sentimental and grossly realistic attitudes toward love and sexuality.[10]   Lawall's approach has the merit of looking beneath the surface-play of rustic repartee and attempting to read the *Idyll* in terms of its own tone and motifs rather than external criteria of "poetical elements." One cannot deny the validity of the erotic elements which Lawall has detected, especially in the light of the close parallels with other *Idylls* (*cf*. especially IV.15-16 and II.89-90; IV.38 and III.6). At the same time, leaving the perhaps forced interpretation of the "gaping" of 53 aside, we may wonder if the contrast between sentimentality and realism does not extend beyond the erotic themes to which Lawall confines it.

Lawall's attention to unity of structure and symbol informs J.B. Van Sickle's more recent discussion of *Idyll* IV.[11] Building upon Lawall, he sees the contrast in the poem as one between styles or modes of poetry symbolized by the two rustics: a sentimental and rhetorical mode (Battus) and a harder, more realistic, yet more accommodating mode (Corydon). The characters and the narrative situation are "all the symbolic representations of the basic problems of a new poetry." These "have to be worked out and settled" in order to accomplish a "work of self-definition."[12] Van Sickle goes further than Lawall in bringing together character, style, and setting into a single perspective. Yet his view too may sacrifice a part to the whole. The characters may, and indeed almost certainly do, embody different voices of poetry. But they may embody other things besides. It is interesting that Lawall had considered Van Sickle's line of interpretation, but rejected it. He saw in the "thin Bull," ($\lambda\epsilon\pi\tau\acute{o}\varsigma\ \tau\alpha\hat{v}\rho o\varsigma$), of line 20 a possible allusion to Callimachus' celebrated advice about a "thin style": "The allusion to contemporary poetical theory is, of course, too slight to break the dramatic illusion."[13] Van Sickle has freed us from excessive bondage to the "dramatic illusion," but he may have freed us a bit too much.

The terms in which Lawall and Van Sickle frame the issues of the poem are not mutually exclusive. The vitality of sex asserted at the end runs parallel to the vitality of art in the *Idyll's* movement toward a sound poetic discourse. Both areas have a further correlative in the beauty and vitality of a natural world presided over by Pan, Nymphs, the Satyrs . These figures are spirits of exuberant sexuality, but they are also powers of nature. At the same time their very presence attests to the creative infusion of myth and imagination into nature.

At the opposite pole from Lawall and Van Sickle stands the approach of Rosenmeyer. He repudiates any attempt at symbolic interpretation. "Theocritus resists decoding."[14] Rosenmeyer's emphasis falls rather on the pastoral's creation of a fruitful *locus* in which can flower "the life of the soul, the *otium* of the free."[15] The philosophical analogue is Epicurus' garden. No one element — word, phrase, or action — is to be isolated as a "condensation of a larger meaning."[16] The meaning is the whole poem, the leisured, beautiful setting populated by naive and essentially happy shepherds. "The poem as a whole is a trope, rather than any one portion of it."[17]

Although Lawall and Van Sickle may be occasionally guilty of what Rosenmeyer warns against, isolating a single element at the expense of the whole, such an approach through metaphor and symbol need not necessarily be the one-dimensional, simplistic "decoding" implicit in Rosenmeyer's phrase. Rosenmeyer's approach risks too complacent an acceptance of the surface elements and involves the old, but unwarranted assumption that poetry of this nature aims primarily at realism. Hence Rosenmeyer's method is descriptive rather than analytical: he offers no unified interpretation of an entire *Idyll.*

The distance between these three points of view is considerable, but an area for agreement might be found in the encompassing vitality of Theocritus' pastoral world. Here where pressing concerns involve nothing more complicated than shooing away greedy cows or extracting thorns, the mind finds rest and takes delight in the goodness of life. Yet our sense of peace and our delight come in part from the knowledge that we are contemplating a world simpler than the one in which we normally live. The basic constituents of life are all present — love, death, the rhythms of toil and ease —, but they are transformed through metaphor and the implications of the setting into clearer, purer, more tangible terms. Hence we enjoy a double perspective: we accept the songful rustics and the verdant setting in their own right, but we also stand above them and relish the aesthetic satisfaction of a sophisticated paradox: leisured simplicity created by consummate art. In this double perspective the question of poetics (Van Sickle's concern) becomes virtually inescapable, for the poet is playing on the antithesis between simplicity and artfulness. The dialogue between Corydon and Battus develops a complex and multi-dimensional statement of this antithesis. Evolving a contrast between different voices of poetry, they also spin a dialogue between naive sentimentality and naive, good-natured practicality; and thus they take us simultaneously through a drama of human relations (Lawall's concern).

The various aspects of this contrast coincide and are resolved, in part, in the vision of an exuberant vitality which is that of art, sexuality, and the pastoral cosmos all at the same time. The movement of the poem is from tight, prickly, line-by-line dialogue to broader, open movement, from suspicion (line 3) to trust and friendship (lines 54-7). One may describe this movement in terms of poetics, love, friendship, or Epicurean notions of tranquility and spiritual pleasure. But each of these descriptions is but one way of concretizing and conceptualizing an aesthetic satisfaction which derives primarily from the resolution of tension into affirmation. That pattern of resolution is fulfilled on a sexual, a stylistic, and a philosophical level simultaneously. The prism of our critical analysis can isolate now one beam, now another. The total luminosity of this magical fusion belongs to art rather than criticism. It can be described, not recreated.

II.

Rosenmeyer has cautioned against reading the *Idylls* in developmental and dramatic terms. Their dominant quality, he suggests, is staticity and calm.[18] This judgment requires qualification in the light of *Idyll* IV. Rosenmeyer is right, however, in so far as the dramatic elements remain low-keyed and do not break through the surface of the pastoral frame. The very quietness of mood and the paucity of events attune our receptivity to the importance of little things. In Virgil, who shatters pastoral calm and smoothness with the *grandia* or *maiora* of war, exile, politics, these "little things," the beech tree or the shadows of *Eclogue* 1 or the little basket of *Eclogue* 10, become especially precious as the reminders and survivors of a beautiful, but fragile Arcadian world. Hence they gain a self-conscious symbolic value. In Theocritus, where the polarity between pastoral landscape and reality, *rus* and *urbs*, is less marked, the scenery shades off less immediately into the realm of symbol. Symbolism there is, but it is more reticent, less obtrusive, less demanding.

Idyll IV has a strong dramatic structure. Contrast is the driving force in the poem.[19] Battus is emotional, sentimental, inclined to exaggeration and despair. Corydon is more even-tempered, calmer, quietly efficient.[20] The differences appear both in language and in situation. Battus is given to poignant exclamations drawn from the tragic stage: φεῦ φεῦ . . . ὦ τάλαν (26); αἰαῖ (40). Corydon's ejaculations are more positive and more practical. His is the herdsman's warning "*sstth . . . sstth*" (45-6) when the cows get too close to the olive trees. "Yes, yes" (ναὶ ναί), he emphatically reassures the worried Battus as he extracts the thorn (54).

Battus describes Aegon's absence in the language of tragedy: ἄφαντος …ᾤχετο ("went off, disappeared," 5). The elaborate hyperbaton of this line, ἐς τίνα . . . χώραν ("to what . . .land"), also suggests a certain pretentiousness and reinforces the tragic tone. Corydon echoes Battus' ᾤχετο, but his tone is dry and matter-of-fact: "Haven't you heard? Milo went off with him (ᾤχετο), to the Alpheus" (6). Battus and Corydon then exchange Homeric phrases (ἐν ὀφθαλμοῖσιν ὀπώπει, "saw in his eyes," 7; βίην καὶ κάρτος, "force and strength," 8). Battus' first declarative sentence, after four consecutive questions, is an ironical allusion to Polydeuces (9). He also criticizes Milo in figurative language (11). Corydon's comparison of Aegon to Heracles, on the other hand, is, as seems probable, naively straightforward rather than ironical.[21] This naivete of Corydon appears elsewhere in the *Idyll*. It is an essential ingredient of his enthusiastic approval of Aegon. He sees in Aegon a kindred spirit and something of a hero. The friendship seems to have been reciprocated, for Aegon left him his pipe (30).

In the ensuing lines Corydon offers matter-of-fact information about Aegon's departure (10), as he did a few lines before. Battus, inclined to see things in terms of extremes, takes a dim view of Aegon's venture: he foresees death for the herd and decay for the pipe with which "poor Aegon" was wont to sing (26-8). Corydon replies vigorously in the negative (οὐ τήνα γ', οὐ Νύμφας, "No indeed, not that, no, by the Nymphs," 29). He is even able to extract something positive from Aegon's departure. He speaks not of his ill-starred "love of victory," as does Battus (27), but of an act of generosity, the "gift'" (δῶρον, 30) of the pipe which Aegon left him. One recalls Aegon's "giving" of his cows to Corydon to pasture at the very beginning (2). Corydon then goes on to present the fullest and most particularized image of Aegon in the poem (33-7). Whereas Battus depicted Aegon in static, despairing terms, Corydon shows us Aegon in the full swing of action, a Heracles-like figure performing acts of strength and gluttony, full of laughter and exuberance (33-7).[22] Corydon is more sanguine about Aegon's aspirations to a life beyond the rustic pale: for Corydon he is "Aegon the boxer," ὁ πύκτας Αἴγων (33-4). It was Corydon, we recall, who compared Aegon to Heracles at the beginning of the *Idyll* (line 8), and we have just noted the Herculean overtones in his recollections of Aegon at 33-7. Correspondingly, Battus uses the rhetorical figure of apostrophe (26, 38);

Corydon speaks of Aegon and of Amaryllis in a third-person narrative (34,36).

Battus and Corydon are both singers. Battus' songs, naturally enough, reflect a poetry of sentimental exaggeration and self-indulgent subjectivity. Corydon, on the other hand, sings of gaiety and action. Hence it was appropriately his line on shovels and sheep (10) that punctured the inflated Homeric and tragic language of lines 5-9. The contrast may reflect the aesthetic debates of Theocritus' contemporaries; but, more important, it may reflect tensions, held in balance through irony, within Theocritus' own pastoral poetry, the dialogue between the high and the low, the "fat" and the "lean" styles. Heroic language for very unheroic situations is a stock-in-trade of Theocritean humor. In *Idyll* XI the lovesick Cyclops looks out to sea like the troubled Achilles brooding on honor and death in the *Iliad* (*Idyll* XI.17-18; *Iliad* I.348-50). Yet the incongruity may contain more than humor. It also helps Theocritus to define the limits and nature of his art. He uses epic only to invert it and to set off the non-epic quality of his pastoral world.

The antithesis between the two rustics also presents itself in terms of a basic difference of attitudes towards life. That difference may be designated crudely as one between revery and realism, love and work, things absent and things present. In one form or another it appears in most of the pastoral *Idylls*, but it is articulated with convenient conciseness at the beginning of the Tenth:

> Bucaeus. Has it never happened to you to long for anything out of reach?
> Milo. No. What longing for things far away can a working man have?
> Bucaeus. Has it never befallen you to stay awake because of love?
> Milo. And may it never befall me. It's hard for a dog to get a taste of leather. (X.8-11)

In *Idyll* IV Theocritus expands this basic antithesis of *Idyll* X by blending into it another antithesis, that between life and death, energy and apathy. Battus' prophecy of death and decay at what Van Sickle calls "the peak of paratragic despair" in line 26-8 [23] is met by Corydon's spirited oath to the Nymphs (29) and his picture of a merry, self-assured Aegon bursting with robust good spirits (33-7).

How fully these contrasts develop from the composite effect of language, character, and situation appears from the apparently trifling discourse in which the two rustics discuss the state of Aegon's herd. It looks as if Corydon is going to take a sentimental turn when he describes the cows' "longing" for their herdsman (12). Battus replies "Poor creatures" (δείλαιαι,13), and his word paints the situation in the emotional colors typical of his view of life. Corydon repeats his "poor things" (14); but he adds the practical cowherd's detail that "they no longer wish to pasture" (14). Battus again enlarges upon the thought: the heifer is all bones and perhaps feeds on dew like the cicada (15-16). The image of the cicada is not only a favorite *topos* of Hellenistic poetry, but is also a self-consciously "fine phrase," a literary conceit.[24] · The lore of the cicada has a natural place in a context like that at the end of *Idyll* I (1.148), with its polite hyperboles and its courtly tone. But in a discussion on agronomy and pasture it introduces a humorous incongruity. Corydon too has used a word precisely appropriate to his cattle (νέμεσθαι, "pasture," 14: *cf.* his βόσκειν , "feed," 2), whereas Battus uses the more general οιτίζεται ("eat," 16), which may also be used of human beings. And yet it was Corydon who endowed the heifers with "longing" (12).

As the dialogue opens from stichomythia into two and three-line exchanges, the contrasts between the two rustics become more marked. Up until line 14 the differences are still blurred, as Corydon's tone in line 12 illustrates. Corydon counters Battus' lines on dew-drops and cicadas with an emphatic denial and an earthy precision about rivers, caves, soft hay (17-19). His practicality and his joy in the countryside save him from lapsing into the negativity and sentimentalism of Battus towards which he was tending in 12 and 14. As he is later to envisage a laughing Aegon, so here he pictures a "leaping" heifer (19). Once more his language suggests the practical workaday life of the cowherd: his νομεύω, ("pasture ," 17), like his βόσκειν and νέμεσθαι in 2 and 14, sounds the note of professional authenticity. No confusion of cows and cicadas here. Battus goes on to describe a bull wasting pathetically away.[25] Corydon describes a bull, nonplussed though it must be, in a gay, festive situation, presented as a love-gift to Amaryllis (35-6). Once more, incidentally, he presents Aegon in the act of "giving" (κῆδωκ', 36; *cf.* δῶρον, 30, and ἔδωκεν, 2). Even before this point is reached, however, Corydon's practical sense of pastures and rivers expands into a quiet settled joy in his countryside and in the specific, familiar places which the cowherd frequents: the river Aesarus, the mountain Latymnos, the stream of the Neaethus where "all lovely things grow, restharrow, fleabane, and sweet-smelling balm":

κaὶ πότὶ τὸν Νήαιθον, ὅπα καλὰ πάντα φύοντι
αἰγίπυρος καὶ κνύζα καὶ εὐώδης μελίτεια.   (24-5)

The herdsman appreciates the goodness of the "soft hay" he gives his "leaping" heifer (καὶ μαλακῶ χόρτοιο καλὰν κώμυθα δίδωμι, 18).[26] And, as suggested above, his feeling for the benignity of nature has a human counterpart in his appreciation of the generosity of Aegon (2, 30, 36). Only Corydon uses the adjective καλός ("lovely,"), and he does so three times, twice of growing things (18, 24), once of a city in a bit of song (32). Battus, on the other hand, uses κακός or its compounds five times (13, 22, 27, 52, 63).[27] Corydon finds the world beautiful. His songs, accordingly, reflect a poetry of praise and affirmation, which is also rooted in a practical realism. Battus observes the world and laments its sorrows; Corydon may resort to banalities and proverbial wisdom, but he can also act. The thorn "smites" Battus (ἐπάταξε, 51), but Corydon would wield a stick to "smite" the greedy cow (πάταξα, 49).[28] It is Corydon who has actually seen the virile old man (60-1) and can give a characteristically precise and concrete answer to Battus' inquiry (cf. ποτὶ τᾷ μάνδρᾳ κατελάμβανον, "I found him at the byre,"61).

Battus, wrapped up in his own emotions, mentions only one specific place by name, and that in a curse (18-20). Corydon, responsive to the concrete details of the world around him, names not only rivers and mountains (17-19, 23-5), but even two of his cows (25-6). The thorn wounds Battus, but to Corydon the luxuriant growth of thorns is also an aspect of the life of an intimately known natural world which also feeds his herd (cf. 57 and 24). These thorns do not merely "grow" (which would be φύοντι, as in 24), but "are in leaf" (κομόωντι, 57).[29] Corydon feels even these bothersome plants are infused with nature's processes and variety.

Corydon's responsiveness to the beauty of place – the shady mountain (19), the "soft grass" (18), the lush and fragrant vegetation (24-5) – not only adds another dimension to the antithesis between death and life. It also sets the divergent attitudes and styles of the two rustics into a larger frame and thus maintains the contrasts in a larger equilibrium. Differ as they may, the two rustics participate in a common pastoral beauty which unites them. Hence the verdant pastoral *locus* keeps the contrasts in check with the suggestion of an underlying harmony. It also adds a touch of graceful humor. Battus may complain, invoke Hades, and lament past loves; but he breathes the same air as Corydon and enjoys the same views. If he gets stuck by one of these "flourishing thorns" instead of enjoying "all the lovely things" of Corydon's lines 24-5, it only serves him right.

III

In *Idyll* IV, as in Old Comedy, the theme of food expresses the poet's concern with vitality in nature, language, human and animal life. Food is a major organizing motif in the poem. It is closely connected with a direct, simple vitality. Over against it stands the motif of love. Love interferes with the natural processes and hinders the workaday task of fattening cattle (cf. βόσκεν ... αὐτάς, 2). The cows refuse to eat because they "long for" the absent Aegon (12). Love does not seem to have affected Aegon's appetite: he courts Amaryllis (35-6), but still performs the considerable feat of consuming eighty cakes (34).[30] At the same time this vignette, given by Corydon, of Aegon's gusto, contrasts with Battus' curse on the sacrificial banquet of the demesmen of Lampriadas (20-22). As the poem moves gradually away from the jaundiced sentimentality of Battus, even the fasting beasts of the opening lines regain their appetite: they reach greedily after the forbidden olive shoots (44-5). Finally, the sexual vigor of the old man at the end appears under a metaphor connected with food: he "mills away" (μύλλει, 58) at the girl.[31]

This concern with food and eating is related, at one level, to the poetics of
Theocritus. It continues his dialogue between the high and low styles; and it
graphically illustrates the contrast between sentimental effusion and a dry,
earthy realism. The very simplicity of the natural functions frames in humorous
perspective the clash between the exaggerations of Battus and the directness of
Corydon, between "pasturing" and cicadas living on dew-drops (14 and 18).

Food also links the absent Aegon to the pastoral situation in which Corydon
and Battus meet. Aegon's ration of twenty sheep as he trains for the Olympic
games (10) might appear as a perversion of a rustic's proper function as a
guardian of his flock (*cf.* line 2). Thus it might hint at the misguided
pretentiousness of a poetry which reaches towards Heracles and Polydeuces
instead of staying with shady mountains, Pan, and the earthy "milling." Yet
Aegon has been a great feeder at less distant festivals too (33-4).

The tension between Battus and Corydon is thus concentrated in a further
tension within the figure of Aegon. He spans both rustic vitality and heroic
aspiration, both the backwoods of Croton and the Panhellenic festival at
Olympia. He is a personage full of life and energy; yet he is deserting the rustic
world. His actions and his personality are ambiguous: they have different values
depending on whether they are seen through the eyes of Battus or of Corydon.
The pastoral *locus* allows the possibility of a sentimental, nostalgic Battus. But it
also contains a rather rowdy Aegon. And there are growing plants, very precisely
denoted (25), and thorns. It is all very well to sing of the lost Amaryllis (38-40),
but one had better wear shoes (56).[32]

Theocritus' humor mocks the very pathos and poignancy of emotion which
he can himself evoke so effectively, as in the tale of Daphnis of *Idyll* I. The
self-mockery and the humor are essential parts of the "thin" style, the refusal to
take oneself too seriously, to become ponderous and self-important. Hence the
deliberately anti-climactic realism at the close of *Idyll* I or the humorous
mocking of the love-sick goatherd at the end of III. But the self-mockery is not
only literary. The antitheses of seriousness and irony also point to antitheses of
introspective sentimentality and resilient, extroverted practicality which have
validity outside the circumscribed and stylized pastoral *locus* as well. The poem
may legitimately be considered a dialogue between a sentimental and realistic
poetics. But it is simultaneously a dialogue between self-centeredness and
self-extension, between the realm of feeling, with its rhetoric of the emotions,
and the realm of action with its practical expertise. As a recent critic has written
a propos of *Idyll* XI, Theocritus is "dealing with rival methods of participation
in experience and with the potential for life and death which each contains." [33]

To go a bit further, the contrast between the two rustics can intimate pulls
within the poet himself, pulls between escapism and reality or between
full-blown lyricism and irony.[34] One might be tempted to hear Theocritus' own
voice in Corydon's resilient realism and his joy in his precisely and concretely
observed surroundings. Bignone has, in fact, interpreted the figure of Corydon
on just such lines.[35] Yet, Battus, sentimental though he is, also has qualities to

which one might expect the poet to be sympathetic, e.g. his irony (9, 11). The issues are larger than biographical self-representation. If Corydon and Battus symbolize conflicts within Theocritus' view of life or view of art or both, the essential fact remains that he has objectified these conflicts through a dramatic situation and thus given them ramifications beyond questions of biography, even spiritual biography. We can probably never know the forces which led Theocritus to create these symbols; but symbols, once created, take on their own life and have their own power to speak to many ages in many ways.

IV

It is illuminating to consider these contrasts through the structure and thematic progression of the *Idyll*. Van Sickle has already made a good case for the structural complexity and artistry of the poem, though my analysis differs from his in a number of points.[36]

Fourteen lines of stichomythia set the stage for the main contrasts. Rustic practicality and specificity stand in the foregound: we hear three proper names in rapid succession (Corydon, Philondas, Aegon, 1-2). The very first line introduces a question about the ownership of cattle, a point of practical curiosity natural enough in this rustic world. The main features of these first fourteen lines have already been discussed sufficiently in Section II above. I would only re-emphasize at this point the tension which develops rapidly between the two interlocutors. Battus' tone is clearly aggressive: he imputes to Corydon the petty crime of "secretly" appropriating the "whole" herd's milk (note κρύβδαν and πάσας, 3). Corydon does not reply in kind (e.g. line 4), but Battus' aggressiveness is established. It moves from the plane of low rustic realism in line 3 to that of mock-heroic irony in 8-9.

After the fourteen lines of stichomythia, there follows a series of three exchanges of two and three lines, culminating in Corydon's nine-line speech (29-37) which contains his description of the exuberant Aegon. These nine lines are the longest stretch of continuous discourse in the poem. The three exchanges (15-16 and 17-19; 20-2 and 23-5; 26-8 and 29-37) all have one feature in common. In each there is a pessimistic and negative statement by Battus answered by a strong denial by Corydon (cf. οὐ Δᾶν, "No, by Zeus," 17; καὶ μάν, "And in truth," 23; οὐ τήνα γ', οὐ Νύμφας, "No indeed, not that, no, by the Nymphs," 29).

In the first two of these exchanges, as we have seen above (Section II), Corydon displays his vivid aesthetic and practical appreciation of the countryside (17-19, 23-5). In the third exchange (26-37) the alternation of Battus' pessimism and Corydon's cheery optimism enlarges to include life and death (cf. "Hades" in 27). Love is also present, but negatively: Battus apostrophizes Aegon and laments his "accursed love of victory" (27). The theme of poetry also makes its appearance: "The pipe you [Aegon] once fashioned," Battus tells Corydon, "is spattered with mold" (28). The more explicitly self-reflective tone of Virgil and later pastoralists is not to be read back into Theocritus. His Aegon is no Miltonic Lycidas or even a Virgilian Manalcas (*E.* 5.85-7). The mouldering pipe or the theme of poetry which it may imply receive no disproportionate emphasis.[37] Theocritus does not pause to single out this element (note Corydon's rapid reply in 29), but includes it in the encompassing irony and "Homeric" objectivity of all the pastoral *Idylls*. Cows, not poetry, receive the main emphasis (note the καί of 26 and the enjambed "Hades" in 27), and the pipe enters on the same plane in a swift, unobtrusive parataxis (χἀ σῦριγξ, 28). The implications of the pipe are therefore subsumed under the antithesis between life and death and between Corydon and Battus, nor are they allowed to project beyond the bucolic frame. The *personae* of the *Idyll* never become one-dimensional representations of aesthetic attitudes, but retain their vivid roles in the narrative framework. In this way the antitheses which they create are not confined to a single theme, but remain large, complex, open.

Corydon's reply begins the nine-line section of 29-37. Here he invokes the Nymphs (29), the first mention of rustic deities in the poem. He then gives a sample of his song. This contains a praise of "a lovely city and Zacynthus": καλὰ πόλις ἅ τε Ζάκυνθος(31).[38] The bucolic singer can appreciate the beauty of "the city" too. Like the grass and the growing plants of 18 and 23, Corydon finds it "beautiful." Unlike Virgil's first or ninth *Eclogues*, the city poses no threat to the country.[39] Corydon's poetry, as observed earlier, emerges as a poetry of joyfulness and praise. The last word of his long speech is "laughed" (ἐξεγέλασσεν, 37), which stands in striking contrast with Battus' lugubrious, tragic exclamations of the preceding lines (26-7). His language once more soars to epic heights (37).[40] One may also contrast Battus' "evil victory" (26) and Corydon's "lovely city" (32). Battus sees the movement out of the pastoral world as the prelude to certain disaster. Corydon can praise the "city," sing of happy festivals (that at the shrine of Lacinian Hera, 33) as opposed to Battus' forebodings about Olympia, and he can call upon pastoral divinities. He lives in a world full of life, song, love and he reaches out beyond it to embrace joyful experiences in the city or at famous temples. The songs he sings on his pastoral syrinx are even those of city-poets, Pyrrhos and Glauke (31).

These two exchanges of 26-8 and 29-37, then, complete and expand to its richest terms the antithesis between the two figures. Both thematically and formally lines 26-37 occupy the center of the poem. There are just twenty-five lines before them and twenty-six after (1-25, 38-63).

The contrast between life and death in the preceding section is developed in another exchange of three lines each (38-40,41-3). Here the differences of character and outlook are crystallized into typical modes of speech. Battus apostrophizes the "lovely Amaryllis," promises that he will never forget her, dead though she is, describes his grief in a rather clumsy rustic simile (39), and ends with a paratragic lament over his hard fate (41). The three lines are an ingenious representation of emotional bathos, in which every word is milked for maximum effect, including the unobtrusive μόνας (38), as if she is his "one and only" true love. Battus' μόνας in 38 echoes Corydon's μόνος in the description of Aegon four lines before (34). Both words occupy exactly the same metrical position (after the feminine caesura). Together they deepen the contrast between the representative gestures of the antithetical figures: Aegon eating eighty cakes "by himself", Battus bewailing his "one and only" Amaryllis.

Battus' "lovely Amaryllis" in 38 echoes the words of the sentimental goatherd of *Idyll* III (line 6) and suggests an affinity, if not an identification, between the two figures.[41] The connection is more important for establishing the poet's attitude of ironical distance from and control of his characters than for filling in details of Battus' background. Correspondingly, lines 38-40 should be read in terms of the themes and structure of the whole poem as much as in terms of character development. Bignone falls into the "documentary fallacy" when he interprets the lines as revealing the reasons for Battus' bitterness. He has, according to Bignone, lost his beloved and suffered an incurable wound in his heart.[42] Corydon understands his pain and behaves accordingly. The speakers, however, are *personae,* not real people with real life-histories.[43] Battus' lament for Amaryllis is a representative gesture, in character, to be sure, but also symbolical of an attitude toward experience and illustrative of a mode of speech or poetry that expresses that attitude. The lines, then, like much else in the poem have three interlocking levels of significance. (1) Literally taken, they tell us something of Battus' character, supporting and filling out the fictional frame of the poem. (2) Read in relation to Corydon's immediately preceding and immediately following statements, they form part of a dramatic progression within the structure of the poem, clarifying the growing terms of the antitheses between the two characters. (3) Taken in relation to all the contrasting utterances of the two characters and the implications of those contrasts, the lament of 38-40 symbolizes an attitude towards life and towards poetry. At this third level, the lines contribute another block in the construction of the total, many-faceted symbol which the Battus-Corydon complex constitutes.

Corydon's reply again takes the side of life. Simplicity and directness of expression characterize his tone: "One must cheer up, dear Battus," he begins. We feel an immediate relief at the change from Battus' cloying emotionality. But relief is shortlived, for Corydon continues with a string of heavy-handed platitudes. "Tomorrow will be better; there's hope in the living; only the dead are hopeless; and Zeus is sometimes bright, sometimes rains" (41-3). The contrast with Battus could not be greater. As Battus' adjective "dead" (θανοίσας, 38) contrasted with Corydon's "laughter" (ἐξεγέλασσεν, 37), Corydon's "cheer up" now answers Battus' "Alas for my hard fate" (40). His "Hopeless only are the dead" (θανόντες, 42) takes up Battus' paratragic melancholy over the "dead" Amaryllis (θανοίσας, 38). Battus' utterance was lyrical and personal; Corydon's is prosaic, not to say pedestrian, and generalizing, gnomic. Both characters are made to parody themselves. The language of Corydon's proverb about rain and shine recalls his earlier statement of delight in the particulars of his pastoral world (cf. ἀλλ' ὅκα μὲν .. ἄλλοκα δέ,

17-19; ἄλλοκα μέν. . . ἄλλοκα δ᾽,"sometimes . . .sometimes ," 43). The echo provides a measure of the falling off. Corydon does indeed have a grasp on the life-giving qualities of his pastoral world, but he expressed it better in that concrete appreciation of his beautiful surroundings (17-19, 23-5) and in his detailed image of the boisterous Aegon (33-7).[44]

The surprising thing is that his banalities prove effective: "Ï do take courage," Battus replies (θαρσέω,44). If we look in Corydon's lines for something that may have produced this effect, we may find it not in the generalities themselves but in the personal address which precedes them. "Dear Battus," he began (φίλε Βάττε,41). It is the first real expression of amity, and it accompanies the active attempt to "cheer" his companion. The ironical banter and suspicion of the beginning (cf. κρύβδαν,"secretly," 3) begin to give way to friendship and commiseration.

The two exchanges of 26-37 and 38-43 set out the contrasts between the two figures in the broadest terms. Upon them follow three further exchanges of six, eight, and six lines respectively. These differ from the previous part of the poem in that they center upon immediate or recent action: the greedy cows attacking the olive shoots (44-9), the thorn in Battus' foot (50-7), and the lusty old man (58-63). Empty talk about wasting cattle or a lost mistress and commonplace generalities yield to specific action and a vivid present. The rustics now express and confront their differences not in song or description, but in shared experience. The shift in the type of action not only enlivens the ending of the poem but also gives movement and development to the hitherto static expression of antithesis.

The first vignette (44-9) furthers the new mood of potential accord between the two rustics. In a sense, it works out the consequences of Corydon's "dear Battus" in 41. Battus, awakened from nostalgic revery, calls attention to the cows' straying after the olive shoots. His speech begins with θαρσέω,"I'm cheered up", and his language is clipped and urgent:

βάλλε κάτωθε τὰ μόσχια· τᾶς γὰρ ἐλαίας
τὸν θάλλον τρώγοντι, τὰ δύσσοα.   (44-5)

(Drive up the cows from below, for they're eating the
olive shoots, the wretched creatures.) (44-5)

The sentimentality of his "poor things" earlier (13) is replaced by the hard practical realism of "wretched creatures." [45] The rustic's curse accompanies the reminder of the realm of rustic work, the herdsman's task. Simultaneously the cows change from lackluster longing to eager appetite. Both men and animals participate in the change of tone. After nostalgic recollection of the past and feeble generalities, the concrete presentness of the pastoral world seems to consolidate and reassert itself. The language returns from a distant to a nearer world. [46] So too the remote olive oil of the palaestra which lured the herd's owner out of his pastoral locus (cf. ἔλαιον ἐν ὀφθαλμοῖσιν ὀπώπει, "He has his eyes on the [athlete's] oil,"7) yields to the growing olives protected by the rustics who have not abandoned their surroundings (ἐλαίας, "olives,"44). Yet Battus is still Battus: he alerts the cowherd to the danger, but does nothing himself to help.[47] There is still a trace of his old pleasure in dwelling on other people's troubles; but it is an exhortation to action that begins his observation (βάλλε, "Drive up," 44).

Corydon's reply sounds the authentic voice of rustic practicality even more strongly. No more trite generalities here (41-3), but the herdsman's sharp "sstth" followed by the call to specific wayward cows: σίτθ᾽, ὁ Λέπαργος, σίτθ᾽, ἁ Κυμαίθα, ποτὶ τὸν λόφον, οὐκ ἐσακούεις ; ("Sstth! Lepargos. Sstth! Kymaitha. Up to the hill. Don't you hear?", 45-46). As the urgency of rustic work and the acrid flavor of the herdsman's world cut more keenly into musing about death and love, so this strange vocable of 45, so different from Battus' tragic cries of αἰαῖ or φεῦ φεῦ, breaks abruptly upon the smooth flow of the hexameter. This "sstth" is the only place in the poem where an interlocutor's reply breaks into the middle of a line.[48] Theocritus is careful to place the break at the bucolic diaeresis, but the interruption is still emphatic. It roughens the easy symmetry of hitherto static contrasts with more colloquial and more abrupt rhythms. The effect is perhaps a humorous reminder of the artificiality of herdsmen discoursing in hexameters and of the tension between the rustic illusion and the literary self-consciousness. At the same time it works within the fictional frame to help bring the two speakers together on a common ground of authentic rusticity. Both meet, finally, in a practical concern for animals and valuable crops. They drop their pretentions in a spontaneous and colloquial response to an immediate situation. Corydon alludes to the herdsman's regular equipment, the "crooked stick" with which he would whack his troublesome cows (49). Longing extends no further than the desire for this useful instrument: αἴθ᾽ ἧς μοι ῥοικόν τι λαγωβόλον ὥς τυ πάταξα , ("I wish I had my stick to whack you," 49). The homely phrase contrasts with the equipment which Aegon took with him to Olympia, a shovel for training (10) — something that no herdsman would ordinarily use. It is also appropriate that this tangy rustic speech of Corydon invokes Pan (47), the pastoral deity par excellence.

If, in this first vignette, Battus was willing to drop irony and sentiment for a limited helpfulness, in the second he proves in need of help himself. He cries out sharply at the thorn in his foot (50). The tone remains clipped and colloquial, but the mock-heroic and mock-pathetic line 55 remind us of his ineffectual sentimentality and threatens a relapse into bathos:

ὁσσίχον ἐστὶ τὸ τύμμα, καὶ ἁλίκον ἄνδρα δαμάσδει.

(So small the wound and so big the man it subdues.)[49]

Battus has revealed his penchant for this kind of literary phraseology earlier in his lament for Amaryllis (ὅσον αἶγες ἐμὶν φίλαι, ὅσον ἀπέσβης, "As my goats are dear to me, so [dear] have you perished," 39). Here the contrast with Corydon's brisk and efficient brevity is especially marked: "Yes, yes, I have it in my nails: here is the thorn itself" (ἅδε καὶ αὐτά, 54). Battus' line 55 contrasts also with Corydon's next two lines, for Corydon goes on to give his friend a bit of practical advice about wearing shoes on brambly mountains (56-7). Here, as earlier (cf. 17-19, 23-5), Corydon remains in touch with the concrete particularity of his surroundings: he names two kinds of prickly growth (ῥάμνοι τε καὶ ἀσπάλαθοι,57). When he counsels Battus not to come unshod "up to the mountain" (εἰς ὄρος,56), he recalls the practical energy with which he sent the cows scampering "up to the hills" a few lines before (ποτὶ τὸν λόφον,46). He knows what grows "on the mountain" (ἐν γὰρ ὄρει, 57).[50] Corydon's sense of place and his practical botanical knowledge in the service of a dry, but kindly efficiency combine to check the threatened relapse into sentimentality.

The third vignette (58-63) closes the poem and seals the confirmation of a new tone and a new contact with a concrete rustic present. At the same time it reiterates in a different atmosphere a number of themes developed earlier. The recapitulatory of this section is heralded in Battus' echo of the opening words of the Idyll (εἴπ' ἄγε μ', ὦ Κορύδων, "Come, tell me, Corydon," 58; cf. εἰπέ μοι, ὦ Κορύδων,"Tell me, Corydon," 1). [51] Now, however, Battus has no aggressive question about ownership of the herd, but a sincere request for information. He wants to know about the old man who has been "milling" the "dark-browed girl." The adjective κυάνοφρυν is perhaps a hint of his old tendencies to romanticize, but the coarse metaphor suggests a harder and earthier view of love, quite far from his misty nostalgia over the lost Amaryllis (38-40). If Lawall is right to see erotic overtones in the heifers of 12 and 53 and in the wound of 55, those hints of bestiality, the more grotesque because of the oblique and metaphorical expression, are dissolved in an open healthy sexuality at the end.

Modes of address also emphasize the change of tone. Battus' sentimental "poor things" addressed to the mournful cattle in 13 now becomes an epithet of endearment and friendly play addressed by Corydon to Battus (ὦ δείλαιε, "my poor fellow," 60).[52] The preceding scene and the shift of tone (cf. "dear Battus", 41) enable even the unsubtle Corydon to turn Battus' sentimentality against him. Battus answers with a strong exclamation, an apostrophe to the lusty old man: εὖ γ', ὤνθρωπε φιλοῖφα, "Well done, old lecher" (62). This apostrophe is quite different from those to "poor Aegon" (26) and "lovely Amaryllis" (38); a cry of approving enthusiasm supersedes those of doleful lament. Φιλοίφης ("lecherous, "loving sexual intercourse,") is a rather rare word.[53] Its overt sexuality signals the presence of a latent earthiness and vigor in Battus too. In his appreciation of the old man's gusto he draws closer to Corydon. He becomes less concerned with asserting himself and his sentiments. He recognizes Corydon's authoritative precision, having just benefited from it in the thorn episode. Hence he asks his question of 58-9 in a spirit of genuine curiosity. In his closing tribute to the old man, he manages, finally, to get outside of himself.[54]

The image of the old man changes too. He is surely Aegon's father, the suspicious and cautious "old man" ($\gamma\acute{\epsilon}\rho\omega\nu$) of line 4. Now he appears as a more positive figure. It is an amusing touch, however, that, as one might expect from Corydon's report of the old man's precautions in line 4, Battus is the greater enthusiast.[55]

Corydon's description of Aegon's bursting vitality in 33-7 finds its pendant and its confirmation in Battus' praise of this old fellow's family ($\gamma\acute{\epsilon}\nu\sigma\varsigma$) which rivals Pans and Satyrs:

$$\tau\acute{o}\ \tau\sigma\iota\ \gamma\acute{\epsilon}\nu\sigma\varsigma\ \mathring{\eta}\ \Sigma\alpha\tau\nu\rho\acute{\iota}\sigma\kappa\sigma\iota\varsigma$$
$$\mathring{\epsilon}\gamma\gamma\nu\theta\epsilon\nu\ \mathring{\eta}\ \Pi\acute{\alpha}\nu\epsilon\sigma\sigma\iota\ \kappa\alpha\kappa\sigma\kappa\nu\acute{\alpha}\mu\sigma\iota\sigma\iota\nu\ \mathring{\epsilon}\rho\acute{\iota}\sigma\delta\epsilon\iota.\ (62\text{-}3)$$

(Your race closely rivals Satyrs or skinny-shanked Pans).

Presumably the "family" ($\gamma\acute{\epsilon}\nu\sigma\varsigma$) means Aegon and his father. By implication, therefore, Battus has accepted Corydon's view of Aegon (33-7). As the two rustics find themselves sharing a common enthusiasm for an earthy sexuality, they also experience a restored stability within the pastoral *locus*. Aegon may be off in vain pursuit of honors beyond the rustic pale, but his father is settled on his farm (*cf.* $\mu\acute{\alpha}\nu\delta\rho\alpha$, 61), watching over the herd (5), and engaged as vigorously as ever ($\mathring{\epsilon}\tau\iota$,58) in his wonted pursuits. As van Sickle nicely puts it, "The old man's in his barton, all's right on the hill."[56]

While reasserting familial continuity and rustic stability, the last two lines also vindicate Corydon's optimism. The feeble banality of Corydon's "Where there's life there's hope" (42) wins authority in the specific images of what he "himself" saw just the other day ($\pi\rho\acute{o}\alpha\nu\ \gamma\epsilon\ \mu\grave{\epsilon}\nu\ \alpha\mathring{v}\tau\acute{o}\varsigma$, 60). These closing lines confirm the poem's insistence on vitality over death and present actuality over dreamy nostalgia or easy generalization.[57]

This victory of "life" parallels the winning of valid, unpretentious, "authentic" rustic language. The coarseness of $\phi\iota\lambda\sigma\mathring{\iota}\phi\alpha$ accompanies the allusion to "Satyrs and skinny-shanked Pans" (62-3). Corydon had mentioned Nymphs and Pan earlier (13, 47), but these rustic deities now receive greater emphasis and are characterized more fully. It is also now Battus who mentions them. Battus may have something to learn from the dryness and practicality of a Corydon, but his world too is populated by these creatures of myth and imagination. Possibly these Pans and Satyrs intimate that this poetry can mediate between realism and imagination, between the raw energies of life-impulses and the delicate artifice of art and emotional sensibilities, between the available "dark-browed" country wench and the dead, nostalgically evoked Amaryllis. Possibly they suggest that Battus' penchant for poeticizing has not vanished, although it has found a healthier and more appropriately "rustic" mode of expression. The last word in the poem is $\mathring{\epsilon}\rho\acute{\iota}\sigma\delta\epsilon\iota$ ("strives against," "contests with"); and it perhaps suggests an atmosphere of openness for a continued meeting of contraries which the poet wishes to maintain.[58]

Pans and Satyrs cap the movement from death to life and from nostalgic pessimism to rustic vitality. But they are also playful figures, and their loves are not to be taken too seriously. They belong to myth, but they stand on an altogether different level from the Heracles or Polydeuces of lines 8-9. Aspirations to this "Herculean" heroism carried Aegon off to Olympia. His father remained close to the Pans and Satyrs, enjoying the good things of his rustic world. Aegon would "contest with" (ἐρίσδεω, 8) a mythical Heracles in trials of "force and strength." His father "contests with" rustic demigods in sexual energy (63). Homeric language (βίην καὶ κάρτος, "force and strength," 8) and heroic legend "contest" with bucolic "Pans and Satyrs" on more than just the level of style.

The dramatic movement of the *Idyll* is carefully controlled by the symmetry of the form. This latter appears both in the rhythmic alternation of two-and three-line exchanges between the two rustics and in the larger structure of the whole. Of this structure I offer the following diagrammatic analysis:

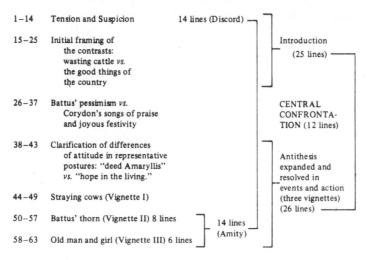

1–14	Tension and Suspicion	14 lines (Discord)	
15–25	Initial framing of the contrasts: wasting cattle *vs.* the good things of the country		Introduction (25 lines)
26–37	Battus' pessimism *vs.* Corydon's songs of praise and joyous festivity		CENTRAL CONFRONTATION (12 lines)
38–43	Clarification of differences of attitude in representative postures: "deed Amaryllis" *vs.* "hope in the living."		Antithesis expanded and resolved in events and action (three vignettes) (26 lines)
44–49	Straying cows (Vignette I)		
50–57	Battus' thorn (Vignette II) 8 lines	14 lines (Amity)	
58–63	Old man and girl (Vignette III) 6 lines		

Somewhat simplified, the structure is as follows:

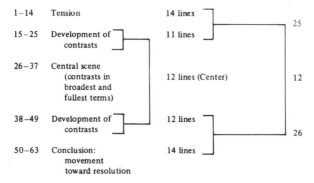

1–14	Tension	14 lines	
15–25	Development of contrasts	11 lines	25
26–37	Central scene (contrasts in broadest and fullest terms)	12 lines (Center)	12
38–49	Development of contrasts	12 lines	
50–63	Conclusion: movement toward resolution	14 lines	26

This diagram must be taken with considerable reservation. While it is clear that Theocritus carefully links beginning and end (cf. 1 and 58) and probable that the fourteen lines at the beginning form a significant unit answered by the fourteen at the end, the symmetry is not perfect. Even more important, the progression of the poem from one exchange to the next is carried so lightly and easily in the flow of rustic discourse that the division into discrete, balancing sections seems in places an artificial imposition.[59] Hence Battus' speech at 26-8, which I have placed with Corydon's nine-line speech which answers it, is also closely linked with the preceding three-line exchanges and especially with Battus' earlier lines about the bull ($\chi\dot{\omega}$ $\tau\alpha\tilde{\upsilon}\rho\sigma\varsigma$, 20; cf. $\kappa\alpha\grave{\iota}$ $\tau\alpha\grave{\iota}$ $\beta\acute{\sigma}\epsilon\varsigma$, "also the cows," 26).[60] Similarly at the end of the poem the parallel with the fourteen-line unit of stichomythia at the beginning is not fully developed, for lines 44-49 are also part of this closing movement. One must beware, then, of insisting too heavily on the static form.[61] The symmetrical design is intimated, but only in the background, as a suggestion of order and artifice behind the apparent easy realism. Continuity and flow predominate in determining the movement of the *Idyll*.

This combination of a dynamic and a symmetrical structure is also expressive of the two planes on which the narrative moves, the dramatic and the symbolical. When the poem is reread, it is clear that the main antithesis and its ramifications are present in every part of the whole, so that even unobtrusive details like Corydon's $\check{\epsilon}\delta\omega\kappa\epsilon\nu$ ("gave,") of 2 or Battus' $\pi\acute{\alpha}\sigma\alpha\varsigma$ ("all [the cows]") of 3 become retrospectively significant. At the same time the antithesis builds toward climax and clarification as the dialogue continues. Thus on the one hand the antitheses grasped in their totality comment on and modify the action which has already developed; on the other hand, the dramatic development of the action articulates the antitheses and gives them a vibrant, concrete energy. The antitheses, like the structure, have both a conceptual and a dramatic aspect. Hence, although the poem attains a clear formulation of its central antithesis in the middle section (26-37), it cannot be satisfactorily described in terms of a static and abstract symmetry. After the central contrast the two characters continue to react upon and influence one another until each occupies at the end a position quite different from that at the beginning. Battus comes around to something of Corydon's gusto; Corydon acquires a little of Battus' irony (cf. 56-7) and a trace of his peevishness (47-9; cf. 20-2).[62] We recall that Battus revealed a strain of aggressiveness and irony along side of his sentimentality. Thus at the end distinctions which had seemed clear threaten to blur, and insight wavers. Yet the symmetrical framing of the central antithesis helps keep clear and firm the poem's conceptual center. Where concrete particulars might carry us back to the apparently aimless quarrelling and inchoate differences of the beginning, form helps stabilize what we have acquired in watching the two *personae* diverge and then unite.

V

Theocritus never tells us at exactly what level we should read his poem. That is part of the "openness" of his "lean" style. He refuses to take himself seriously while at the same time dealing in issues of importance: death, love, poetry, friendship. Hence the serious and the playful interpenetrate and infuse each other; and the poem slides easily, sometimes with a touch of disconcerting irony, from one level to another.

Two factors contribute to this elusiveness of his "seriousness." One is the ironic humor, which often derives from the discrepancy between mock-heroic sentiments and rustic setting. This discrepancy finds its stylistic expression in the presence of epic and tragic language in the mouths of rustic personages. The other element is the ultimate peacefulness, stability, and beauty of the pastoral world. Ultimately these two features of the *Idylls* are one. The serenity of the pastoral realm and the modest aspirations which it enforces within its well-demarcated boundaries provide a norm from which deviations appear grotesque and comic. This norm of rustic good sense tends to keep excess emotionality within definite limits.

The beauty and bounty of the pastoral world also check tragic seriousness.[63] Daphnis' death has a haunting pathos, but the rutting goats still frisk lustily (I.151-2). The lyrical flight can always be chastened, the heavy made "lean" by the down-to-earth realities of country life. For these reasons too the poem can often change tones quickly, from the sweet to the acrid, from the high to the low: compare *Idyll* V (especially 116-50) or the movement from the rustic beating of Pan to the Castalian Nymphs and Demeter in *Idyll* VII (106-10, 148-57). Correspondingly, the atmosphere of simplicity and utter naivete created by the pastoral setting puts us in the role of superior observers, looking down upon the loves of desperate rustics with a cool, amused irony (e.g. III or XI).

The movement of a Theocritean pastoral *Idyll* appears, at least at first glance, to be disjunct and paratactic.[64] But for this very reason major antitheses can merely be stated simply in concrete situations and descriptions. As in Homer, the reader is left to make as much or as little of the text as he may. Yet the sophisticated structure, the parallels and repetitions, the hints dropped and then taken up later invite the reader to make as much as possible. At the same time Theocritus teases him with the danger of making too much and becoming rather like Battus: ὁσσίχον ἐστὶ τὸ τύμμα, καὶ ἁλίκον ἄνδρα δαμάσδει ("So small the wound and so big the man it subdues," 55). In the ironic mode, self-importance is the biggest target. In a genre in which we constantly laugh at the exaggerations of others, we are invited to reserve a little laughter for ourselves.

Looked at from this point of view, Corydon's proverbs in 39-42 reveal another level of irony. They relate directly to the central themes of the *Idyll* and illuminate the development of the antitheses between the two rustics in terms of life and death, hope and despair. Yet they do so in so obvious and heavy-handed a way that we cannot doubt the deliberate mockery of any didacticism. Theocritus lures us into pointing a moral. Then, just as we begin to congratulate ourselves on our insight, he makes fun of his own subtlety, and ours.

One might, therefore, approach Theocritean pastoral as an exercise in ironic self-deprecation. The irony is keen, but benign; yet it is also puzzling, for it consists in leaving us never quite sure how seriously we are to take the self-deprecation. When Comatas in *Idyll* V attributes his bowl to Praxiteles (105), we laugh at the rustic's pretensions to culture. Sharper and more startling is Corydon's knowledge of the songs of Glauke, a contemporary of Theocritus then fashionable in Alexandria, and the even more obscure Pyrrhus in *Idyll* IV (31).[65]

What, then, is one to make of the fact that the low-keyed "realism" of the first two lines of the *Idyll* echo one of the most tense and terrible scenes in all Greek literature, Oedipus' interrogation of the Messenger in the *Oedipus Rex*?[66] It is probably impossible to decide whether the echo is intentional or not, but one cannot exclude the possibility that Theocritus is taking a special delight in a surprising and impish collocation of high solemnity and utter triviality. If the echo is intentional, then the whole of the *Idyll* appears in the light of a gigantic burlesque of tragedy. The paratragic language of Battus throughout thus gains a sharper point and an even broader humor. Yet even this humorous incongruity has a counterbalancing and restorative irony, for Theocritus suggests everywhere that his humble and trivial frame may glance at matters which are far from trivial: death and love, sentimentality and realism, and so on. He, however, is not going to wax ponderous or didactic about them, and he lightly mocks the reader who would do so.

In so shifting a sequence of tones unity comes from the beauty of the setting and the clearly defined limits of this artificial world. Artifice and realism can here come together and interact, for the rustics are both singers of lovely melodies and down-to-earth workers (cf. *Idyll* X.9), dependent on the rhythms of nature and experts in the practical problems of the pasturage and increase of their flocks. In such a setting the high and the low, triviality and profundity, jest and seriousness, lyricism and prosaic realism can jostle one another easily and rapidly. There is nothing dreamy about Corydon's milking (IV.3-4); yet Pans and Satyrs are, as it were, just around the corner (62-3).

Where time seems suspended and where nature is bountiful, serious and trivial can appear as aspects of the same thing. The effect is the humble, rustic equivalent of the humor of Homer's Olympus. The pastoral perspective endows us with infinite time, few cares, and simple wants. In such an atmosphere we awaken to the light side of "great" issues, and we appreciate the "seriousness" of little things. On the one hand we contemplate the humorous side of supposedly mighty passions; on the other, we give full attention to the modest delights of a stream, a tree, a grasshopper, a special kind of grass. The particular and the universal stand in harmony rather than discord. Pastoral speaks a language of potential universals in a world of lovely particulars.

The specialness of the bucolic setting, its beauty and leisure and songfulness, invite us to understand its elements as more than just the pieces of our every-day world transferred to the countryside or to a simpler economy. Here the usual problems of life recur, but the consequences are lighter and the interconnections clearer. The pastoral frame, like all art, refines, purifies, clarifies.

This clarity is the external, formal and aesthetic equivalent of that spiritual "inner harmony" which the refugee from the violence and confusion of the urban and political world seeks in the pastoral realm.[67] Here opposites need not necessarily be resolved; yet the very creation of clear and plastic symbols for the antitheses brings a sense of intellectual control and aesthetic satisfaction. The Fourth *Idyll* brings something more, a healing accord which runs beneath the antithetical structure. This accord might be termed moral in so far as it rests on the experience of an encompassing natural order and the mutual perception, by both figures, of the beauty and vitality of that order. In the sheltered hospitality of the pastoral *locus* the two figures converge and assert out of dissonance a harmony in several different modes. Here the life-instincts, practical knowledge, the desire for beauty and the attempt to find the poetic style and tone appropriate to it, the need for friendship, impulses to generosity, joy, and festivity, and the flowering of imagination in talk of "rivaling" Pans and Satyrs can all meet, interfuse, and clarify one another as the expressions of a larger, more elusive unity.[68]

Brown University and
*Intercollegiate Center for Classical Studies
in Rome.*

NOTES

1. See, for instance, M.C.J. Putnam, *Virgil's Pastoral Art* (Princeton 1970) 8ff. and *passim*; Eleanor Winsor Leach, "Nature and Art and Vergil's Second *Eclogue*," *AJP* 87 (1966) 427-45; and, with a more historical orientation, Brooks Otis, *Virgil* (Oxford 1963) chap. 4, especially 128ff.
2. See Thomas G. Rosenmeyer, *The Green Cabinet* (Berkeley and Los Angeles 1969) 52-3, 249ff.
3. See, for instance, Ph.-E. Legrand, *Étude sur Théocrite*, "Bibl. des Écoles françaises d' Athènes et de Rome," 79 (Paris 1898) 92-103; Albin Lesky, *A History of Greek Literature*[2], transl. Willis and de Heer (London 1966) 725 on the significance of ἐκπονεῖν in *Idyll* VII. 51.
4. L.E. Rossi, "Vittoria e sconfitta nell' agone bucolico letterario," *GIF* n.s. 2 (1970) 24.
5. See C. Segal, "Vergil's *Caelatum Opus*: An Interpretation of the Third *Eclogue*," *AJP* 88 (1967) 286-92.
6. Kénneth Quinn, *The Catullan Revolution* (Melbourne 1959) 32-43.
7. Rosenmeyer (above, note 2); Gilbert Lawall, *Theocritus' Coan Pastorals, A Poetry Book* (Cambridge, Mass. 1967).
8. Legrand (above, note 3) 411.
9. A.S.F. Gow, *Theocritus*[2] (Cambridge 1952) II.76. Similarly H. Fritzsche and E. Hiller, *Theokrits Gedichte*[3] (Leipzig 1881) II (". . . in sich abgeschlossene Scenen des landlichen Lebens in poetischer Form"); Augusto Rostagni, *Poeti alessandrini* (Torino 1916) 99 ("la realtà rude e volgarissima dei campi"); R.J. Cholmeley, *The Idylls of Theocritus* (London

1919) 220 ("realistic sketches of the rougher side of Greek country life"); Ettore Bignone, *Teocrito* (Bari 1934) 217; and, with some qualifications, Ulrich Ott, *Die Kunst des Gegensatzes in Theokrits Hirtengedichten,* "Spudasmata" 22 (Hildesheim 1969) 49-50, 56.

10. Lawall, "Theocritus' Fourth Idyll: Animal Loves and Human Loves," *RFIC* 94 (1966) 42-50 = *Coan Pastorals* (above, note 7) 42-51. References to this study are to the article in *RFIC*. For criticism of Lawall's thesis see Ott (above, note 9) pp. 44-5, note 124 and my review in *CJ* 63 (1967-68) 228.

11. John B. Van Sickle, "The Fourth Pastoral Poems of Virgil and Theocritus," *Atti e Memorie dell' Arcadia,* ser. 3, vol. 5, fasc. 1 (Rome 1969) 1-20; also "Poetica teocritea," *QUCC* 9 (1970) 67-82.

12. Van Sickle, "Fourth Pastorals," 7.

13. Lawall, *RFIC* (above, note 10) p. 44, note 1, citing *Aetia* I, frag. 1 23-4 (Pfeiffer), to which add Callimachus, *Epigram* 27. Further support for this view might be found in the allusion to the τέττιξ in IV.16, which also occurs in this passage of the *Aetia* (lines 29-35).

14. Rosenmeyer (above, note 2) 279.

15. *Ibid.,* 280.

16. *Ibid.,* 279.

17. *Ibid.,* 278.

18. *Ibid.,* 96-7; also 47-8.

19. For the importance of antithesis as a literary device of the *Idylls* generally see Legrand (above, note 3) 407-12 and Ott (above, note 9) 7-9 with the further literature there cited in notes 12 and 14.

20. For the different temperaments see Legrand (above, note 3) 175-6; Bignone (above, note 9) 231ff.

21. IV.8 and Gow (above, note 9) *ad loc.*

22. *Cf.* Theocritus' image of Heracles as a great eater of bread in *Id.* XXIV.137-8.

23. Van Sickle, "Fourth Pastorals" (above, note 11) 10.

24. On the cicada see Rosenmeyer (above, note 2) 134-5 with notes 14-15 on p. 313; also A. Dihle, "The Poem on the Cicada," *HSCP* 71 (1966) 112 with note 17; Steier, s.v. "Tettix," *RE* A 9 (1934) 1114-5, 1117. For a pastoral context see Virg., *E.* 5.77.

25. *Id.* IV.15-16 echoes the love-plaint of a human figure, Simaetha in II.89-90, as Legrand (above, note 3) 353 long ago noted.

26 See the good observations of Bignone (above, note 9) 231-2 on Corydon's feeling for the benignity and richness of nature.

27. See Legrand (above, note 3) 363. Corydon's one use of κακός (line 47) comes when his professional capacities are engaged, but even here he speaks with a half-playful exaggeration. See below, note 62.

28. Legrand, *Bucoliques Grecs,* I, *Théocrite* (Paris 1925) *ad loc.,* points out that the verb πατάσσω ("Strike") is rather inappropriate for the thorn and hence is an intentional echo of Corydon's word in 49.

29. On the striking quality of the word see Gow *ad loc.*

30. These "eighty cakes" constitute the only real hyperbaton which the otherwise plain-speaking Corydon indulges in (*cf.* his very slight hyperbaton in 30). Compare Battus' hyperbaton in line 5: Battus waxes rhetorical on parting and doom, Corydon on feasting. Note also Battus' hyperbata in two similar situations, both times to emphasize disaster: κακᾶς . . . νίκας ("evil . . . victory," 27) and σκληρῶ . . . δαίμονος ("hard . . . fate," 40).

31. For a different view see Van Sickle, "Fourth Pastorals" (above, note 11) 16.

32. Ott (above, note 9) 47 suggests that the reference to shoes also contains a malicious jibe at the inferior status of the goatherd.

33. Anne Brooke, "Theocritus' Idyll 11: A study in Pastoral," *Arethusa* 4 (1971) 80.

34. For an approach to the *Idylls* in general along these lines see Lawall, *Coan Pastorals* (above, note 7) chap. 1, especially 13, and also 101,105-8; Van Sickle, "Fourth Pastorals" (above, note 11) 14-15.

35. Bignone (above, note 9) 232 finds in Corydon "quasi un presentimento del poeta e del musico che e in Teocrito," "un aspetto della sua ricca anima che sa l'ideale e il reale, il dolce e l'amaro delle cose . . . ."

36. Van Sickle, "Fourth Pastorals" (above, note 11) 11ff. and "Poetica" (above, note 11) 74-5.

37. See, *contra,* Van Sickle, "Fourth Pastorals" (above, note 11) 10: "The climax of the first two sections of the poem thus touches a motif which is the key to the implicit and perennial subject of pastoral, art itself. All the questions of property, responsibility, place are hints and preparation for the poetic question." "Poetica" (above, note 11) 75 is more cautious.

38. For the text and interpretation of the phrase see Gow (above, note 9) *ad loc.* Conceivably the τε could be regarded as postponed, so that the phrase could be translated,

"And Zakynthus is a lovely city," as Emil Staiger, *Theokrit, Die echten Gedichte* (Zürich 1970) 82 takes it ("Schön ist Zakynthos . . .").

39. Note also the mention of the polis in *Id.* V.78 and VII.2. Ott (above, note 9) 54-5 remarks that in *Id.* IV and V the rustics "nicht einsame Bewohner abgeschiedener Gegenden sind, die sich nur mit Hüten und Musik beschäftigen, sondern dass sie im Umkreis von Städten zuhause sind . . ."

40. The expression μακρὸν ἀνάυσαν ("they shouted greatly") has Homeric echoes (cf. *Il.* 3.81; *Od.* 6.117): cf. Fritzsche-Hiller (above, note 9) *ad loc.*

41. Lawall, *RFIC* (above, note 10) 46 suggests that "Battus is the unnamed goatherd of the earlier poem."

42. Bignone (above, note 9) 233-4: "Batto amò e perdette il suo amore: quella sventura ha lasciato nel suo spirito un solco indelebile di amaro e di aspro," whereas Corydon "sa e comprende; e perciò non si stupisce nè si ribella."

43. See the useful strictures of Van Sickle, "Poetica" (above, note 11) 75-6 and the same author's "Studies of Dialectical Methodology in the Virgilian Tradition," *MLN* 85 (1970) 889-96.

44. Critics have been hard, perhaps too one-sidedly so, on Corydon's proverbs: Lawall, *RFIC* (above, note 10) 46-7; Van Sickle, "Fourth Pastorals" (above, note 11) 11; Rosenmeyer (above, note 2) 28-9.

45. On this progression in the attitude toward the animals see Lawall, *RFIC* (above, note 10) 47.

46. On this movement from distant things to the present see Van Sickle, "Fourth Pastorals" (above, note 11) 12-13. The beginning of *Id.* X is again relevant here.

47. See Legrand (above, note 3) 176, who stresses the continuing self-centeredness and *Schadenfreude* of Battus here.

48. See Van Sickle, "Fourth Pastorals" (above, note 11) 13. In the other places where this *"sstth!"* occurs it still does not break into the verse so abruptly: V.3 and 100 and *cf.* VI.29 and V.89 with Gow's note on the last passage. The imitator of Theocritus in the spurious *Id.* VIII.69, however, has completely lost the dramatic touch of this exclamation, as is nicely observed by L.E. Rossi, *Mondo pastorale e poesia bucolica di maniera: L'idillio ottavo del corpus teocriteo* (Florence 1971) 5ff. = *Studi ital. di Filologia Classica* (1971) 5ff.

49. For this figure in a highly self-conscious and "literary" context see Ps.-Theocr. XIX.5-8. Legrand (above, note 3) 176 suggests, with some justification, that even the experience of the thorn doesn't really affect Battus: "L'aventure lui fournit simplement une occasion de s'admirer lui-même."

50. On the importance of the hill or mountain in the poem see Van Sickle, "Fourth Pastorals" (above, note 11) 12.

51. Such symmetry is a marked feature of other bucolic *Idylls* as well: *cf.* I. 1-3 and 146-8, V. 1 and 145, XI. 7 and 81. The significance of such internal echoes has been well stressed by Lawall, *Coan Pastorals* (above, note 7) *passim* and Rossi (above, note 4) 21-4.

52. On the importance of δείλαιος see Van Sickle, "Fourth Pastorals" (above, note 11) p. 17, note 21.

53. On φιλοίφης in the poem see *ibid.* 18 and "Poetica" (above, note 11) 76. Also E.A. Schmidt, "Φιλαλήθης. Zu Theokrit, Idyll IV," *Philologus* 112 (1968) 131-2.

54. Van Sickle's interpretation of the contrast between the two rustics in terms of poetics leads him to underestimate the growth in Battus at the end. He speaks of "Corydon's obvious growth" in "the acquisition of capacity to deal with love and poetry," which he regards as climaxed in line 54, but passes over Battus very summarily (p. 18): "Fourth Pastorals" (above, note 11) 15-16.

55. The importance of the old man's "milling" for the poem as a whole is perhaps also recognized in the punning title, Φιλαλήθης, as interpreted by Schmidt (above, note 53).

56. Van Sickle, "Fourth Pastorals" (above, note 11) 18.

57. Bignone (above, note 9) 235-6 nicely observes the fusion of rustic earthiness and universal vitality in the closing lines: "Un soffio di paganesimo campestro, che e di tutti i tempi e della vita universale alita di questi versi . . . ."

58. On ἐρίσδεμ see Van Sickle, "Fourth Pastorals" (above, note 11) 18. The word is regularly used of the rustic singing match (*Id.* I.24, V.23, VII.41, etc.).

59. For this fluid movement, achieved largely through repetitions, pronouns, and particles, see Legrand (above, note 3) 384. Question and answer, statement and denial contribute further to the sense of a continuous, rapid onward flow. Note also the repetitions of ᾤχετο ("went off") in 5 and 6, the combination of repetition of words and of sounds in 12-14 (δαμάλαι . . . δειλαιαί γ' αὖται . . . ἦ μὰν δειλαιαί γε, "The heifers . . . Poor things . . . yes, poor things"), the repetitions of "Amaryllis" in 36 and 38 and of θαρσεῖν in 41 and 44.

60. So Van Sickle, "Fourth Pastorals" 10-11 and "Poetica" 74 (both above, note 11),

and see also Ott (above, note 9) 43-4. Van Sickle proposes a more complex scheme based on "increments" of fourteen verses. This works well for the beginning and (to some extent) for the ending of the poem, but involves an arbitrary isolation of line 32 (cf. "Fourth Pastorals," p. 11 with note 11) which I find unconvincing. For other forms of organization and symmetry see Legrand (above, note 3) p. 387, note 1. On the dangers of pushing this kind of analysis too far, as a number of critics in the nineteenth century did, see the salutary warnings of Legrand, 394, and the acerbic comments of Fritzsche-Hiller (above, note 9) p. 16 with note 36 on "Zahlenspielerei" and "mystische . . . Zahlenverhältnisse."

61. From this point of view Van Sickle's emphasis on the "incremental" movement of the poem (preceding note) is valuable, even if his units are not always convincing.

62. Hence we may contrast Corydon's talk of "giving an evil end" to the cows (47) with his more generous "giving" earlier (2,18,36).

63. As Bignone (above, note 9) 5 puts it, "Anche l'intensità tragica del dolore si placa nella modulazione lirica della sua implorazione solitaria."

64. See Rosenmeyer (above, note 2) 46ff., especially 52-4, 59-62.

65. See Legrand (above, note 3) 143-4, who wisely rejects Reitzenstein's attempt to "unmask" Corydon as a disciple of the two poets in question. The incongruity is regarded by Gow, ad loc. (above, note 9) as a mere oversight, but taken more seriously by Rostagni (above, note 9) 101-2 and by Ott (above, note 9) pp. 53-4 with note 155 and p. 56. Glauke's compositions included μεμεθυσμένα παίγνια Μουσέων , "drunken/trifles of the Muses" (Athenaeus 4.176 d).

66. Oed. Rex 1039-40; Ott (above, note 9) 50. The parallel was noted, without comment, by Fritzsche-Hiller (above, note 9) ad loc.

67. Thus Staiger (above, note 38) 19 describes the pastoral Idylls "kleine Gemälder ausgesparter, von der Welt und ihrem ruhelosen Treiben verschonter Räume, denen sich ein Geist zuwendet, der in der politischen Öffentlichkeit und in der höheren Gesellschaft kein antwortendes Gegenbild für seine innere Harmonie mehr kennt und eine seelische Heimat sich vielleicht sogar, dort wo er nicht realistisch verfährt, erfinden muss."

68. I thank Professor John Van Sickle for his helpful and friendly discussion of this essay with me.

CHARLES SEGAL / PROVIDENCE, R. I.

Theocritus' Seventh Idyll and Lycidas

I.

In the Theocritean corpus Idyll 7 has always held a place apart[1]). Until recently the principal task of interpreters was the "unmasking" of Lycidas, Simichidas, and the other characters. But even those who devoted themselves to this problem betrayed

---

[1]) I shall refer to the following works by author's name only: Archibald Cameron, The Form of the ‚Thalysia', Miscellanea di studi alessandrini in memoria di Augusto Rostagni (Torino 1963) 291—307; Quintino Cataudella, Lycidas, Studi in onore di U. E. Paoli (Florence 1955) 159—169; A. T. H. Fritzsche and E. Hiller, edd., Theokrits Gedichte³ (Leipzig 1881); Giuseppe Giangrande, Théocrite, Simichidas, et les Thalysies, AC 37 (1968) 491—533; A. S. F. Gow, Theocritus² (Cambridge 1952); idem, The Seventh Idyll of Theocritus, CQ 34 (1940) 47—54; Alfred Körte and Paul Händel, Die hellenistische Dichtung² (Stuttgart 1960); Josef-Hans Kühn, Die Thalysien Theokrits, Hermes 86 (1958) 40—79; François Lasserre, Aux origines de l'Anthologie: II. Les Thalysies de Théocrite, RhM 102 (1959) 307—330; Gilbert Lawall, Theocritus' Coan Pastorals: A Poetry Book (Cambridge, Mass. 1967); Ph. E. Legrand, Étude sur Théocrite, Bibl. des Écoles françaises d'Athènes et de Rome 79 (Paris 1898); idem, Bucoliques Grecs, I, Théocrite (Paris 1925); Gerhard Lohse, Die Kunstauffassung im VII. Idyll Theokrits und das Programm des Kallimachos, Hermes 94 (1966) 413—425; Georg Luck, Zur Deutung von Theokrits Thalysien, MH 23 (1966) 186—189; Pierre Monteil, Théocrite, Idylles (Paris 1968); Ulrich Ott, Die Kunst des Gegensatzes in Theokrits Hirtengedichten, Spudasmata 22 (Heidelberg 1969); Mario Puelma, Die Dichterbegegnung in Theokrits ‚Thalysien', MH 17 (1960) 144—164; Thomas Rosenmeyer, The Green Cabinet: Theocritus and the European Pastoral Lyric (Berkeley and Los Angeles 1969); Gregorio Serrao, Problemi di poesia alessandrina: I, Studi su Teocrito (Rome 1971); B. A. Van Groningen, "Quelques problèmes de la poésie bucolique grecque", Mnemosyne ser. 4, 12 (1959) 24—53; U. von Wilamowitz-Moellendorff, Hellenistische Dichtung II (Berlin 1924); Frederick Williams, A Theophany in Theocritus, CQ n. s. 21 (1971) 137—145. I owe warm thanks to Professor Michael C. J. Putnam and to Professor John B. Van Sickle for helpful and attentive criticism.

thereby their reluctance to let the poem remain at "the ordinary level of bucolic fictions"[2]).

The notion of the "bucolic masquerade" dominated interpretation to such an extent that even those who rejected it still retained the premises of the historical and biographical approach and clung to a literalist reading of the poem and thereby of the figure of Lycidas[3]). The final result was a reductio ad absurdum of the whole method. As late as 1955 it could be suggested that Lycidas was a real goatherd whom Theocritus knew on Cos, a rustic endowed with natural poetic gifts[4]). Only a few years earlier an interpreter could maintain that Lycidas was an actual poet, a bizarre and eccentric contemporary of the author, accustomed to go around dressed as a goatherd in an attempt to "return to nature"[5]). Eventually the failure of the allegorizing approach which centered on deciphering the bucolic masquerade led to a fresh interpretation of the poem. This interpretation based itself on the text itself rather than on a conjectural biography of the poet.

Gow helped clear the way in 1940 by firmly rejecting the idea of the bucolic masquerade[6]). Even so, he could make little sense of Lycidas' song and declared the whole poem an "enigmatic masterpiece"[7]). The last fifteen years have brought us closer to understanding the "enigma". There has been a remarkable shift of emphasis in the method of interpretation. Van Groningen and Lasserre, who both published their studies in 1959, were the last of recent interpreters to explain the poem primarily as an allegory

---

[2]) Lasserre 310.

[3]) Puelma, for instance, though he places his emphasis elsewhere and accepts the "Mythisierung des Lycidas" (150), still believes that he represents a real person (p. 145 with note 8, p. 151). See also Lohse, 424, criticizing Van Groningen. For a survey of the literature see Cataudella 159—161; Cameron 291 ff.; Ott 164/65 with notes 450—452.

[4]) Cataudella 169: "Licida non è un poeta travestito da capraio, ma un capraio-poeta, un capraio cioè dotato di naturali qualità poetiche, e non del tutto privo di qualche infarinatura di conoscenze letterarie."

[5]) Ph. Legrand, REA 47 (1945) 214—218, who finally identifies the eccentric in question with Astacidas (A. P. 7, 518 = Callim. Epigr. 36 Pf. = 1211 Gow-Page).

[6]) Gow, CQ 34, 47—51. The idea of a masquerade is firmly rejected by Körte-Händel 221: „Unsere Unruhe über die hochgestimmt singenden Hirten sollte nicht so groß sein, daß wir sie als verkappte Poeten ansehen."

[7]) Gow, CQ 34, 47.

of actual events in Theocritus' life or literary milieu[8]). In 1958, in an important article in Hermes, J.-H. Kühn struck out on a new and fruitful line of interpretation. He laid aside completely the question of the masquerade and concentrated instead on the poem's structure and symbolism. This approach has been followed up, with much individual variation, by Puelma (1960), Cameron (1963), Luck (1966), Lawall (1967), Ott (1969), and most recently Serrao (1971)[9]).

On one aspect of the poem there has been a fair degree of consensus, namely the importance of the references to Hesiod's "Dichterweihe"[10]). Idyll 7 is Theocritus' "Dichterweihe", his initiation into the realm of the Muses. As Puelma suggests, it occupies a place in Theocritus' work analogous to Callimachus' proem to the Aitia or to Virgil's Sixth Eclogue or Propertius 3, 3[11]).

As a result of the criticism of the last three decades it will never again be possible to read Idyll 7, as could Legrand nearly a century ago, as "le recit d' 'une bonne journée de Théocrite à Cos' "[12]). Yet the symbolical approach to Theocritus does not appeal to all critics. Rosenmeyer remains skeptical[13]). More particularly Giangrande has launched a polemical attack upon the symbolist interpretation[14]). Giangrande is particularly concerned

---

[8]) Lasserre's approach is discussed critically by Giangrande 493 ff. How tenacious is the habit of searching for poets behind herdsmen appears from S. L. Radt's recent remarks on Comatas: "Theocritea", Mnemosyne, ser. 4, 24 (1971) 254/55.

[9]) I have not been able to consult Margrit Sanchez-Wildberger, Theokrit-Interpretationen (Diss. Zürich 1955) 62—69 nor G. Weingarth, zu Theokrits 7. Idyll (Diss. Freiburg i. Br. 1967).

[10]) See especially Puelma 156—158 and Van Groningen 30 ff.

[11]) Puelma 161.

[12]) So Legrand, Étude, 411. Yet in his review of Gow, REG 64 (1951) 376, more than half a century later, he still calls Idyll 7 a "récit d'une aventure vécue". In his Bucoliques Grecques, 2—3, the only question is whether the poem describes an old Theocritus looking back nostalgically on his youth or a young Theocritus caught up still in the vivid happiness of that glorious day.

[13]) E. g. Rosenmeyer 278 ff. On the question of symbolism in Theocritus see also my essay, Theocritean Criticism and the Interpretation of the Fourth Idyll, Ramus 1 (1972) 4 ff.

[14]) Giangrande 515 ff. See also his review of Lawall in JHS 88 (1968) 171/72 and his essay, Theocritus' Twelfth and Fourth Idylls: A Study in Hellenistic Irony, QUCC 12 (1971) 106, note 35.

to show that the elements of the Hesiodic Dichterweihe are pervaded
by irony, wit and parody. In the Theogony the Muses in fact
insult the shepherds (Theog. 26). Instead of Hesiod's "Olympian
Muses, daughters of aegis-wielding Zeus" (Theog. 25) who bestow
"a scepter, branch of rich-blooming laurel" (Theog. 30), Theocritus
describes a smelly goatherd who gives his lowly herdsman's staff
(κορύναν, 43; λαγωβόλον, 128). Now, the irony and the tone of
parody are undeniable, but they are not so irreconcilable with
symbolism as Giangrande suggests. Rather, they indicate that
Theocritus handles his symbols with dexterity and lightness.

The lack of agreement among symbolist critics need not, as
Giangrande thinks, discredit the symbolist approach, but points
rather to the complexity, elusiveness, and richness of the symbols
themselves. Symbols are not signs. The richer the symbol, the
wider the range of its meanings and the more complex its relation
to the total literary construct in which it stands.

To call Lycidas or Simichidas symbols or symbolic does not
imply a one-to-one equation with a single idea or object or person[15]).
Symbolism here means not something arcane and apart from the
poem, some secret, cabbalistic system superimposed by the poet
for a few initiates, but rather a meaning inherent in the subject
matter itself. A literary work and its elements (character, setting,
action) are symbolic in the way that all art is: they point beyond
themselves to something universal, something which enables art
from remotely different times and cultures still to speak to us.
Symbol in this sense refers to that fusion of concrete particular and
universal meaning which takes place in all poetry. Through this
fusion the poet focuses, unites, and raises to new levels of intensity
and thereby of comprehension clusters of ideas, relationships,
emotional tonalities which together constitute the "meaning" of
the poem. A symbol, in the sense here defined, operates within a
structure. It could, in fact, be described as an operative counter
within a structure which is itself symbolic, i. e. a structure which
creates fresh collocations, fresh points of reference, and vivid,
concrete enactments of ideas, relationships, aspects of experience

---

[15]) Symbols of this limited nature are what G. S. Kirk, Myth, Its
Meaning and Function in Ancient and Other Cultures, Sather Classical
Lectures 40 (Berkeley and Los Angeles 1970) 278—280, aptly terms "static
symbols". The symbols I am discussing are "dynamic".

in order to clarify and expressively represent those areas of reality with which the poem is concerned.

Precisely because a symbol's meaning depends on its place within the structure of the whole work, it will reveal different facets of its meaning as the critic stresses one or another aspect of the work. A symbol, therefore, cannot "mean" whatever the critic wants it to mean; but it is important to recognize that a symbol may have several related and interconnected meanings. Precisely because of the range of such interrelated meanings we can return to a literary work again and again and never fully exhaust its significance. The figures of Oedipus, Hamlet, Faust are such symbols; and Lycidas, though on a far lower plane, belongs in the same category. Thus there is no necessary contradiction in regarding him as a god, as an aspect of Theocritus' poetic personality, or (as I suggest inter alia here) as a symbol of bucolic inspiration in general.

In stressing the irony of Theocritus, Giangrande has in fact made a valuable contribution. This irony points to a crucial ambivalence in Theocritus' pastoral. His subject-matter often involves fundamental issues of human life: passion and order, the nature of poetry, aggressiveness and amity in human relations. But Theocritus masks the seriousness of the subject by a light and playful tone. By its very nature bucolic poetry is inclined to this ambivalence[16]). "The pastoral process of putting the complex into the simple", writes Empson, is "in itself a great help to the concentration needed for poetry". Pastoral presents a narrative surface of playful, basically happy country folk in a peaceful setting in which life's gravest concerns are locating stray cows or meditating ditties on rustic amours. Yet the very artificiality of the genre and the very contrast between the rusticity of the setting and the sophistication of the language call this simplicity into question.

---

[16]) See Bruno Snell, Arcadia: The Discovery of a Spiritual Landscape, in The Discovery of the Mind, tr. T. G. Rosenmeyer (Cambridge, Mass. 1953) 285—288: "The dissonance between the bucolic simplicity of the pasture and the literary refinement of the city is never completely resolved, nor was it ever intended to be, for the whole point of Theocritus' humour lies in this dissonance" (286). On later uses of the convention see W. Empson, Some Versions of Pastoral (New York 1960) 11/12, 23; Renato Poggioli, "The Oaten Flute", Harvard Library Bulletin 11 (1957) 167/68 and 177—179, citing the second book of Boileau's Art Poétique: Telle, aimable en son air, mais humble dans son style / Doit éclater sans pompe une élegante idylle.

From this contradiction in pastoral between content and form, between the narrative surface and the refined style, spring other contradictions, ironies, ambiguities. The very form poses a contrast of simplicity and artfulness. Pastoral appeals to man's need for a return to nature, which is also a need for simplicity; but it does not lose touch with the complexities and polarities of the human condition: man's place between νόμος and φύσις, civilization and nature, restraint and freedom.

The allusions, even in parody, to Homer and Hesiod reinforce, rather than destroy, the multiplicity of levels of meaning, for they call attention to the discrepancy between the author's world of art and learning and that of the characters whom he depicts. Theocritus compounds this difficulty by refusing to indicate at exactly what level his poems should be read[17]). They fluctuate between the highest and the lowest styles; between crude realism and high, mythical lyricism; between (ostensibly) simple paratactic narrative and learned, even obscure allusions[18]).

Like his contemporary, Callimachus, Theocritus prefers to retain a certain distance and coolness toward his art. The refined, polished surface shuns too open a display of enthusiasm or involvement. In this respect he partakes of a quality of the Hellenistic poetic mentality which Van Groningen has defined with exemplary clarity: "Ce badinage avec les choses très sérieuses est un des caractéristiques du siècle de Théocrite. Ce que les générations antérieures exprimaient ou racontaient dans une langue altière, solennelle, héroïque, est dépouillé par la plupart des auteurs hellénistiques de sa grandeur et de sa noblesse, est abaissé au niveau des choses de tous les jours"[19]).

When Theocritus, therefore, adapts his "Dichterweihe" to the low realism of the bucolic mime and lets us catch a whiff of his passing goatherd, he is not excluding symbolical overtones, but rather rendering these overtones even more complex because he

---

[17]) See my remarks in Ramus 1. 20ff. (above, note 13).

[18]) In Id. 7, e. g., note the erudition of 114—116 or the contrast between high and low styles in 7, 16 and 7, 74ff. Or cf. Id. 1, 150—152 or Id. 5, 50—54, 84—87, 108—116. The later imitators of Theocritus tend to smooth out these abrupt shifts of tone and aim at a more uniform "poetical" style: cf. ps.-Theocr. 8, 12—20 with Theocr. 5, 23—30, and see in general L. E. Rossi, SIFC 43 (1971) 5—25; R. Merkelbach, ΒΟΥΚΟΛΙΑΣΤΑΙ (Der Wettgesang der Hirten), RhM 99 (1956) 117—122.

[19]) Van Groningen 30.

handles them with an ironical self-awareness. The poet himself
peeks around the structures he creates. He recognizes the seriousness
of his themes (hence the allusions to Homer and Hesiod and the
rich myths of Daphnis and Comatas), but he also avoids the
"heaviness" (παχύτης would be the Alexandrian equivalent) of
unqualified seriousness. As 7, 45—48 implies, Theocritus would
agree with his contemporary's famous dictum, "To thunder is not
mine, but of Zeus"[20]).

II.

The plot of Idyll 7 is dramatic in nature. Two figures from
different realms encounter one another and thereby create a
confrontation of different sets of attitudes and experience. In this
meeting between the urban Simichidas and the goatherd Lycidas,
the realm of the mountains, of pastoral life, intersects the realm
of the city and the plain. For a brief time the two travelers are
united on a "common road" (35). The structure of the poem is
linear: a journey from one point to another, from city to country.
But into this linear progression intrudes a foreign and distinctive
element, the strange goatherd, Lycidas. One could chart the meeting
as the intersection of a horizontal direction (the movement from
the city to the Harvest Festival) by a vertical direction (the
appearance of Lycidas from his mountain (cf. 51).

Lycidas serves to bring the city-based Simichidas into contact
with a remote, mysterious, mythical realm. Like Socrates and his
young companion in Plato's Phaedrus, Simichidas journeys from
polis to country; and in the process he draws upon the country's
magic and music[21]). The use of the journey as symbol is deeply
rooted in the Greek literary tradition[22]). Theocritus himself ex-

---

[20]) Callim. Aitia I, fr. 1. 20 (Pf.). Lines 45—48 have often been taken
as a sign of Theocritus' adherence to Callimachus' aesthetic: cf. E. Schwartz,
Theokrits Daphnis, NGG (1904) 298, note 3. See, however, the qualifica-
tions of Lohse 424/25 and Körte-Händel 212/13.

[21]) See Cameron 306; Clyde Murley, Plato's Phaedrus and Theocritean
Pastoral, TAPA 71 (1940) 281—295.

[22]) Parmenides' proem (DK 28 B1), the Odyssean and Orphic katabases,
and the metaphor of journey in Pindar are perhaps the most familiar examp-
les: see O. Becker, Das Bild des Weges und verwandte Vorstellungen im
frühgriechischen Denken, Hermes Einzelschrift 4 (1937).

ploited the motif of the symbolical journey at length in what is
perhaps his earliest poem (Id. 16, 8—15, 68—70).

Simichidas' journey can be understood in a number of different
ways. Biographically, it reflects Theocritus' attempt to explore the
nature and origins of his inspiration to write pastoral poetry. More
generally, it brings this local encounter with the mystique of the
country in touch with ancient myths of finding an unfamiliar,
unknown realm. Here the poet's model is the voyage of Odysseus,
to which, as we shall see, the Idyll alludes. Third and last, this
journey focuses the ironies, inherent in the very genre of pastoral:
the poet "from the city" (2) who would make his way to the
country has an unexpected encounter with a figure who embodies
a sharper and more disturbing, more independent kind of rusticity
than he expected.

Neither Simichidas nor Lycidas need represent Theocritus or
the inner life of Theocritus[23]. Both characters are symbolic figures
in a drama which has to do with the balance between imagination
and reality, the distant and the tangible, artifice and nature,
complexity and simplicity. The emphasis throughout on Muses,
song, myths of singers makes the elements of this drama converge
unmistakably upon the theme of poetry and specifically bucolic
poetry. The work, however, invites extrapolation from poetics
to other areas of human experience.

For Kühn, Ott, and Lawall, the figures of the poem are not
allegories, but multivalent symbols of inward tensions or conflict.
On their view the meeting of Lycidas and Simichidas embodies a
contrast of passion and irony, romantic unreality and a harder,
more aggressive attitude[24]. This view is valid up to a point, but
does not cover every aspect of the poem. Particularly, it does not
take account of the superiority which the poem assigns Lycidas.
The two singers do not stand on an equal footing, perfectly balanced
in their art and therefore representing two balanced tendencies

---

[23]) Even in antiquity the identification of Simichidas with Theocritus
was not regarded as certain: see the scholion ad 21. Even scholars who have
maintained the identification have become aware that there may be more
than one Theocritus in the poem and that the confrontation is as much
between ideas and views of art as between actual persons: see Ott 167/68;
Lawall 80; Kühn 57—61; Körte-Händel 217—219. One should keep in
mind also the tendency toward detachment in Theocritus and other pastoral:
see Rosenmeyer 15—16.

[24]) See Lawall 101; Ott 160—173; Kühn 64—74.

within Theocritean poetry. As Van Groningen rightly saw, Lycidas
is the master[25]). He bestows his staff; Simichidas gives nothing in
return. On the other hand, this fact does not necessarily justify
Van Groningen's view that Simichidas' song is an inferior pro-
duction[26]).

Despite the preliminary agonistic mood, there is no real
contest between the two singers[27]). Lycidas gives his crook to
Simichidas not as the insignia of victory, but as a mark of friendship
and as a token of his "initiation" into the joys of rustic song and
rustic life[28]). Simichidas' hope to "equal" (ἰσοφαρίζειν, 30) his
companion is not an eristic desire for victory so much as a reflection
of a desire to emulate a singer of established superior talent[29]).
Simichidas is not entirely without aggressiveness and egotism[30]).
Yet on the whole he presents himself as rather agreeable. Lycidas'
excellence in song "warms his heart" (θυμὸν ἰαίνει / ἀμέτερον, 29f).
In his very next line he goes on to the happy subject of the Thalysia
and lays stress on the "common" journey (ξυνὰ ὁδός, ξυνὰ δὲ καὶ
ἀώς, 35) and on mutual help or benefit (τάχ' ὥτερος ἄλλον ὀνασεῖ, 36).
Lycidas not only promises the gift of his herdsman's staff (43);
he also praises his companion (44), prior to inviting him to bucolic
song in 49. Idylls 6 and 10 and the pseudo-Theocritean Idyll 8
attest that in bucolic singing matches amity is just as possible as
contentiousness. In 7, despite some background contentiousness
on the part of Simichidas, subtly and humorously conveyed[31]),
harmony prevails. It is in this mood of friendship, laughter, and
concord that the songs begin.

Merkelbach has emphasized the fact that a certain amount of
rustic banter is to be expected in the genre[32]). Even so, the banter is

---

[25]) Van Groningen 26/27.

[26]) Serrao 64 rightly rejects this view.

[27]) See Puelma 152/53 with notes 27—28; Ott 145; Lohse 423; Merkel-
bach (above, note 18) 116.

[28]) See Puelma 154/55 with note 36.

[29]) Puelma 152/53, with note 28.

[30]) Puelma 152 goes too far, however, in stressing that Lycidas is all
courtesy and friendliness. For the sarcastic side of Lycidas see Ott 169,
Williams 142, and especially Giangrande 503—508.

[31]) Lines 42—44 are a focal point for this humor; and Lycidas' repartee
cleverly and amusingly parries his friend's exaggerations: see my essay,
Simichidas' Modesty: Theocritus, Idyll 7, 44, in AJP (forthcoming).

[32]) Merkelbach (above, note 18) 110—122, especially 116. See also
Lawall 54.

about evenly divided between the two characters. Simichidas is perhaps indulging in irony when he calls Lycidas the best syrinx player among "shepherds and reapers" (28/29). Reapers are often connected with song, but nowhere in Theocritus does a reaper play the syrinx[33]). Yet Lycidas also scores his points, particularly in his hint, nicely observed by Giangrande, that Simichidas may be going to the Harvest Festival as a workman rather than as a guest (25/26)[34]), and possibly in his laughter (42) and statement of 44.

Lycidas clearly has a strong independent status. As Puelma suggests, he is "the embodiment of the αἰπόλος; and since this class of herdsmen is the lowest in the bucolic hierarchy and thereby represents the most distinctive level of the herdsman's existence, (he appears) as the exemplary or ideal herdsman in general"[35]). His striking appearance reinforces this quality, for he goes walking about dressed in goatskin, smelling of the cheese-making, and carrying his staff, though goats are nowhere in sight[36]). He is a kind of distillation of the rustic world, the very essence of its acrid flavor, its strange, uncitylike, unassimilable particularity, smell and all[37]).

Lycidas is a distillation of rustic song too, for he is "the best piper among herdsmen and reapers" (συρικτὰν μέγ' ὑπείροχον ἔν τε νομεῦσιν / ἔν τ' ἀματήρεσσι, 28/29). If Simichidas' compliment can be taken at face value, it unites in Lycidas' superlative talent the realms of both herdsman and farmers, both pastoral and agricultural settings. As in Idyll 10, Theocritus self-consciously brings these

---

[33]) In Id. 10, 15 a girl plays the aulos to mowers, but the aulos seems to be a lower-class instrument: cf. Id. 5, 4—7. So in Tibullus 2, 1, 51—54 a farmer plays on the avena or aulos: see P. L. Smith, TAPA 101 (1970) 508. Mowers are sung to again in Iliad 18, 569, but it is the two herdsmen who "take joy in the syrinx" (Iliad 18, 525/26). For the mowers' song see Gow ad Id. 7, 29 and 10, 41.

[34]) Giangrande 503—508.

[35]) Puelma 148: „Lykidas wird so geradezu als ideale Verkörperung des aipolos und, da diese Hirtenart in der Hierarchie der Bukolik die niederste und damit markanteste Stufe des Hirtendaseins darstellt, als Muster- oder Idealhirt überhaupt vorgestellt."

[36]) See Cataudella 161/62; Kühn 62. Lawall 80 remarks, "In fact, he is described in greater detail than almost any other character in Theocritus' Idylls".

[37]) See Lohse 424.

two divisions of rusticity together. This praise of Lycidas' art
spans in microcosm the two aspects of the country which the
Idyll encompasses, a herdsman and an agricultural festival;
thus it hints at the inclusiveness of the rustic frame.

A goatherd who plays the syrinx is an unusual phenomenon.
He unites the coarsest and the richest possibilities offered by the
bucolic world. Lycidas and the anonymous goatherd of Idyll 1
are, in fact, the only two goatherds in the Theocritean corpus to
play the syrinx[38]. They are also the two most talented herdsmen
in the Idylls.

Appearing at the noon hour, time of supernatural interven-
tions and of danger, Lycidas carries with him the "mystique of the
wilderness"[39], the wild flavor and remoteness of the mountains.
We may compare Idyll 1; the Goatherd evokes "bitter Pan" in a
calm and songful setting (1, 15—18). In the Greek world, even
today, the division between city and country, πόλις and ἄγρος, is
far more stark and abrupt than what most of us urban and suburban
moderns are familiar with; the ἄγρος can contain something strange,
if not actually forbidding, to the city-dweller. The allusion to Pan
in Idyll 1 shows that such settings may be tinged with an element of
danger: they produce in the urban reader a frisson as at something
uncanny. As Bardon has recently remarked, "Il est toujours
dangereux que l'homme, — être social, — retrouve la campagne:
celle-ci n'est pas son cadre naturel d'action"[40]. Finding himself
outside the safety of the town (ἐχ πόλιος, 2) and sharing a "common
road" with an archetypal rustic, Simichidas may expect a more
significant experience than an hour's casual companionship. To
anticipate our argument, Lycidas embodies, among other things, a
mysterious creative power, the gift of pastoral song which the
countryside can bestow on the would-be pastoralist "from the
city" (2).

---

[38]) Note the conflict between syrinx and aulos in Id. 5, 4—7, and
see above, note 33. The status of players of the syrinx in the Theocritean
corpus is as follows:
Cowherd: Id. 1, 4, [9], [20], [27], Epigram 2.   Goatherd: Id. 1 and 7.
Shepherd: Id. 4, 5, 6 [8].   Unidentified: Bion, 2.
For the importance of the syrinx as „ein Instrument der technischen Musik"
which demands high art see E. Schwartz, Theokrits Daphnis, NGG (1904) 301.
[39]) See Cameron p. 296 with note 13.
[40]) H. Bardon, Bucolique et politique, RhM 115 (1972) 8.

If Theocritus, as seems probable, is the inventor of pastoral poetry as a separate literary genre, then he is using the figure of Lycidas in part to point toward the uniqueness, specialness, and elusiveness of the art itself. Through Lycidas he explores the mystery of the creative power which enabled him to invent this new form. The ancients are especially sensitive to tradition and to past models. Hence the creation of a new genre must have seemed a striking and almost miraculous occurrence. Hesiod talked with the Muses; Callimachus had a dream. Theocritus, to grapple with the mysterious nature of this new poetic inspiration, uses the rich and vivid figure of Lycidas. Through this character the poet makes contact with something beyond rational explanation, a beckoning, foreign realm which he can approach only through myth and symbol.

From the very first a supernatural atmosphere surrounds Lycidas. His sudden appearance, his smile, the noon hour, the sudden disappearance, the Homeric phraseology of the lines, οὐδέ κέ τίς νιν / ἠγνοίησεν ἰδών ἐπεὶ αἰπόλῳ ἔξοχ᾽ ἐῴκει (13/14), all draw heavily on epic encounters between a god and mortal[41]. The arrival of Hermes in Odyssey 5, the meeting of Odysseus and Athena in Odyssey 13 and of Odysseus and Hermes in Odyssey 10, the nocturnal encounter of Priam and Hermes in Iliad 24 are the most relevant parallels. Lycidas' bestowal of his staff is like the gift of the god in many such encounters[42]. His sudden and silent disappearance — prepared for, as Lohse points out, because the staff has already been introduced[43] — is like the mysterious vanishing of the god after his epiphany[44]. The parallels extend from Homer to the Gospels. Cameron, who has made the fullest study of this dimension of Lycidas, points out how Theocritus has adapted the form and terminology of a supernatural encounter to a totally secular situation[45]. This use of supernatural motifs has caused readers and editors to find something puzzling in the language of the passage and indeed in the atmosphere of the whole poem. F. Williams has now made a convincing case for identifying Lycidas

---

[41]) See Cameron, passim; Puelma 147—149; Luck 186—189; Ott 170 with note 470, and now RhM 115 (1972) 142ff.

[42]) See Odyssey 5, 333 and 10, 277; Pindar, Pyth. 4, 35; Hdt. 6, 61. See in general Cameron 304/05.

[43]) Lohse 421.

[44]) See Cameron 305.

[45]) Ibid., 303.

with Apollo[46]). An understanding of Lycidas' role in the poem, however, does not depend upon a full identification with a god. It suffices to recognize the supernatural and mythic features of the narrative. Lycidas' divinity remains a hint only, a suggestion which the alert reader will keep in the back of his mind.

The supernatural elements surrounding Lycidas are an important indication that for Theocritus the power of myth is not entirely dead. "What takes place in the encounter", as Cameron observed, "is not to be treated entirely on the plane of mundane reality"[47]). In Lycidas the magic of the countryside and, behind that, the mystery of the unknown step forth to greet the "new" pastoral poet[48]). He brings the narrator into intense, exposed contact with something demonic. This contact with a mysterious numinous power can shake a poet's whole being and demands transmutation into art:

> Denn das Schöne ist nichts
> als des Schrecklichen Anfang, den wir noch gerade ertragen,
> und wir bewundern es so, weil es gelassen verschmäht,
> uns zu zerstören,

wrote Rilke in a famous passage of the Duino Elegies. Ancient poets have expressed similar ideas in mythic form: the birth of the Graces and the Muses, the bard Thamyris' encounter with the Muses in the Iliad, the Muse who takes coral from the "hoary sea" in Pindar (N. 7, 77—79), his tale of Athena's inventing flute music from the wail of the dying Medusa (P. 12)[49]).

When Theocritus feels this demonic quality in the beauty which inspires and calls forth his art, he can no longer describe it in the traditional mythology or with the deep and serious religiosity of a Hesiod or a Pindar. For these writers there is no sharp split between myth and reality, for reality is still, in a certain sense, mythical. Hence they have available to them a narrative style which can report an encounter with the Muses as a straightforward,

---

[46]) Williams 137—145.

[47]) Cameron 306.

[48]) Luck 187 remarks that „... mit Lykidas das Imaginäre, rein Dichterische beginnt".

[49]) On N. 7, 77—79 see my remarks in TAPA 98 (1967) 460—462. On Pyth. 12 see E. Schlesinger, Hermes 96 (1968) 280—283. He aptly cites Aristotle, Poet. c. 4, 1448 b 10 ff.

literal occurrence. Theocritus cannot permit himself such naiveté. He can signal the wonder of his new creation only by an allusive restructuring of a past tradition and by a careful, self-deprecatory irony. Like Callimachus in his treatment of the Hesiodic Dichterweihe (Aitia, frag. 2 Pf.), Theocritus secularizes and personalizes a religious and impersonal (or suprapersonal) motif. Wit and parody take the edges off the demonic and supernatural violence of the old myths. It belongs to Theocritus' irony and delicate ambivalence between seriousness and parody that he gives his "Hesiodic" encounter the peculiar off-color tang of the art which he has invented[50]).

Lycidas may manufacture his cheeses with his own hands, but like Daphnis in Idyll 1 he is in touch with a remote world of bucolic demigods. His being embraces both the all too palpable marks of the rustic's trade and "divine" singers (83, 89), both down-to-earth work in the country and a view of nature as animate and responsive to human grief (74—77), both prosaic reality and miraculous salvation from death (78—89)[51]). Like Daphnis, he is "dear to the Muses" (7, 95 and 1, 141). Yet, unlike Daphnis, he is wholly in accord with his world; and he is not torn by the mysterious dichotomy, the struggle of instinct and aspiration, that seems to destroy the melancholy cowherd of the first Idyll[52]). From Lycidas' own harmony with his world there flow intimations of a larger accord achieved at the end of Idyll 7 between art and the physical setting, herdsman and farmer, Pan and Demeter.

The Harvest Festival itself celebrates the moment when the human world and the cosmic order come most closely together. Here nature reveals its full bounty to man, and man rejoices in his harmonious relation with nature[53]). As the goatherd par excellence who is also a celebrated singer, Lycidas stands between the mystery,

---

[50]) See Lohse 424.

[51]) On this tension between realism and the supernatural in Lycidas see Serrao 27/28; Luck 187. Lohse 424 suggests that Theocritus may have developed this tension in Lycidas to answer objections to his portraits of rustics, demonstrating „daß die theokritischen Hirten mit den wirklichen so viel und so wenig zu tun haben wie Lykidas der Hirte mit Lykidas dem Dichter".

[52]) On these tensions in Daphnis see Lawall 19 ff. and my essay 'Since Daphnis Dies': The Meaning of Theocritus' First Idyll, MH 31 (1974).

[53]) The thalysia as a point of contact between man and nature can also

beauty, and soulfulness of the country on the one hand and the
more ordered, but also more constrained city-world of Simichidas
on the other hand. As Demeter, presiding over the physical nurture
of life, is the mediator between the human world and nature's
tangible gifts, so Lycidas in the realm of mind and art touches both
the natural and supernatural poles of the physical world. He is
grounded in both the earthiness of nature's processes and what
Marie Desport calls "the sympathy of nature for those who hold
the gift of poetry, the friends of the Muses"[54]).

Lycidas thus embodies some of the polarities of art itself:
something which is both human and divine, physical and spiritual,
both suffers death and transcends it (74—85). Hence his appearance
and disappearance both stand under the sign of the Muses (12, 129).
He is "dear to the Muses" (95) and mentions the Muses in his
statement of poetic preferences (47). His song contains a mythical
goatherd saved from death "because the Muse poured sweet nectar
on his mouth" (82). Simichidas, by contrast, refers to the Muses
only once in his own behalf (37), and that in a context (possibly
ironical) of self-deprecation. It is the Nymphs, not the Muses,
who instructed him on the mountains (92).

Lycidas' connection with the peculiar otherness of the country-
side and the mystery of its poetry is a serious obstacle to Kühn's
(and in part) Lawall's attempt to identify him with aspects of
Theocritus[55]). On the contrary, Lycidas carries with him an elixir
of a world of which Theocritus, as poet, has intimations; but this
world is something which poetry reaches toward rather than
possesses. Simichidas too cannot simply be identified with Theo-
critus, for Theocritus the poet also embraces the realm of a Lycidas
which intersects Simichidas' world at only one point, the moment
of encounter described in the Idyll. After the meeting Lycidas goes
back to his mountain, where Simichidas has no place, and the
poem turns decisively to the plain, with a wish for some sort of
permanence there (155—157).

---

be dangerous. Artemis inflicts the destructive boar upon the Calydonians
because Oeneus did not perform the thalysia-sacrifices due her (Iliad 9,
534/35).

[54]) Marie Desport, L'incantation virgilienne (Bordeaux 1952) 115.
See Van Groningen 30, who considers Lycidas "l'intermède entre Simichidas,
le jeune poète, et les Muses, déesses et protectrices de la poésie".

[55]) Kühn's point, for example, 72, that the Daphnis of Id. 1 occurs

It is significant that Theocritus makes us see the bucolic world
of Lycidas through the eyes of Simichidas, the narrator. He thereby
presents Lycidas' world in contrast to something else, as reflected
or "refracted", as Kühn puts it[56]). His bucolic world does not stand
on quite the same level as the world presented in a poem like
Idyll 4 or 5. In those poems the pastoral setting is simply given:
it occupies the first plane of the narrative. In Idyll 7 the bucolic
realm, which is the realm of Lycidas, is one degree removed. The
narrative frame delineates it as something on the fringes of the
narrator's normal world, beyond, though intersecting, the axis
that runs between the city and Phrasidamus' farm. Over against
these two ordered and social realms, city and farm, Lycidas'
mountainous habitat and his isolated, non-social life stand apart
as something alien.

Theocritus might have treated the meeting between the two
characters as a dialogue in the present tense, like the encounters in
Idylls 4 or 5. By enclosing the encounter within a frame and making
it the subject of recollection by a first-person narrator (ἦς χρόνος
ἀνίκ' ἐγών ... in the first line), he forces us to see Lycidas from the
point of view of Simichidas' "I." This is not the device one would
expect if the poem were merely trying to contrast two sides of
Theocritus' poetry or personality, for then the two figures ought
each to stand on the same level of reality and objectivity. Instead
the Idyll anchors us in Simichidas' world and presents the encounter
with Lycidas as an extension outward from that. This meeting,
then, is not simply a balanced dialogue of opposites, but a reaching
forth on the part of Simichidas into a foreign realm.

At the very center of the poem stands the tale of Comatas.
As the "divine" goatherd, Comatas is the mythic archetype of all
goatherd-singers. Indeed, he is an archetype behind Lycidas himself,
and the two figures have much in common. Both are associated
with sweetness (20/21, 42; 82, 89); both "recline" (66 and 89);
both have "toiled" (ἐξεπόνασα, 51; ἐξεπόνασας, 85).

---

in Lycidas' song is indecisive; it could as well serve for identifying Thyrsis
with Theocritus or Tityrus with Theocritus. In fact these songs need not be
interpreted biographically. They can be seen rather as elements of a bucolic
world which the poet can enter and exploit in many different ways and
through many different personae, all of which are in some sense "Theocritus"
since he is their creator.

56) Kühn 69.

The tale of Comatas is doubly removed from the realm of the present "I" of Simichidas. First, it stands within Lycidas' song; and, second, it is projected by Lycidas from a hypothetical song of Tityrus. It is Lycidas who again mediates this remote, mythical world of the dead Comatas to the living, present, urban world of Simichidas and his companions. Illuminated by this glow of myth, even the crude realism of the goatherd's work is transfigured. As Lycidas concludes his song with an apostrophe to Comatas, the goats which he pastures "on the mountains" become "beautiful goats" (87—89):

> ὥς τοι ἐγὼν ἐνόμευον ἀν' ὥρεα τὰς καλὰς αἶγας
> φωνᾶς εἰσαΐων, τὺ δ' ὑπὸ δρυσὶν ἢ ὑπὸ πεύκαις
> ἁδὺ μελισδόμενος κατεκέκλισο, θεῖε Κομᾶτα.

Lycidas would "hear the voice" of Comatas (88) as he pastures his goats, while Comatas, like the songful herdsmen of other Idylls, reclines "under oaks or pines" (88/89)[57]). This wished-for vignette is the bucolic, Lycidan equivalent of what the city-people do at the Thalysia: listen to the birds and insects of their rustic surroundings (139—141). Yet whereas they hear only these lower creatures, real and tangible, Lycidas would "hear the voice" of the divine goatherd himself, a figure shadowy with myth and death (86). The bees which buzz around Simichidas and his friends (142) are, for all their beauty, a prosaic echo of those mythical bees which kept alive the fabled herdsman (81, 84).

From the first, the surroundings in which Lycidas appears have an archetypal bucolic quality. The spring and its shady setting (even though not physically present to the travelers), the midday heat, the stillness (6—9, 22/23), even the tomb (10) are a distillation of the settings of all the rustic meetings in the bucolic Idylls[58]). One element is conspicuous by its absence. There is no song, no sound, no "whispering pine" or sweetly plashing water, as in Idyll 1 or even in Simichidas' first-person narrative in 6—9. By the end of the

---

[57]) Cf. Id. 1, 1—8, 21—23; see also 12, 8; 18, 46; 22, 76.

[58]) For the spring of water cf. Id. 1, 1—8; 6, 3; for the mid-day setting, Id. 1, 15ff; 6, 4; 10, 5. Even the tomb occurs elsewhere: 1, 125 and 5, 121. For "the Harvest Festival as Recapitulation" see Lawall 110—117. He has conveniently collected all the echoes of the other bucolic Idylls which occur in Id. 7: 136—138, note 43.

poem, in the grove of the Nymphs on Phrasidamus' estate, larks will sing (ἄειδον κόρυδοι καὶ ἀκανθίδες, 141). But here "not even . . . the larks (οὐδ' . . . κορυδαλλίδες) wander about" (23).

Here at the beginning Simichidas and his companions "have not yet completed the midpoint of their road" (κοὔπω τὰν μεσάταν ὁδὸν ἄνυμες, 10). Having set out "from the city" (2) they are in a kind of mysterious no-man's land between city and the easeful, cultivated setting in which they will refresh themselves at the end, immediately after Lycidas departs (131—157). The shaded Burina spring and the heroic Chalco who actually "made the spring" (ἄνυε κράναν, 6) and caused the water to gush forth (6/7) put the travelers in touch with the very origins of bucolic beauty and, given the poetical associations of springs, with the possibility of bucolic poetry. But that spring is, presumably, distant. The three friends have ventured out of the city and far from its heroic personages.

Here, on the road, it is the "road-traveler," ὁδίτας, Lycidas, who describes the scene. Whatever we learn about this point in "mid-journey" we learn from the description by this ὁδίτας. The birds do not sing, but Lycidas evokes song in his cheerful image of the pebbles "singing" against Simichidas' sandals (πᾶσα λίθος πταίοισα ποτ' ἀρβυλίδεσσιν ἀείδει, 26). The line is Lycidas' last in this passage, and it ends emphatically with the key word, "sings" (ἀείδει). This word and its cognates occur eight times in the Idyll, but this is the only place where it has a metaphorical meaning. Here, then, where the city-dwellers have left behind their familiar realm, Lycidas is in control. His description in 21—23 sketches in the concrete reality of the place in which they find themselves. His metaphor and the gaiety of line 26 create the first evocation of song in this still "midpoint of the road". From his evocation of song derive, in a sense, the two songs which constitute the centerpiece of the poem; and it is he who first mentions "bucolic song", βουκολικὰ ἀοιδά (49), although the invitation to "bucolicize" originated with Simichidas (36).

The motif of the journey, so central to the poem, has not received the attention it deserves. Encounters "on the road" often have a special significance and a supernatural character. Poets especially are prone to important meetings "on the road": so Thamyris meets the Muses, so Pindar meets Alcmeon (Il. 2, 594—596; Pyth. 8, 56—63). In Theocritus himself there is Poly-

phemus' fateful journey on which he falls passionately in love
(11, 25—27) and the journeys of Hylas and the Dioscuri (Idylls
13 and 22). Theocritus still uses, though indirectly and allusively,
the mythical force of the initiatory passage between worlds, like
Odysseus' in the Apologoi or Priam's in Iliad 24. Beyond that, he
is drawing upon the literary use of movement between city and
country as a means to explore complex relations between culture
and nature which has very deep roots in the Mediterranean cultural
heritage[59]).

A carefully contrived correspondence between beginning and
end of the poem emphasizes the motif of the journey: εἴρπομες
ἐκ πόλιος (2); εἶρφ' ὁδόν (131). This motif gives the poem a dynamic,
linear movement, a feeling of progress toward a fixed goal. But
between "city" of line 2 and Phrasidamus' estate of line 131
stands the "midpoint of the road" (11), the point of encounter
with a strange "road-traveler" (ὁδίτας), who tells them of the
still noon hour and of singing pebbles (21—26).

Though this quality of "traveler" first introduces and defines
Lycidas, he is no ordinary ὁδίτας. He is ἐσθλός (12), "noble," like
Sicelidas and like the songs of Simichidas and the old stock of Cos
(4, 39, 92); and it is "with the Muses' help" that the city-dwellers
meet this traveler (11/12). This phrase, σὺν Μοίσαισι, goes syntacti-
cally with εὕρομες, as Gow takes it (καί τιν' ὁδίταν / ἐσθλὸν σὺν
Μοίσαισι Κυδωνικὸν εὕρομες ἄνδρα, 11/12). Yet its position in the
verse also associates it with Lycidas. On this road he stands in a
special connection with the Muses; and, as Simichidas later says,
he is "dear to the Muses" (95).

That the journey will have a positive outcome is indicated by
Simichidas' invitation (35/36):

ἀλλ' ἄγε δή, ξυνὰ γὰρ ὁδὸς ξυνὰ δὲ καὶ ἀώς,
βουκολιασδώμεσθα · τάχ' ὥτερος ἄλλον ὀνασεῖ.

He is open to what Lycidas' realm may contain and welcomes this
strange figure as one who shares "a common road". Simichidas
himself enters into the "bucolic" realm with the verb which fills

---

[59]) See Kirk (above, note 15) chap. 4, especially 146—149, on
the Gilgamesh Epic: "At all events, in order to make a name, to overcome
death in a modified way, Gilgamesh has to move from culture and the city
into the mountain wilderness ..." (147).

the first half of line 36, "Let us bucolicize". His journey, he says, is "of a harvest festival" (ἁ δ' ὁδὸς ἅδε θαλυσιάς, 31). In this phrase he gives his journey a shape and a direction, and he asserts his own city-linked, agricultural identity over against the herdsman's world at this undefined point between defined realms.

These two realms, Lycidas' and Simichidas', are thus clearly demarcated as separate, but at the same time as open to each other (ξυνὰ ὁδός). The content of the meeting will be primarily the two songs, which expand and clarify the nature of the realm to which each character belongs. As soon as the songs are finished, Lycidas gives his staff (128; cf. 42/43). At once Muses recur (129 and 12). Lycidas then "goes off on his road" (131; cf. 2 and 10); Simichidas and his companions turn off into their sheltered, well tended grove of the Nymphs (131ff). The shade, water, and trees that were only distant evocations of a heroic past at the beginning (6—9) are now tangible realities (135ff).

III.

Idyll 7 contrasts not only city-dweller and rustic, but also herdsman and farmer, pastoral and agricultural rusticity, animal husbandry and the tilling of the earth[60]). This latter contrast was prepared for in the combination of "herdsmen" and "mowers" in lines 28/29 (ἔν τε νομεῦσιν / ἔν τ' ἀματήρεσσι), but it acquires greater importance as the poem progresses. The city-dwellers, Simichidas and his friends, though venturing "out of the city", are still heading for a natural world controlled by human purposes, the well tilled fertile fields over which Demeter presides. Their road is that of the Harvest Festival (31) where their companions are making offerings to "rich-robed Demeter" (32), for she "filled their threshing floors with fat measure" (πίονι μέτρῳ 33). When they reach the scene of "fat" summer (θέρεος μάλα πίονος, 143) and drink "by the altar of Demeter of the threshing floor" (155), they are safely ensconced within the very heart of agricultural bounty and order. In between, on the "common road" shared with Lycidas,

---

[60]) Most interpreters fail to distinguish the types of rusticity involved in the poem: so Wilamowitz 137 („echt ländliches Naturgefühl"); Monteil 103 ("Cette poésie des nourritures terrestres imprègne finalement, du premier vers jusqu'au dernier, la pièce toute entiére"); Legrand, Étude 412.

they are exposed to a less controlled, more mysterious aspect of
the country. As the scene at the altar at the end (155—157) embodies
the very essence of agricultural rusticity, so Lycidas at the be-
ginning embodies the very essence of pastoral rusticity (15—16):

ἐκ μὲν γὰρ λασίοιο δασύτριχος εἶχε τράγοιο
κνακὸν δέρμ' ὤμοισι νέας ταμίσοιο ποτόσδον.

His "smell of fresh rennet" contrasts sharply with the "smell of
fat summer" emphasized near the end of the poem (143):

πάντ' ὦσδεν θέρεος μάλα πίονος, ὦσδε δ' ὀπώρας.

His "old peplos", drawn tight by a broad belt (17—18) is quite
different from the "rich peplos" which the grain goddess wears
(εὐπέπλῳ Δαμάτερι, 32). Even the "rennet" (τάμισος, 16) of which
he smells belongs purely to pastoral rusticity. It is not a vegetable
substance, like fig juice, but, according to the scholion on Nicander's
Theriaca 77, an enzyme obtained from the stomachs of the herds-
man's own beasts.

Smell, as Marcel Detienne has recently re-emphasized, played
a far larger and more significant role in Greek mythological and
religious thought than we usually attribute to it[61]). The contrasting
odors of Lycidas in 16 and of the enclosed farmstead and its fruits
in 143 articulate one of the basic antitheses of the Idyll. That
aspect of the ἀγρός which is close to the harsh remoteness of nature
and involves the rearing and killing of the animals which supply
this τάμισος contrasts with the aspect of the ἀγρός which gives its
fruits more willingly, gently, with less violence. The first realm
stands under the protection of Pan, ambiguous deity of the wild
and the mountains, who has no place in the πόλις. The second
stands under Demeter, more adaptable to the πόλις and its civilized
manners.

These contrasting scents also adumbrate the deeper contrast
between φύσις and νόμος alluded to above. Though both Lycidas'
realm and the farm of Phrasidamus belong to "nature", Lycidas'
world retains its independence from the city-world and therewith

---

[61]) M. Detienne, Les jardins d'Adonis (Paris 1972). For further details
on τάμισος see Gow ad 7, 16.

a certain otherness, mystery, and even potential violence (cf. Id. 1, 16—18); Demeter's realm, which does not require animal substances or the killing of animals, is more adaptable to city ways. Lycidas' pastoral ἀγρός, therefore, stands in a closer relation to φύσις; Demeter's agricultural ἀγρός is more easily included within νόμος.

The setting of the Harvest Festival implies the plain, or at least the rolling hills suitable for wheatfields and orchards. But Lycidas is a man of the mountains. "On the mountains" he fashioned the song he sings (51); "among the mountains" he pastures his "lovely goats" (87). These mountains in Theocritus often stand at the border between myth and reality. Such are the distant mountains from which Hermes comes to Daphnis (1, 77), the mountains on which the wild beasts dwell (1, 115), and where Pan lives (123 ff). The Goatherd of Idyll 3 pastures his flock on the mountain (3, 2), but it is also "among the mountains" that Adonis inflamed with love "the beautiful Cythereia" (3, 46). The Cyclops falls in love when he accompanies Galatea "to pluck hyacinth leaves from the mountain" (11, 26—27; cf. Sappho 105a, 105c L-P). The mountainous setting is also prominent in the Dionysiac celebration which Pentheus fatally violates (26, 2 and 26). In the Epitaphios Bionis Chelidon sings her lament "among the broad mountains" (Ps.-Moschus 3, 39).

We may recall here too the role that the mountain-dwelling herdsman plays in Greek myth and tragedy. It is such a figure — shepherd or goatherd or, like Anchises in the Homeric Hymn to Aphrodite, cowherd who meets goddess or nymph in uninhabited places (cf. Boucolion in Iliad 6, 22—26). In tragedy such a figure often discovers the foundling and thereby brings the remote, but heavy and disruptive past into the stable life of the city. Commenting on such myths, Kirk has recently remarked, "... It is nearly always a shepherd or goatherd who finds an exposed child, because they are the people most likely to be roaming around in the deserted uplands and least likely to be deterred by the cultural inhibitions of the city"[62]. This simple fact of experience may have helped give herdsmen and their mountainous domain an added dimension of literary significance. Commentators have often noted that the opening of Theocritus' Fourth Idyll echoes

---

[62] Kirk (above, note 15) 190.

the fateful meeting between Oedipus and the ποιμήν in Sophocles
(O. T. 1039/40; cf. also 1026—29).

Although "the common road" unites plain and mountain for
a moment (35), the sharing of these two realms is never complete.
Simichidas remains a figure of "velléités pseudopastorales", in
Legrand's apt phrase[63]). When he speaks of "mountains", there
is always a certain incongruity or wishfulness. The Nymphs "taught
him as he was herding cattle on the mountains", he says (92).
He is imitating not only Hesiod, but also Lycidas who spoke of
"herding lovely goats on the mountains" in 87. For Lycidas the
mountain is a place of "work", whether with poetry (ἐν ὄρει τὸ
μελύδριον ἐξεπόνασα, 51) or with goats (87). Simichidas, alluding
perhaps to the Pindaric (and Sophistic) antithesis between φύσις
and διδαχή, ingenium and ars, to which he referred in 47/48, did not
"work" at his song on the mountain, but had it as the "teaching"
of the Nymphs (92). (The Nymphs' "teaching", of course, implies
the opposite of the "learning" which Pindar scornfully opposes to
φύα in O. 2, 86—88.) Simichidas' κἠμέ, "me too", emphasizes the
derivative and artificial quality of his expression (compare his
similar καὶ γὰρ ἐγώ, 37). Furthermore, he has replaced "goats" by
"cows", thereby moving himself up a notch in the bucolic hierarchy.
Perhaps he also reveals his incongruity with a pastoral setting in
another way too, for cows, though possible on mountains, are less
appropriate there than Lycidas' goats or Hesiod's sheep[64]).

Immediately after envisaging himself as a Nymph-taught
cowherd, Simichidas boasts that "report carried his songs to the

---

[63]) Legrand, Étude 152. Cf. Giangrande 511 and 532.

[64]) None of the genuine Theocritean pieces have a cowherd in the
mountains, although mountains appear in Daphnis' lament in Id. 1, 76, 115,
123. Cf. ps.-Theocr. 20, 30 and 34/35 and 8, 1/2 (in the latter sheep and cows
occur together on the mountains). Theocritus' phrase, "herding cattle on
the mountains", found literary imitators: cf. Giangrande, 511 with note 49.
Outside of bucolic poetry, there is of course, Anchises who herds his cattle
on Mt. Ida in the Homeric Hymn to Aphrodite. For the incongruity of the
phrase in Simichidas' mouth see Legrand, REA 47 (1945) 218; Gow, CQ 34.
48; Cataudella 165/66. It would intensify the incongruity even further if
line 92, like lines 47/48, contained a Pindaric echo, namely an allusion to
Pyth. 3, 89/90. Here Cadmus and Peleus hear the "Muses singing on the
mountain" (χρυσαμπύκων μελπομενᾶν ἐν ὄρει Μοισᾶν ... ἄϊον) as the token
of the highest happiness that a human life may encompass (βροτῶν ὄλβον
ὑπέρτατον, Pyth. 3, 88/89).

throne of Zeus" (93). This lofty claim clashes violently with the pastoral image of 92. If "Zeus" alludes to Ptolemy Philadelphus, Simichidas is juxtaposing the circle of courtiers at Alexandria with herdsmen and mountains[65]). Such an incongruity would not only play humorously on the pastoral fiction, but would also emphasize how far the character Simichidas stands from the bucolic world. Simichidas is artificial and condescending when he pictures himself as a neatherd-poet[66]). Lycidas is content to regard his work as "a little song" (μελύδριον, 51). He has no need to take it beyond the realm of the "mountain" where he fashioned it.

When Simichidas alludes to mountains again, it is in his curse on Pan, the herdsman's god, and the mountains are in far off Thrace (111): εἴης δ' Ἠδωνῶν μὲν ὤρεσι χείματι μέσσῳ. His third and last mention of mountains comes when he is settled in his farmer's world. There he alludes to the grotesque, mythical "shepherd", (ποιμένα, 151), "the strong Polyphemus who pelted ships with mountains" (152): τὸν κρατερὸν Πολύφαμον, ὃς ὤρεσι νᾶας ἔβαλλε. Here he is in the realm of Homeric myth, and his tale is not especially flattering to herdsmen (see infra, section VI).

The very first words of the true rustic — and the first words of dialogue in the Idyll — call attention to the incongruity of Simichidas' appearance in the country. Lycidas convicts Simichidas of pseudo-rusticity on three counts. First, he remarks that Simichidas is out in the midday heat (21—23)[67]). Second, he teases him about going to a "townsman's winepress" (24/25), as if Simichidas were still enclosed in his city-world (τινος ἀστῶν, 24). If Giangrande's interpretation of the insult is correct, namely that Lycidas is

---

[65]) The identification Zeus = Ptolemy is accepted by most recent interpreters (see Gow and Monteil ad loc.), but rejected by Puelma 153, note 29, by Williams 143, note 2, and by R. J. Cholmeley, The Idylls of Theocritus (London 1919) ad loc.

[66]) Legrand, REG 64 (1951) 375/76 remarked, "Je suis frappé avec la condescendance avec laquelle Simichidas, qui vient d'être traité en citadin égaré sur les routes aux heures les plus chaudes de la journée, accepte de feindre que les Nymphes lui ont enseigné bien des chants pendant qu'il gardait les vaches dans les montagnes (v. 92)". The scholiast ad loc. finds a touch of ironical condescension to the goatherd in the fact that Simichidas replaces "Muses" with "Nymphs".

[67]) Cf. Id. 12, 8/9, where the idea of seeking shade when walking on a road at the hot hours is made part of a simile: σκιερὴν δ' ὑπὸ φηγόν / ἠελίου φρύγοντος ὁδοιπόρος ἔδραμον ὥς τις.

humorously comparing Simichidas to a farm-worker employed for the harvest[68]), the humor still lies in an incongruity between city and country identities. Third, Lycidas' lovely lines about the pebbles singing against Simichidas' sandals (25/26) calls attention to the fact that the latter has shoes, whereas the goatherd, like Battus in Idyll 4 (cf. 4, 56), is naturally unshod[69]).

Simichidas' rusticity is less than skin deep. Whereas Lycidas gives particular details of the country scene (21—26) and is totally in harmony with his setting, Simichidas trails a larger social world behind him (cf. 4—7). Lycidas stands alone as an individual. Even in his song his herdsmen friends are present at a purely private gathering (71/72). Simichidas, on the other hand, refers three times to a wider context of public opinion (27, 37/38, 93). He tends to place himself against a background of society and its judgments and to assert his personal opinion against these. In both 27—31 and 37—40 he establishes this contrast between what "all say" and what he thinks "in (his) own mind". The expressions are closely parallel: φαντί τυ πάντες ... καίτοι κατ' ἐμὸν νόον ἰσοφαρίζειν / ἔλπομαι (27, 30/31); κἠμὲ λέγοντι πάντες ἀοιδὸν ἄριστον· ... / οὐ γάρ πω κατ' ἐμὸν νόον οὔτε ... νίκημι (37—40). Simichidas carries with him even into the country the opinions of his urban society. As the necessary complement to that social consciousness, he brings with him also the city-dweller's compulsive need to assert his individuality.

Lycidas, on the other hand, reveals himself as he is, with no such need for self-assertion. His being is far more unified: "He was a goatherd, nor could any one have mistaken him when he saw him, since he was excellently like a goatherd" (13/14).

Though mysterious, Lycidas has a directness and a simplicity lacking in his companion. Simichidas is cordial and generous (27—36), but he cannot help mingling praise of himself with his praise of Lycidas (27—31). Even the language in which Simichidas disclaims special preeminence hints at an agonistic, competitive spirit (cf. ἰσοφαρίζειν, 30; νίκημι, 40; ἐρίσδω, 41). Nor can we be entirely sure that his "express purpose" (cf. ἐπίταδες, 42) in praising Lycidas is not to lull him into a false sense of security, while he expects to dazzle him with his own display of poetic talent (91 ff)[70].

---

[68]) See Giangrande 504/05.

[69]) See Cataudella 164/65.

[70]) See Gow ad 42; Kühn 70/71.

Whereas Lycidas modestly hopes that his song will "please" his friend (ἀρέσκει, 50), Simichidas introduces his song with an elaborate hyperbole (93) and Homeric talk of "honoring" his companion (γεραίρειν, 94)[71].

Simichidas is ready to enjoy a little taste of country life, but he does not want to dirty his hands in the process[72]. In meeting the archetypal herdsman, he gets more than he bargained for: goatskins, the smell of τάμισος, pastoral mythology (71—89). Through the sharpness of this contrast and through the wit and humor accompanying it Theocritus selfconsciously explores the ambiguity of his own bucolic poetry. He reflects upon the very pastoral metaphor in which this and related Idylls are based, i. e. the juxtaposition of simple rustics and the utmost literary sophistication. This contrast between form and content lays bare the paradox that the desire for the country is bred by the extremes of urbanity. The humor and irony allow Theocritus to reach toward the country and utilize it as a symbolical source of spiritual refreshment on the one hand while still marking out the reality of his distance from it on the other hand.

IV.

If it is surprising to find Simichidas ponderously challenging a goatherd to "bucolicize" (36)[73] and learning from Nymphs as he pastures cows on the mountains, it is no less striking that the goatherd, whose rough and malodorous dress receives such painstaking description, should sing one of the most delicate songs in all bucolic poetry, a refined composition full of sentiment and nostalgia[74]. The characters in Lycidas' song, Tityrus, Daphnis, Comatas, are figures from the bucolic fictions of other Idylls (cf. 1, 3, 5)[75]. Occupying the space between country and city, Idyll 7 elegantly focuses upon the nature of the bucolic fiction in general. At the same time its world of pastoral fantasy is transfigured by

---

[71]) See Iliad 7, 321; Odyssey 14, 437 and 441.

[72]) Giangrande 532.

[73]) Kühn 69 observes the strangeness of βουκολιασδώμεσθα in Simichidas' mouth.

[74]) See Kühn 62/63; Ott 170.

[75]) Cf. also "Lycopas the neatherd" of Id. 5, 62 and Lycidas' friend "from Lycope" in 7, 72. See also note 58 above.

a tone of lofty, pathetic myth. Comatas, for example, is not the prosaic and cantankerous Comatas of Idyll 5, but a divine singer. Here again Lycidas brings to the city-realm of Simichidas not just bucolic rusticity, but that rusticity distilled to a concentrated, mythic essence.

By their very nature the songs of the two protagonists push the discrepancy between rusticity and urbanity, simplicity and artificiality, to its furthest point, for their styles are as polished as the most demanding of city poets could wish. Scarcely any other place in the Idylls offers so prolonged and dense a display of erudition[76]). Both singers, despite their difference of subjects, display this erudition equally. The verb which the goatherd uses to describe his song, ἐκπονεῖν (51), has associations elsewhere with the artistic finish in which Hellenistic poets took pride[77]).

Van Groningen has claimed that Simichidas' erudition is less relevant and more self-conscious than Lycidas', the mark of a less experienced poet[78]). Lawall has remarked a somewhat lower tone in Simichidas' song: he begins with sneezes and ends with spitting; in between he alludes to guts, bones, flanks and shoulders, nails and skin[79]). These details point to a real difference between a higher and lower style. Lycidas' tone is loftier[80]), for he is reaching for higher themes, and he is in touch with the mysteries of pastoral myths that pass Simichidas by.

On the other hand, the narrative framework and dialogue which surround the songs do not permit us to generalize this contrast between high and low tones. Lycidas, for example, has the only fully developed simile in the first third of the poem (45—

---

[76]) Legrand, Bucoliques grecs 5. Cholmeley (above, note 65) observes ad 111ff. that "Such recondite allusions are remarkably rare in Theocritus". Simichidas' lines on the Erotes in 115—117 present the closest parallel to the refinement of the Hellenistic epigram: cf. A. P. 12, 166 (Asclepiades) and 12, 45 (Posidippus), although Lycidas' lines on the Halcyons are a close second: cf. A. P. 9, 271 (Apollonidas). See in general Lasserre 312ff., 319.

[77]) See A. P. 4, 1, 4 (Meleager); 7, 11 = 942 Gow-Page: Callimachus Epigr. 6 Pf. = 1293 Gow-Page; cf. also A. P. 6, 61; 9, 200; 12, 257 = 4724 Gow-Page; Thucyd. 3, 38, 2.

[78]) Van Groningen 78.

[79]) Lawall 97/98. There are guts in 99, bones in 102, flanks and shoulders in 107, nails and skin in 109/10. See also Kühn 55—57 and Ott, 157, note 435.

[80]) See Ott, 157, note 435; Kühn 51.

48); yet he is also capable of direct, straightforward observation
(21—25) and a simple, lean style (e. g. 42/43, 50/51). Conversely,
Simichidas, while he disclaims the high skill attributed to him
(27—41), can also make extravagant claims in extravagant language
(91—95). The alternation of high and low styles in Simichidas runs
parallel to the alternation of bragging and modesty, inflation and
self-deprecation, which also characterizes him. His boastfulness
in 91—95 balances his modesty and self-effacement before Lycidas
in his first speech (27—31). The balance is strengthened by the
fact that both passages begin with the same phrase in the same
metrical position: Λυκίδα φίλε (27 and 91). And if one seeks for
loftiness of language and elaborate similes, Simichidas' enthusiasm
over the wine in 149—155 outdoes Lycidas' indignation over
Homerid mountain-building poets in 45—48. Hence one cannot
divide the two figures neatly in terms of an antithesis of high
versus low styles, somewhat after the antithesis of Corydon and
Battus in Idyll 4. Here in 7 the two positions overlap.

The most widely accepted view of the two songs is that they
reflect an antithesis between subjectivity and objectivity, passion
and coolness, or, in Lawall's words, "romance and reality"[81]).
On this view the differences between Simichidas and Lycidas are
analogous to those between Corydon and Battus in 4, Milo and
Bucaeus in 10, and, as I have suggested elsewhere, between Thyrsis
and Daphnis in 1[82]). Lycidas' song is full of a beautiful lyricism,
but also full of unreality. Simichidas' song is closer to reality, but
is in large part clever play. Theocritus as the poet who controls
both characters brings the two sides together in his narrative
framework of a "common road", meeting place of rustic and urban
worlds[83]).

This dramatic, objective portrayal of the two opposing
personalities in the no-man's-land of the road depicts the tensions
within which bucolic poetry exists. Without the opposite pole of
the city, the simplicity of the rustic setting loses its charm. That
urban pole is implicit in the sophisticated language of the Idylls
even when it makes no actual appearance in the content. Dealing

---

[81]) Lawall 101. See in general Kühn 48—64.

[82]) See the essay cited above, note 52; also my remarks in Ramus 1
(1972) 7.

[83]) See Ott 158/59, 171—173; Kühn 64.

in archetypal bucolic mythology, Lycidas brings Simichidas into contact with remote pastoral myths which would not otherwise impinge on his urban existence. At the same time Simichidas does not lose his city existence. Over against Lycidas' pastoral themes he asserts his own urban themes in an urban setting. Each figure presents himself as what he basically is. Out of the encounter are born a broad tolerance of the limits of both the bucolic and the urban and a healthy irony which can cut through the pretensions and hold in humorous balance the discrepancies and improbabilities inherent in the genre itself.

The two songs, though presenting different attitudes toward love, both seek to achieve emotional tranquillity and equilibrium. As Lawall puts it, "The one is overwhelmed by desire, the other calmly rational, but their ultimate wishes are the same, peace and quiet"[84]). Both songs move from violence to rest, and both end in images of calm[85]). Lycidas moves from the disturbed ocean and the fire of love to a quiet banquet and then from the myth of a herdsman who dies of love to a goatherd saved from death. His last vignette pictures himself enjoying Comatas' sweet song as Comatas "reclines beneath oaks or pines" (88/89). Simichidas moves from Aratus' love for a boy and violent curses upon Pan to talk of ἀσυχία and an old woman who will "keep away what is not good" (126/27). Here, as in other Idylls — notably 2, 11, 30 — the achievement of peace out of passion is a major theme[86]).

There are, however, different levels of calm achieved. The contrast between a sentimentally inclined lyricism and an ironical realism may not necessarily be the controlling factor in the contrast between the two songs, nor is Simichidas, with his realism, necessarily superior to Lycidas, with his imaginative lyricism. It is true that Simichidas mentions "calm", ἀσυχία, explicitly (126/27):

---

[84]) Lawall 101.

[85]) See Ott 155/56; Serrao 59—61.

[86]) See Anne Brooke, Arethusa 4 (1971) 73—81; N. Spofford, AJP 90 (1969) 34/35; E. B. Holtsmark, TAPA 97 (1966) 253—259 (all à propos of Id. 11). Cf. also Phanocles frag. 1, lines 3—4 (Powell) on the grieving Orpheus, where hesychia is used of the serenity of mind that a tormented lover lacks; here too there is a quasi-pastoral setting of "shady groves":

πολλάκι δὲ σκιεροῖσιν ἐν ἄλσεσιν ἕζετ' ἀείδων
ὃν πόθον, οὐδ' ἦν οἱ θυμὸς ἐν ἡσυχίη.

Cf. also Asclepiades' epigram, A. P. 12, 166, 2.

ἄμμιν δ' ἀσυχία τε μέλοι, γραία τε παρείη
ἄτις ἐπιφθύζοισα τὰ μὴ καλὰ νόσφιν ἐρύκοι.

Serrao has laid great stress on these lines and considers them "probably the most important verses of the entire poem"[87]). If the first third of the poem develops a concept of truth, ἀλάθεια, these lines, he argues, reveal "another concept, no less important than the first, that of ἀσυχία". Theocritus presents "in poetical terms the 'ideal of the sage' as it was theoretically conceived in the Hellenistic philosophies"[88]), but now that ideal can be realized through song and poetry. Such a view, however, isolates a part at the expense of the whole. Simichidas' single word, ἀσυχία, should not obscure the movement from passion to calm which occurs also in Lycidas' song.

Ott, rather more precise than Serrao, describes Simichidas' song as moving from "spiritual unrest to an image of spiritual peace" (,,von seelischer Unruhe zu einem Bild seelischer Ruhe")[89]). This "spiritual peace", he suggests, is capable of realization and, unlike Lycidas' conclusion, is not a mere wish. If one examines Simichidas' lines closely, however, there is not very much that is "seelisch" or spiritual about his calm. He and his friend are to concern themselves with ἀσυχία, true. But they are to make use also of magic and superstition, the spitting of this old hag (ἐπιφθύ-ζοισα, 127). These urban sophisticates descend to the level of the superstitious goatherd of Idyll 3, 31, the uncouth Polyphemus of 6, 39/40, and the desperate Simaetha of 2, 90/91. Whatever "spirituality" the generalizing ἀσυχία evokes is undercut by the antirational, superstitious reliance on the old woman's spit.

The analogy between Simichidas' ἀσυχία and the calm at the end of Idyll 2 is quite misleading. That poem eventually relinquishes magic for nature, inner for outer space, enclosedness for expansiveness. It moves from the circling iynx of passion to the broad circling movements in the night sky (2, 165/66)[90]). Simichidas' movement, however, is back into magic. His curse on Philinus (121) implies

---

[87]) Serrao, 67.

[88]) Loc. cit.

[89]) Ott 172.

[90]) For this aspect of Id. 2 see my essay, Simaetha and the Iynx Theocritus, Idyll II), in QUCC 15 (1973) 32—43.

a regression into violent emotions and passion. The parallel of
language and situation between this curse and Simaetha's plight
in Idyll 2, 83 and 88—90 suggests that Philinus' beauty will
disappear because he wastes away with unrequited love (cf. also
Id. 4, 15f). Hence Simichidas' calm is purchased at the cost of
another's unhappy passion. The familiar situation of the desperately
unhappy, suffering lover is still present near the end of his song[91]).

The curse on Philinus is characteristic of Simichidas' approach
to ἀσυχία, for he achieves calm in largely negative ways. He curses
Pan if he fails to bring aid (106—114) and exhorts Aratus "not
to wait at the doors" (122). This negative tendency extends also
to the way in which he speaks of "the beautiful", τὸ καλόν. Philinus
is to lose "the lovely flower" (τὸ καλὸν ἄνθος) of his beauty (121),
and the old woman will keep away "what is not beautiful" (τὰ
μὴ καλά). Lycidas, by contrast, began with "a beautiful voyage"
(καλὸς πλόος, 52) and ended by finding beauty even in his every-
day surroundings, his "beautiful goats" (τὰς καλὰς αἶγας, 87)[92]).
He utters not a curse, but a blessing: "May all things be pro-
pitious", he had wished Ageanax (ὥρια πάντα γένοιτο, 63; cf. ἔτος
ὥριον, 85). His song is full of images of sweetness (81/82, 89). It
is true that he prays for distant and impossible events and ends
with a contrary-to-fact wish that Comatas were alive to sing
(86—89). Yet Simichidas too ends in wishes, more immediate and
not impossible of fulfilment, to be sure, but still shading off into
superstition and magic.

The level of Lycidas' wishfulness is, in fact, higher and far more
positive and creative than Simichidas'. Ending with the supreme
peace of bucolic song (86—89), Lycidas, far more than Simichidas,
points to the ideal of what bucolic poetry can bestow. In reality,
his song is more "seelisch" than Simichidas'. The conclusion of
his song comes closer to the advice proferred by Theocritus himself
in his own person: the use of poetry as the remedy against passion
(Id. 11, 1—6, 17—18, 81/82).

---

[91]) Serrao 64—66 regards Simichidas' song as ending in the success
of his prayer: a supposed change in Philinus from the παῖς καλός to a mature
man. This view, though ingeniously argued, does not follow easily from the
text.

[92]) In the narrative frame, however, Simichidas does praise τὸ καλόν
in a more positive way; cf. the "dear lovely Amyntas" of 132.

Although concerned with his own love affairs to a greater degree than Simichidas, Lycidas has actually achieved a much greater distance from passion through poetry. In his fine lines on the calm waves he comes closer to the calm sought and finally achieved in Idyll 2, where the sea at rest symbolizes a peace lacking in the soul of the girl (2, 38/39 and cf. 163). Although "burned" or "roasted" by "warm love" (55/56), Lycidas can conjure up an image of a fire of another kind, the fire by which he reclines in contentment and tranquillity (πῦρ, twice in the same line, 60). This scene of Lycidas' imaginary banquet has close affinities with the peaceful symposia of an ideal happiness sketched by Xenophanes, Aristophanes, and Plato[93]). His passion here is quiet, controlled by the mental functions of memory (69) and song (71ff.). Even the "remembering" is gentle: πίομαι μαλακῶς μεμναμένος Ἀγεάνακτος, (69), if the adverb can be taken with "remembering" as well as with "drinking"[94]).

In this delight in memory Lycidas approaches the calm of the Epicurean philosopher. For Epicurus memory is an important and valid spiritual pleasure which outweighs the short-lived physical pleasures and provides a consolation to pain and suffering[95]). The philosophical "ideal of the sage" which Serrao invoked to describe Simichidas[96]) appears here as in fact far more appropriate

---

[93]) Xenophanes, frag. 1 and 22; Aristoph. Pax 1131ff.; Plato, Repub. 2, 372 b—c. See Gow ad 7, 66, 67. The following parallels are especially close: Id. 7, 66 and Xenophan. frag. 22; Id. 7, 67 and Xenophan. frag. 1, 11; Id. 7, 66—68 and Plato, Repub. 2, 372b 5 6:

Theocr.: πὰρ πυρὶ κεκλιμένος, κύαμον δέ τις ἐν πυρὶ φρύξεῖ.

χἀ στιβὰς ἐσσεῖται πεπυκασμένα ἔστ' ἐπὶ πᾶχυν
κνύζᾳ τ' ἀσφοδέλῳ τε πολυγνάμπτῳ τε σελίνῳ.

Plato: κατακλινέντες ἐπὶ στιβάδων ἐστρωμένων μίλακί τε καὶ μυρρίναις.

[94]) Gow ad 7, 69 notes the connection of μαλακῶς with sleeping, sitting, and lying. Yet the word is used of songs or enchantments (cf. μαλακαὶ ἐπαοιδαί, Pindar, Pyth. 3, 51), of friendly disposition (cf. μαλακὰ φρονέων, Pindar, N. 4, 95 and cf. Ol. 2, 90, Pyth. 1, 98), of a "tender look" (Aristoph. Plut. 1022). It is also used of language, music, character (often in a pejorative sense), docility.

[95]) See especially Epicurus' deathbed letter to Idomeneus in which he opposes to his present sufferings τὸ κατὰ ψυχὴν χαῖρον ἐπὶ τῇ τῶν γεγονότων ἡμῖν διαλογισμῶν μνήμῃ (D. L. 10, 22 = frag. 138 Usener). See also D. L. 10, 137 = frag. 452 Us. and Plutarch, Non posse suaviter vivi sec. Epic. 18, 1099 d = frag. 436 Us. On the Epicurean affinities of Theocritus see Rosenmeyer 42—44, 54/55, 69—70, 81/82.

[96]) See above, note 88.

to Lycidas. We may recall here also the "calm" of Lycidas' smile early in the poem (ἀτρέμας εἶπε σεσαρώς, 19)[97]).

The first song which Lycidas quotes, that of Daphnis, ends as a victory of love (cf. ἠράσσατο, 73). But the passion of love is itself presented in a remote, elegiac tone where nature's sympathy consoles the lover. Here too song of a sort — the θρῆνος (74) of the oaks — answers and calms the wildness of passion.

It is with the victory of poetry over death and with the wish for the revival of the dead poet that Lycidas ends. The address to Comatas in 83—89 closely parallels in its form Simichidas' address to the Erotes and the subsequent prayer against Philinus in 115—121. In each case there is a second-person address — ὦ μακαριστὲ Κομᾶτα, 83; ὔμμες ... / ὦ ... Ἔρωτες (115—117) — which devotes three lines to the attributes of the addressee (83—85; 115—117). Then there comes a wish or prayer in four lines (86—89, 118—121). The parallelism helps to underline the differences. Lycidas addresses a mythical herdsman-singer for an impossible wish which concerns only himself (note the first-person pronouns and verbs in 86—89). Simichidas addresses the conventional figures of the Erotes to curse another. With this idealized pastoral scene Lycidas ends; Simichidas goes on to an urban setting of house doors, palestra, cold, hard paving stones, and the bit of social realism in the old hag and superstitious practices[98]).

Lycidas' song does not merely embody a fanciful unreality over against Simichidas' hard-headed clarity. It reaches beyond ordinary experience and brings to bear upon the passion and suffering of love a poetic reality which transcends the limits of the ordinary. Hence it presents a way of dealing with passion without violence or aggression. Through the magic of poetry, mythology, and that mysterious calm which he possesses from his first appearance (19; cf. 69), Lycidas sets his love into a larger setting. Thereby he not only masters his passion, but gives it a new beauty and delicacy. His entire song exemplifies the capacity of art to transcend immediate circumstances, to extend present life into timeless myth.

Seeking to emphasize Lycidas' wishfulness, Kühn remarks that he makes only one reference to the present, and that in a

----

[97]) Of this "calm smile" Puelma 150 remarks, „Es bezeichnet die Haltung ruhiger Selbstsicherheit und Gelöstheit, wie sie bei Homer vor allem Göttern und Helden im Kampfe eignet".

[98]) See Kühn 63.

statement of his subjection to love, line 56: θερμὸς γὰρ ἔρως αὐτῷ με καταίθει[99]). There are, however, three other instances in which Lycidas uses the present tense; and in each case he is describing phenomena of the natural world: the constellations (διώκῃ, ἴσχει, 53/54)[100]), the winds (κινεῖ, 58), the oaks that grow by the banks of the Himera river (φύοντι, 75). His song, then, is anchored also in a larger world, namely the external reality of nature. It is more than „die confessio eines schwärmerisch-begeisterten Herzens", as Kühn considers it[101]).

Nor is all Lycidas' bent toward a vague, dreamily felt future. He can speak with confidence of the waves' calm and the sea (57): χάλκυόνες στορεσεῦντι τὰ κύματα τάν τε θάλασσαν ... He thus brings into this urban-agricultural world the vastness and the potential serenity of nature[102]). Hence he, far more than Simichidas, points toward a remote, ideal realm in which poetry can heal the passion-vexed soul. The actual "seelisch" element in the poem lies with him. Simichidas, whose origins are in the city, is closer to "reality", but this reality remains earth-bound. It is Lycidas who gives a hint, fleeting and elusive, of what the world might be if transfigured by poetry.

Theocritus has placed Simichidas' song second, for one cannot dwell long in the realm of a Lycidas, with his stars, halcyons, and Nereids (53—60). The urban, practical, ironical world is there to answer it and to assert its harsher, more strident voice. Whether or not he is actually Apollo in disguise, Lycidas brings a divine dimension into human experience. Such contact is necessarily momentary, even dream-like. It is enough to have joined with him for a moment "on the mountains" where one "hears the voice of divine Comatas" (87—89).

Journeys, to say nothing of sea journeys, are beyond the grasp of most rustics. We may compare Battus' reaction to Aegon's Olympian trip at the beginning of Idyll 4. But Lycidas, in the very first line of his song, mentions a journey over the sea (42) which in

---

[99]) Ibid. 52.

[100]) The mss. vary between indicative and subjunctive in line 54. Gow prints the indicative (ἴσχει) in both his Cambridge and Oxford editions.

[101]) Kühn 52.

[102]) Compare the marine setting of Id. 11, 14, αὐτὸς ἐπ' ἀϊόνος κατετάκετο φυκιοέσσας, with Id. 7, 58/59. Note too the connection between sea and passion in 2, 38/39.

turn sets his song's tone of expansive reaching outward. His connection with the life of the sea, so strange in a goatherd from the mountains, is an important element in a complex of motifs which compose this symbol-character. The voyage of which he sings continues the motif of the journey, with its mythological overtones, from the narrative framework at the beginning of the Idyll. At the same time his associations with the sea are in keeping with the mystery and suggestiveness that the sea conveys throughout the Idylls[103]).

Simichidas, by contrast, begins with the Erotes, scarcely anthropomorphic figures drawn from conventional Alexandrian topoi and containing little plastic, mythic power. He has the city man's distance from divine powers. His allusions to Pan are learned and literary (103, 106ff.)[104]), and he teases the god with playfully exaggerated threats (note the marked κν- alliteration in 110). There is a humorous incongruity in the fact that this urbane figure should compare his love to the love of goats for the spring (97) and should dwell at length on Arcadian rites involving Pan (106—108). The only way, in fact, in which Simichidas can approach Lycidas' pastoral realm is through irony and mock aggressiveness. Whereas Lycidas would "pasture (ἐνόμευον) his lovely goats on the mountains, hearing the voice" of "sweetly singing Comatas" (87—89), Simichidas threatens Pan with "pasturing" (νομεύοις) among the "furthest Ethiopians" (113—114). The first instance of "pasturing" implies union with a far-off beauty, the second contains ironical sophistication and mockery.

Simichidas' address to Pan is symptomatic of an attitude toward nature which contrasts with Lycidas'. Lycidas knows of a harmony between man and nature. He sings of nature's sympathetic response to human emotions: the calm sea of 57—60, the weeping oaks, lamenting mountain, and melting snows of 74—76, the saving bees of 80—85[105]). Simichidas, on the other hand, sings of constraining nature: he would have Pan whipped to punish nature's

---

[103]) See especially Idylls 2; 6; 11. See Brooke 74 and Holtsmark 256/57 (both in note 86, above).

[104]) The scholiast ad 103 suggests that Simichidas invokes Pan as a pederast god. But this aspect of Pan is rare (cf. Lasserre p. 318 with note 19), and nothing in Theocritus' text supports this view. See also Kühn 53; Pfeiffer ad. Callimach. frag. 689.

[105]) Kühn 52 suggests that Lycidas subordinates the reality of nature

stinginess (107—108)[106]). He evokes here an image of dearth in the herds (ὅτε κρέα τυτθὰ παρείη, 108), which contrasts strikingly with the bounty of nature both in the bees which feed Comatas (80—85) and in the Thalysia itself. Lycidas sang of distant mountains and snow, but even they exemplify sympathy between man and nature (76/77). Simichidas sings of snow and distant places, but his purpose is to threaten the pastoral god with these extreme points of north and south, barren places where nothing grows (111—114). Of the two springs with a "sweet stream" (ἁδὺ . . . νᾶμα) which he mentions in the next line (115), one at least is associated with an unhappy and incestuous love, a flagrant violation of the natural order (Byblis, 115).

Not only does Lycidas present the natural world as embracing human life in a large, sympathetic frame, but he also conveys the autonomous power and mystery of natural processes. He knows of the connection between the stars and the sea and between the sea and the winds. He is keenly aware of the movement of the seasons (53/54), when the sea is calm (57/58), when the snows melt on the mountains (76). He speaks of sprigs and grasses, trees and rivers (44, 68, 74/75), as well as remote constellations and mountains. He builds his song upon a rich sensitivity to the mythology of nature: the halcyons, the Nereids, the "pathetic fallacy" of oaks lamenting Daphnis. At the same time he reveals nature's intimate life and its violence: the "deepest sea weed" (ἔσχατα φυκία, 58), the prey on which the halcyons feed (ὅσοις τέ περ ἐξ ἁλὸς ἄγρα, 60). The verbs with which he describes the movements of nature convey this feeling for its dynamic forces: διώκη (53), στορεσεῦντι (57), κινεῖ (58), φύοντι (75).

The natural world of Simichidas' song is distant and static, a matter of literary convention and learned allusions. His only references to the processes of nature are negative: the shortage of

to the power of love. From Theocritus' text it is at least equally likely that Lycidas understands and calms the passion of love by setting it into the larger framework of nature. In any case Kühn does not take account of Lycidas' description in 22/23 and his metaphor of the sprig in 44. For this healing function of nature see also Id. 2, 147/48 and 163—66.

[106]) Kühn, following up his view of the pederastic Pan (see above, note 104) suggests that he is „die Verkörperung der vitalen Naturkraft selbst" (53). Lines 106ff., however, associate him with that "vital power of nature" in its retrograde movement.

meat (108), presumably because of the flocks' failure to increase, and the wasting away of Philinus' "bloom" (ἄνθος, 121). Philinus is to become "riper than a pear" (120). Here the cycle of growth is downward, to decay and loss of sexual attractiveness or potency. This negative overripeness contrasts with the positive ripeness (where a species of pear is also involved) at the Thalysia (143—146)[107].

When not checked by irony, Simichidas' world is demarcated by the small, human-scaled limits of the city dweller, like the rooster which crows at dawn (123/24). Lycidas, however, grasps tensions whereby he creates a far richer picture of nature. He combines both a mythical and a scientific view of natural phenomena. He can both regard nature as process and also assimilate nature to human emotion. Thus he mentions the star calendar, the winds, the sea-weed on the one hand (53—55, 58), and the Nereids and "pathetic fallacy" on the other (59, 74—76).

Lycidas' song contains still another tension of opposites, that between the enclosed, tranquil inner world of his feast, where he "remembers" Ageanax (61—70) and the external, mythologized world of constellations, halcyons, Nereids, and potentially violent winds and sea (52—60). Theocritus emphasizes this balance by a formal device. The first lines of each passage echo one another in close verbal parallels:

Ἔσσεται Ἀγεάνακτι καλὸς πλόος ἐς Μιτυλήναν (52).

Ἀγεάνακτι πλόον διζημένῳ ἐς Μιτυλήναν (61).

Further, if we exclude the initial line or lines wishing Ageanax a good journey (i. e. lines 52 and 61/62), there are exactly eight lines of description in each passage (53—60, 63—70).

Even this indoor scene contains a sympathetic correspondence between man and nature, for here are flowers in abundance (62/63) and a deep coverlet of fragrant grasses and herbs (67/68). The richness here prepares for and balances the richness of the outdoor scene of the Thalysia later, a point to which we shall return.

This movement between outer and inner worlds, between the violence of sea and remoteness of the stars on the one hand and the

---

[107]) Maas' emendation μαλαπίοιο in 120 would make an even more pointed contrast with the scene of the Thalysia: cf. μᾶλα, 144.

safe, comfortable interior where Lycidas "remembers" on the other hand, is essential for grasping what Lycidas means. Even in his song of love he retains the mythical removal and calm which he possessed at the Idyll's beginning[108]). At moments he may seem akin to the "sentimental" figures of other Idylls, one who emerges from his inner subjective world of myth and dream for a moment and then loses himself in it again. But his affinities with a Battus or a Bucaeus are superficial. In fact he possesses an inward calm which is both stable and deep. With this calm, whether or not due to his divinity or quasi-divinity, he can embrace a vast range of nature's phenomena in the outside world; yet he can also repose in a private chamber to dwell upon love (69) and share in song with friends (71 ff).

The antithesis between sentimentality and realism, then, explains only a small part of Lycidas. He is also a symbol of what the bucolic world has to confer on the city poet: an expansive, mythologized nature, a feeling of sympathy between man's emotional life and nature's processes, a tranquil private world of gentle sentiment shared in a society of fellow-singers amid the rich gifts of nature which are yet cherished in an imagined setting, a realm of the mind (63/64, 67/68). And all this is permeated with a sense of divinity and a feeling of open access to mythic power. Divinity is present at the Thalysia too (155—157). Lycidas is the pastoral equivalent, "on the mountains" (cf. 87), of the agricultural harvest-festival celebrated on the plain.

With the musings of his song and the earthiness of his dress and pursuits, Lycidas mediates between this remote, private, inward enjoyment of nature's bounty and the more matter-of-fact, more tangible city world of Simichidas. The result is the public celebration of nature's generosity, the Thalysia which ends the poem. It is right for Lycidas to disappear at this point (130/31), for he has no place in that public and agricultural setting. Yet his open and expansive view of nature is the mythic and private prerequisite of that public celebration. It is what the city poet needs to experience on his "journey" if he would transcend the limitations of urban realism and become a part of the country, the ἄγρος, with all that it may hold. Simichidas does not abandon the

---

[108]) From this point of view Williams' identification of Lycidas with Apollo is attractive.

plains for the mountains, nor is this ever a possibility for him. But he at least hears of the magical herdsmen who sang "on the mountains" (51, 87); and he can fancy, albeit in a spirit of half-joking imitation and rivalry, being instructed in song there himself (92/93).

V.

The end of Simichidas' song and the return to the narrative frame — that is, the return to the "road" or journey — is carefully demarcated. The phrase τόσσ' ἐφάμαν (128) echoes χὢ μὲν τόσσ' εἰπών (90) at the end of the first song. The gift of the goatherd's crook (128/29) formally closes the interlude of the songs (cf. 43), and Lycidas' "sweet laughter" now recurs (42, 128). The expression, "as before" (ὡς πάρος, 129) makes the repetition even more evident. The Muses (129) recall not only the scene of the challenge (37), but also the first sight of Lycidas (12). Correspondingly Lycidas turns off and "goes along his road toward Pyxae" (τὰν ἐπὶ Πύξας / εἶρφ' ὁδόν, 130/31). This phrase not only concludes the "road" motif (ὁδός, ὁδίτας, in 10, 11, 31, 35), but also completes the journey "from the city" (εἴρπομες ἐκ πόλιος, 2). The journey from city to country is now accomplished, and with it Simichidas' "initiation" into the realm of rustic singers. Hence the gift of the goatherd's crook.

Yet the matter is not quite so simple, for the poem goes on for another thirty lines with a rich and brilliant ekphrasis of rustic exuberance, the Harvest Festival, for which the opening scene has prepared us (3, 31—34). This description requires close attention if we are to grasp the implications of Simichidas' "initiation" by a songful goatherd.

This final scene (132—157) presents a tamer world than Lycidas'. It is an agricultural, not a pastoral setting. The presiding deity is Demeter, not Pan (155; cf. 106 ff, 31—34). Lycidas' departure in 130/31 marks the end of Simichidas' contact with the foreign, remote, mythical element. His encounter with Lycidas, as Lawall has noted, appears as a purely private experience. Eucritus and Amyntas, his traveling companions, are never brought into contact with the goatherd[109]). When Lycidas departs,

---

[109]) See Lawall 80.

Eucritus, Amyntas, and Phrasidamus forthwith reappear: "He turned off to the right and went along on the road toward Pyxae, but I and Eucritus and my handsome Amyntas headed off to Phrasidamus' farm ..." (130—132). The proper names, following in the very same line as Lycidas' disappearance (131), not only hark back to the narrative frame of the beginning (1—4), but also bring back the specific Coan reality. Thus they remind us of the narrator's place in a society, his ties with a community, a πόλις, Eucritus and Amyntas being, presumably, his friends from the πόλις (cf. 2).

The celebration of the Thalysia has both a public aspect and a tangibility, a concrete rootedness in the fertility of nature, lacking in the private feast of Lycidas (63ff.). As opposed to Lycidas' mountain realm, with its archetypal myths of death and rebirth (73—89), the world of the Thalysia is sheltered, enclosed, unambiguously fruitful. Nature here appears in terms of its usefulness to man, as a nurturer of human life. The smell is not of acrid enzymes obtained from slaughtered animals (the τάμισος of 16), but of "the rich harvest time" (143; cf. 16, 33).

The presiding deity, Demeter, is a civilizing power. Everywhere the mark of man, taming and using, is evident. There are vine shoots, newly cut (134); pears, apples, and plums — cultivated as well as wild fruit. The wine has been aged for four years in casks (147). These details all attest to human order imposed upon nature, to conservation and planning.

After the longing for absent lovers, the public festival returns us to the practical workaday world, somewhat as in Idyll 10 or Virgil's second Eclogue[110]). After the sea, which Theocritus often associates with what is distant and unreachable, we come to the land, indeed to the very essence of stable and settled life on the land. The midday hour (21) was the moment for a mysterious meeting with an alien figure. Then birds and insects slept. Now we return from the mysterious to the normal, from Pan's heavy hour to a gentler time of day. Noon sleep passes, and those skylarks and insects which "did not wander" before (23) wake up and sing (141). So in the tenth Idyll the waking of the skylark calls the mowers

---

[110]) See Ecl. 2, 10—13, 66—72, and Eleanor Leach, Nature and Art in Vergil's Second Eclogue, AJP 87 (1966) 442—445. Mrs. Leach's suggestion, however, that "In Alexandrian pastoral the natural world is completely absorbed into art" (444) greatly oversimplifies the situation of the Idylls.

from their midday sleep (50/51) and leads into the ensuing contrasts between "love" and "work", ἔρως and μόχθος (10, 56/57).

Through the Thalysia at the end, as through Milo's invocation to Demeter in Idyll 10, 41ff., Theocritus indicates that his poetry does not exist within its own enclosed realm only. It has a place within a larger context of reality: the cycles of nature, productive work, settledness on the land, and the cosmic and social orders which these processes presuppose and in turn support. On the level of style and genre, the purely bucolic elements are balanced by Hesiodic, georgic reminiscences. On the socio-economic plane the (relatively) free and unbound life of the herdsman contrasts with the settled, agrarian wealth of a Phrasidamus, who, with his brother Antigenes, seems to belong to an ancient landed aristocracy on Cos (3—7). Of Simichidas' origins we are told virtually nothing, save that his roots are in the city (2) and therefore he can learn from both aspects of the country, the bucolic and the Hesiodic. But Simichidas still appears against a social background, whether a πόλις or a community of well-to-do landowners. He holds down a human, social reality over against the supernatural, mysterious reality to which Lycidas points.

The lushness and order in the scene of the Thalysia may be read as a symbol of the joyousness, exuberance, harmony between man and the cosmos from which the highest art can flow. A mysterious goatherd may compose his songs "on the mountain", but a singer "from the city" will have to find his place in a human environment, closer to the senses and to the life-processes. The relation between man and nature symbolized by Demeter is predictable, tangible, productive rather than imaginative or emotional. It is also tougher, for the winnowing fan at the end is a reminder of hard physical labor.

In Lycidas' world the poet can penetrate the barrier between matter and spirit (74—89), like Orpheus in Virgil's Sixth Eclogue or Daphnis in the First Idyll (cf. 1, 115—136). No such crossing of boundaries is possible at the Thalysia. Nature is more distant from man, but less mysterious. At the same time she is more regular, more reliably generous. Hence Lycidas cannot be invited to the Harvest Festival. He does not belong in that world, any more than Simichidas belongs in his. Yet it is important for Simichidas, journeying from city to country, to have had converse with Lycidas and to have heard of Daphnis and Comatas.

The feast of Lycidas and the feast of Thalysia share a number
of parallel motifs through which the contrasts between herdsman's
world and farmer's world stand out more sharply[111]). In both
cases the principal figure is accompanied by two or three friends
who remain obscurely in the background: Amyntas and Eucritus
on the one hand, Tityrus and two unnamed shepherds on the other.
Eucritus and Amyntas are, presumably, men of the city. Their
friends, Phrasidamus and Antigenes, are men of the country, but
since they belong to the old stock of Cos (3—7) and are well off,
they move easily among the urban gentry. They are not to be
thought of as simple rustics. Lycidas' friends are all herdsmen, two
explicitly (δύο ποιμένες, 71), the other by implication. In both cases
there is song: bucolic song on the one hand; the Nymphs, water,
and symbols of poetry on the other[112]). Lycidas' feast took place
inside, with grasses and flowers made into garlands or carpets.
His pallet is artificial (67/68). The Thalysia, however, is celebrated
in the open sunlight, amid live, growing plants; and the guests
recline amid the rushes and vine shoots (133/34). The spring,
remote at the beginning (6—9), is now present in its movement
and sound (κατειβόμενον κελάρυζε, 137; cf. 142); and at the same
time its associations with poetry become stronger (cf. διεκρανάσατε
in 154 and κράναν in 6). Lycidas had imagined "reclining" as he
thinks of Ageanax (κεκλιμένος 66), and had pictured a scene of
listening to "divine Comatas" as he "reclined" in a mountainous
setting (κατεκέκλισο, 89). But now Simichidas and his friends
actually "recline" in one of the most concrete and tactile images
of the poem, "in the deep beds of sweet rushes and the newly cut
vine shoots" (132—134):

> ἔν τε βαθείαις
> ἀδείας σχοίνοιο χαμευνίσιν ἐκλίνθημες
> ἔν τε νεοτμάτοισι γεγαθότες οἰναρέοισι.

In this scene they achieve a harmony between nature and civiliza-
tion, natural process and human control. The rushes are, presumably,

---

[111]) Van Groningen 37 compares the two feasts, but only to support
his biographical interpretation of the poem, i. e. the view that "Theocritus"
(= Simichidas) has now surpassed his old master.

[112]) For a watery locus involving nymphs as symbolic of poetry see
in general A. Kambylis, Die Dichterweihe und ihre Symbolik (Heidelberg
1965) 23—30 and 44; also Puelma 156/57 with note 44.

growing wild, whereas the vines are carefully tended for human purposes (νεότματοι, 134)[113]). This harmony is both the basis and the logical concomitant of their joy (γεγαθότες, 134).

Instead of the metaphorical singing of stones (26) Simichidas and his companions hear the actual singing (ἄειδον, 141) of birds. The bees here (142) have nothing supernatural about them (contrast 80—84). The chirrupping cicadas "toil" (ἔχον πόνον 139), but it is a more concrete and less mysterious "toil" than the mountains "toiling about" Daphnis in grief (ἀμφεπονεῖτο, 74). It is also less remote or inward than the poetical "toil" (ἐκπονεῖν) of Lycidas and Comatas on their mountains (51 and 85). There is "laughter" here, but it belongs to the grain goddess, not to the semi-mythical herdsman (cf. ἁδὺ γελάσσας 42 and 128; ἇ δὲ γελάσσαι, 156)[114]). The optative mood in the last passage, "May she laugh ..." (156), implies a clarity about the division between reality and imagination which is not present in the parts of the poem dominated by Lycidas. In all of these details of the Thalysia nature shows its benignity and sympathetic cooperation with human life, but in a far more realistic and far less mythical way than did nature in Lycidas' song. The Thalysia celebrates fertility, but it also makes clear that order and fertility go together. The "alte terminus haerens" between matter and spirit and between man and nature stands as the necessary condition of this exuberant fertility.

The feast at the end presents what seems at first to be a paradoxical inversion of the two chief characters' previous relation to nature. In their songs Lycidas had been in touch with nature's rhythms and processes, whereas Simichidas had sung of an artificial, urban world. Now the real scene out in the open air and sun, amid living grasses and growing vines (132—134) contrasts with the interior, fire-warmed, projected feast of Lycidas (63—70). The previous antitheses have not been cancelled out, but they have been lifted to a vantage point which takes fuller cognizance of the complexity of man's — and art's — position in the world.

---

[113]) Similarly the fruit includes both wild and cultivated varieties: apples (143) and (wild) sloes (146). The pears (ὄχναι, 144) can be either: see Gow ad 7, 120. The βράβιλοι of 146 are probably sloes, i. e. wild, but this is not absolutely certain: see Gow ad loc.

[114]) For other aspects of this echo see my review of Lawall in CJ 63 (1967/68) 228.

The antitheses so far generated in the poem may be expressed in diagrammatic form:

LYCIDAS	SIMICHIDAS
Country	City
Herding	Agriculture
Mountains	Plain
Muses	Nymphs (42)
Wish	Reality
Mystery of Nature (imaginative harmony between man and nature expressed through pastoral myths, 74—85)	Tangible fertility of nature (physical harmony between man and nature in terms of productivity: grain, fruit, wine, etc.)
Pan	Demeter
Feast indoors, by the fire	Feast outside, by the altar of Demeter (155)
Imagined or future "reclining" (66, 89) (inside)	Actual "reclining" in deep rushes (132/33) (outside)

VI.

The symbolical locus amoenus at the end does not entirely resolve these antitheses. In fact, a new and disturbing element enters at the culmination of the feast, when a cask of four-year-old wine is broached (147). Addressing "the Castalian Nymphs who hold the Parnassian height", Simichidas asks if this is the wine that Chiron gave to Heracles or "the nectar that persuaded the shepherd by the Anapus, strong Polyphemus who hurled stones at the ships, to dance in his sheepfold" (149—153). The address to "Castalian Nymphs" suggests not only poetry, but a higher level of poetry. As Delphi's divinities, they introduce an international and universal note above the local happenings on Cos. These Nymphs can claim a far wider celebrity than such as might frequent the little Burina spring. "Castalian Nymphs" (148) also contrast with the unnamed Nymphs whose water refreshes the grove of the Thalysia in 137 (Νυμφᾶν ἐξ ἄντροιο). The "stony cave" (κατὰ λάινον ἄντρον, 149) of Pholus contrasts with the actual "cave" in this local setting (137). There is thus a double contrast: one between myth and present reality, and one between epic and bucolic tones.

The myths of Heracles, Pholus, and Polyphemus alluded to
in these lines, though pastoral in setting, reveal a more violent
side of pastoral mythology. They also sharpen the larger antithesis
of νόμος and φύσις behind the bucolic contrast of city and country,
for Centaurs and Cyclopes are the two orders of creatures that
throughout Greek art and literature most fully embody the world
of φύσις in its ambiguous and potentially dangerous, anarchic
aspects[115]). It is interesting that precisely these two ambiguous sets
of beings occur when the passage between city and country is
almost over and when the travelers seem snugly ensconced in a
totally protected corner of the country. Pholus and the Cyclops
are a reminder, however faint, that the realm of φύσις has other
faces to show.

The caves and mountains involved in these closing myths of
Simichidas are more ominous than those in Lycidas' world. Pholus
is, to be sure, a "good" Centaur, like Chiron; but his invitation
to Heracles resulted in the drunkenness of the Centaurs, as a result
of which this hero slaughters them in battle[116]). "Strong Poly-
phemus" appears not in the light and humorous bucolic guise of
Idylls 6 and 11, but as the uncouth, dangerous monster of epic.
His "casting rocks at the ships" (152) recalls Odyssey 9, 481/82:

$$\tilde{\eta}\varkappa\epsilon\ \delta'\ \dot{\alpha}\pi o\rho\rho\dot{\eta}\xi\alpha\varsigma\ \varkappa o\rho\upsilon\phi\dot{\eta}\nu\ \ddot{o}\rho\epsilon o\varsigma\ \mu\epsilon\gamma\dot{\alpha}\lambda o\iota o,$$
$$\varkappa\dot{\alpha}\delta\ \delta'\ \ddot{\epsilon}\beta\alpha\lambda\epsilon\ \pi\rho o\pi\dot{\alpha}\rho o\iota\vartheta\epsilon\ \nu\epsilon\dot{o}\varsigma\ \varkappa\upsilon\alpha\nu o\pi\rho\dot{\omega}\rho o\iota o\ \ldots$$

The allusions to Heracles and Polyphemus are the only place
where Simichidas recounts myths. Lycidas' myths (73—89) were
purely pastoral and were pervaded by a gentle, if melancholy,
wistfulness. The myths of Simichidas are heroic and violent. And

---

[115]) See Kirk (above, note 15) chap. 4, especially 152—171. Pierre
Vidal-Naquet, Valeurs religieuses et mythiques de la terre et du sacrifice
dans l'Odyssée, Annales E. S. C. 5 (1970) 1285—87. The violence implicit
in Simichidas' myths is neglected by Monteil ad 148—155 (p. 123), who
sees only "un parallèle entre le bonheur sensuel de Simichidas et le bonheur
de deux héros mythologiques, Héraclès et Polyphème, dont le drame
satyrique a popularisé le penchant pour les plaisirs gastronomiques".

[116]) For the myth and its sources see Höfer in Roscher, Ausführliches
Lexicon der griechischen u. römischen Mythologie 3, 2 (Leipzig 1902—09)
2416—23, especially 2423. For a recent discussion of the myth and its
implications see Kirk (above, note 15) 158, 161/62, 170.

yet they occur within a setting of utter peacefulness and benignity. The ripe, abundant fruit comes just before (143—146), the "altar of Demeter of the threshing floor" comes immediately after (155).

Simichidas' mythology, with its different view of the bucolic world, continues at the end the dialectics that pastoral tends to create within itself, from the contrasted rustics of Theocritus and Virgil down to the philosophic, if practical, meditations of Shakespeare's Touchstone[117]).

To the antitheses listed above, therefore, these myths now add a further set of contrasts:

LYCIDAS in 73—85 (bucolic)	SIMICHIDAS in 149—153 (epic)
Myths of pastoral heroes (Daphnis, Comatas)	Myths of epic heroes (Heracles, Cyclops)
Gentleness and melancholy	Violence and drunkenness
Archetypal themes of death and rebirth	Heroic themes of hybris and battle
Myths of singers	Myths of fighters and wanderers

Simichidas' myths have another side. They also evoke a distant, mythical, heroic geography within the framework of a peaceful, local harvest festival on Cos. The drunkenness which plays a large part in both of Simichidas' myths points to the realm beyond normal, every-day experience and brings him a little closer to Lycidas' world. Centaurs and Cyclopes with their mountainous habitats belong more appropriately to Lycidas than to Simichidas' realm. Here, then, is another inversion between the two figures. Lycidas, though he has vanished, has left his staff behind. Is it possible that Simichidas, plainsman though he is, is now the possessor of this symbolical instrument and through it, can be in touch with the mountainous, herdsman's realm from which it came?

---

[117]) "Truly, shepherd, in respect of itself, it is a good life; but in respect that it is a shepherd's life, it is nought. In respect that it is solitary, I like it very well; but in respect that it is private, it is a very vile life. Now in respect it is in the fields, it pleaseth me well; but in respect it is not in the court, it is tedious. As it is a spare life, look you, it fits my humour well; but as there is no more plenty in it, it goes much against my stomach. Hast any philosophy in thee, shepherd?" (As You Like It, 3, 2, 11ff.).

Simichidas' safe ensconcement in his lush grove, his reclining
in the deep rushes (132/33) when the "journey" is over, mark the
city poet's acceptance of his limitations. He cannot enter the
goatherd's mysterious sympathy with nature. He has his own
equivalent in the fertile agricultural realm where Demeter is
celebrated. At the same time this rustic realm of productive work
and fertility is not all calm and simplicity. There is the address
to remote mountain nymphs at Delphi and the violent mythical
events in mountainous places (149—153). Through these elements
Theocritus restates at a deeper level the tension and ambivalence
of his bucolic poetry. Mountain mythology and mountain nymphs
point, like Lycidas himself, to something beyond safe georgic
enclosure.

The "Castalian Nymphs holding the Parnassian height" (148)
have always troubled commentators[118]). In Greek poetry, unlike
Latin, they are not identified with the Muses or with poetry gene-
rally. Yet they seem to have a place in a grove associated with
springs and poetry, and the language suggests the invocations
to the Muses in Homer and Hesiod[119]). Lines 100—101 may suggest
a solution. Simichidas there joined together Apollo and the Delphian
shrine: (Ἄριστις) . . . ὃν οὐδέ κεν αὐτὸς ἀείδειν / Φοῖβος σὺν φόρμιγγι
παρὰ τριπόδεσσι μεγαίροι. The phrase παρὰ τριπόδεσσι makes clear
the precise localization at Delphi. The reference is surely to musical
contests at the Pythian festival[120]). If this is so, then that association
of Delphi and music may be relevant also to the Castalian Nymphs
at 148. This association, in turn, juxtaposes a rustic singing match
on Cos with a grand musical contest at a great Panhellenic festival,
song on the plain with song on the "Parnassian height", simple
harvest feast and grandiose Delphic celebration. For this antithesis
between a Panhellenic contest and a rustic competition there is a

---

[118]) For example, Monteil ad 148: "On comprend mal l'appel au
témoinage des Nymphes si l'on n'admet point (v. 92) leur assimilation
implicite aux Muses". See also Wilamowitz 136, note 3.

[119]) Iliad 2, 484; Hesiod, Theog. 1—2 and 25. See Puelma, 156, note 37.
Cholmeley (above, note 65, ad 150 accepts Wilamowitz' view of the
Castalian Nymphs here as being merely "queen of all fountains, and therefore
the source of all fountains", but he also calls attention to the Pindaric
associations of fountains, water, and poetry: e. g. Isth. 6, 62—64, 74—76.

[120]) See Gow ad 7, 101. Compare Pindar, Pae. 6, 5—18. We may call
attention again to the Pindaric echo of line 42. Idyll 24 is sufficient testimony
to Theocritus' keen interest in Pindar (cf. Nem. 1).

close parallel in Battus' disparagement of Aegon's departure for Olympia in Idyll 4 (4, 5—12). Here too Theocritus exploits a contrast between distant, international celebration and a local festival, for the Olympian celebration is balanced by the South Italian celebration at the shrine of Hera Lacinia (4, 33—37). This hint of an unequal comparison between Delphi and Cos, rustic "bucolicizing" (36) and professional competition, is also part of the pervasive dichotomy between great and small, Homeric heroes and Coan rustics, throughout the poem. The discrepancy, as noted earlier, is the poet's way of ironically masking the seriousness of his themes with an ostensibly trivial and humble exterior.

Here at the end Theocritus not only juxtaposes high and low styles, but combines descriptive realism with mythical narrative. Possibly he is hinting at another kind of relevance for Hesiod and another level of importance for the Hesiodic "Dichterweihe". The description of the grove and the rustic exuberance of Demeter suggest the georgic poetry of the Works and Days[121]. Hesiodic didactic poetry began to enjoy a new vogue in Hellenistic times, as the works of Aratus and Nicander indicate. On the other hand, the mythological references, like the allusions to meeting Nymphs and pasturing on the mountains in 87 ff. and 91 ff. suggest the Hesiod of the Theogony, the poet of the high style in touch with cosmogonic myth and heroic legend. Theocritus is exploiting an antithesis present in Hesiod himself, farmer and shepherd, agrarian didacticism and encounters with goddesses on a mountain. Hence the poem's insistent counterpoint between Homeric grandeur and bucolic leanness (see especially 45—49) is enriched by a counterpoint between bucolic and Hesiodic rusticity and between two aspects of Hesiodic poetry, the mythic and the agrarian, the mountain and the plain.

The last lines of the Idyll convey an image both of fixity and of sensuous concreteness. Simichidas would "fix his great winnowing

---

[121]) The image of nature in Hesiod's agrarian poetry, of course, has nothing even remotely "pastoral" (in the Theocritean sense) about it, and is quite remote from the easy abundance of Theocritus' grove. The point has been well made again by C. R. Beye, The Rhythm of Hesiod's Works and Days, HSCP 76 (1972) 33; see also L. A. Stella's sensitive discussion, Esiodo poeta georgico? PP 4 (1949) 201—216. On the distinction between the Hesiodic and the "idyllic" elements in the bucolic tradition see Rosenmeyer 20—29.

fan in (Demeter's) heap", while she is to "laugh" and hold "sheaves
and poppies in both hands" (155—157):

$$
\begin{array}{l}
\text{ἇς ἐπὶ σωρῷ} \\
\text{αὖτις ἐγὼ πάξαιμι μέγα πτύον, ἃ δὲ γελάσσαι} \\
\text{δράγματα καὶ μάκωνας ἐν ἀμφοτέραισιν ἔχοισα.}
\end{array}
$$

The goddess' firm grasping of the grain itself in the poem's last line
(157) ánchors the elusiveness and mystery of a Lycidas in a gesture
of solidity with a fruitful, tangible present. "Fastening" the
winnowing fan is another image of fixity and calm. It seems to
complete the journey from movement to calm reflected in the
structure of the poem as a whole and in each of the two songs.
In Demeter's fertile presence we regain the mysterious "calm"
of Lycidas' smile (19), just as Demeter's "laughter" continues the
mysterious laughter of Lycidas (42, 128, 156).

The gesture of planting the winnowing fan inevitably recalls
the end of another journey, that of Homer's Odysseus. The allusion
to the Odyssey is all the more likely here in 156 because of the
adaptation of Odyssey 9, 481—2 just five lines before (152). In
Odyssey 11, 121—137 Teiresias tells Odysseus that his journeys will
end when he meets "another traveler", ἄλλος ὁδίτης (127), who
mistakes his oar for a winnowing fan. The hero must "plant in the
earth" (γαίη πήξας) his oar and sacrifice to Poseidon. Then he will
return home, and death "will come, mild, far from the sea"[122]).
Lycidas had sung of a journey over water. The winnowing fan in
the grain-heap of this land goddess seems to return us definitively
to the known and the finite, to a more familiar, rooted, and less
fantastic natural world. This movement from fantasy to natural,
orderly process corresponds to the change from Lycidas' sea and
its green Nereids (57—60) to "the sacred water" of kindly Nymphs
(136/37). Simichidas, like Odysseus, does not belong in the world
of marine mythology. The Harvest Festival, with its earthy pro-
ductivity, is his Ithaca. He plays Odysseus to the Calypso-like
allurements of Lycidas' imagination. Like Odysseus, he must
return from the fantasy-world of a Comatas or a Daphnis and

---

[122]) Odyssey 11, 126—137 = 23, 267—284. It is an old problem whether
ἐξ ἁλός in 11, 134 means "from the sea" or "away from the sea", i. e. "far
from the sea", but the context suggests that the latter view is probably
the correct one.

their mountains (bucolic equivalents, perhaps, to an Ogygia or a Scheria) to the Coan plain. Like Odysseus too, he will plant a winnowing fan to mark the end of travel.

Yet an element of mystery remains, even in this peaceful and fertile grove. The "sacred water" bubbles forth from a cave (137), and soon after come the Centaur Pholus' "stony cave" (149) and hints of the Cyclops' cave (153/54). These last two passages, as noted above, suggest violence and point back toward Odyssean, heroic myth. The fastening of the winnowing fan also contrasts with the movement and activity within the grove itself. This setting is hardly static. Not only does water "bubble forth" (137), but the trees move violently in the wind (135)[123]), the cicadas "toil" (139), bees "flit about" (142), and fruit "rolls down" (ἐκυλίν-δετο, 145).

Most important of all, the verbs, "fix" and "laugh" (πάξαιμι, γελάσσαι, 156) are optatives and express a wish, albeit one capable of fulfilment (cf. 86—89, 125—127). The optative mood contrasts with the descriptive imperfects used of the actual grove (135—147) and with the past tenses in the references to the Nymphs and the wine immediately before (148—154). The grove and the wine belong to an actual reality, enjoyed and captured as part of an historical past. Yet the poem ends not with the real, historical moment, but with a wish, a wish which involves "fastening" and "holding" (156, 157). Staticity, therefore, does indeed close the poem, but it is still a desiderated ideal, not a solidly attained fact. Thus the entire dialogue between reality and imagination, like that between real and mythical loci, remains open. Odyssean reminiscence in a Thalysian grove encapsulates the poem's tension between concrete sensual richness in the present moment and extension toward what is distant, ungraspable, imaginary.

Theocritus faces, but does not resolve the problem of whether the myths and the idealized images of bucolic, and perhaps of all, poetry are an evasion of reality or an intensification and clarification of reality, whether such poetry merely expresses longing for an unattainable and unreal peace and calm or whether it halts the flux of the every-day particulars so that an underlying "fixity" —

---

[123]) The verb in 135, δονέοντο, especially emphasizes the violence. It echoes the violent storms in two similes of the Iliad: 12, 156—158 and 17, 55/56.

a stable, eternal, but usually hidden truth — can emerge. In any
case it seems that for Simichidas, both in his song (cf. 126) and in
his last words of narrative, "calm" ἀσυχία and fixity constitute
something to be wished for rather than something fully attained[124]).
Lycidas, for all his wishfulness, seems to have his calm as a part
of his very being (cf. 19). But he is not a permanent inhabitant of
Simichidas' world.

VII.

Precisely because movement and rest are so important in
the poem and because journey is one of the Idyll's central symbols,
the locus and its atmosphere form the point around which crystalize
the polarities of imagination and reality, inner and outer worlds.
To make this tension as powerful as possible, Theocritus creates
a narrative frame in a real place with (presumably) real people.
The opening lines are studded with proper nouns: the names of
Simichidas' friends (Eucritus, Amyntas, Phrasidamus, Antigenes,
Lycopeus), the names of places on Cos (Haleis, the Burina spring),
the names of remote figures of Coan legend (Clytia, Chalco). Here
Theocritus gives the actual social and geographical environment
of his poetry. With Lycidas' entrance he will give its inward and
mythical "environment".

As opposed to this local and factual Coan world, the songs deal
with distant, literary places (cf. 76, 103, 111—116) or, in the case
of Lycidas' song, with nameless mountains (74, 87), meadow (80),
or sea (57, 60). Lycidas, it is true, refers to places on Cos also (46,
72)[125]). But these local references are swallowed up in the remote
and mythical setting of constellations, Nereids, Sicily, Thrace
(53—60, 75—77). At least one of the shepherds at his banquet is

---

[124]) See the interesting remarks of Serrao 68: "Ma l'idealizzazione
del mondo pastorale portava inevitabilmente all' evasione dalla realtà:
può essere paradigmatico il caso di Licida e Simichida i quali, per raggiungere
la hasychia, sono costretti ad immaginare, l'uno che Ageanatte sia stato
con lui compiacente, l'altro che Filino sia diventato improvvisamente brutto.
Difatti il genere bucolico fu soprattutto poesia di evasione." Serrao, however,
neglects the calm that Lycidas possesses by his very nature and the images
of tranquillity in his song even before his final wish (cf. 86—89).

[125]) For the problems of identifying Ptelea in 65 and Acharne in 71
see Gow ad locc.

from the Coan Lycope (72) and thus may have some connection with Lycopeus (4), father of one of Simichidas' friends[126]). His wine too may be Coan (65). Yet the location of this banquet remains as vague and mysterious as the "day" on which it will be celebrated (62). Its affinities, as noted earlier, are with the idealized symposia of the literary tradition. Hence it stands off as an interior realm, a "soulscape", or, better, "wishscape", sharply distinguished from the immediate Coan geography and even from the external reality of Ageanax' voyage to Mytilene.

Simichidas and Lycidas embody very different relationships to place. The opening lines not only pinpoint Simichidas within specific, highly particularized geographical and social coordinates; they also define exactly the nature of his journey. It has a precise beginning and a precise end: "from the city" (line 2) and "to the Haleis" (line 1). No such spatial or social relations define Lycidas. He is a "Cydonian man" (12), but scholars are still arguing about which of the three or four different Cydonias is meant[127]). More important, the poem gives no clear starting point or destination for Lycidas' journey. At the end of the encounter he "turns off to the left on the road toward Pyxae" (ἐπ' ἀριστερὰ τὰν ἐπὶ Πύξας / εἶρφ' ὁδόν, 130f.). The road, but not necessarily Lycidas, goes to Pyxae. We are left with a description of the road he takes, not his actual goal[128]). Whereas Simichidas arrives at his destination and settles down, in the deep grass, Lycidas is last seen "on the road" (εἶρφ' ὁδόν 131), i. e. in the same condition of journeying and passage as he, along with Simichidas and his friends, was at the beginning (cf. εἴρπομες, 2; ὁδόν, 11). Lycidas is free of the fixity and definiteness of place which define Simichidas. His is a mysterious, non-purposive movement from his vague "mountains" (51, 87) along this "road". He is simply a part of the countryside, moving in it, but not within clearly defined points or between set limits, like those of city and farm for Simichidas.

---

[126]) See Wilamowitz 138.

[127]) For the identification of Cydone see Gow ad 12. Most scholars now agree on Crete, but there is no absolute certainty, nor was Theocritus necessarily concerned with providing any. See, however, Williams 139/40.

[128]) See Kühn 69ff. Gow ad 7, 29 would make Lycidas' journey a little more purposive in suggesting that he was called in to help in the harvest, but nothing in the text actually supports this view and the description of 13—19 is rather against it.

Naturally we should not push these or similar distinctions too far[129]). Yet it is valid to see in Lycidas' undefined geography and lack of stated goal a quality of freedom of imagination and poetry which inhabit their own autonomous realm. The nature of Lycidas' movement across Simichidas' "road" embodies something of what Kühn calls "the freedom of an unbound poet-existence" („die Freiheit ungebundenen Dichterdaseins")[130]). Without ties, restrictions, or responsibilities, Lycidas is also the embodiment of bucolic freedom par excellence[131]).

The "real" Theocritus — that is, the poet who shaped both Simichidas and Lycidas and their confrontation in the poetic construct that is Idyll 7 — lives in both realms, both in the world of human relationships and real places and in the timeless world of the spirit, of symbol and myth. The two realms are brought together and in part reconciled in the setting of the Thalysia at the end. This place has a firm physical existence: the river Haleis and the owner, Phrasidamus, are its coordinates: but it is touched by the imaginative, mythical aura of Lycidas' placeless realm. Not only is it an actual farm on Cos, but it becomes transmuted into a symbolical locus amoenus, a magical grove where Nymphs and Demeter are present, where song pours forth from the spring and the trees (136—142). The real spring of Burina (6) and the spring of the grove (136/37, 142) blend with a metaphorical "spring" of wine from which Nymphs profer their intoxicating nectar (διεχρανά-σατε, 154; cf. χράνα, 6). This beverage is so splendid that it too reaches back to the realm of myth and demands a mythical ge-nealogy, like the scepter of Agamemnon or the cup of Nestor in the Iliad (cf. 149—154). Although the Castalian Nymphs are not

---

[129]) As Kühn 76—79 tends to do. See the criticisms of Lasserre 309.

[130]) Kühn 75.

[131]) On this creation of an autonomous freedom through the pastoral locus see especially Marvell's "The Garden" and what Renato Poggioli calls "the pastoral of the self": Daedalus 88 (1959) 686—699. At the same time one must recognize that this autonomy in Theocritus is only half of an antithesis. Demeter and rustic work prevent his bucolic world from being a place of escape only. Writers in the Christian tradition, like Marvell, draw on images of a prelapsarian Garden of Eden which are not present for the Greek pastoralist: see Poggioli, Harv. Lib. Bull. 11, 150—152. Rosenmeyer devotes a chapter to "Freedom" (98—129), but does not discuss this kind of "freedom". He offers some interesting remarks, however, on pastoral freedom and the autarkeia of the Hellenistic philosophers: 105/06.

Muses (148), they connect the grove with a famous Panhellenic sanctuary far away. The Nymphs' association with "sacred water" throughout the passage sets this locus, as Puelma saw, among "the familiar images of the Muses' springs", like those of Callimachus and Propertius[132]).

This interchange between the specific and the imaginary, place and placelessness, applies also to time. Theocritus' opening lines create a striking and at first baffling fusion of precision and vagueness: ἧς χρόνος ἀνίκ' ἐγών ..., "Once upon a time ..." Wilamowitz noted the fairytale atmosphere of these opening words and their "undefined distance, as if it were a fairy-tale" („eine unbestimmte Ferne ..., als ob es ein Märchen wäre")[133]). Yet he went on to deny that Theocritus intended such an aura of remoteness since the subsequent details made the experience seem so vivid and fresh. Without fully realizing it, Wilamowitz put his finger on a subtle and important ambiguity, a kind of intentional contradiction. The poem's first line suggests a mythical distance which the subsequent details belie.

This blending of imprecision and specificity can now be seen as part of the dialectic between imagination and reality which controls the entire work. The very first lines create this ambivalence[134]). The tone continues a few lines later in the introduction of Lycidas which echoes line 1, ἧς δ' αἰπόλος ... (13).

In the vignette which closes the poem this complex, shifting presentation of place and time seems to be resolved in an image of fixity: πάξαιμι μέγα πτύον (156). Yet, as we have seen, the verb introduces a distant, wishful note into this concrete, past experience. And the very gesture of fixing the winnowing fan harks back, as we have observed, to the mythic exemplar of change and movement, Odysseus, at the point when he is to conclude his long battle with the sea and its mystery.

Simichidas' desire to "fasten his great winnowing fan" is a gesture of kinship and solidarity with the agricultural world and

---

[132]) Puelma 148; cf. also 156 with notes 37/38; Giangrande 519 with note 67 and JHS 88 (1968) 172. See also above, note 112.

[133]) Wilamowitz, 142 with note 1. See also Körte-Händel 216/17.

[134]) Lasserre 324 remarks that the meeting described in the poem is situated "dans l'histoire, à une date que la formule initiale ... fixe d'une manière volontairement imprécise et cependant réelle". See also Gow, CQ 34, 52.

with the social and cosmic order behind it. Yet the gesture does
not entirely close off the elusive Lycidan realm, for it recalls myths
of distant, fabulous voyaging. The wish for the grain-goddess'
laughter in the same line and in the same optative construction
(ἃ δὲ γελάσσαι, 156) confirms Simichidas' arrival in the land's
concrete, workaday reality, with its regularity, settledness, and
rewards of bountiful productivity. Yet that laughter also conceals,
through an unmistakable verbal echo (cf. 42, 128), a reminiscence
of the wandering goatherd's mysterious grin.

Conclusion

The origins of Theocritus' bucolic poetry are shrouded in
mystery[135]). Idyll 7 allows us to glimpse at least some elements
which entered into that creation. Through the figure of Lycidas, as
through the herdsmen of the other bucolic idylls, Theocritus makes
contact with a world which was already becoming increasingly
inaccessible in his time. The herdsman serves as a means for the
poet in the Hellenistic age to find his way back to the potent grip
of myth. In the country he could still feel the sense of awe, the
frisson, produced by the unknown; and yet he could contain those
sentiments through the self-protection of irony and a sophisticated
aesthetic framework.

Some six centuries after Theocritus an anonymous poet was to
announce the death of the gods in language borrowed in part from
the bucolic locus amoenus which Theocritus had so richly elaborated:

εἴπατε τῷ βασιλῆι· χαμαὶ πέσε δαίδαλος αὐλά·
οὐκέτι Φοῖβος ἔχει καλύβαν, οὐ μάντιδα δάφναν,
οὐ παγὰν λαλέουσαν· ἀπέσβετο καὶ λάλον ὕδωρ[136]).

For Theocritus Pan was not yet dead. The search for the living
Pan, "bitter" and dangerous though he might be (Id. 1, 16—18)

---

[135]) See Körte-Händel 219.

[136]) An oracle given to Oribasius at Delphi in the reign of Julian the
Apostate: text in Oxford Book of Greek Verse, no. 627, and the "Appendix
Nova" of the Firmin-Didot Edition of the Epigrammatum Anthologia
Palatina, vol. 3 (Paris 1827) cap. 6, no. 122 (p. 487, with the note ad loc,
p. 543).

was also the search for the vitality of myth and mythic poetry in
an age which no longer took the old myths seriously[137]). Poems like
Idylls 1, 13, or 26 amply testify to the power and fascination which
myth still held for Theocritus. Yet it could not speak to him and
his contemporaries as it had to Greek poets of the past centuries.
He had to find a new medium and a new setting to express the
relation between myth and reality for himself and his time. For
this relation the pastoral framework offered rich expression. It
could contain the beauty, even the majestic and awesome beauty,
of nature, and yet balance them harmoniously against the achieve-
ment of art and the self-assured grace of wit and humor.

The divine too, obviously, had to appear in new garb and a new
setting. In Idyll 7 Theocritus went to the heart of the matter. He
created an encounter between country and city which was in turn
a selfconscious reflection upon the question of myth and reality
posed by the bucolic genre itself. By the typical Hellenistic device
of inset poems within a poem he could play upon the paradoxes of
naiveté and simplicity, factuality and imagination. At the same
time he could lightly finger the trappings of the old myths:
mysterious journeys, strange meetings, divine epiphanies, hopeless
love, death and rebirth, sheltered and beautiful gardens, nymphs
and mountains, centaurs and cyclopes. He created a character so
quintessentially bucolic that around his presence there crystalizes
a summation of the bucolic world.

The differences between two friends meeting by chance on a
country road soon ramify to broader antitheses: φύσις and νόμος,
mountain and plain, Pan and Demeter, passion and playfulness,
local and universal ambitions, rustic excursion and Odyssean
voyage, inner and outer worlds. Theocritus revivifies and trans-
figures the lonely herdsman who appears in earlier Greek literature
in Homer, Hesiod, the Homeric Hymns, and tragedy; though
sparkling with genial humor, he is not entirely divested of his
ancient aura of strange knowledge and his experience of strange
companionships.

---

[137]) See the chapters of Bruno Snell, Art and Play in Callimachus,
and Arcadia: The Discovery of a Spiritual Landscape, in the Discovery
of the Mind (above, note 16), especially 284ff., and my remarks in: Ovid's
Metamorphoses: Greek Myth in Augustan Rome, Studies in Philology
68 (1971) 371—373. I do not, however, accept Snell's implicit assumption
of a decline in energy and a "post philosophical exhaustion" (274).

Contemporary allusion and ancient myth, humor and erudition, sophistication and naiveté, city and country, Cos and Parnassus: Theocritus subtly balances these and related themes against one another to create an extraordinary masterpiece as enjoyable for its surface beauties of sound and sense as for its complex cross-references, analogies, symbolism, and structure. There is doubtless much more that we can only vaguely surmise. The reading offered here will not exhaust these meanings, but hopefully may suggest a framework and a context for their further exploration.

SIMICHIDAS' MODESTY: THEOCRITUS, *IDYLL* 7.44

ὥς ἐφάμαν ἐπίταδες· ὁ δ' αἰπόλος ἁδὺ γελάσσας,
'τάν τοι', ἔφα, 'κορύναν δωρύττομαι, οὕνεκεν ἐσσί
πᾶν ἐπ' ἀλαθείᾳ πεπλασμένον ἐκ Διὸς ἔρνος. *(Id.* 7.42-44)

Of *Idyll* 7.44 Gow remarks, "The phrase has been suspected, and if taken at its face value is certainly odd. If allowance is made however for Lycidas' playful mood and the faded character of both metaphors, it does not seem improbable."[1] The particular phraseology, he suggests, is to be explained by the accompanying gift of the goatherd's crook: "It seems probable that Lycidas' choice of words is connected with his gift, and that he means *I give you my staff, a piece of wood as unblemished as yourself."* The phrase ἐπ' ἀλαθείᾳ could mean merely "really and truly," but more probably goes closely with πεπλασμένον, i.e. "formed for truth," and refers to "the candour with which Simichidas has admitted his inferiority to Asclepiades and Philetas."[2] So much may be regarded as fairly certain. The exact nature and function of Lycidas' "candour" remain to be clarified.

Puelma accepted Gow's interpretation of ἐπ' ἀλαθείᾳ and carried it further. According to Puelma the words carry the connotation, "formed for the true art," "'im Geist, in der Gesinnung der Wahrheit,' d.h. der 'wahren Kunst.'"[3] Lycidas thereby marks out Simichidas as being "'in ehrlicher Gesinnung geformt,'" "ein edler Jünger der 'wahren Kunst.'"[4] This "wahre Kunst" is the λεπτότης of Asclepiades and Philetas whom Simichidas has just praised (39-41), in contrast to the Homeric, mountain-building poetry criticized in his next verses

---

[1] A. S. F. Gow, ed., *Theocritus*[2] (Cambridge 1952) *ad* 7.44.

[2] Loc. cit. Earlier interpreters had been inclined to take ἐπ' ἀλαθείᾳ as "in truth," "really" (= ὡς ἀληθῶς): see C. Hartung, *Philologus* 34 (1876) 603; Th. Roeper, *Philologus* 18 (1862) 191.

[3] Mario Puelma, "Die Dichterbegegnung in Theokrits 'Thalysien,'" *MH* 17 (1960) 160, note 55.

[4] Ibid. 159, 160.

(45-48). Lycidas, then, is taking Callimachus' side in the famous literary quarrel with Apollonius of Rhodes. Theocritus thus is also pronouncing for Callimachus. Puelma's interpretation has one difficulty, namely that the scholion to the proem of the *Aitia* places Asclepiades (= Sicelidas) among the Telchines, i.e. among the detractors of Callimachus and his "lean" style.[5] And an epigram of Asclepiades attests to the fact that he did not share all of Callimachus' views on style *(A. P.* 9.63). Hence both Lohse and Cataudella have rejected Puelma's interpretation.[6] Lohse, however, grants that in line 44 Lycidas recognizes that his companion's last utterance "concerns very serious things which touch his entire artistic existence."[7]

There can be little doubt that lines 39-41 and 45-48 touch upon important literary questions of Theocritus' day. Yet line 44 may also have a more immediate and less exalted meaning than most scholars have seen, a meaning more directly related to the dramatic structure of the *Idyll* and the interplay of character. The strangeness of the language suggests that Lycidas is being ironical. Fritzsche-Hiller long ago observed the "playful expression."[8] In Theocritus playfulness need not exclude seriousness. The problem is what Lycidas is being playful about.

This playfulness, I suggest, lies in the alternation between modesty and boastfulness in the way in which Simichidas presents himself. The irony of Lycidas in 44 is directed against Simichidas' protestations of modesty in the face of the attitude which the preceding discourse has illustrated.

Crucial for understanding Lycidas' irony is the word ἐπίταδες, "on purpose," in 42. Why has Simichidas made his speech "on purpose," and what is the meaning of Lycidas' "sweet laughter" which introduces his reply (42)? For the first

---

[5] Schol. Flor. *ad Aitia* I, proem, vv. 1-12 (Pfeiffer, *Callimachus* [Oxford 1949] vol. 1, p. 3, line 4).

[6] G. Lohse, "Die Kunstauffassung im VII. Idyll Theokrits und das Programm des Kallimachos," *Hermes* 94 (1966) 413-25, especially 420-25 and p. 421, note 1; Q. Cataudella, "Lycidas," *Studi in onore di U. E. Paoli* (Florence 1959) 159-69, especially p. 167 with note 2.

[7] Lohse (preceding note) 421.

[8] A. T. H. Fritzsche and E. Hiller, eds., *Theokrits Gedichte*[3] (Leipzig 1881) *ad* 44 ("ein scherzhafter Ausdruck").

question Gow's explanation is the most probable: Simichidas "seems to mean that his modesty was calculated to induce Lycidas to take part in the friendly exchange of songs suggested at 36."[9] This "modesty," which Gow accepts at face value,[10] is deceptive. It is, I think, the point of one of the sharpest ironies in the poem.

Simichidas' statements, in fact, indicate that he does not believe that he is as poor a singer as he says, that actually he considers himself quite superior to Lycidas. He makes an effort at politeness, however, hoping above all to encourage his friend to sing. Nevertheless his very attempt at politeness contains a trace of condescension and egotistical insensitivity. As F. Williams has observed, the word ἐπίταδες depicts a man "confident of his ability to manipulate the reactions of others."[11]

Nearly all interpreters have neglected a small, but crucial word in Simichidas' protestations of his inferiority to Sicelidas and Philetas, the adverb πω (39-41):

οὐ Δᾶν· οὐ γάρ πω κατ' ἐμὸν νόον οὔτε τὸν ἐσθλόν
Σικελίδαν νίκημι τὸν ἐκ Σάμω οὔτε Φιλίταν
ἀείδων . . .

Eduard Schwartz seems to be the only one who has taken any notice of the word at all, but his interpretation is unsatisfactory. He claimed that it does not mean "not yet," but rather "not at all," on the (quite dubious) analogy of Homeric phraseology.[12] Not only is the alleged Homeric meaning "not at all" uncertain, but there is also the occurrence of this same οὔπω thirty lines

[9] Gow (above, note 1) ad 42. See also J.-H. Kühn, "Die Thalysien Theokrits," Hermes 86 (1958) 70-71, who also notes the contradiction between 37-38 and 90-95, to be discussed infra.

[10] Gow (above, note 1) ad 47f.: "Lycidas commends the modesty with which Simichidas declines to compare himself with Sicelidas or Philetas . . ."

[11] F. Williams, "A Theophany in Theocritus," CQ N.S. 21 (1971) 142. If Williams is right about Lycidas being Apollo in disguise, then the idea of Simichidas boasting before the god of the lyre is even more amusing.

[12] Eduard Schwartz, "Theokrits Daphnis," Nachr. Gött. (1904) 299, note 1, citing the scholion to Iliad 14.143. Gow translates the phrase in 39 by "as yet." The meaning "not at all" (instead of "not yet") for οὔ πω in Homer is far from certain: see Leaf ad Il. 14.143; West ad Hesiod, Theogony, 560; J. E. Fontenrose, AJP 62 (1941) 65-79; contra, W. J. Verdenius, Mnemosyne, ser. 4, vol. 24 (1971) 4, à propos of Theog. 560, with further bibliography.

earlier in the poem, where the meaning is unambiguously "not yet" (10): κοὔπω τὰν μεσάταν ὁδὸν ἄνυμες . . . Hence Simichidas qualifies even his statement of poetic inferiority: he does "not yet conquer" Sicelidas or Philetas.

Through the οὐ . . . πω of 39, the ἐπίταδες of 42, and other touches which will appear later, Theocritus shows his distance from his characters. He does not simply identify with Simichidas, but with an amused removal observes certain of his idiosyncrasies. Simichidas' "modesty" of 37-41 was a pose, assumed "on purpose" to entice Lycidas to sing. But his friend has a little surprise in store for him. He plays along and takes him up on his humility. When he calls him "a sprig formed from Zeus all for truth," he is in effect saying, "Yes, you are quite right: your reputation as the best of singers is, just as you say, undeserved. You are to be congratulated on your absolute (πᾶν) truthfulness." On this view πᾶν also gets its due. Simichidas did not intend to be taken literally at all. The "sweet laughter" (ἁδὺ γελάσσας, 42) which precedes Lycidas' words prepares for the light touch of malice.[13]

The double edge of Lycidas' "truth" in ἐπ' ἀλαθείᾳ πεπλασμένον appears sharper if we remember that the verb πλάττειν commonly connotes falsehood or fiction (LSJ s.v., V). Plato uses πεπλασμένος and ἀλήθεια as *antithetical,* not complementary, terms: μὴ πεπλασμένως ἀλλ' ἀληθῶς φιλόσοφος *(Rep.* 6.485D); μὴ πλασθέντα μῦθον ἀλλ' ἀληθινὸν λόγον *(Tim.* 26 E). Aeschylus uses the same antithesis in *Prometheus* 1030-33, where we may note the implicit equation of πεπλασμένος with a compound of *pseudos* (ψευδηφορεῖν):

> ὡς ὅδ' οὐ πεπλασμένος
> ὁ κόμπος, ἀλλὰ καὶ λίαν εἰρημένος·
> ψευδηγορεῖν γὰρ οὐκ ἐπίσταται στόμα
> τὸ Δῖον . . .

---

[13] H. Kynaston (formerly Snow), ed., *The Idylls and Epigrams of Theocritus*[5] (Oxford 1892) sees irony in 43-44, but understands the lines merely as a compliment to Simichidas. On line 42 he remarks, rather cryptically, "ἐπίταδες, 'purposely' depreciating my own talents. Lycidas was however not to be taken in; his gift of the crook and accompanying words are evidently ironical." It is hard to see what Lycidas is being ironical about, if he is merely complimenting his friend.

There is no good English equivalent to this double meaning, but we may convey something of the paradox and irony if we translate "fictioned for truth."

On the whole Lycidas is friendly, but a witty jibe at a foible is not inconsistent with the amiable character which Theocritus gives him. In stressing the antitheses between Lycidas and Simichidas, Ott has mistakenly made Lycidas out to be "ganz Wohlwollen und Freundlichkeit"[14] and his "sweet laughter" to be "ein freudiges Lachen."[15] For the possibility of a gentle mockery in this laughter, however, there is the parallel with the "sweet laughter" of Aphrodite in *Idyll* 1.95, which also has an ironical edge.[16] Giangrande and F. Williams have recently pointed out other traces of a teasing and playfully malicious character in Lycidas' speeches.[17]

Theocritus need only hint lightly at this aspect of Lycidas, for in the bucolic convention the meeting of two singers is regularly accompanied by an exchange of insults or jibes.[18] In *Idyll* 7, unlike *Idyll 5*, there is a free sharing of songs rather than a formal contest. Yet the eristic element, with its accompanying badinage, remains in the background.[19] It may be implicit in the verb βουκολιασδώμεσθα (36), which probably suggests competition.[20]

Two details prepare us for a more acrid discourse between the two figures: first, there is Lycidas' smell (16), which connects him with a goatherd as earthy and contentious as Comatas in

[14] Ulrich Ott, *Die Kunst des Gegensatzes in Theokrits Hirtengedichten*, Spudasmata 22 (Hildesheim 1969) 169.

[15] Ibid. 169, note 463.

[16] For the interpretation of *Idyll* 1.95 see G. Zuntz, *CQ* N.S. 10 (1960) 37-40; R. Ogilvie, *JHS* 82 (1962) 107.

[17] Giuseppe Giangrande, "Théocrite, Simichidas, et les *Thalysies*," AC 37 (1968) 491-533, especially 503-8 on lines 24-25; Williams (above, note 11) p. 142 with note 1.

[18] See R. Merkelbach, *"ΒΟΥΚΟΛΙΑΣΤΑΙ* (Der Wettgesang der Hirten)," *RhM* 99 (1956) 110-22, especially 116; also G. Lawall, *Theocritus' Coan Pastorals: A Poetry Book* (Cambridge, Mass., 1967) 54.

[19] A number of scholars have pointed out that *Idyll* 7 proceeds *as if* there will be an actual contest which, however, never develops: see Lohse (above, note 6) 422-23; Puelma (above, note 3) 154-55; Ott (above, note 14) 145.

[20] See Gow (above, note 1) *ad* 7.36 and 5.44; Schwartz (above, note 12) 302.

Idyll 5 (cf. 5.51-52). Second, there is a trace of amused surprise, verging on the rustic's condescension for the city-dweller, in Lycidas' comment on Simichidas' *passeggiata* in the noonday sun, when even *(καί)* the lizards and birds have sense enough to sleep (21-23; cf. *Id.* 12.8f.).

Once we recognize this ironical streak in Lycidas, we may wonder whether there may not be some irony toward his friend in his lines on Homerid mountain-building (45-48). A verbal link between the Homerid poets and Simichidas' report of his own exalted reputation leaves this possibility open: Χῖον ἀοιδόν (47); ἀοιδὸν ἄριστον (38).

To these lofty, mountain-like structures (45-48) Lycidas a-bruptly *(ἀλλ' ἄγε)* opposes "herdman's song," βουκολικὰ ἀοιδά (49). For us "bucolic" has the romantic associations conferred upon it by centuries of literary tradition. "Bucolic" is itself a literary word in our vocabulary. But for Theocritus, who stands at the beginning of that tradition, the word evokes still the toil of the countryman and the smell of his beasts.[21] It stands out sharply against the Homeric and Pindaric echoes of lines 45-48 which immediately precede it. It deepens the distance between Simichidas and Lycidas and emphasizes the humility of Lycidas' song.

The humility is especially marked in the way Lycidas goes on to describe his own work. It is merely a little song *(μελύδριον)*, which even so cost him much effort on his mountain *(πρᾶν ἐν ὄρει τὸ μελύδριον ἐξεπόνασα,* 51). Whereas Simichidas ended his speech with talk of "conquest" and "rivalling" *(νίκημι, ἐρίσδω* 40, 41), Lycidas ends with amity *(φίλος,* 50), and con-cerns himself not with competing, but with "pleasing" his friend *(ὅρη, φίλος, εἴ τοι ἀρέσκει / τοῦθ' ὅτι . . . ἐξεπόνασα,* 50f.).

Within his first speech (27-41) Simichidas begins with a generous praise of Lycidas. Lycidas' supremacy as a piper *(συρικτάς)* warms Simichidas' heart *(τὸ δὴ μάλα θυμὸν ἰαίνει*

---

[21] Aside from the "Bucolic" mouth of the Nile in Hdt. 2.17 the adjective βουκολικός seems not to occur before Theocritus. The adjective would, of course, suggest the *boukolos,* or "cowherd," who, from Homer on, stands low on the social scale: cf. βουκόλος δοῦλος in Plato, *Ion* 540 c.

/ἁμέτερον, 29-30). Yet in his own opinion Simichidas believes that he can "equal" his friend (30-31). His verb here, ἰσοφαρίζειν, recalls the challenges of Homeric heroes in battle.[22] But it also may hint at Simichidas' ambition.

In this speech, nevertheless, Simichidas still balances his high claims with modesty. This balance is expressed in a repetition of phrases between 27-31 and 37-40:

> Λυκίδα φίλε, φαντί τυ πάντες
> ἦμεν συρικτὰν μέγ' ὑπείροχον . . .
> . . . καίτοι κατ' ἐμὸν νόον ἰσοφαρίζειν
> ἔλπομαι.
> καὶ γὰρ ἐγὼ Μοισᾶν καπυρὸν στόμα, κἠμὲ λέγοντι
> πάντες ἀοιδὸν ἄριστον· ἐγὼ δέ τις οὐ ταχυπειθής,
> οὐ Δᾶν· οὐ γάρ πω κατ' ἐμὸν νόον οὔτε τὸν ἐσθλόν
> Σικελίδαν νίκημι . . . οὔτε Φιλίταν
> ἀείδων.

In the first passage Simichidas asserted that, despite what "all say," he can "equal" the "best of pipers." In the second passage he asserts that, despite what "all say," he cannot (yet) defeat Asclepiades or Philetas. Initial boastfulness is checked by restraint at the end.

However, Simichidas still shows himself concerned with public opinion. Twice he reports what "all say" (φαντί τυ πάντες, 27; λέγοντι πάντες, 37-38). Though he speaks of mutual help or benefit (36), he still thinks in competitive terms. His verbs are ἰσοφαρίζειν (30), νίκημι (40), ἐρίσδω (41), and we may probably add βουκολιασδώεσθα in 36.[23] His last word is ἐρίσδω, and he does not speak again until line 91. This eristic tone stands out all the more sharply against Lycidas' indifference to such matters, his generosity in giving his staff, and his simple desire to "please" (ἀρέσκει, 50).

Simichidas' second speech (91-95) is clearly intended to recall the first, for it begins with the same address to "dear Lycidas" (Λυκίδα φίλε) in the same metrical position (27 and 91). The word κἠμὲ in the next line also recalls κἠμὲ λέγοντι in 37. Yet the disclaimer is now replaced by self-importance: the Nymphs

---

[22] E.g. Iliad 6.101, 21.194 and 411.
[23] See above, note 20.

have taught him, like Hesiod, on the mountains, and report has carried his songs to the throne of Zeus (92-93), which may refer to Ptolemy Philadelphus.[24] The claim is extraordinary in any case. "Zeus" in 93 also echoes Lycidas' "sprig of Zeus" in 44.

The parallels and contrasts continue further. In his opening compliment Simichidas had called his friend "by far the best" of pipers: μέγ' ὑπείροχον (28). He now repeats that phrase, in the same metrical position, but applies it to his own song: τόγ' ἐκ πάντων μέγ' ὑπείροχον (94). Whereas Lycidas was concerned with "pleasing" his friend (50), Simichidas will "honor" Lycidas (ᾧ τυ γεραίρειν / ἀρξεῦμ', 94f.), a word which once more suggests the heroic gestures of epic figures.[25] Here again he reaches toward grandiosity where Lycidas was simple, and again we may wonder whether Lycidas' warnings about rivalling Homer (47f.) may not have had some relevance to Simichidas' character.

Simichidas concludes with a compliment to his friend: "Listen, for you are dear to the Muses" (95). Given the context, we may suspect that the phrase contains a trace of condescension.[26] Such a tone was present earlier in ἐπίταδες of 42 and possibly also in the offer of "mutual benefit" in 36.

In Simichidas' first speech modesty and pretention strove against one another, but modesty won the upper hand (οὐ γάρ πω ... νίκημι ... , 39-41). Simichidas' second speech reverses the proportions. Now his true opinion of his merits breaks out. He had reason to restrain himself earlier, for he wished to encourage Lycidas to sing. Lycidas has sung his song, and Simichidas' second speech confirms the hints conveyed earlier.

---

[24] Most commentators accept the identification. R. J. Cholmeley, *The Idylls of Theocritus* (London 1919) ad loc. rejects it on rather uncertain chronological grounds. Recent interpreters have reservations for other reasons: e.g. Puelma (above, note 3) p. 153, note 29; Williams (above, note 11) p. 143, note 2.

[25] Cf. *Iliad* 7.321; *Odyssey* 14.437 and 441.

[26] Puelma (above, note 3) p. 152 with note 27 takes lines 91-95 differently. In his view Simichidas here recognizes the excellence of Lycidas' song and desires to reciprocate. The γέρας, therefore, reveals a mood of "galante Höflichkeit." Yet the differences between Lycidas' μελύδριον and Simichidas' ἐκ πάντων μέγ' ὑπείροχον remain, as Puelma realizes; and Simichidas' compliment still is self-centered. See also Williams (above, note 11) p. 143.

The hyperbole of 93 finally resolves the tension. Self-importance wins.

With Simichidas' opinion of his own talents clarified, we understand in retrospect why he felt it necessary to speak "on purpose" of his inferiority to other poets and why Lycidas thereupon laughs when he congratulates Simichidas on his absolute bent for truthfulness.

CHARLES SEGAL

BROWN UNIVERSITY

CHARLES SEGAL / PROVIDENCE

Thematic Coherence and Levels of Style in Theocritus' Bucolic Idylls

1.

It is the thesis of this paper that the seven genuine bucolic Idylls of Theocritus — 1, 3, 4, 5, 6, 7, 11 — should be read not as isolated poems, but as the consciously varied expressions of a unified poetic vision and concern[1]. The elements which compose the bucolic landscape and action of these poems are not to be regarded as parts of a static, decorative stage-setting of "little weight and complexity" and little differentiated from poem to poem, as they are in the "generic" approach of E. R. Curtius' influential chapter on "Ideal Landscape" and more recently in Rosenmeyer's The Green Cabinet[2]. Instead, these elements stand in complex, dynamic, and dramatic

---

[1]) With most recent scholars I regard Id. 8 and 9 as not by Theocritus: see the Introduction to the poems in A. S. F. Gow, Theocritus (Cambridge 1952), Commentary, and the discussion in L. E. Rossi, Mondo pastorale e poesia bucolica di maniera: L'idillio ottavo del *corpus* teocriteo, SIFC 43 (1971) 5—25, with the bibliography, p. 5, nn. 1—3. For the older literature see also Ph.-E. Legrand, Étude sur Théocrite, Bibl. des Écoles françaises d'Athènes et de Rome, 79 (Paris 1898) 14—17. See also my Appendix, infra. Id. 10, though it has some affinities with the bucolic poems, is Hesiodic or agrarian rather than genuinely bucolic, and its characters are reapers, farmworkers, not herdsmen.

[2]) Ernst Robert Curtius, European Literature and the Latin Middle Ages (1948), tr. W. Trask (London 1953) 183—202, especially 194ff.; Thomas Rosenmeyer, The Green Cabinet: Theocritus and the European Pastoral Lyric (Berkeley and Los Angeles 1969) 186—192, 198f. (the quotation is on p. 199). Rosenmeyer is followed by Eleanor W. Leach, Vergil's Eclogues: Landscapes of Experience (Ithaca, N. Y. 1974) 81f., who stresses the "consistency and uniformity" of the "entire, unchanging landscape" over against its "visual complexity" (82). See also G. Soutar, Nature in Greek Poetry (London 1939) 223, who, like Rosenmeyer (186), sees the Theocritean bucolic landscape in terms of a set of stage-properties. For a basic critique of this leveling, generic approach to Theocritean bucolic see John Van Sickle, Epic and Bucolic (Theocritus, Id. VII; Virgil, Ecl. 1), QUCC 19 (1975) 45—72, especially 49, 67f.

relationship to one another. They constitute a code of signifiers whose signified is as much a set of relations as a concrete, objectively "real" bucolic world.

Theocritus' manipulation and variation of the terms in this "code" not only express the relation between the different parts of the bucolic world, but also contain implicitly the individual character of each particular poem in its relation to the rest of Theocritean bucolic. The interplay between myth, character, landscape, and bucolic song in each poem both articulates the structure and meaning of that poem and also reflects a larger structure within the seven bucolic Idylls.

Taken together these seven Idylls delineate a hierarchical structure of different levels of poetic and mythic intensity within the bucolic corpus. There is, in other words, a gradation or sliding scale among the seven bucolic Idylls, from the low-toned realism of 4 and 5 to the more mythical subject matter and loftier tone of 1 and 7.

The thematic approach that I shall set forth here receives independent confirmation in the area of style from Fabiano's recent analysis of the fluctuation between epic and realistic, literary and colloquial language in Theocritus[3]). The shift between different levels of style within the individual Idyll and within the Theocritean corpus as a whole, Fabiano argues, is a function not of chronological development, but of deliberate thematic variation. Unlike the more or less unified poetical tone of Virgil's bucolics, Theocritus' pastoral Idylls display a sharp discontinuity of style: "What seems chiefly to characterize Theocritus' poetic language is the instability of the system at every level"[4]). This "instability" and discontinuity of style, however — and here I would qualify Fabiano's remarks — operate within a set of flexible limits and conform to a larger pattern within the corpus of bucolic Idylls. Over and above the mixture of "high" and "low" diction, each Idyll also has its own unity of style and tone which in turn is related to the systematic variation of mythic and poetic levels among the seven bucolic Idylls.

In this structure Idyll 7 holds a privileged position. Recently

---

[3]) Gianfranco Fabiano, Fluctuation in Theocritus' Style, GRBS 12 (1971) 517—537, especially 524—528; see also Van Sickle (preceding note) 54—56.

[4]) Fabiano (preceding note) 528.

Lawall has stressed its synoptic, recapitulatory function[5]). With most recent scholars, Lawall is surely right ro regard 7 as the high point of Theocritean bucolic, a work written after the other pastoral Idylls and self-consciously reflecting on the nature of bucolic poetry and on the poet's own artistic achievement in these poems[6]). But Lawall's stress on a specifically Coan element as a basis of unity and his notion of a "pastoral-urban diptych" formed by Idylls 1 and 2 shift the basis of interrelation in the bucolic corpus from the plane of aesthetic essentials to externals and accidents[7]). Whereas for Lawall Idyll Seven's reuse of phrases and motifs of other Idylls creates "an autobiographical reminiscence"[8]), the important thing about 7 from the point of view which I am putting forth here is the mythic quality of the locus it creates and its heightened realization of the mythic and poetic possibilities of the bucolic world.

We cannot, of course, reconstruct Theocritus' creative processes. But we can imagine him composing the seven pastoral Idylls each with a view to the others, consciously experimenting with the different formal properties, the different tonalities, the different linguistic registers — lyrical and mime-like, mythic or prosaic — of his pastoral fiction, carefully adjusting landscape, character, style, narrative, the presence or absence of myth to suit the particular level of each of the seven poems, trying out different combinations or juxtapositions of motifs. He could expect the sophisticated readers among whom he circulated these poems — Aratus, Asclepiades, Philitas, Nicias — to savor these formal variations and nuances. And of course at some level every poet works for himself alone, for the integrity demanded by the text as it creates its own laws and patterns.

It would be convenient for our thesis if Theocritus put to-

---

[5]) Gilbert Lawall, Theocritus' Coan Pastorals: A Poetry Book (Washington, D. C. and Cambridge, Mass. 1967) 110 ff.

[6]) For discussion see C. Segal, Theocritus' Seventh Idyll and Lycidas, WS 87 (N. F. 8, 1974) 20—76, especially 32 ff., 57 ff., 72 ff. To the bibliography (p. 20, n. 1) add now William Berg, Early Virgil (London 1974) 22—25; Ulrich Ott, Theokrits „Thalysien" und ihre literarischen Vorbilder, RhM 115 (1972) 134—149; Ernst A. Schmidt, Poetische Reflexion: Vergils Bukolik (Munich 1972) 227—238; E. R. Schwinge, Theokrits „Dichterweihe" (Id. 7), Philologus 118 (1974) 40—58.

[7]) See the reviews by J. Griffin, CR, N. S. 19 (1969) 39 and C. Segal, CJ 63 (1967/68) 228.

[8]) Lawall (above, note 5) 116.

gether these seven Idylls into a libellus of bucolic poems. Unfortunately the solid evidence all points in the other direction. The manuscript tradition, papyri, and the two epigrams prefixed to the bucolic corpus indicate that the "boukolika" were not brought together as a unit until late Hellenistic times[9]). Irigoin's recent argument for an "Idyll Book" organized by multiples of nine is an unfortunate attempt by a distinguished scholar to apply to Theocritus, inappropriately, certain tendencies in Virgilian scholarship, especially the work of Maury[10]). Irigoin's thesis requires that we accept Idylls 8 and 9 as authentic and Idyll 10 as bucolic, nor does he account for the disturbing place of Id. 2 in the Vatican Family of manuscripts nor for the variation in the order of the poems in the papyri.

Theocritus' bucolic Idylls, therefore, do not have the same kind of unity as Virgil's "Eclogue Book". The symmetries and contrasts which Virgil achieves by the placement of poems within the collection, the repeated characters, the attribution of the songs within the collection to the various pastoral singers, the developing theme of a poetical Arcadia do not have a precise counterpart in Theocritus[11]). Yet here, as elsewhere, Virgil may have been enlarging upon hints already present in Theocritus. Although Theocritus does not have Virgil's well defined cast of bucolic characters, he does repeat certain proper names as a link between Idylls. The mythical Daphnis occurs in 1, 5, and 7, and "Daphnis the neatherd" sings in 6. Tityrus appears in 3 and 7; Amaryllis in 3 and 4; Comatas in 5 and 7. Lycopas is a herdsman in 5, and a shepherd from Lycope is a companion of Lycidas in 7 (5, 62; 7, 72). The Haleis River occurs in both 5 and 7 (5, 123; 7, 1). There are also a large number of

---

[9]) See Gow (above, note 1) 1. lix—lxii; U. von Wilamowitz-Moellendorff, Die Textgeschichte der griechischen Bukoliker, Philol. Untersuch. 18 (Berlin 1906) 102ff.; Legrand (above, note 1) 9—17; A. Rostagni, L'idillio VIII di Teocrito e la sua autenticità, Scritti Minori, II. 1 (Torino 1956) 214—216; G. Giangrande, JHS 88 (1968) 173.

[10]) Jean Irigoin, Les bucoliques de Théocrite: la composition du recueil, QUCC 19 (1975) 27—44.

[11]) For a unified "Eclogue Book" see Carl Becker, Vergils Eklogenbuch, Hermes 88 (1955) 314—349, especially 323ff.; J. Van Sickle, The Unity of the Eclogues: Arcadian Forest, Theocritean Trees, TAPA 98 (1967) 491—508 and his forthcoming survey, The 'Bucolics' of Virgil, Aufstieg und Niedergang der römischen Welt, II, Prinzipat (Festschrift J. Vogt, Berlin 1975); Leach (above, note 2) 245ff.; Karl Büchner, s. v. Vergilius, RE VIII A 1 (1955) 1254—1257.

verbal echoes among the bucolic Idylls, and in a few cases whole
verses are repeated[12]).

Idyll 7, with its elaborate structure, its myths of Daphnis and
Comatas, and above all its elusive figure of Lycidas, represents the
fullest actualization of the mythic and poetic potential of the
bucolic world. Close to 7 stands 1, with the "sufferings of Daphnis"
(1, 19), the archetypal bucolic singer and the mythical creator of
bucolic poetry (Diodorus 4, 84, 3). Only in these two of the seven
bucolic Idylls does nature become animate with sympathy for the
suffering of the herdsman-singer-poet (1, 71 ff.; 7, 74—77). Here too
the mythopoetic imagination has the broadest scope and the
greatest seriousness. In Idyll 1 the story of Daphnis' death involves
pastoral and non-pastoral divinities like the Nymphs, Hermes,
Priapus, Aphrodite, Pan. Idyll 7 not only revolves around the
enigmatic Lycidas and the mythic archetypes behind him, but has
as its center the symmetrical myths of Daphnis and the "divine
Comatas" (7, 73—89). The one is mourned in death by mountains
and oaks; the other is kept alive, or virtually brought back to life
after death-like concealment, by bees (7, 74—85).

The full mythical consciousness of these two poems goes hand
in hand with a full achievement of a beautiful bucolic locus. Idyll 1
begins with a setting of whispering pines and songfully plashing
water, itself symbolic of song (1, 1—7)[13]). It then goes on to a kind
of quintessential bucolic locus with its "shepherd's seat" (ὁ θῶκος /
τῆνος ὁ ποιμενικός, 1, 22—23), its elm tree and oaks, statue of Priapus,
spring sacred to the Nymphs (1, 21—23). This calm and happy
place, established at the very beginning of the poem, is the foil
to the work-world described on the cup (1, 39—54) and also to the
mourning bucolic world of the song of Daphnis. The full development
of the locus encourages both the amity between the two characters
of the Idyll and the expansiveness of the song, by far the longest
pastoral song in the Idylls[14]). The death of the archetypal herdsman-

---

[12]) See Lawall (above, note 5) 111 ff. and his lists on 133—138; also
Ernst A. Schmidt, Der göttliche Ziegenhirt: Analyse des fünften Idylls als
Beitrag zu Theokrits bukolischer Technik, Hermes 102 (1974) 213 f., 219, 221,
236 ff.

[13]) For the water-symbolism see in general A. Kambylis, Die Dichter-
weihe und ihre Symbolik (Heidelberg 1967) 23—30; W. Wimmel, Kallimachos
in Rom, Hermes Einzelschr. 16 (Wiesbaden 1960) 222 ff.; M. Puelma, Die
Dichterbegegnung in Theokrits „Thalysien", MH 17 (1960) 156; C. Segal,
'Since Daphnis Dies': The Meaning of Theocritus' First Idyll, MH 31 (1974) 10 f.

[14]) The song of Lycidas in 7 is the closest, with 36 lines; Simichidas'

singer within the song then calls the whole bucolic world into question and elicits its fullest degree of participation in human emotions: Nymphs, jackals, wolves, cows and shepherds, Pan himself are all involved (1, 66—75; 115—126). "All the springs" and "all the groves" — that is, the totality of the bucolic setting — are touched by Daphnis' suffering (1, 83). The end of the song brings an inversion of the beauty and fertility of nature (1, 132—136), until the poem finally returns at the end to songful sweetness and water (1, 146—150). The "Springs of the Seasons" in which the cup is washed at the end (1, 150), however, take us beyond the present and tangible springs of the rustic conversation of the beginning (1, 2 and 1, 22) to a distant and mythical realm[15]). Even the realism of the leaping she-goats (1, 151—152) complements the remote, quasi-imaginary wolves, lions, and jackals who weep for Daphnis (1, 71f.; 115f.)[16]), just as their exuberant caprine sexuality complements the troubled and denied sexuality of Daphnis (cf. 1, 139 and 152)[17]).

Whereas oaks and mountains lament in 7 and jackals, lions and wolves mourn in 1, the "lower" pastoral realism of Idyll 4 permits only cows and bulls to moo with longing for an absent (not dead) herdsman (4, 12). Corydon's animals lose their appetite and grow thin; but this event is, after all, within the possibilities of actual experience. In the pseudo-Theocritean Eighth Idyll the sympathy between nature and man is trivialized and sentimentalized even further (8, 43—48).

Idyll 7 goes even beyond 1 in the creation of the bucolic locus, for it actually shows that locus coming into being in the creation of the Burina spring (7, 5—7). The trees there "weave" the shady grove which forms part of the Thalysian setting too (cf. αἴγειροι πτελέαι τε, 7, 8 and 7, 136). This "weaving" of a bucolic locus is

---

song has 32 lines. Thyrsis' song in 1 has 58 lines of narrative, 2 lines of introduction, and 18 of refrain, making a total of 78.

[15]) G. Giangrande, Eranos 71 (1973) 73 stresses the Horai's connection with rain, another possible point of relevance, which, however, does not change the mythical status of their spring here.

[16]) G. Jachmann, Die dichterische Technik in Vergils Bukolika, NJbb 49 (1922) 102f. stresses „die grandiose Phantastik" of this motif in Id. 1. F. Williams, ʽΩ in Theocritus, Eranos 71 (1973) 66, suggests that the epicletic ὦ with its hint of a hymnic formula, conveys a certain mythical distance.

[17]) On the mythic element of this frame at the end and its relation to the Idyll as a whole see Segal, First Idyll (above, note 13) 1—22, especially 8—11.

to be compared with the boy's "plaiting a lovely grasshopper cage" on the cup in 1, 52. Both images suggest the making of poetry, for the association of "weaving" and poetry goes back to archaic times[18]. But the boy's cage will enclose the songful insects who in the purely bucolic locus (as opposed to the artificial inset of the cup) sing freely in the trees (5, 34; cf. 7, 139).

This scene on the cup is already once removed from the living vitality of the pastoral frame: it is a work of art within the work of art that is the poem itself. The cup creates a second degree of removal from the bucolic locus because its scenes belong to the rustic work-world, not the leisure of herdsmen (see especially 1, 41—44). There is ripe fruit here, as in the Thalysian grove (1, 46 and 7, 146), but these grapes are menaced by foxes as the grapes on 5, 108—109 are threatened by grasshoppers. In 7, 134, on the other hand, the "newly cut vines" in which the companions "rejoice" at the very beginning of the description of the locus amoenus indicate the safe, well cultivated condition of these grapes.

The boy in 1 is plaiting his cage with "asphodel stems" (ἀνθέρικοι) and "rushes" (σχοῖνος, 1, 52—53). Both of these plants occur in only one other place each in the bucolic Idylls. Asphodel is part of the couch or στιβάς of Lycidas in 7, 68; "sweet rushes" line the place where Simichidas and his friends recline in 7, 133[19]. In both instances the locus of 7 is a safer, more restful, more harmonious setting. Here bucolic song reaches its richest form amid human companionship, abundance, inward and outward peace. The enclosed work-world on the cup contains song only in the symbolical form of the cage; and the singers will be imprisoned by an artful device which is analogous to the cup itself[20]. We can present these contrasts in diagrammatic form:

---

[18]) See Sappho, 188 LP; Pindar, Ol. 6, 87 and Nem. 7, 77; Bacchyl, 5, 9 and 19, 8; Virg. E. 10, 71 and Servius ad loc. See in general C. M. Bowra, Pindar (Oxford 1964) 16; H. Fränkel, Dichtung und Philosophie des frühen Griechentums[2] (Munich 1962) 369 with n. 38; O. Skutsch, HSCP 73 (1969) 166.

[19]) For the connection of the ἀνθέρικος of 1, 52f. and the ἀσφόδελος of 7, 68 see Kurt Lembach, Die Pflanzen bei Theokrit (Heidelberg 1970) 32.

[20]) There are, of course, other tensions between the cup, Daphnis, and the pastoral setting which I cannot discuss here: see Segal, First Idyll (above, note 13) 5ff.; Lawall (above, note 5) 27—31; Ulrich Ott, Die Kunst des Gegensatzes in Theokrits Hirtengedichten, Spudasmata 22 (Heidelberg 1969) 132—137.

Idyll 1	Idyll 7
plaiting of a cage	trees weaving shade
caged grasshoppers	freely singing cicadas
endangered grapes	"newly cut vines" and abundant fruits
work	ease
frustrated and teasing love	happy love (Ageanax)

These differences are indicative of Seven's more positive image of the bucolic world. The sympathy between man and nature in One's lament for Daphnis appears in Seven as a grander, bolder, and more confident fiction. Not just Nymphs or wild animals lament the herdsman-singer, but, more miraculously, the voiceless mountain and the oaks of the bucolic landscape itself (7, 74). In 7 too Daphnis' death is balanced by Comatas' resurrection. Analogously the inset of 1 presents a world of fruitless amorous play and hard work, whereas 7 describes a deep and passionate love and a scene of pastoral festivity (7, 63 ff.) and ends with the most bountiful locus amoenus in the corpus (7, 132 ff.).

Both of these loci of 7, Lycidas' pastoral gathering in 63 ff. and Simichidas' Thalysian festival in 132 ff., constitute virtually a mythic transfiguration of the bucolic world. Metaphorical and actual song, the singing of birds and cicadas and the singing of herdsmen, including "divine Comatas", combine to create a setting of quintessential bucolic songfulness (cf. 7, 26; 41; 139—141). In the story of Comatas the bucolic motif of reclining under trees and listening to song reaches its highest point (7, 86—89). Here touched by the glow of remote myth, these motifs recur on a lower, but more concrete and immediate plane at the Thalysian festival (7, 133). Similarly the mythical bees which fed Comatas recur as real bees on Phrasidamus' farm (cf. 7, 81 and 142).

Elements that appear in the inversion of the natural order at Daphnis' death in 1 recur as part of the richness of the Thalysian grove in 7: cactus and thorns (1, 132 and 7, 140); pears (1, 134 and 7, 144); birdsong (1, 136 and 7, 141; cf. also the violets of 7, 132 and the white-violet chaplet of 7, 64). The "sacred water" which keeps the Nymphs from mourning Daphnis (1, 69) is part of the charm of the grove of 7 (7, 136 f.). Here not only does water plash melodiously (7, 136 f.), as in 1, 7—8; not only do cicadas and birds sing (7, 138—141); but the very pebbles "sing" in the road (7, 26). In a different realm the loves in 7, though intense (7, 55 f.), are mastered, happy, and moving toward "calm" (ἀσυχία, 7, 126), whereas in all the other bucolic Idylls, with the exception of Daphnis and Damoetas in 6, love is unhappy, unattainable, or unfulfilled.

The motif of the "road" in Idyll 7 (10; 11; 35; 131) and the journey "from the city" (2) to the country present the bucolic locus there as itself the goal of a journey[21]), the endpoint of a spatial as well as thematic progression toward friendship, fertility, song, a fusion of rustic reality and suggestive myth (cf. 7, 137; 148 ff.). Although this locus is agrarian rather than strictly bucolic, Theocritus so manipulates the narrative structure of the poem that access to this wondrous place is conferred immediately after Lycidas' bestowal of his crook as a "guest-gift of the Muses" (128 f.). In this way the locus of 7 is demarcated as a special place attainable only after the privileged contact with the archetypal goatherd-singer and the "initiation" into the realms of myth and song which that contact brings.

If Idyll 7, and next to it Idyll 1, represent the highest poetic and mythic realization of the bucolic world, Idyll 5 represents the lowest[22]). Like 7, Idyll 5 contains an implicit poetics by virtue of its very form as a singing contest[23]). Its poetics, however, contrast with and complement those of 7. Whereas 7 uses ancient mythic archetypes to create a bucolic "Dichterweihe" against the background of a harmonious natural order and amicable personal relations, 5 presents song as another item of discord amid the disiecta membra of a bucolic locus whose surface beauties only mask contentiousness. Its tone of insult and banter contrasts markedly with Seven's courtesy[24]). Yet without this "lower" limit Theocritus'

[21]) See Schwinge (above, note 6) 40; Segal, Seventh Idyll (above, note 6) 71.

[22]) On the realism of 5 see Gow (above, note 1) 2, 76, who, however, neglects the literary stylization. For the interaction of the two elements see L. E. Rossi, Vittoria e sconfitta nell' agone bucolico letterario, GIF, N. S. 2 (1971) 13—24, especially 22 f., and above all Gregorio Serrao, L'*Idillio* V di Teocrito: realtà campestre e stilizzazione letteraria, QUCC 19 (1975) 73—109, who carries the formalistic analysis of 5 to its furthest point. Rosenmeyer (above, note 2) 137 f., approaching the poem from the "generic" view, can do little with it: "The poem is unusual, an extreme realization of certain tendencies that elsewhere are largely sublimated or held at arm's length."

[23]) See Schmidt, Id. 5 (above, note 12) 208: „Der Wettgesang mit Zuweisung des Sieges an einen der Rivalen ist eine Poetik."

[24]) On these contrasts of 5 and 7 see Williams (above, note 16) 60 f.; Giangrande, JHS 88 (1968) 172, both of whom, however, draw no conclusions from their observations.

bucolic world would lack its range and its stylistic and thematic variety, and Seven would stand out less clearly as the extraordinary achievement it is. Between the limits set by 5 and 7, as we shall see, all the other bucolic Idylls take their place in a definable continuum of styles, themes, landscapes, and mythical consciousness.

Whereas the Daphnis of 7, like that of 1, is an involving figure who enlists the sympathy of all of nature, the Daphnis of 5 is only a vague, quasi-proverbial symbol of pastoral suffering (5, 21) or pastoral song (5, 80 f.); his aura of myth and magic is dim and distant. Likewise in 5 being loved by the Muses appears only as a boast at the beginning of the contest (5, 80 f.), whereas in 7, as in 1, being „dear to the Muses" has a more concrete reality (cf. 1, 141 and 7, 95), just as the Muses themselves are more real (cf. 7, 82) and less incongruous with the surrounding frame (cf. 7, 45—51).

In 5 Comatas is an ordinary goatherd, poetically more talented, presumably, than Lacon, but also possibly more lecherous. Comatas in 7, however, is the "divine Comatas" (7, 89), the center of a miraculous event at the mythical center of this bucolic world[25]. The bees feed him with honey from the soft flowers of the meadow "because the Muse poured honey into his mouth" (7, 80—82). Lycidas can celebrate and presumably invent his own lofty bucolic mythology. This mythic transfiguration of the bucolic world stands at the furthest remove from the mime-like atmosphere of 5. In like manner Lycidas' delicately "remembered" (7, 69) and poetically rendered love for Ageanax (7, 55 ff.), with its generosity toward the beloved (7, 52; 61 f.), contrasts with the brutal and painful intercourse between the herdsmen of 5. The "grin" of Lacon contrasts with the "grin" of Lycidas (5, 116 and 7, 19), as the "pain" which Comatas inflicts in 5, 41 contrasts with the "pleasure" which the "divine" Comatas experienced in 7, 83.

Though 5 contains four descriptions of bucolic landscape, the two speakers cannot agree on where to sing. Thus the locus itself, quite unlike the "common road" of 7, 35, is drawn into their quarrel[26]. In like manner the opening accusations of the theft of

---

[25]) See Schmidt, Id. 5 (above, note 12) 208—210; schol. ad Id. 7, 78/79a and also ad 83.

[26]) See Rosenmeyer (above, note 2) 188: "Each remains where he is, and the invocations of the bower remain abortive, In fact they serve to sharpen the sense of loss; the difference between what a pastoral is expected to accomplish, and what the present contest does, is bitingly defined by the quadrupling of the pastoral arbor." See also Schmidt, Id. 5 (above, note 12)

a goatskin and of a flute infect both bucolic labor and bucolic music with the contentious tone. The spring, from which the flock is pushed away (οὐκ ἀπὸ τᾶς κράνας, 5, 3; cf. 5, 100) here introduces not amity as at the opening of Idylls 1 and 7, but hostility and suspicion (5, 3—4):

Won't you move away from the spring? Sstt, sheep!

Don't you see Comatas who yesterday stole my pipe?[27]

The shade, a basic component of bucolic ease (1, 21f.; 7, 8f. and 138; cf. 12, 8f.) also becomes an item in the contest (5, 48f.). The "here" or "there" (τεῖδε, τηνεί) which attends the coming together of the bucolic characters into friendship, song, the sharing of festivity or beauty (cf. 1, 12; 1, 21; 4, 35; 11, 45) here points to division rather than accord (5, 32; 45; 60). The bad smell of the goats in 5, 52 is at the opposite extreme from the rich smell of summer in 7, 143. Even Lycidas' rennet smell in 7, 16, though pungent, has the redeeming quality of its quintessentially bucolic character (7, 14).

To "bucolicize", βουκολιάζεσθαι, the verb denoting the rustic singing contest, marked a friendly meeting attended by mutual "help" in 7, 36; here it is combined with "strife" (ποτέρισδε, 5, 60; cf. 67f.) and contains a veiled threat (44): "Come here and you'll bucolicize for the last time"[28]). No wonder Comatas replies, "I won't go there" (45).

In Idylls 1 and 7, as also in 6, "singing", ἀείδειν, springs easily from the peace and leisure of the bucolic world and the friendly feeling of its inhabitants for one another. In Idyll 5 "singing" is an instrument of aggression and violence (5, 22): διαείσομαι ἔστε κ' ἀπείπῃς[29]). The intensifying prefix (δια-) directs this singing not to the calm and friendship of the other Idylls, but to exhaustion, collapse, failure of speech: δι-αείδειν produces ἀπ-ειπεῖν (5, 22). Thus the negative modality of the "singing" of 5 closely parallels that of

---

231—234; Serrao (above, note 22) 80—82; Adolf Köhnken, Gnomon 44 (1972) 756, who stresses the lack of agreement („von Konzilianz keine Spur").

[27]) On the expression in 5, 3 and 5, 100 see the detailed remarks of Rossi, Id. 8 (above, note 1) 10—18.

[28]) See Lawall (above, note 5) 113f. for a different view of the echoes between 7, 36 and 5, 44. For the aggressiveness of the latter passage see Schmidt, Id. 5 (above, note 12) 231, 242. Virgil, E. 3, 51, caught the tone but carefully restricted the scope to song: *efficiam posthac nec quemquam voce lacessas.*

[29]) See Serrao, Id. 5 (above, note 22) 86f.

its "bucolicizing". Idyll 5 shares with the other poems the comparison of one songful bird or insect to another: owl to nightingale, cicada to frog, magpie to nightingale (1, 136; 7, 41; 5, 136f.); but it adds the more grotesque instance of pig against Athena (5, 23). The tomb that in Idyll 7 marks the point of meeting on a "common road" propitious for song (7, 10f.) or in Idyll 1 was a haunt of Pan admired even by the gods (1, 125f.) is here a lowly old woman's tomb where herbs for purgative and punitive purposes are gathered (5, 120f.).

The only myths alluded to in 5 occur as brief, proverb-like passing remarks (e. g. 20; 23; 149f.), as if the poem cannot break through its coarse rustic surface to deeper elements. When Lacon, asking Comatas to stake a kid, urges, ἔστι μὲν οὐδέν / ἱερόν (5, 21f.), the words, with their harsh enjambment, remind us also of the absence of τὸ ἱερόν, the sacred or numinous element prominent in the settings of 1 and 7 (cf. ἱερὸν ὕδωρ, 1, 69 and 7, 136). Finally the cup of cypress wood which Comatas inappropriately attributes to Praxiteles (5, 104f.) is a reduced and trivialized form of the wondrous cup of Idyll 1.

Though the couplets of the singing contest contain many fine "poetic" details, they too dwell on the destructive features of the natural world (cf. 5, 107—115), including wolves and grape-devouring grasshoppers, foxes and beetles. Then, after a probably obscene allusion to eating figs[30]), song nearly breaks down into insults about buggery, beatings (116—119), and taunts about magic (120—123), in immediate juxtaposition with the "highest" poetical element of the poem, the miracle of rivers flowing with milk and honey (124—127). Only in Idyll 5 are the cicadas or grasshoppers possibly harmful insects, destroying grapes and annoying reapers (5, 108—111). In 1 and 7, as also in 5, they are symbols of song (cf. 1, 148; 5, 29; 7, 139). Whatever the exact manner in which the cicadas "provoke" the reapers in 5, 110—111, they certainly do not invite to the restful mood of their Thalysian counterparts (7, 139). Idyll 5 ends with the washing of real goats in a real river (5, 145/146), whereas the loftier and more mythically oriented First Idyll ends with the "washing" of the beautiful cup, an elaborate work of art, in the remote "springs of the Horai" (1, 150; cf. 1, 27).

In 5 too the economic and class considerations of possession and slavery make themselves sharply and discordantly felt (5, 6;

---

[30]) See Schmidt, Id. 5 (above, note 12) 228f.

10; 73 ff.). The possessive "my" and "mine" in the first lines (1; 2; 4) become increasingly important as claims of "theft" and "possession" begin to be bandied about or denied (2; 4; 6; 7; 10).

In these "lower" themes Idyll 4 stands close to Idyll 5 (cf. 4, 1 and κρύβδαν, 4, 3). But the tone of Idyll 4 is much more amicable, and the quarrel soon fades from sight. The realism of the beginning is answered by the glimpse of the mythical gods of the country, Pans and Satyrs, at the end (4, 62f.). In keeping with that eventual, if fleeting, emergence of a mythical element is the image of a happy and fertile bucolic locus which Corydon consistently opposes to Battus' melancholy[31]). Yet the remote Olympian festival where Aegon has gone, unlike the Coan Thalysia of 7, is disruptive rather than affirmative of rustic leisure and amity. Even the local festival of Hera Lacinia, though it has a happier mood, is a distant and brief memory (4, 33—37) whose past "laughter" (4, 37) is abruptly followed by grief, loss, and death (4, 38—40). The Thalysian festival of 7, by contrast, is tangible, immediate, expansive.

With the disagreement over a bucolic locus in Idyll 5 we may contrast the "one place" of Idyll 6[32]). The herdsmen-lovers, Daphnis and Damoetas, are the mirror-image of Comatas and Lacon. They drive their flocks "together" (συν-, 6, 2). The harmony of this "one place" of 6 is the spatial analogue to the singers' love and exchange of gifts. All three elements — place, love, and gifts — are in strong contrast with 5. This unity of place finds stylistic expression in the symmetries of the two songs which Damoetas and Daphnis sing[33]), and then in the balanced phrases of the closing frame: pipe and flute are answered by flute-playing and pipe-playing in 43f., "victory" is balanced by "unconquered" in 46. The two herdsmen of the first line become syntactically, as physically, interwoven at the end (Δαμοίτας καὶ Δάφνις, 6, 1; τὸν Δάφνιν ὁ Δαμοίτας, 6, 42), as they become also musically interwoven, as it were, in the exchange of instruments linked chiastically with the proper names in 42—44: Daphnis - Damoetas (42); syrinx - aulos (43); aulos - syrinx (44); Damoetas - Daphnis (44). Here, then, place, narrative frame of the song (prize and victory), emotional tone,

---

[31]) Contrast 4, 17—19; 23—25; 41—43 with 15f.; 20—22; 26—28; 38—40, and see in general C. Segal, Theocritean Criticism and the Interpretation of the Fourth Idyll, Ramus 1 (1972) 6ff.; S. Lattimore, Battus in Theocritus' Fourth *Idyll*, GRBS 14 (1973) 319—324.

[32]) See Lawall (above, note 5) 67.

[33]) See Ott, Kunst d. Gegensatzes (above, note 20) 72ff.

and the gentler mood of the songs themselves are all calibrated with the positive and harmonious atmosphere.

The pull between land and sea, between tangible reality and the inaccessible longings of love and imagination, is less violent here in 6 than in its companion piece, Idyll 11. The Polyphemus of 6 plays his pipe sweetly, but does not "waste away" (6, 9 ~ 11, 14; 69). It is the dog, not the wishful and lovesick master who looks out to sea (6, 11 ~ 11, 18; cf. 6, 25). Though Polyphemus is doubtless equally vain and equally deluded by "appearances" (6, 35ff. ~ 11, 79), it is the Nymph of 6 who abandons her element, the sea, to pursue him. In 6, unlike 11, she seems to be the more active partner in this unequal and improbable relationship (cf. 6, 17 and 11, 19; 75; 6, 27 and 11, 14; 11, 69). With its carefully modulated dissonances between the happy love of the narrative frame and the unattainable love of the songs, Idyll 6 achieves an overall harmony absent from 11 and exemplifies a quality which lies at the heart of the bucolic corpus as a whole: the "coming together" of different voices "into one place". Here, then, 6 stands close to 1 and 7 over against the discordant locus of 5.

The lovesick Cyclops of 11 tries to create a seductive locus to lure Galatea from her sea-world (11, 44—49), but his concern with the grosser physical comforts and material wealth of this locus cancels out its more refined, aesthetic attractions (cf. 11, 34—37; 40f.; 46—48; 51). To an even greater extent than in 6, his locus remains torn between land and sea. Whereas Lycidas, the quintessential goatherd of Idyll 7, arrived smelling of rennet (7, 16), the Cyclops fancies the sea-nymph, Galatea, putting rennet into the milk (11, 66), an improbable exchange of land and sea which dissolves bucolic reality into wishful imagining.

The bucolic locus of Idyll 3 is even more elusive and remote than that of 11. Here the palpable realities of the pastoral place belong only to the distant Tityrus and his mountain (3, 2—3), whereas the goatherd who addresses us seems to live in an imaginary world of his own, defined by only the vaguest spatial terms. Even Amaryllis' cave (3, 6) blends into fancy and poetic conceit (3, 12—14), in contrast to the all-too-solid cave of the pastoral capitalist, the Cyclops of 11 (11, 34—51).

If, then, on our scale of bucolic values we place the harmonious "one place" of 6 just below the songful loci of 7 and 1, the contentious locus of 5 stands at the bottom of the scale, and the landscapes of 3, 4, and 11 (not necessarily in that order) come in between. To this gradation of landscape, as we shall see, corresponds also a gradation of other elements.

II.

In Idyll 7 and to a lesser degree in Idyll 1 Theocritus is able to generate an inclusive mythical frame for his bucolic world. We have already noted how far Idyll 5 stands from this mythical side of the bucolic world, with its earthy, not "divine", Comatas. Likewise the unmythic, though amiable, Daphnis of 6 contrasts with the mysteriously suffering Daphnis of 1. Similarly the Tityrus of 3, who herds another's goats to permit him to sing, contrasts with the Tityrus of 7, who will himself sing wide-reaching and evocative songs. Even the buffoonish Polyphemus of 6 and 11 can reacquire in 7, for a moment, his serious, and dangerous, character as a Homeric figure, "the strong Polyphemus who pelted the ships with mountains" (7, 152; cf. Od. 9, 481 f.)[34]). Whereas the Cyclops of Idyll 6 "pelts" with apples (6, 6 ff.), this Cyclops' pelting is grimmer and closer to the epic model (7, 152). The unhappy love of which Daphnis sings in 6 is trivial (cf. δυσέρωτα, 6, 7), in contrast to the serious and indeed fatal consequences of Daphnis' condition as δύσερως in Idyll 1[35]). The verbal echo between these two passages is unmistakable:

>   ... ἃ δύσερώς τις ἄγαν καὶ ἀμήχανος ἐσσί.
>   βούτας μὲν ἐλέγευ, νῦν δ᾽ αἰπόλῳ ἀνδρὶ ἔοικας. (1, 85—86).
>
>   ... δυσέρωτα καὶ αἰπόλον ἄνδρα καλεῦσα (6, 7).

Just as Idyll 7 raises the theme of bucolic song and bucolic gift to its fullest seriousness and highest poetic and mythic value through the echoes of the Hesiodic Dichterweihe[36]), so Idyll 1 raises bucolic love, pathetic, but light and humorous in the other Idylls, to its highest seriousness and its closest approximation to tragic and heroic models[37]).

---

[34]) See Segal, Seventh Idyll (above, note 6) 64.

[35]) See E. A. Schmidt, Die Leiden des verliebten Daphnis, Hermes 96 (1968) 539—552, especially 543 ff.; Segal, First Idyll (above, note 13) 10.

[36]) See Segal, Seventh Idyll (above, note 6) 31 ff., with the references cited in notes 41—42; now Schwinge (above, note 6) 42 ff.

[37]) See Lawall (above, note 5) 19—22; Segal, First Idyll (above, note 13) 17—19.

The λαγωβόλον or goatherd's crook which in Idyll 7 echoes the Hesiodic σκῆπτρον as the Muses' gift (7, 128—129) appears at a lower level in the more realistic Idyll 4, where it performs its regular practical function of hitting stray goats (4, 49). Or, to work from the middle stratum of the bucolic corpus toward the lower, the leap into water and the cloak in Idyll 3, 25 reflect the exaggerated sentimentality of love, whereas in the closely parallel passage of Idyll 5 the same two elements are connected with accusations of thievery:

τὰν βαίταν ἀποδὺς ἐς κύματα τηνῶ ἀλεῦμαι. (3, 25).

τὰν βαίταν ἀπέδυσ' ὁ Καλαιθίδος· ἢ κατὰ τήνας
τᾶς πέτρας, ὤνθρωπε, μανεὶς εἰς Κρᾶθιν ἀλοίμαν. (5, 15—16).

Lacon's willingness to "leap into the Crathis" is then answered at the end by Comatas' exultant, "I will leap to the sky" (5, 144, imitated in 8, 88), a naive impulse which reiterates the painful division between the two herdsmen, the winner and the loser. "Leaping" ends the First Idyll too, but here it reflects not a division within the bucolic world as in 5 (Comatas against Lacon), but the amity and joy of the whole bucolic locus as the goats frisk about (1, 152). We may recall also the contrast between the washing that ends the two Idylls (1, 150; 5, 145ff.). In 6 too the herd's leaping has an equally happy aspect, for the heifers dance to the neatherds' music (6, 45); and in 6, as in 1 but unlike 5, the two herdsmen are brought together in friendship and a common delight in song.

Idyll 5 is the only poem which has an umpire to judge the bucolic contest, a detail in keeping with the seriousness given to the agonistic element per se. This umpire, moreover, cuts down oak trees as his profession (5, 64), i. e. destroys a part of the bucolic locus (cf. 45; 61). He also lives in the city, which is his present destination (ἐς πόλιν, 5, 78); we may contrast the movement "out of the city" in 7, 2 (ἐκ πόλιος).

In 1 and 7 the comparison of musical talent takes the form of friendly banter or compliment (1, 7—8; 19ff.; 7, 27ff.) not insult, as in 5 (cf. 5, 23—29)[38]. In Idyll 1 the "contest" (ἐρίσδων) is in the remote past (1, 24). Thyrsis receives the cup and goat as a reward

---

[38]) On the urbane refinement and friendly tone of this banter in 7 see C. Segal, Simichidas' Modesty: Theocritus, Idyll 7, 44, AJP 95 (1974) 128—136.

for song, not as a prize for victory. In 7, though competition is mentioned (7, 30; 7, 41), "contest" gives way to mutual "help" (36) and "pleasure" (50). Eventually it fades away entirely before the theme of the "gift" (7, 43; 128/29)[39]. The harmonious "one place" of 6 likewise prefigures the harmonious closure of the "contest" (ἔρισδεν, 6, 5), which ends not with a victory at all, but a friendly exchange of the instruments of bucolic song (6, 42—46). Here, as in 1 and 7, the gift or prize is awarded spontaneously[40]), whereas in 5 the participants haggle at length over the wager (5, 21—30). Every aspect of the singing in 5, then, reflects discord, the place as well as the terms of the contest. Analogously the lamb which is finally bestowed as the victor's prize in 5 is sacrificed to the Nymphs in a judgment not entirely free of suspicion about the umpire's interest in the tasty meat (καλὸν κρέας, 5, 140; cf. 1, 6). In 1, however, the she-goat which the goatherd gives to Thyrsis is not killed, but milked, and the milk is offered not to the Nymphs, but to the goddesses of song, the Muses (142—145)[41]). Idyll 1 also ends with frisky she-goats who may excite the billy, but the goatherd's tone is friendly and in fact establishes a return to the vitality of natural energies after Daphnis' refusal of love and consequent death (1, 151/52). The goatherd of 5, however, speaks more sharply, threatens to castrate the butting billy if he mounts any of the she-goats, and ends with an oath to Melanthius (5, 146—150), the evil goatherd of the Odyssey who himself is finally castrated. Between the endings of 1 and 5, then, there is a four-fold contrast: Muses and Nymphs, offering of milk and blood sacrifice; virile he-goat and castrated he-goat; friendly goatherd and threatening goatherd.

Not only do the happy and musical movements of the heifers[42])

---

[39]) See B. A. Van Groningen, Quelques problèmes de la poésie bucolique grecque, II, Mnemosyne, Ser. 4, 12 (1959) 27, 29. On the different conditions of the bucolic singing contest see Gow (above, note 1) 2, 92—94 (Introd. to Id. 5).

[40]) Schwinge (above, note 6) 56 rather neglects the close parallel with the end of Id. 1 when he remarks of 7, 128f., „Nur Theokrit bekommt ein Geschenk; sein Partner zieht mit leeren Händen weiter. Diese Äußerlichkeit hebt den Wechselgesang des Thalysiengedichts von denen der parallelen Idyllen ab."

[41]) It is true that Muses and Nymphs are often closely associated: see Schwinge (above, note 6) 44 with n. 15, Puelma (above, note 13) 156 with n. 37; but here the difference seems to be more important than the association.

[42]) We are not to think here of a bucolic hierarchy reaching from cows

at the end of 6 connect it with 1 and 7 over against 5, but in 6 also, as in 1 and 7, the prize is connected with art (flute and pipe). In Idyll 1 one of the two gifts is a wondrously fashioned cup; and in 7 the gift is Lycidas' staff, a "guest-gift from the Muses" (7, 129). In 5, on the other hand, the prize is the "good meat" which Morson contemplates with some eagerness (note αὐτίκα, "send it at once", 5, 140).

Between the two poles of 1 and 7 on the one hand and 5 on the other we may situate the remaining four bucolic Idylls. Six, as we have seen, is close to 7 and 1 in the felicity of its "one place" which makes possible friendly song and exchange of gifts pertaining to art. Three and Eleven, which are dominated by longing for an absent beloved and pervert the pastoral locus with desires inappropriate to it, stand somewhere in between. Four also has affinities with this group (3; 6; 11); but its proper place is at the lower end of the scale, close to Five. Four has no singing contest, only a bucolic conversation[43]. The amity of the speakers and the helpfulness of Corydon (4, 54; 56/57), however, draws it toward the "higher" group, 1; 7; the frame of 6. On the other hand it shares with 5 an interest in earthy sexuality, albeit of a less aggressive type (4, 58—63).

Idyll 3 is the only one of the bucolic poems presented without a narrative frame. It is a monologue from start to finish. The unnamed speaker is sometimes identified with the Battus of Idyll 4 because both indulge a sentimental passion for Amaryllis (cf. 3, 6 and 4, 38). Having given his goats to Tityrus, for whom he also feels a special affection (3, 3), to pasture on the mountains (3, 3—5), this herdsman, like Battus in 4, is without a flock[44]. The reference to the butting billy-goat in these lines recalls for a moment the realistic rusticity at the end of 5 (cf. 3, 5 and 5, 147; ἐνόρχαν in 3, 4 also suggests the theme of castration at the end of 5). But

---

to goats: see Ernst A. Schmidt, Hirtenhierarchie in der antiken Bukolik? Philologus 113 (1969) 183—200; contra B. A. Van Groningen, Mnemosyne, Ser. 4, 11 (1958) 313—316.

[43]) See above, note 31.

[44]) The identification between the goatherd in 3 and Battus in 4 goes back to the ancient commentators: see schol. ad Id. 3, a (p. 116 Wendel), 3, 1a (p. 117 Wendel), 4, 38/39d (p. 147 Wendel); also Lawall 47, with n. 1, p. 128; Gow (above, note 1) ad 3, 1 regards the connection as "absurd". For Battus' lack of a herd see Lattimore (above, note 31) 321ff.

Three is much further from pastoral realism than 5, and the actualities of bucolic life soon disappear.

The virtual absence of a real bucolic world in Three is in keeping with the self-enclosed, fanciful character of the speaker[45]). Perhaps it is significant that we do not learn his name or any concrete particulars of his life, his origins, his locality. Hopelessly out of touch with reality, he lives not in a precisely defined pastoral geography, like the herdsmen of 4 and 5, but in a mental world of his own distant imaginings and immature emotions.

Idyll 11, like Idyll 3, consists mostly of a monologue about the love of an inaccessible girl. Unlike 3, however, the narrative frame and a concrete pastoral locus play a prominent role. The contrast between land and sea, possible and impossible, naturally groups 11 with 6, as does of course the subject matter, the romance of Polyphemus und Galatea. By creating false images both of himself (6, 33—39; 11, 77—79) and of his beloved (6, 31—33; 11, 20ff.), Polyphemus destroys the peace and happiness that his own pastoral world might give him[46]). The theme of impossible desire and the amusingly naive juxtaposition of irreconcilable elements, nevertheless, brings 11 close to 3. Each speaker begins with a similar address to his beloved: ὦ λευκὰ Γαλάτεια (11, 19); ὦ χαρίεσσ' Ἀμαρυλλί (3, 6). On the other hand the second-person address to a real contemporary outside the bucolic fiction also links 6 and 11 (Ἄρατε, 6, 2; Νικία, 11, 2).

The criteria of myth, mutual amity, poetic elevation, and the realization or neglect of a bucolic locus allow us to place 6 next to 7 and 1 at the "upper" end of the pastoral scale, 3 and 11 close to one another (along with the songs of 6), 4 close to 5 in its rustic realism, initial banter, and earthy sexuality, but akin to 6 in the amity between the speakers. It must be stressed that these groupings are thematic only; they do not necessarily reflect order of composition or placement in an original book of Boukolika.

---

[45]) See Lawall (above, note 5) 34—41; Schmidt, Poet. Reflexion (above, note 6) 53: „Das dritte Idyll ist nicht eine im Lied sich darbietende bukolische Szene, sondern eine liedhafte Schaustellung."

[46]) For this aspect of Idd. 6 and 11 see C. Segal, Landscape into Myth: Theocritus' Bucolic Poetry, Ramus 4 (1975) 128—130, = Ancient Pastoral, Ramus Essays on Greek and Roman Pastoral Poetry, ed. A. J. Boyle (Melbourne, Australia 1975) 46—48, with the bibliography cited there in notes 37—43.

The large mythic frame of Idylls 1 and 7 not only form the highest level of the pastoral corpus, but also enable Theocritus to express, in symbolic form, the poetic essence of his bucolic world and his bucolic art. The other five Idylls, less complete in their synthesis and less wide-ranging in their themes, operate more through surface detail and wit than mythic depth.

The three Idylls primarily concerned with longing for an impossible or distant love, namely 3, 4, and 11, also share the common theme of the neglected flock. In 3 the Goatherd has left his herd to be tended by Tityrus. In 4, Aegon, "in love" with athletic victory (4, 27), has gone off to Olympia, leaving his cows to get thin with longing for their master (4, 12—16; 26—27). In 11 the love-sick Cyclops neglects his sheep as he sits looking out at the sea and thinking of Galatea (11, 10—18): "By themselves the sheep often came back to the steading from the pale grass" (11, 12—13)[47]. In the gentler and less disruptive love of the companion-piece, Idyll 6, the more confident and more stolid Polyphemus (cf. 6, 34—38 and 11, 30—33) neither wastes away nor looks out to sea; and correspondingly the bucolic setting is more whole, less torn by the inversions of land and sea that mark 11. The herdsman himself is a more content, well integrated part of his bucolic world (cf. 6, 9—10; 21; 28).

The "sentimental goatherd" of Idyll 3 is further out of touch with this bucolic world than any other figure in the Idylls. His having left his goats to Tityrus on the mountain is emblematic of his detachment from (bucolic) reality. On the other two occasions in the Idylls when a goatherd minds a friend's flock, it is to listen to the other's song (1, 14; 7, 87), not indulge his own talent.

The pastoral locale of 3 reflects the character of the speaker. The cave and the buzzing bee, both regular parts of the bucolic locus[48], here blend into his own erotic fantasies (cf. 3, 6 and 12/13). The garland with its fragrant herbs and flowers which adorn the happy bucolic feast of Tityrus in 7 (cf. 7, 63 and 68) is here a mark of the speaker's frustration as he threatens to tear it apart (3,

---

[47]) The spontaneous return of the herd has a very different significance in the pastoral Golden Age of Virgil (E. 4, 21 f.) or Horace (Epode 16, 49 f.): see Schmidt, Hirtenhierarchie (above, note 42) 190; Bruno Snell, Hermes 73 (1938) 240 f.; Becker (above, note 11) 347 f.

[48]) Bee: 1, 107; 5, 46; 7, 141 f.; [8]; 45 f.; cave: 6, 28; 7, 137; 11, 44; cf. [8], 72 and [9], 15.

21—23)[49]). The flowers which are elsewhere offerings of love[50]),
even unhappy love (5, 92f.; 11, 10f.; 11, 56ff.) have here "withered
on the soft arm" of the speaker (3, 30), where "soft", ἀπαλῷ, adds
to the humorous pathos and irony. In the happy locus of 7 "every
stone sings" (7, 26)[51]); here the stone is absorbed into the singer's
unfulfilled longing, his own self-centered emotions, and becomes an
emotion-charged metaphor in a "fantastically extravagant address"
(3, 18f.)[52]):

ὦ τὸ καλὸν ποθορεῦσα, τὸ πᾶν λίθος, ὦ κυάνοφρυ
νύμφα. . .

This perversion of the happy bucolic locus is especially marked
at the end of 3. Whereas Tityrus in 7 sings the appropriately bucolic
myths of Daphnis and Comatas, the goatherd of 3 sings a series
of amatory myths which reach grotesquely beyond the pastoral
world[53]). Through this and the other aspects of the poem already
discussed, the Idyll appears as a kind of comic inversion or distorted
mirror-image of 7, the fullest realization of bucolic scenery and
bucolic myth in the corpus.

Just before his catalogue of myths, the goatherd touches on the
familiar pastoral motif of reclining under a pine as he sings (3, 38):
ᾀσεῦμαι ποτὶ τὰν πίτυν ὧδ' ἀποκλινθείς. This motif finds its richest
poetic formulation in the wishful reclining of Tityrus/Lycidas in
7, 86—89 (cf. also 7, 66 and 133): Here the reclining is part of
Tityrus' offer to the "divine Comatas" as he recognizes the latter's
extraordinary gift of song (7, 86—89):

Would that you were numbered among the living in my day, that
I might have pastured the lovely goats on the mountains,
hearing your voice, and you would have reclined under
oaks or pines, singing sweetly, divine Comatas.

The goatherd of 3, however, will hear only his own voice and hope
to attract a glance from Amaryllis (3, 38—39):

---

[49]) For the garland and love cf. also 2, 153 and 10, 29.

[50]) See Lembach (above, note 19) 151—154.

[51]) See Lawall (above, note 5) 104f.; Segal, Seventh Idyll (above,
note 6) 37.

[52]) Williams (above, note 16) 53.

[53]) See Lawall (above, note 5) 40f. Even the story of Adonis and
Aphrodite (3, 46—48), though vaguely bucolic (cf. 1, 109), destroys the
modest limits of pastoral: see C. Segal, Adonis and Aphrodite: Theocritus,
Idyll III, 48, AC 38 (1969) 82—88.

I shall sing reclining thus against the pine, and perhaps
she would look toward me since she is not adamantine.

The promise of songful reclining just before the goatherd's cata-
logue of myths (3, 38) is framed by a cessation of song and a total
collapse at the end (3, 52—54):

I have a pain in my head, but you don't care. I sing no
longer (οὐκέτ' ἀείδω; cf. ἀσεῦμαι 38), but
I shall fall down and lie there, and the wolves will eat
me up. May this be as sweet to you as honey in your throat.

This passage may be compared not only to the conclusion of Lycidas'
song cited above (7, 86—89), but also to the story of Comatas him-
self just before (7, 78—85)[54]. Comatas' "pleasure" (τάδε τερπνά, 83)
contrasts with the goatherd's trivial "pain" (ἀλγέω, 3, 52). The
honey of the bees which keeps Comatas alive contrasts with
Amaryllis' supposedly honey-sweet pleasure in the goatherd's
death (3, 54; cf. also 5, 126). Wolves, dangerous predators generally
remote from this bucolic world (see supra), will now, as the goatherd
imagines, attack the herdsman himself (cf. also 5, 38 and 106), a
reflection of a hostility between man and nature quite different from
the helpful and fostering relation between man and nature in
Seven's myth of Comatas or in One's cosmic sympathy for Daphnis,
where wolves are also involved (1, 71f.; 115). In the goatherd's
overheated imagination the wolf motif also destroys the playful
eroticism in the stylized wolves of the familiar bucolic simile
("You flee me as the ewe when she sees the grey wolf", 11, 24;
cf. 10, 30)[55]. Finally the refusal of song contrasts both with the
songful reclining of Comatas (ἀδὺ μελισδόμενος κατεκέκλισο, 7, 89)
and with Comatas' special relation to the bees who feed him honey
and to the Muse who pours nectar into his mouth (7, 80—82). These
contrasts will appear more clearly in tabular form:

Idyll 3
Tityrus pastures goats to allow goat-
herd to sing
inappropriate myths

---

[54] For other aspects of these contrasts see Segal, Landscape (above,
note 46) 133f., = Ancient Pastoral 51f.

[55] Van Groningen (above, note 39) 47f., remarking the figure of Lykos,
"Wolf", in Id. 14, calls attention to a possible erotic significance of the
wolf-motif in the pastoral Epigram 6 as well.

silly goatherd
no song (3, 52)
"Wolves will eat me" (death)
honey connected with refusal of song
          and with death
reclining under a pine followed by
          collapse in silence and despair

Idyll 7
Tityrus pastures goats to allow
          Comatas to sing
myths of bucolic hero-poets, Daphnis
          and Comatas
divine goatherd (7, 89)
Muses and exquisite song
bees feed Comatas (rebirth, life)
honey connected with Muses and life-
          giving bees
reclining under oaks or pines for
          "sweet singing"

If we accept the identification of the Tityrus of 3 with the Tityrus of 7, we might go even further and reflect on the irony of this awkward goatherd-poet of 3 giving his goats to the herdsman who sings one of the most haunting myths in the bucolic corpus (7, 72—89) while he himself indulges his considerably lesser talent and his penchant for emotional pathos. Lycidas in 7, so tactful in eliciting song from Simichidas (7, 42—51)[56]), seems to have known, as the goatherd of 3 does not, how to enjoy Tityrus' gifts at their best.

III.

So far we have compared and contrasted individual Idylls. It is also possible to proceed by taking a cross-section of separate motifs. The changing values of these motifs can be traced across the various poems. Each motif, as we move farther down the scale, has a different value, higher or lower, in accordance with the different level of poetic or mythic elevation in the respective Idyll.

---

[56]) See above, note 38. If the Goatherd of 3 is in fact identified with Battus in 4 (see above, note 44), there is perhaps a common element of the distracted herdsman relying upon a more practical and experienced pastoral colleague: see Segal, Fourth Idyll (above, note 31) 14—16.

Such a procedure is analogous to following the melodic line of a single instrument through the movements of a quartet or symphony. But since such a motif, like the single melodic line, has its aesthetic significance only in relation to the harmony created by the simultaneous presence of all the motifs, this procedure suffers from the disadvantage of artificially isolating details not really detachable from the whole.

Another limitation must also be considered. Many of these motifs exert a bonding force in several different directions at once, i. e. are related to several different elements simultaneously in the complex web of the poem. The motif of the cicada or tettix (item 9, infra), for example, pertains to the physical beauty of the pastoral locus, to the theme of song, to love and longing, to the balance between the life-giving harmony or the potential hostility of nature. The motif of mountains cuts across the themes of love, poetry, helpful sympathy between man and nature, delusion and down-to-earth work.

Theoretically, it would be possible to construct a grid showing how each of these motifs functions across the various spheres of the bucolic world and bucolic activity (song, love, friendship, etc.) in accordance with each particular Idyll's place in our sliding scale. The two coordinates of the grid we may loosely call v a l u e (fuller or lesser realization of the possibilities of the pastoral locus) and f u n c t i o n (the relation of the given motif — trees, water, pipe, cicada, etc. — to the general bucolic themes of song, love, harmony with nature, delusion, etc.). Such a grid, using a few of the motifs we have discussed, might appear as follows:

Value| higher: (more elevated, happier, etc.) → lower: (less elevated, etc.)

Function	Song	Thyrsis in 1, Lycidas and Comatas in 7	→ Imagined breakdown of song in 3		→ Quarrelsome singing contest of 5
	Friendship	Herdsman of 1; 6; 7	→ Use of Tityrus in 3	→ banter of 4	→ accusations of 5
	Nature	Bees and Comatas in 7	→ Sympathy for Daphnis in 1	→ Inversions of 1, 132 ff.	→ Harmful creatures of 5, 108—115
	Love	Lycidas and Ageanax in 7; Daphnis and Damoetas in 6	→ Deluded loves of 3; 6 (songs); 11	→ Love for dead Amaryllis in 4	→ Aggressive sex and violence of 5

The list of the motifs that follow could obviously be lengthened and more details could be offered, especially on items 11 and 12, trees and plants. I shall confine my remarks to the most salient examples.

1. Truth. As a number of scholars have pointed out, truth occupies a major role in Idyll 7. Lycidas calls Simichidas "a sprig from Zeus formed all for truth" (7, 44). The vegetative metaphor, the reference to Zeus, the probable allusion to the "truth" of the Muses in Theogony 27, the delicate irony all contribute to making this elusive line the poetically richest, and at the same time, the most explicit statement of the motif[57]). The goatherd of Idyll 3 reports that a soothsayer named Agroio told him the "truth" about Amaryllis' indifference (3, 31—38). Here we descend from myth to magic and superstition. We also drop from the bucolic to the agrarian work-world since Agroio is a gleaner (3, 32). More important, the speaker has not been able to profit from this truth, for he goes right on to offer his gifts and sing his myths to the unheeding girl. In 5, as Van Sickle, Serrao, and Schmidt have pointed out, truth-fulness, mentioned at the very center of the poem (5, 76/77), is a major element in the quarrel between the two herdsmen and possibly the decisive element in Comatas' victory (cf. 134/35 and 4)[58]). Here, typically, truth is itself an element in the quarrel, and the point is the absence of truth, not the celebration of truth (even with some irony), as in 7, 44. If Schmidt is right to suppose that Lacon's remark on the syrinx in 134/35 reveals the "truth" about his "stolen" syrinx, truth still remains hidden and evasive.

2. Syrinx and Aulos. The lowest level of the motif, as we have seen, occurs in Lacon's possibly mendacious allegations that Comatas stole his syrinx (5, 4ff.). At the other end of the scale stands the mythical framework of the motif in 1, where the dying Daphnis describes at length his pipe with its "honey-sweet breath ... curved around lovely lip" which he bestows upon Pan himself (1, 127/28). Happier, though on a more human and realistic plane, is the exchange of pipe and flute between the two cowherds of 6. A sentimental and unmythical version of the syrinx of 1 occurs

---

[57]) For the significance of "truth" in Id. 7 see Puelma (above, note 13) 156—160; Gregorio Serrao, Problemi di poesia alessandrina: I, Studi su Teocrito (Rome 1971) 39—54, especially 47 and 50ff.; Segal, Seventh Idyll (above, note 6) 22ff. and Simichidas' Modesty (above, note 38) 131ff.

[58]) On "truth" in Id. 5 see Van Sickle, Unity (above, note 11) 495f.; Schmidt, Id. 5 (above, note 12) 240; Serrao, Id. 5 (above, note 22) 88f., 108.

in Battus' lament for the mouldering pipe of the absent Aegon (4, 28). The syrinx plays no major role in 7, though Simichidas calls Lycidas" the best player of the syrinx among herdsmen and reapers" (7, 28/29). The syrinx-motif, then, conforms to the scale we have suggested: Idylls 1 and 5 are at the greatest distance from one another; 6 is close to 1, and 4 beneath 6.

3. Memory. The finest and most elevated remembering occurs in Lycidas' song in 7, 69, where in a peaceful, happy, and musical setting he will "gently remember Ageanax" (taking μαλακῶς with μεμναμένος)[59]. At the opposite extreme from this rather delicate and spiritualized love (despite 55/56) stands the unhappy "remembering" of sexual brutality in 5 (40; 116; 118)[60]. Typical of the tone of 3 is the sentimental motif of "reminding" or "remembering" through the clack of the petal of "love-in-absence", which naturally gives a negative response (3, 28/29). Closely parallel, though in a (characteristically) negative vein is the sentimental Battus' resolve never to "forget" Amaryllis, not even in death (4, 38/39).

4. The noon hour. The mysterious noon hour has its fullest supernatural and mythic resonance in 1, 15ff., the time of "bitter Pan's rest" when herdsmen dare not sing (cf. Epigram 5, 6). The noon hour of 7, 21 is also a time of heavy sleep for living creatures (7, 21—23) and of course a fitting moment for the encounter with the mysterious Lycidas. In 6, 4 noon is only an indication of the time of day, with the suggestion of ease, calm, and rest in the seeking of a spring of cool water (6, 3). If we may digress from the bucolic corpus proper for a moment, we may note the two references to noon by the hard worker, Milo, in 10, 5 and 10, 48. In both places the noon hour marks the practical exigencies of the mower's toil, the rhythms of work and rest.

5. Sea. The most expansive and mythically richest development of sea occurs in the song of Lycidas (7, 52—62). Here a strong and happy love accompanies images of the calm sea (57). Lycidas' large perspective takes in both sea and stars, both the surface and the seaweed in the depths (57), both the predatory life of marine fowl (60) and the mythical "grey Nereids" (59)[61]. In contrast to

---

[59] See Segal, Seventh Idyll (above, note 6) 51.

[60] Schmidt, Id. 5 (above, note 12) 231.

[61] Segal, Seventh Idyll (above, note 6) 53ff.; Landscape (above, note 46) 128ff., = Ancient Pastoral 46ff.

7 stands the sea of 6 and 11, where the sea-calm mirrors back illusory appearances (6, 35) or else holds out hopes of an impossible change of one's basic constitution (11, 54—66). Rather than being comprehended in its natural rhythms, like the sea in Lycidas' song, the sea here either mocks the lover in its "calm laughter" (6, 12) or else symbolizes a hopelessly distant love in contrast to the immediate and earthy realities of the herdsman's land existence (cf. 11, 12—18; 73 ff.). At this same level of emotional immaturity belongs the lover's leap "into the waves" in 3, 25, where the sea, at the opposite extreme from Ageanax' "lovely voyage" in 7, is associated with unfulfilled love.

6. Mountains. The mountains of 1 are a haunt of Pan (1, 123—125), of the Nymphs (1, 66/67), of Aphrodite and the mythical Anchises (1, 105/106) and also of the wild beasts which lament Daphnis' death (1, 115). In 7 the mountains are the place where Lycidas fashions his song (51) and where Simichidas meets the Nymphs (7, 92). There are also the distant mountains of the Edones in the curse on Pan (7, 111) and the mountains which Polyphemus threw at Odysseus' ships (7, 152). More important than these mythical mountains is 7, 74, the only place in the bucolic Idylls where mountains become animate with sympathy for the archetypal herdsman-singer, Daphnis. The mountains of 11, like the sea, reflect the distant, wistful hopes of inaccessible love as the Cyclops recalls how he fell in love with Galatea when she came to pluck hyacinth leaves on the mountain (11, 25—27)[62]. Idyll 3 mentions the mythical mountains where Adonis pastured his sheep (3, 46), but its mountain at the beginning is the prosaic pasture for goats (3, 2). In the more realistic Fourth Idyll mountains are the setting for the exuberant Aegon's great feat of strength (4, 35 f.), but they also have thorns which enable the practical Corydon to teach the sentimental Battus a lesson (4, 56/57).

7. Cool Water. No more need be said of the elaborately described springs of 1 and 7 or the movement "away from the spring" in 5, 3. It is, however, worth adding that the Cyclops' lovely description of "cool water which many-treed Aetna sends forth from its white snow, ambrosial drink" (11, 47/48), is the only place in the bucolic Idylls which talks of actually drinking this

---

[62] Cf. Sappho 105c LP; see Lembach (above, note 19) 174—179; E. W. Spofford, Theocritus and Polyphemus, AJP 90 (1969) 31f.

water. Despite the melodiousness of the verse the bumptious
Cyclops remains concerned with material comforts (cf. 11, 35f.; 51).

8. Cave. Close to the fusion of wishful sentiment and reality
in 3 is the Cyclops' image of a passionate Galatea looking toward
his cave in 6, 28. In 11 the Cyclops' cave, like his water (preceding
item), is a place of physical comfort (11, 44) and, probably, of
wished-for love. Idyll 7 again has the fullest mythical development:
in the Thalysian grove "sacred water came bubbling forth from
the cave of the Nymphs" (136/37). The wine broached at that happy
feast invites comparison with the wine which old Chiron offered
Heracles "in Pholus' stony cave" (7, 149/50).

9. Cicadas and Grasshoppers. In 7, 139 the cicada is
part of the happy and bountiful Thalysian setting, and in 7, 41
the grasshopper is the symbol of superior song (βάτραχος δὲ ποτ'
ἀκρίδας ὥς τις ἐρίσδω). In 5, 34 grasshoppers also sing in a bucolic
locus, but later in 5 both grasshoppers and cicadas are destructive
or annoying (5, 108—111). The grasshopper of 1, 52, as we have
seen, is associated with artistic creation and song, but this singer
will exchange his freedom in grove or tree for a plaited cage.
Idyll 4, 16 makes a passing allusion to the cicada's love of dew-
drops, a motif connected with the purity of song elsewhere in
Hellenistic poetry[63]). But in the "lower" bucolic realism of this
setting the cicada's modest diet reflects only (or primarily) the
longing of the heifer as it wastes away for the absent herdsman
(4, 15f.), itself a sign of deficiency and sadness in the bucolic locus.

10. Hag/Soothsayer. I have already discussed the "old
woman's" tomb in 5, 121 and the sieve-soothsayer of 3, 31 whose
"truth" teaches the goatherd nothing. The old woman who taught
the Cyclops how to spit into his bosom (6, 40) is an amusing re-
flection on his uncouthness. This passage, like the prophet of 6, 23
(from whose lessons Polyphemus seems to have learned as little as
the goatherd of 3, 31), links Polyphemus and the goatherd of 3 as
foolish and sentimental lovers. The old woman who appears at the
end of Simichidas' song, 7, 126/27 (a partial echo of 6, 39/40) would

---

[63]) See especially Callim. Aet. 1, fr. 1. 29ff. Pf.; Wimmel (above, note 13)
224f. with n. 1, p. 225; Rosenmeyer (above, note 2) 134f.; Gow (above,
note 1) ad 4, 16; A. Dihle, The Poem on the Cicada, HSCP 71 (1966) 112
with n. 17; G. Giangrande, On the Text of the Anacreontea, QUCC 19 (1975)
196, à propos of Anacr. 32 (Bergk).

bring not only a superstitious averting of evil, but also "inner calm, ἀσυχία"[64]).

11. Trees. This is a complex topic involving Homeric models and sacred or medicinal associations of which we cannot always be certain. Lembach's monograph marks an important beginning, but more work needs to be done on the literary associations.

Two extreme points are offered by 7, 74 and 5, 117 respectively. On the one hand the oaks reflect nature's cosmic sympathy with the dead poet-herdsman, Daphnis; on the other hand the oaks are part of a sordid scene of low rustic life, Comatas' alleged intercourse with the shepherd Lacon.

Oaks play an important role in the bucolic locus of 5, possibly because of their unhappy associations for one of the interlocutors[65]). The umpire is an oak-cutter (64). But in 7 it is under "oaks or pitch-pines", ὑπὸ δρυσὶν ἢ ὑπὸ πεύκαις (7, 88) that Tityrus/Lycidas would have the "divine Comatas" recline while he sang. Not only is there a Homeric echo (Iliad 23, 328), but this is also the only place in the bucolic Idylls where the πεύκη occurs, a tree which Theocritus remarks for its height elsewhere (ὑψηλαὶ πεῦκαι, 22, 40). This lofty tree, along with the noble oak, forms an especially appropriate setting for the "divine" Comatas' song. Elsewhere in the bucolic corpus herdsmen recline under the πίτυς, but not the πεύκη (e. g. 3, 38; 5, 49)[66]). Is being pelted with pine-cones from high up in the latter passage (5, 49) an ironical touch, a rather dubious attraction in this contentiously reached locus? According to Lembach Comatas reckons these cones "among the positive aspects of his place", and Cholmeley considers them "a great recommendation because these pine cones were used for food"[67]). It is true that κῶνοι can be somewhat ambiguous (see Athenaeus 2, 57b—c) and that with the cones fall also the edible pine nut, the much prized pignolo[68]). Yet, as Serrao has pointed out, "a pine-cone

---

[64]) On the importance of ἀσυχία here see Serrao, Problemi (above, note 57) 67f.; Segal, Seventh Idyll (above, note 6) 48f., 70.

[65]) See Schmidt, Id. 5 (above, note 12) 229; cf. Id. 5, 45; 61; 102.

[66]) For the pines in Theocritus see Lembach (above, note 19) 99f.

[67]) Lembach (above, note 19) 100; R. J. Cholmeley, The Idylls of Theocritus (London 1919) ad 5, 44.

[68]) At the time of writing (August/September, 1975) I have observed families eagerly gathering these nuts under the tall umbrella pines of the Villa Doria Pamphili in Rome.

that falls on one's head cannot certainly be enumerated among the 'positive aspects', not even by a goatherd"[69]).

"Myricae (tamarisks) are common in the Theocritean landscape"[70]). This innocent statement is typical of the tendency to level Theocritus' bucolic landscapes down to a vague and static unity. In fact, tamarisks occur only twice in Theocritus. This infrequency is surprising in the light of the fact that "they belong among the most widespread and most common vegetation of stream and forest"[71]). The two passages where tamarisks do occur, moreover, echo one another, and this echo is significant:

λῆς ποτὶ τᾶν Νυμφᾶν, λῆς, αἰπόλε, τεῖδε καθίξας,
ὡς τὸ κάταντες τοῦτο γεώλοφον αἵ τε μυρῖκαι,
συρίσδεν; τὰς δ' αἶγας ἐγὼν ἐν τῷδε νομευσῶ.

(1, 12—14)

σίττ' ἀπὸ τᾶς κοτίνω, ταὶ μηκάδες· ὧδε νέμεσθε
ὡς τὸ κάταντες τοῦτο γεώλοφον αἵ τε μυρῖκαι.

(5, 100—101)

In 1 the tamarisks form part of the gentle and songful setting where two friendly herdsmen meet in the mysterious quiet of noon. In 5 the trees (and the same line) occur within a contentious atmosphere, the contest of Lacon and Comatas, and create no easeful locus. In 1, Thyrsis, like Tityrus in 7, 87, offers to pasture the goatherd's animals in order to make song possible. In 5 the realities of the herdsman's work are present in the energetic interruption, σίττ' ἀπὸ τᾶς κοτίνω (100), with its vivid onomatopoetic evocation of the noises of the country, the strange vocable σίττ'. This interjection, characteristically, occurs only in the two lower-level, realistic bucolics, 4 and 5 (cf. 4, 46 and 5, 3) and is inappropriately imitated in the spurious 8, 69[72]). The wild olive and the oak in 5, 100 and 102 are also not places of rest, like the oaks and pines of 7, 88, but, like the spring of 5, 3, are places where the herdsman has to stay alert and show his mettle. In 5 too it is Comatas' goats, not the herdsmen themselves, who will enjoy the sloping hill and its tamarisks (5, 101; 1, 13).

---

[69]) Serrao, Id. 5 (above, note 22) 80f., n. 14.
[70]) Leach (above, note 2) 249.
[71]) Lembach (above, note 19) 105.
[72]) See Rossi, Id. 8 (above, note 1) 7 ff.

The Cyclops has laurel and cypress growing outside his cave, partly a reminiscence of Od. 9, 109 and 182. But the laurel is connected with dangerous magic in the Second Idyll, and the cypress is a funereal tree. Cypresses stand outside Calypso's cave in the Odyssey (5, 64), no cheerful place for the hero (5, 151 ff.). Cypress trees occur nowhere else in the bucolic Idylls save for the bowl of cypress-wood, also in 5 (104). Cypress and laurel occur together as part of the setting of a locus sacer in the fourth Epigram (4, 7), the shrine of Priapus. The sacral associations may possibly point to the less than inviting aspects of the Cyclops' cave. On the more positive side, and in keeping with the happier associations of their respective bucolic loci, are the elms and dark poplars which weave their shade in the seventh Idyll (7, 8 and 135) and the elm which adds its charm to the spring and shrines to form the "shepherd's seat" in Idyll 1, 21.

12. Flowers and plants. Idylls 7 and 5 again provide two points of contrast. The "soft flowers" with which the bees feed Comatas in 7, 81 certainly have a loftier tone than the flowers in which Lacon "sullies the unripe boy" in 5, 87. Somewhere in between can be located the petals of 3, 29f. and 11, 55—59 with their sentimental tone or the hyacinth leaves, with their Sapphic reminiscence (105 c LP), which provided the occasion of Polyphemus' falling in love with Galatea (11, 25—29). The rich ivy which entwines the cup in 1, 29/30) marks the abundance and reality of the natural world, in contrast to the ivy which forms part of the Goatherd's erotic daydream in 3, 14. On the other hand the thistles (βάτοι, ἄκανθαι) which are part of the inversion of nature at Daphnis' death (1, 132) reflect the fruitfulness of the Thalysian grove in 7, 140. Those same thistles mark the coyness of Galatea and a paradoxical shifting between sea and land in the simile of 6, 15/16, but they have all their nasty thorniness in the more realistic 4, 50. Analogously the herb fleabane, κνύζα, forms part of the bed or στιβάς of Lycidas in 7, 68, but is fodder for cows in 4, 25. The "sweet-fruited vine" on which the Cyclops prides himself as part of the rustic wealth and comfort of his cave is threatened by grasshoppers in Comatas' couplet of 5, 108/09 (cf. also 1, 49).

In the enumeration of the possibly questionable blandishments of Comatas' unachieved locus amoenus of 5 occur two lines which mention galingale (κύπειρος) and bees, virtually identical with lines in the first Idyll (5, 45/46 = 1, 106/07). The context in the first

Idyll is the setting of Anchises' meeting with Aphrodite in Daphnis' taunt to that goddess, a not altogether propitious association. Whichever poem was written first, the echo links Comatas' locus with one of the more discordant scenes in the bucolic world, Daphnis' bitter speech to the goddess allegedly responsible for his doom. The only other place where galingale (κύπειρος) occurs also has ominous associations: the ill-fated landing place of the Argonauts in 13, 34. The description of the bees too in 5, 46 seems to echo a passage in Hesiod's Theogony which compares the evils of woman to bees' nurture of useless drones (Theog. 594), a negative association (toil versus pastoral ease) appropriate to both contexts.

Not all these contrasts and comparisons carry the same weight. Yet the evidence accumulated above is sufficient to establish my main thesis, that the specific elements of the bucolic world are significant and closely correlated with the poetic and mythic elevation of the individual Idylls, from the fully realized locus of 7 to the disiecta membra of a bucolic locus that form the quarrelsome, realistic, and unmythical fifth Idyll.

How conscious Theocritus was of these relationships, to what extent he wrote and then rewrote the Idylls as Virgil certainly did the Eclogues, with such cross-references in view we cannot say. It is, of course, possible, though unproven, that Theocritus brought these poems together in a form which has left no subsequent trace on the transmission of the text. It is also possible that the poet's desire to vary, experiment with, and self-consciously connect a body of poems on similar themes led him to carry his thought over from one poem to the next and helped shape the patterns which we have here attempted to follow. These patterns and hierarchical relationships seem too consistent to be the result of fortuitous similarities between works belonging to the same genre. Whatever the process of composition, revision, and publication, the bucolic Idylls illuminate one another in their multiple interconnections of theme and verbal echo, and they should no longer be treated as discrete, unrelated poems.

Appendix: Idylls 8 and 9

I shall not repeat here the arguments that have been put forth for and against the authenticity of these poems[73]), but rather comment

---

[73]) See above, note 1.

on them from the point of view of the results of this study. With the majority of recent scholars, I regard these two Idylls as spurious. Their imitative quality results in the loss of the thematic coherence and gradations which have been traced above. Both 8 and 9 mix elements from the "higher" and "lower" levels in a way which does not occur in the genuine bucolics.

Idyll 8 begins on a note of spatial remoteness (κατ' ὥρεα μακρά, 8, 2) which recalls the mountainous setting of 7 (cf. 7, 92) and 1 (cf. κατ' ὥρεα μακρὰ Λυκαίω, 1, 123; also ps.-Mosch., Epitaph. Bion. 39). Likewise the stress on mutual amity in the fourfold anaphora of ἄμφω (8, 3/4) echoes the beginning of 6. But that tone of friendliness is then mingled with the more quarrelsome, "lower" themes of Idyll 5 in the discussion of the stakes (8, 12—17). Like 5, 8 introduces an umpire (8, 25—29), who, however, is himself a herdsman and remains further in the background than the woodcutter-umpire of 5. The genuine Idylls do, of course, mix high and low tones within the same poem; but, as I have tried to show, their thematic coherence is greater, and they generally effect their mixture of literary and bucolic worlds with less heavy-handed artificiality than a passage like 8, 6—10 with its labored pastiche of Homeric phrases.

The songs of 8 are in keeping with its mannered and artificial tone. The first set develops the familiar theme of the sympathy between man and nature (8, 33—48). In effect, this section imitates the sentimentality of 4, 12ff., but without the saving ironies produced by the contrast between Battus and Corydon (cf. 4, 17—19 and 23—25), and also without the broad mythic resonances of Idylls 1 or 7. The motif of the wolf (8, 63ff.) that Theocritus uses either as a touch of remote fantasy (e. g. 1, 71f.), or as a bit of proverbial pastoral lore (4, 11; 5, 38) in the more "realistic" poems, or as an indication of humorously exaggerated violence (3, 53) here becomes a gently pathetic element in a static tableau which resembles the stylization of the Sixth Epigram. The closest parallel to this address to the wolf is 1, 115, but the grand mythical fantasy and elegiac sympathy of the latter passage differ toto caelo from the unreal and derivative pathos of this poem.

The ending of 8 tries to combine the calm, symmetrical, amiable closure of 1 and 6 (cf. 8, 81—87) with the violent, more "realistic", and more insensitive gestures of victory and defeat at the end of 5 (cf. 8, 88—91 and 5, 142—144). The next lines, "And from this time Daphnis was first among shepherds and, still a youth, wedded the Nymph Nais" (8, 92f.) abruptly freezes pastoral song and pastoral love into a conventionality, artificiality, and fixity which are different from the openness with which the genuine Idylls end. The closest analogy to this kind of self-conscious, static closure is perhaps the picture of Demeter at the end of 7. Yet even that scene is continuous with the preceding descriptions of rustic activity and maintains those tensions between fixity and movement, imagination and reality, which pervade all of Seven.

Idyll 9 presents some equally odd collocations. Most striking is the juxtaposition of the "cool water" and the rustic couch or στιβάς, familiar from the calm pastoral loci of 1 or 7, with the violent and grotesque detail of goats blown off a cliff (9, 7—11). Lines 15ff. draw upon Idyll 11 in the description of the material comforts of a cave, but lack the ironies which the themes of hopeless love and the contrasts of sea and land give to that motif in its original context. Instead, this section of 9 introduces a total discontinuity of tone in the realistic proverb about a toothless man and nuts (9, 20f.). The concern with food continues into the next section. Lines 22—27 juxtapose the gift of a shepherd's staff drawn from Seven (but without Seven's mythical overtones) with the unpastoral theme of seafood (9, 25f.). Theocritus' careful gradation of higher and lower elements in a coherent framework of style and setting here gives way to a deliberate and often mechanical play upon discontinuity: the proverbs at the end of the first two songs (9, 12f.; 20f.), the shell at the end of the third (9, 25—27). The last line abruptly introduces Circe. This sudden intrusion of a mythical figure might be compared to Demeter at the end of 7 or Melanthius at the end of 5, but both of these figures have a thematic relevance which is hard to discover here.

Lacking this coherence of the motifs in the genuine Idylls, 8 and 9 also lack their clarity and firmness of locus and encounter. We do not feel that particularity and concrete rootedness in bucolic place and bucolic character which enable the genuine Idylls to combine, interweave, and play off against one another realism and myth, banter and lyricism, irony and fantasy.

LANDSCAPE INTO MYTH: THEOCRITUS' BUCOLIC POETRY

Charles Segal

'I no longer look upon *Theocritus* as a romantic writer,' wrote Lady Montagu to Alexander Pope; 'he has only given a plain image of the way of life amongst the peasants of his country . . . I don't doubt, had he been born a Briton, but his *Idylliums* had been filled with descriptions of thrashing and churning.'[1] Thanks to greater sophistication about the nature of pastoral and a better knowledge of Hellenistic poetry we have probably left behind forever the notion of Theocritus as the conveyor of a 'plain image' of rustic life.[2] The alternative is not, of course, the 'romantic' Theocritus, but a poet of consummate literary artistry, wit, and irony.

Besides the critical commonplace of rustic realism the other stumbling block to a satisfactory appreciation of Theocritus has been the inevitable comparison with Virgil. Critics who have viewed Theocritus through lenses adjusted to Virgil have tended to emphasize the emotional complexity, inwardness, and seriousness of the Latin poet over against the outward-facing playfulness and lightness of the Greek.[3] Theocritus certainly lacks the tension between historical reality and poetry which gives the *Eclogues* their special depth and poignancy; but he has a seriousness of a different sort. The simplicity and trivial realism which are sometimes attributed to the bucolic *Idylls* are in fact themselves part of the poetic fiction and often stand in deliberate self-contradiction with mythical elements in the form and structure of the work.

The descriptive elements in Theocritus' pastoral landscape are not purely ornamental, but are related to one another both within the individual poems and across separate poems as constituent parts of a total design, like letters in an alphabet which we can eventually learn to read. To describe these landscapes as 'symbolic' is to say both too much and too little. The uniqueness of Theocritus' bucolic corpus (by which I mean essentially *Idylls* 1, 3-7, 11, with the 'Hesiodic' 10 and *Epigrams* 2-6 on the periphery) lies in the complete fusion of surface and latent meaning. As Rosenmeyer has emphasized, the bucolic convention is itself the trope; the pastoral frame is its own metaphor.[4] The bucolic fiction, with its implicit contrast of country and city, the simple and the elaborate, signifies something beyond itself, a desiderated ideal of calm and harmony with self and with nature.

Not realism *per se*, but the tension between realism and artificiality, the actual and the imaginary — whether in love, art, human relationships, or the search for spiritual peace — form the primary concerns of Theocritus' bucolic poetry.⁵ This poetry, as Ott has shown at length, is an 'art of contrasts'. On the level of poetics the contrasts take the form of opposing voices of poetry, sentimental and ironic, as in *Idyll* 4.⁶ In love the tension is between the absent and the present, imaginary and real possibilities for happiness (*Id.* 3, 10, 11). In personal integration *hasychia*, 'calm' or 'serenity', contrasts with delusion or emotional violence (*Id.* 3, 5, 6, 7).⁷

By the end of the fifth century B.C. and especially in Euripides nature, no longer part of a divinely governed world-order, is free to become a vehicle for purely poetic signification, resonant with human feelings and sensitive to human emotions. 'The disintegration of the belief in the cosmos released nature for an interpretation in the language of human pathos in much the same way as, *mutatis mutandis*, the decline of the teleological metaphysics in the eighteenth century released nature for a response to that romantic yearning which made the poet discern in the murmur of wood and river "the still, sad music of humanity".'⁸ This is not to say that there is not an immense difference between nature's sympathetic response to Prometheus' suffering in Aeschylus (*P.V.* 406-35) and the natural world's mourning for Daphnis (*Id.* 1.132-6; 7.72-77). Theocritus' transformation of this tragic trope displaces the emphasis from the isolation of the hero — a Prometheus, an Ajax, a Philoctetes — to the emotionality and soulfulness of the world itself. The lament of nature for the dying Daphnis in both the above passages is carefully enclosed by the framing motifs of refrain or the act of singing: 'Cease, Muses, come cease your bucolic song' (1.131 and 137); 'Tityrus . . . will sing . . . and he will sing' (7.72 and 78). This framing calls attention to the artificiality of the situation and scales the cosmic reference down to a lighter, more manageable tone. The art-world enframing the suffering tempers the questions of ultimate meaning which had their full scope in the open social and ritual contexts of epic and tragedy.

Tityrus' song of Daphnis will bear closer examination (*Id.* 7.72-77):

> ὁ δὲ Τίτυρος ἐγγύθεν ἀσεῖ
> ὡς ποκα τᾶς Ξενέας ἠράσσατο Δάφνις ὁ βούτας,
> χὼς ὄρος ἀμφεπονεῖτο καὶ ὡς δρύες αὐτὸν ἐθρήνευν
> Ἱμέρα αἵτε φύοντι παρ' ὄχθαισιν ποταμοῖο,
> εὖτε χιὼν ὥς τις κατετάκετο μακρὸν ὑφ' Αἷμον
> ἢ Ἄθω ἢ Ῥοδόπαν ἢ Καύκασον ἐσχατόωντα.

Tityrus close by will sing how once Daphnis the cowherd loved Xenea and how the mountain toiled in grief for him and the oaks mourned him, they which grow by the river Himera's banks, and how he melted away as the snow melts down great Haemus or Athos or Rhodope or Caucasus at the world's end.

The parataxis, the melodious cadences, the 'objective' elements in the information about Himera's oaks, the Homeric epithets, and indeed the Homeric catalogue-geography of the last line deliberately recall literary tradition and literary convention and thus keep the emotion under control, while the suggestive 'melts as the snow' awakens a gentle and familiar pathos tinged with the erotic connotations which the verb 'melt' carries in Greek poetry and elsewhere in Theocritus (*Id.* 1.66 and 82; 2.29, 6.27, etc.).[9]

A passage from the third *Idyll* provides a different, but complementary perspective on the relation between Theocritean landscape and its more expansive predecessors (3.12-16):

> Look, then! Grievous is the ache to my heart. Would that I were the buzzing bee and might come into your cave, penetrating the ivy and fern that densely closes it. Now I know Eros. Harsh god! A lioness' breast he suckled . . .

'Would that I were . . .' The phrase echoes the familiar 'escape' motif of Greek tragedy: 'Would that I were a high-flying eagle that I might take wing over the swell of the unharvested grey sea', wrote Sophocles in the lost *Oenomaus* (frag. 476P = 435N). 'Would that I were among the concealing hollows of the rocks, that a god might make me a winged bird among the soaring flocks' (Eurip., *Hippol.* 723ff.); 'Would that we were winged birds where they flock to leave Libya's wintry storm, obeying their shepherd's flute . . . O winged long-necked cranes, companions of the clouds' courses' (Eurip., *Helen* 1478ff.). The Goatherd of Theocritus may be unhappy, but his ambitions and his needs are modest. He would be a humble bee, not an eagle or a crane. His flight blends with the restful sound of the bee, a familiar inhabitant of the bucolic locus (*Id.* 1.107 = 5.46; 7. 141-2; [8.] 45-6). Within the framework of the *Idyll* the 'here' of the present and the 'elsewhere' of the evasion are both places of wishful escape. The 'would that I were' motif becomes a parody of itself, escape within escape. As in the 'melting' of 7.76, the erotic overtones fuse the external reality of nature with subjective desire. The boundaries between objective nature and inward emotion become blurred. But the possible sentimentality of the effect is checked both by the parodistic echo of the literary tradition and by the paratragic 'Now I know Eros', with its abrupt asyndeton. The vacillation, characteristic of this speaker, between sentimentality and realistic apprehension is reinforced by the close metrical parallel, in two lines of unusually choppy rhythm, between the wish and the understanding (3.12 and 3.15).

This tension of the bucolic *persona* between sentimentality and realism has its counterpart in the landscape. On the one hand there are fresh, crisp details of wild roses growing by a stone wall (*Id.* 5.93) or a ring dove in a juniper tree (5.96-7) or dry thistledown in late summer (6.15-16). On the other hand the landscape is often sketched out in a few essential features, concrete enough to avoid seeming stereotypic, but yet conventional and generic in the actual descriptive words.[10] Grass and flowers are 'soft' (4.18, 6.45, 7.81) and cypresses are 'slender' or 'sweet-smelling' (11.45; *Epigr.* 4.7). A stream is 'great' (1.68) and its water is 'holy' or 'lovely' (1.68 and 118), all echoes of Homeric epithets, as are also the 'dark grapes' with which the vineyard on the cup is heavily laden (1.46; cf. *Iliad* 18.561; Hesiod, *Scutum* 296). The richest pleasance in Theocritus, the setting of the Harvest Festival of 7, is remarkable for the restraint and paucity of adjectives. Rushes are 'sweet' and 'deep' (7.132-3), water is (again) 'holy' (136); branches are 'shady' (138); thorns are 'dense' (140); bees 'yellow' (142) and summer 'rich' (143).

Like Homer, whom the *Idylls* so often have in mind, Theocritus has an eye for the practical and human reality even amid the clearly symbolical richness of this place of songful bounty. The 'deep' rushes of 7 relate immediately to the 'reclining' of the happy picnickers (132-3); and the 'newly cut' vines (134), like Odysseus' remarks on the suitability of Goat Island for agriculture (*Od.* 9.131-5), are a reminder of the toilsomely gained order which promotes the fertility of this flourishing farm, a practical aspect of that harmony between man and nature of which the laughing Demeter holding sheaves and poppies is the mythical emblem at the end (156-7).

All these details, like the tangibility of the winnowing fan and Demeter's 'holding', point us back to a familiar, enclosed world, a solid, well-known reality based on the rural economy of Greece and southern Italy. The recurrence of the same features throughout the bucolic *Idylls* reinforces the plausibility and familiarity of this landscape: pines, oaks, grass for pasture, olive trees wild and tame, vineyards, rubble walls, springs and marshes, the sea and mountains nearby. This is a landscape of the known rather than of the bizarre or exotic.[11] Details tend to arise naturally and easily from the narrative frame and from the characters' regular activities in their world. Even the metaphorical cave of *Idyll* 3.13-4 discussed above has a certain concrete particularity in 'this cave here' from which Amaryllis glances out in line 6.

All this constitutes the familiar world of the 'realistic' Theocritus, the poetry which relaxes and dissolves tensions by its very limitations, by its rootedness in the soil and the earthy life of herdsmen and, on the periphery, farmers, vintners, woodcutters, and fishermen.

Surface calm and static beauty, however, are often deceptive. The mellifluous line αἱ δὲ καλὸν βομβεῦντι ποτὶ σμάνεσσι μέλισσαι

The bees buzz beautifully around the hives

occurs in contexts which hardly lull our senses to ease. In one place it is part of Daphnis' bitter reproach to Aphrodite (1.107); in another it is an item in the quarrel of two cantankerous herdsmen (5.46). The peaceful rustic scenery of the latter poem clashes with its vivid details of aggressive and sadistic homosexuality (contrast 5.29-34 and 45-59 with 41-44).[12] Legrand, stressing Theocritus' preference for 'calm aspects of nature', says of the songful 'toil' (*ponos*) of the chirping cicadas in 7.139, 'What Theocritus, it seems, values in his favored localities is their aptitude for fostering indolence'.[13] But he is overlooking the significance of that word 'toil' and paying too little heed to the intense movement, the kinetic as well as the static joy, which the Thalysian grove contains. The image of the traveller reclining 'under a shady beech tree when the sun's heat parches' is elsewhere (*Id*. 12.8-9) part of the rather fatuous speaker's 'bucolic' sentimental expatiation on his romantic bliss.[14]

How misleading it may be to savor the melodious serenity of a Theocritean landscape without an eye to the ironic and dramatic tensions can perhaps best be illustrated from this charming passage:

ἔστι ψυχρὸν ὕδωρ, τό μοι ἁ πολυδένδρεος Αἴτνα
λευκᾶς ἐκ χίονος ποτὸν ἀμβρόσιον προΐητι.

There is cold water which many-treed Aetna sends forth
for me from its white snow, a drink ambrosial.

But these lines occur in the mouth of the uncouth Cyclops (11.47-8), whose cloying exaggerations in his opening eulogy of Galatea (11.20-1) have already supplied an ironical perspective for the descriptive luxuriance of 'many-treed', 'white snow', 'ambrosial drink'. He can scarcely use a noun without a modifier of some sort, generally trite (e.g. 'smooth poppy with red petals', 57). The discrepancy between the speaker's bourgeois mentality and the rustic beauty of the setting places him in an ironic relation to his landscape and creates a tension analogous to that between locus and character in *Idyll* 5. It is perhaps a subtle detail of this irony that although cold water is a regular feature of the bucolic setting, Polyphemus is the only character in the genuine pastoral *Idylls* to speak explicitly of drinking it.[15] What is a symbol of poetry or a setting for song elsewhere in the *Idylls* (e.g. 1.1-9, 5.33 and 47, 7.136) is here part of the grosser creature comforts with which this boorish lover hopes to win a nymph whose very element is water.

As Eleanor Leach has recently emphasized once more, Theocritus does not present the range and variety of Virgil's landscapes.[16] His settings do not span Virgil's distance between history and quietism, between peaceful streams and the stellar reaches of *Eclogues* 4, 5, or 6. Though Theocritus' forests do not contain 'things worthy of a consul', his bucolic world, in a different way, can rise above its 'lowly tamarisks' and incorporate some very unrustic themes. Simichidas' song in *Idyll* 7 certainly has its natural place in an urban setting (especially 116-27); and the prologue of *Idyll* 11 implies an urban world of professionalism and amateur poetry, self-consciously played off against the rustic themes of the center: note the juxtaposition of the 'shepherding' of love and (medical?) fees in the last two lines (80-1). More important are the mythical background of *Idylls* 1, 6, 7, 11 and the learned framing device, with its Homeric resonances, of the cup in *Idyll* 1.

Across the coherent, continuous, and gradually unfolded bucolic backdrop there flits also an occasional reminder of the country's mysterious, invisible inhabitants: the 'bitter Pan' of *Idyll* 1, the briefly mentioned Pans and Satyrs who conclude *Idyll* 4, the traces of the uncanny in Lycidas' appearance in *Idyll* 7. This element is more fully, though allusively, developed in the pastoral *Epigrams* (2, 3, 5). The effect is to deepen the atmosphere of pastoral removal by evoking the otherness of the country's mythical life. It appears only at rare moments in the *Eclogues* (e.g. *Ecl.* 6. 13-26), but it is this mythic aura of the country which Lucretius evokes as the negative, superstitious side of pastoral 'rusticity' (4. 580-9):

> These places the inhabitants imagine to be held by goat-footed Satyrs and Nymphs, and they say that there are Fauns there whose night-wandering riot and sportive play, as they claim, break the still silences and create the sounds of music and the sweet plaints which the lyre pours forth as it is struck by the fingers of the singers; and the farmers far and wide hear it as Pan, shaking the piny garlands on his half-wild head, runs over the open reeds with curved lip, that the pipe may not cease to pour out the forest muse.

Lyrical effects are at home in such a blend of myth and pastoral removal (*Id.* 1.66-9):

πᾶ ποκ' ἄρ' ἦσθ', ὅκα Δάφνις ἐτάκετο, πᾶ ποκα, Νύμφαι;
ἦ κατὰ Πηνειῶ καλὰ τέμπεα, ἦ κατὰ Πίνδω;
οὐ γὰρ δὴ ποταμοῖο μέγαν ῥόον εἴχετ' Ἀνάπω,
οὐδ' Αἴτνας σκοπιάν, οὐδ' Ἄκιδος ἱερὸν ὕδωρ.

> Where were you when Daphnis was wasting away,
> where were you, Nymphs? By Peneus' lovely vales or
> Pindus'? For you held not the great stream of the
> river Anapus nor Aetna's crag nor Acis' holy water.

The rhythmical balances, the rhyme of *Pêneiô . . . Pindô . . . Anapô*, the alliteration of *p* and *k* throughout, the assonances of 'Peneus . . . Pindus' and 'Anapus . . . Aetna . . . Acis' combine with the sudden address to the Nymphs, hitherto a static and distant feature of the landscape (12 and 22) and with the suggestive 'was wasting away' to produce a landscape which might plausibly contain the semi-mythical Daphnis and sympathetic deities. The Peneus and Pindus are remote, almost literary allusions; but the Anapus, Acis, and Aetna (the last is Thyrsis' place of origin in 65) keeps the coherence and continuity of the present locale. Yet even the local streams acquire a touch of mythic distance through the Homeric 'great stream' and 'holy water'.

Lycidas' song in *Idyll* 7 has several analogous effects, notably in the sudden evocation of the movements of the sea and its depths, its harsh marine life, and its mythology, an effect all the more striking because everything in the poem up to that point has focussed on the land (7.57-60):

> And the halcyons will calm the waves and the sea and
> the south and east wind that stirs the sea weed from
> the furthest deep, the halcyons, to the grey-green
> Nereids dearest of all birds that have their prey from
> the sea.[17]

Removed still one degree more by the song-within-a-song device are the mountains which mourn Daphnis and the sudden and distant landscapes of Himera's banks (7 is set in Cos) and northern mountains (74-77, cited above). The geographical discontinuity broadens in Simichidas' threats of removing the pastoral and Arcadian Pan to wintry Thrace or torrid Ethiopia (106-14). Even at the very end of the poem, in our safe enclosure in the low-lying Coan farm, we glance at the remote mountains of Parnassus and Peleon (148-50).

The more modest poems too can exhibit this tension between a realistic and a lyrical landscape. The cave of *Idyll* 3, cited above, stands somewhere in between; and indeed the blurred status of that cave is itself characteristic of the fantasizing and inappropriate mythologizing of the speaker. *Idylls* 6 and 11 both use the sea as a focal point for the contrast of the present and the distant, the real and the imaginary. The Cyclops' hopeless love leads him to neglect the routines of his solid land-existence for an unattainable beauty for whom he longs and must long (11.12-15):

> Often the ewes by themselves left the pale grass for
> the steading. But the shepherd himself wasted away as
> he sang of Galatea from sunrise on the seaweed-
> covered strand, holding beneath his heart a wound
> most hateful which a dart from great Kypris fixed in his
> liver.

The conventional love-mythology of 'great Kypris' and her 'most hateful
dart' adds to the mythic atmosphere, viewed with mildly amused *Selb-
stironie* through the epithet 'great' and the (inconsistently) repeated
physiological details of heart and liver. The expansiveness of the land-
scape and the mythical overtones interlock for an even more amusing
pathos in the next lines (11.17-18), where the picture of the Cyclops
singing as he 'sits on a high rock looking out into the sea' echoes the
situations of the Homeric Achilles or Odysseus (*Iliad* 1.350; *Odyssey*
5.156-7). The pseudo-Theocritean eighth *Idyll* imitates this passage, but
replaces the Theocritean interweaving of spaciousness, myth, and melan-
choly with the warm, comfortable presence of the girl in the singer's
arms and his flocks nearby (8.55-6):

> But beneath this rock I shall sing holding you in my
> embrace as I look upon the herds grazing together and
> the Sicilian sea.

In like manner the 'wasting away on the seaweed-covered strand' (11.14)
uses the suggestive marine image to convey pathos and unhappy love
more effectively than pseudo-Moschus' 'empty sands' where the grieving
Galatea sat 'forgetting the sea' (*Epitaph. Bionis* 62-63).[18] The Cyclops'
plea, 'Let the grey-green sea reach to the dry land' (11.43), like the fine
contrast between the agitated barking and running dog and the calm of
the sea 'on its quietly gurgling strand' in the sixth *Idyll* (10-12)[19] portrays
the mystery and autonomy of the sea's movements which the quasi-
mythic Lycidas of 7 somehow understands (7.57-60) and the bumptious
Cyclops of 6 and 11 would try, in vain, to assimilate.

Like all great pastoral poets, Theocritus is 'directly concerned with the
extent to which song that gives present pleasure can confront and, if not
transform and celebrate, then accept and reconcile man to the stresses
and realities of his situation'.[20] In that wonderful continuity of surface
and depth which is one of Theocritus' most unique qualities,[21] this
'present pleasure' and the present setting which contains, reflects, and
creates it also exist in and for themselves in a coherent, experientially

livable natural world. The *hasychia* or 'calm serenity' of Theocritus' bucolic realm has little or nothing of the later pastoralists' search for escape from a fallen world into a prelapsarian paradise, like Marvell's 'Fair Quiet, have I found thee here / And Innocence, thy sister dear'.[22] Theocritus' 'Fair Quiet' (*hasychia*), itself a part of the natural world in 6.12, is closer to hand and more in touch with the exigencies of human relationships.[23] His pastoral world is a place for the achievement and testing of clarity and spiritual harmony, not an escapist retreat; the tensions between art and life and the realities of sexual instincts, in men as in animals (1.141-52, 4.58-63, 5.41-2), are there to be dealt with. The gods who address Daphnis in *Idyll* 1 — Hermes, Priapus, Aphrodite — are there not so much to reveal the herdsman's isolation from nature as to rescue him from that isolation.[24]

The ending of the non-bucolic Second *Idyll* provides a useful parallel and incidentally confirms the continuity within the totality of Theocritus' *oeuvre* (2.163-6):

> But you, Lady Goddess, farewell and turn your horses
> toward Ocean, and I shall bear my longing as I have
> borne it. Farewell, Selene of the brilliant throne; fare-
> well, you other stars who follow in the train of calm
> Night's chariot.

The expansive vision of the 'calm' of the night sky creates a continuum both of myth and of nature which matches a new spiritual resourceful-ness in Simaetha ('I shall bear my longing as I have borne it . . .') and reintegrates her too into a larger universe, a more coherent world where nature's order can answer magic just as 'enduring' can replace hopeless 'passion'. The cosmic, mythic, and psychological levels of integration work together to counterbalance, if not entirely to replace, the mental dis-orientation of love and the logical and physical disorientations brought by magical incantation.[25]

How much the lyricism of Theocritus is supported and enlarged by the mythic coherence of his natural world appears from comparison with a not dissimilar context of a modern poet, Pablo Neruda's

> He aquí la soledad de donde estás ausente.
> Lleuve. El viento del mar caza errantes gaviotas.
>
> Here is the solitude from which you are absent.
> It is raining. The sea wind is hunting stray gulls.

or   Los pájaros nocturnos picotean las primeras estrellas
        que centellean como mi alma cuando te amo.
        Galopa la noche en su yegua sombría
        desparramando espigas azules sobre el campo.

        The birds of night peck at the first stars
        that flash like my soul when I love you.
        The night gallops on its shadowy mare
        shedding blue tassels over the land.[26]

Leaving aside the modern version of the 'pathetical fallacy', the elements of nature — the wind, gull, the stars — remain as incoherent points surrounded by the vast spaces of a barely understood desolation. In both the ancient and the modern poet, the large framework of the natural world intensifies pathos, but the ancient presupposes, even if distantly, an underlying harmony, a cosmic order which will eventually make itself felt, while the modern exploits the dissonance of the small lost irrecoverably in a mute, formless universe.

Thus the reversal of nature's fertility in Daphnis' lament (1.132-6) or the wasting away of the cows with longing (4.26-7) or the mouldering of the syrinx in Battus' jaundiced sentimentality (4.28; cf. 38-40 and 1.62-3) all have their place in a balanced, ironic structure and the larger compass of nature's rhythms and man's necessary participation. Daphnis' death is viewed against the background of frisky goats (1.151-2), the mournful loss of Amaryllis against flourishing thorns and the lecherous old man (4.38-40 and 56-63). Virgil's *iam fracta cacumina* ('now broken trunks') in the midst of the vague and gentle landscape of the Ninth *Eclogue* (7-9) is closer to Neruda's poignant discontinuity of nature than the oaks, grass, and bees with which the dying Daphnis reproaches Aphrodite (*Id.* 1.106). The comfort which rustic work holds out to Virgil's Corydon (*E.*2.70-2), though important, is more ambiguous than his Theocritean model's turn to baskets and fodder for his ewes (*Id.* 11.73-5). The coarse, 'Milk the one at hand' (11.75), has a stringent, if crude, sanity far from Corydon's involuted 'plaiting with twigs and the soft rush' (*viminibus mollique . . . detexere iunco, E.*2.72), just as the Cyclops' brief allusion to night and the lascivious laughter that it holds (11.77) is abrupt and cleansing by contrast to Corydon's more sensitive perception of growth and farewell in the lengthening shadows of nightfall (*et sol crescentis decedens duplicat umbras,* 'And the sun, departing, doubles the growing shadows', *E.*2.67), a typical instance of that exquisite 'vespertinal mixture of sadness and tranquillity' so much admired by Panofsky.[27] The broad irony of the Cyclops' last line, 'It's clear that I too seem to be somebody in the land' (11.79), tells us just where we stand with regard to this pathetic buffoon, and the subtler irony attaches to the closing two lines of the frame ('So then Polyphemus shepherded his love by playing at the muse and got along more easily than if he had given gold', 11.81-2), whereas our judgment of Corydon is left more suspended thanks to the abruptness of the closure, the still hopeful 'if' and the ambiguity of 'another Alexis' (*E.2.73*):

> invenies alium, si hic fastidit, Alexin.

> You'll find another Alexis if this one scorns you.

What is true of love and death applies also to poetry itself. Theocritean continuity, limited though it is between myth and realism, precludes the divorce between the pastoral setting and the pastoral singer that is so painful in the First and Ninth *Eclogues,* and so elusive and despairing in the Tenth, with its nostalgia for a now remote Arcadia and its ominous bucolic shadows 'heavy for singers'. That 'contingency' of the human voice which the *Eclogues* dramatize[28] is untheocritean. The heavy stillness of noon and 'bitter Pan' (1.15ff.) is only a momentary scruple, soon overcome. The mysterious noon hour may add a *frisson* of the supernatural,[29] but that fleeting glimpse of the remote and mythical side of the country only enhances the charmed beauty of the songs sung at that hour (*cf.* 6.4 and 7.21). If the 'enchantment' (*thelxis*) of Daphnis' syrinx robs Pan of his midday sleep, there seem to be no recriminations (*Epigram* 5).

Theocritus' large frame of myth is built into his diction, meter, and rhythm, all resonant with Homeric and Hesiodic echoes. This mythic relevance is surely as important as any 'generic' consideration for Theocritus' decision to write his bucolics in the hexameter and not in a more colloquial meter like the iambic. The description of the sweetly falling water at the beginning of *Idyll* 1, for example (7-8), is not just a felicitous piece of onomatopoeic scene-painting, but, as its unmistakable echoes of *Odyssey* 17.209-10 and *Theogony* 785-7 imply, an evocation of a mythic and poetic tradition. The Thalysian grove of *Idyll* 7 gains something of its symbolic force from echoes of passages like the garden of Alcinous, the cave of Calypso, or the cave of the Nymphs in the *Odyssey*.[30] Homeric formulas like 'great stream' and 'holy water' provide a *basso ostinato* against which Theocritus can counterpoint his hexameter's new fluidity and susceptibility to emotion in the small words, repetitions, pauses of that first line (1.66) which floats up with surprising, unpredictable lightness from Thyrsis' formal announcement of his title (*Id.* 1. 65-6):

Θύρσις ὅδ’ ὡξ Αἴτνας, καὶ Θύρσιδος ἁδέα φωνά.
πᾷ ποκ’ ἄρ’ ἦσθ’, ὅκα Δάφνις ἐτάκετο, πᾷ ποκα, Νύμφαι;

This is Thyrsis from Aetna, and the sweet voice of
Thyrsis. Where were you when Daphnis was wasting
away, where were you, Nymphs?

Virgil's adaptation has a strength and firmness perhaps made necessary
by his lack of a crystallized epic diction to play against (E.10.9-10):

Quae nemora aut qui vos saltus habuere, puellae
Naides, indigno cum Gallus amore peribat?

What groves or what meadows held you, maiden Naiads,
when Gallus was perishing of cruel love?

The names of Greek mountains in the following lines, especially *Aonie
Aganippe* and *gelidi . . . saxa Lycaei* ('the cold rocks of Lycaeon', 12
and 15) have an even more remote, exotic ring than Theocritus' 'lovely
vales of Peneus . . . Pindus . . . crag of Aetna' (*Id.* 1. 67-9). They carry
suggestions of erudition and a self-conscious blending of cultures foreign
to the concreteness and uniformity of detail which Theocritus' place in
his literary tradition assures him.[31]

The kind of discontinuity between the pastoral fiction and the poetic
tradition which *E.*10.9-15 illustrates can, of course, be a resource as well
as a limitation, as is clear if we leap the centuries to Milton's version of
the Theocritean lines, the 'Where were ye Nymphs' and 'Return, Alpheus'
passages of *Lycidas*, with the almost epic expansion of nature from rivers
and mountains to continents and 'resounding seas', the spanning of
pagan and Christian divinity, northern and Mediterranean geography,
classical dirge and Christian consolation ('Look homeward Angel now,
and melt with ruth').[32]

For Virgil and for Milton the problem of transmuting Theocritus'
pastoral world is, in one sense, only a matter of degree, to find a personal
voice in their native tongue that can fuse traditional elements into a
valid artistic unity and thereby allow the tradition, absorbed and recast,
to fructify the poetry and sensibility of their own time. Theocritus, how-
ever, enjoys two advantages. First, he writes in the same language
(Greek) and essentially the same poetic vocabulary as the literary tradi-
tion which is his point of reference. Second, as the first real pastoral poet
he enjoys a freedom and an ease which are never again recoverable
because his own verse, whether directly or through Virgil's mediation,
is itself the point of reference for later bucolic poetry.

As the founder of pastoral poetry, Theocritus stands in closer connection with its mythical elements and their doubtless ritual origins: the story of Daphnis was already sung by Stesichorus, and far back in Mediterranean culture lay the ritual lament for a beautiful, beloved shepherd-king and singer whose death is intimately bound up with death and renewal in nature (*cf.* 1.132-6, 7.74-6).[33] The myth of Daphnis provided a framework for bringing together nature, art, and love, the analogies and discrepancies between the creativity of nature and the creativity of art.[34] About the waning singer Daphnis and the concealed and then reborn singer Comatas, as about Adonis in the Fifteenth *Idyll,* the whole cosmic order symbolically revolves (1.132-6, 7.74-6).

In *Idyll* 7 echoes of Homeric and Hesiodic encounters with divinity surround the figure of Lycidas with a mythical aura[35] which makes him not only the archetypal bucolic singer and a kind of hypostatization of the bucolic world, but also the embodiment of the vital inspiration which poetry can find when it moves 'out of the city' (2) towards the mountains (51, 87, 92). Lycidas embodies a quality that can only come unexpectedly and fleetingly. The rich *locus amoenus* of the grain-goddess' Thalysian festival, as quintessentially agrarian as Lycidas is pastoral, is a symbolical realization of energies which poetry both requires and releases, celebrates and denies. At the same time there are hints that this agrarian bounty is not an altogether satisfactory compensation for the bracing air of Lycidas' mountains and all that they symbolize. The fixing of the winnowing fan (156) signals the end of an Odyssean voyage (*Od.* 11.126ff; *cf. Id.* 7.152-3) and of that 'road' (10) on which Lycidas still continues to travel (132), leaving the city-dwellers down in their fertile, but perhaps too sheltered farmland.

The complex structuring and allusive techniques of the two great poems, *Idylls* 1 and 7, enable Theocritus to recover, in a sceptical and self-conscious age, something of the power and range of myth available to earlier poets. Or, to put it the other way round, his need to find a mythic actualization of the essence of his bucolic world and therefore of his bucolic art, to portray in its widest implications the remoteness, beauty, hardness, and *difference* of that bucolic realm, generates the mythic structures and allusive techniques. Through the culminating creation of that art, the figure of Lycidas in 7, poetry can once more mediate between the demonic and the intelligible; the expansiveness and the threatening, disruptive otherness of all intense experience; the ordering continuity which can make that experience a fruitful part of our lives and the intuition of its irreconcilability, even hostility, to our lives.

That elusive, more mysterious and recalcitrant (and, one may add unepicurean) aspect of the bucolic world is closely associated with two elements in the landscape which Lycidas knows with special intimacy:

sea and mountains. Played off against the shady trees, soft grasses, cool water, and the soothing sounds of bees, cicadas, or birds, sea and mountain help shape that rhythm of closed and open, finite and infinite, which is so fundamental a part of the inner dynamics of Theocritean bucolic.[36]

Lycidas can evoke a sheltered land-scene of friends reclining by the fire (7.66), but his previous song embraces a purview which extends from the sea to the constellations (7.53ff.), from the sea-birds' harsh search for their 'prey' (60) to the 'grey-green Nereids' (59), from the calm surface brought by the halcyons (57) to the disturbed seaweed of the depths (58), where literary echoes also add their resonances: *cf.* *Iliad* 23.692-4 and Sophocles, *Antigone*, 590-3. Despite his 'fiery' love (55-6), he is actually in touch with that sea-calm (57) which eludes all the other bucolic lovers. Singing of harmony rather than dissonance between man and nature (*cf.* 57-60, 74-6, 80-5), he possesses from the beginning the large perspective and its accompanying spiritual health that Simaetha glimpses uncertainly only at the end (*cf.* 2.163 and 7.54; also 2.39-41 and 7.57).

Both the Polyphemus *Idylls,* 6 and 11, are built around a contrast between the herdsman's earthy reality of flocks, caves, trees and the elusive Nymph, as inaccessible to the Cyclops as her marine element itself. The clash of marine life and pastoral life which marks the unhappy love of Polyphemus and Galatea in *Idyll* 6 is enclosed by the harmonious bucolic land-world of Daphnis and Damoetas who come together, with their herd, 'to one place' (6.1) for happy singing (contrast 11.13 and 18) and happy love (6.42-4),[37] a framing device analogous to the contrast between the dying Daphnis and the exuberant rustic world of Thyrsis in *Idyll* 1.

The situation of 6 unfolds *in mediis rebus* with a highly visual vignette (note *ide,* 'look' in 9) that sketches the basic contrast of sea and land, rest and movement, the rustic sounds of pipe and dog and the marine sounds of the shore (6.9-13):

> She again — look there! — pelts the dog who watches
> your flock, and the dog barks looking to the sea, but
> the lovely waves show her (Galatea) as she runs along
> the calmly laughing strand.

There is no romantic longing in this seaward look, for it is the dog, not the Cyclops (as in 11.18), who is doing the looking. The sea retains its remote, objective beauty ('lovely waves'), in contrast to the subjective perception of what is 'lovely' (*kala*) in Daphnis' last lines (18-19): 'For often to love (or, 'through love'), Polyphemus, the unlovely has seemed lovely.' Even more significant is the 'calm' of the sea's 'laughter' (*hasycha kachlazontos,* 12), in contrast to the external agitation of the 'running' sea-nymph and the internal agitation of the seated (8) lover. The *hasychia* or 'calm' of the sea is just what the animate figures in this landscape lack. The contrast is deepened by the lovely comparison of Galatea's fickle and inconstant movements to the dry thistledown in summer (15-17). The simile's implicit contrast of land and sea (the 'dryness' and 'parching' of the simile being paradoxical when applied to Galatea) once more underlines the nymph's inaccessibility to the land-based herdsman. Here again the emotional agitation of love and land contrast with the 'calm' of the sea (12).

In the Cyclops' first-person reply (Damoetas' song) the sea loses this objective reality and becomes absorbed into the lover's erotic imagination. Using the pastoral (and bestial) image of the gadfly (*oistrei*, 28) Polyphemus conjures up a passionate Galatea who will come 'from the sea' (27) to share his terrestrial world of 'cave' and 'flocks' (28). The lovely coverlet that, in his imagination, she will 'lay flat' (6.33) contrasts with the halcyons' 'laying flat' of the sea in Lycidas' mastery of love (7.57). The quiet of the sea (*galana*, 35) in his next lines, like the 'calm laughing' of the sea in the first song, ironically points up his own amorous disquietude. Even this sea-calm becomes an instrument of his own delusion in the false 'appearances' which it mirrors back (35-8), an ironical verification of Daphnis' prediction about love's distortion of what 'appears lovely' (18-19 ∼ 36-37). 'Appear', *phainesthai*, is a leitmotif, and verbs for 'seeing' run throughout the poem.[38] 'I saw' is the Cyclops' first word (21), and in his last line he makes use of a magical charm to avert the danger of seeing one's reflection (6.39, with Gow's note). But the real danger of mirror-images here lies beyond the Cyclops' comprehension.

By creating a false Galatea who will live on the land (6.31-3), the Cyclops distorts and agitates the potential calm of his own pastoral world. *Idyll* 11 adds the complementary image of a false Cyclops who could join a responsive Galatea in the sea (11.54-62). There the Cyclops' malaise is prefigured in his anomalous place in a marine landscape, between land and sea, as he 'wastes away on the seaweed-covered strand', and, though on the land, has eyes only for the sea (11.14-18).[39] His pastoral world, like that of the absent Aegon in *Idyll* 4, suffers decline (11.11-13). The contrast of land and sea in 11.12-15 sets *amour-passion*, with its fruitless imaginings, over against practical work and finite, attainable desires. The sea itself holds the elusive mystery of love: it is the unreachable otherness which it is the nature of Eros to yearn after.[40] The grass which should nurture the flock (11.13; *cf.* 4.18) is here as 'pale' as the conventionally unhappy lover (Sappho 31.14 LP; Longus 1.17.4). The verb 'wasted away' in the next line enhances the division between the lovesick herdsman and the vitality of the world from which he is alienated, rather like Daphnis in the First *Idyll* (*cf.* 1.82-93 and 139～152). The epithet 'seaweed-covered' (14) reinforces the non-bucolic remoteness of that sea-world on which the shepherd so hopelessly broods.

The implications of the 'pale grass' and the neglected flock find a different but analogous expression later, when the land-dweller who once led a flower-picking expedition in the mountains (11.25-27) momentarily forgets the seasons of the flowers which he would present to the nymph in her own watery realm (56-59). The conjunction of flowers on the mountain and sea-nymph is itself an uneasy union of dissimilars which in turn reflects the hopelessness of the love itself. The occasion of falling in love holds the microcosm of the entire experience. In *Idyll* 6 too the amour develops from the scene of Galatea 'from the sea' pelting a dog with apples which, of course, like the flowers of 11, belong to the land. Polyphemus' mother who is present at the flower-picking scene of 11 recurs throughout the poem at key points of the Cyclops' dissatisfaction with his pastoral existence (54, 67). In the mythological tradition she is herself a sea-nymph and thus a reminder of Polyphemus' ambiguous biological status.[41] He is a being constitutionally drawn to what he cannot have, a mythical emblem and expansion of what the goatherd-lover suffers in *Idyll* 3.

The movement of *Idyll* 11 follows a restless rhythm of inert despair and confident persuasion, acknowledgment of the remoteness of the sea and the hope to win Galatea over to his pastoral life.[42] His one admission of the sea's remoteness and autonomous processes, 'Let the grey-green sea reach toward the land' (43), comes almost exactly in the middle of his long enumeration of the good things of his land-wealth with which he would persuade Galatea to abandon the sea (36-42, 44-51). When he then turns back to the sea in 54, it is for the impossible wish that he had gills. At the same time his offer to Galatea of his 'one eye than which nothing is sweeter to me' (53) negates that more realistic appraisal of that 'one eye' (32) at the beginning of the speech (note the important *ginôskô*, 'I know', 30). Velleitarian fancies about the outside world of sea and land go hand in hand with unreal suppositions about the inner world of personal identity and personal appearance. When in his last line he does accept his place 'in (on) the land', it is only by dint of surrendering to another 'appearance' or delusion: 'It's clear that in the *land* I too *appear* to be somebody' (79).[43]

As the flower-picking passage of *Idyll* 11 shows (11.25-27), mountains can function in a way analogous to the sea in indicating a remote, wistful, or mysterious quality in experience. In this particular case Virgil, for once the more 'realistic' poet, changed Theocritus' mountains to hedges (*E*.8.37). Theocritus has behind him Sappho's verses on plucking hyacinths in the mountains (105c LP), which confer an even more delicate and distant atmosphere.[44] The haunt of Nymphs, Pan, and wild beasts in *Idyll* 1, mountains are the appropriate place for the confluence of death and love for Daphnis (1.66ff., 105-7, 115, 123-6) and for Adonis (1.109f., 3.46ff.; cf. ps.-Theocr. 20.35, Bion *Epitaph. Adon.* 7). Here Daphnis the hunter is himself hunted, erotically, by Pan and Priapus (*Epigram* 3.2).[45] In a non-pastoral *Idyll*, the *Bacchants*, a movement 'to the mountain' and 'from the mountain' frames the savage dismemberment of Pentheus (26.2 and 26). In the deceptively peaceful *locus amoenus* where Castor and Polydeuces meet the uncouth Amycus they 'behold a wild wood all about them on the mountain' (22.36). Callimachus' Astacidas epigram (22 Pf. = 1211-14 Gow-Page) or the noon silence that holds the mountain in Teiresias' sinister meeting with Artemis (Callim. *Hymn* 5.72-4) exploit the same quality of mountain landscape.[46]

Sometimes Theocritus can play the numinous atmosphere of mountainous settings off against the triviality of pastoral actions. Thus in 7.92 Simichidas' Hesiodic claim that the Nymphs taught him too as he 'pastured cows on the mountains' is probably to be understood as an attempt to match Lycidas' easy contact with the mythical and magical aspect of mountain life (*cf.* 7.51, 74, 87).[47] In any case the urban Simichidas' cows are far less appropriate in the mountains than Lycidas' goats, although Anyte, in a pastoral epigram, has Pan pasturing heifers 'on dewy mountains' (*Anth. Plan.* (A) 231 = 738-41 Gow-Page). The sentimental goatherd of *Idyll* 3 has left his goats for Tityrus to look after 'on the mountain' (3.1-2), while he indulges his amorous fancies for Amaryllis. Whereas the mountains of Idyll 4 are appropriate to the elusive vitality of the absent Aegon (4.35-6), they give the sentimental and impractical Battus his come-uppance (4.56-57). One can trace a kind of gradation in this mountainous atmosphere from full mythic value in 1 and 7 (and, for a moment, in 11.25-27) to more prosaic function in 3 and 4. Only in 7, the *Idyll* most deeply imbued with the power of myth, does a mountain itself become animate with grief for a herdsman-singer (7.74).

The parallels between the mountainous settings of the bucolic *Idylls* 1 and 7 and the non-bucolic 13, 22, or 26 bring us back to our earlier point about the continuities of landscape within Theocritus' total *oeuvre*. In the *Epithalamion for Helen*, for example, 'meadowy leaves', a fragrant garland (*cf.* 7.63-64), a 'shady plane tree', and a bucolic simile of lambs and ewes contribute to the blissful mood of this section of the poem (18.39-48). In such numinous places — the mountains of 7, the grove and pool of 13, the wild wood of 22 or 26 — the normal restrictions on human vision are temporarily lifted; and for good or ill men come into more direct contact with nature's creative and destructive powers and with the secrets of their own strengths and weaknesses.[48]

Yet the bucolic landscapes have a coherence of their own too; and the purely mythical, non-bucolic *Idylls* have features which have no place in the bucolic poems. Thus Hylas' mysterious pool contains a spring (13.39), but not the plashing water of *Idylls* 1, 5, or 7; and its vegetation is quite different from pastoral vegetation (13.39-42). The water itself is ominously 'black water' (13.39), not the 'holy' or 'cold' water of the pastoral poems. *Idyll* 22 describes water flowing down from a steep rock (22.37), as in 1.7-8, and flowers and bees (42-43) that recall *Idylls* 1, 5, or 7. But its 'wild forest' (22.36) is closer to the mountainous setting of the *Bacchants,* with its 'wild foliage' (26.2-3). The pebbles visible through the clear water (22.38-40), the loftiness of the pines (22.40; *cf.* 7.88), the 'white plane trees' (22.41) occur nowhere in the bucolic poems, nor are cypresses 'high-leaved' in those works (*akrokomoi kyparissoi,* 22.41).

Though the *Idylls*, lacking the coherence of an Eclogue Book, have nothing quite like that progression toward a poetic and symbolical Arcadia that Van Sickle has attempted to trace in Virgil's bucolics,[49] there seems to be, as we suggested above, a significant gradation of certain elements in the landscape varying in accordance with the nature of the individual poem. The poems imbued with the fullest mythical consciousness seem to contain also the fullest realization of the bucolic setting, i.e. *Idylls* 1, 6, 7, 11. In 5, though there are some detailed descriptions of bucolic landscape, the bucolic locus itself is an element in the contest between the two herdsmen.[50] In 6, on the contrary, the 'one place' of the opening line creates a locus where the herdsmen's love is happy and mutual, not exploitive. Here too the instruments of pastoral song are given in free and generous exchange (6.42), not stolen as in 5.4, nor decaying as in 4.28 nor (at a higher level) given over *in extremis* to Pan as in 1.128-30.

In *Idyll* 7, the most 'mythical' of the bucolic poems, the landscape is the most expansive in both space and time. The *Idyll* moves from the local Burina spring on Cos, with its epichoric divinities (7.4-6), to the Castalian spring on Parnassus (148). The cave, associated with unreal fantasy in *Idyll* 3 or with physical comfort and material wealth in *Idyll* 11, is here a Nymphs' cave, like that of the *Odyssey,* with its revivifying 'holy water' (137), or the mythical cave of a hospitable (though not entirely unambiguous) meeting between the greatest of the heroes and Centaurs on remote Peleon (149-50). The sea that expresses the follies and delusions of love in *Idylls* 6 and 11 or violence and emotional immaturity in *Idyll* 3 (25) is here the calm sea comprehended in the breadth of its mythical and natural life (52-60).

At times this mythic aspect of the landscape can co-operate with the recurrent theme of song to make the bucolic setting a kind of *Dichter-*

landschaft, a space coterminous with the easeful calm (*hasychia*), beauty, and reflectiveness that poetry itself can confer (*cf.* 11.1ff. and 80f.). So too the alternation between 'realistic' and 'mythical' landscapes can help create the alternation of contrasting styles or voices of poetry: lyrical and ironic, expansive and contained, outward-facing or introspective. Hence the two herdsmen's respective visions of the pastoral locus in 4, fertile or declining, particularized or general, both shape and are shaped by their predilections for a realistic or sentimental style and outlook (e.g. 4.22-25 *versus* 26-28; 55 *versus* 56-57; *cf.* also 11.12-18).

This landscape is not only instinct with song, but actually fuses with the songs which it contains. The beginning of *Idyll* 1 is the clearest example, and perhaps for that reason Theocritus' ancient editors placed the poem first in the collection (1.1-3):

> Ἁδύ τι τὸ ψιθύρισμα καὶ ἁ πίτυς, αἰπόλε, τήνα,
> ἁ ποτὶ ταῖς παγαῖσι, μελίσδεται, ἁδὺ δὲ καὶ τύ
> συρίσδες· μετὰ Πᾶνα τὸ δεύτερον ἆθλον ἀποισῇ.

> Sweet the whispering and sweetly sings that pine, Goatherd, there by the springs; but sweetly do you too play the syrinx. After Pan you will win the second prize.

The sweetness of the sounds of the locus itself blends with the sweetness of the Goatherd's pipe.[51] The parataxis, anaphora, and repeated sounds and rhythms reinforce the virtual identification of place and song. In the Goatherd's reply the verbal echo between the sweet 'singing' (*melisdetai,* 2) of the pine and the 'song' (*melos,* 7) of Thyrsis once more puts human and natural music on the same level and even suggests that the former surpasses the latter on its own terms.[52]

This bucolic 'songscape' exhibits the same kind of inner logic and coherence that seems to pervade the landscape as a whole. The Cyclops of 11 sits on his 'high rock' and 'sings' to cure his love; but the rocky setting of *Idyll* 1 is, as we have just seen, itself songful. The goatherd of 3 will sing under a tree in a typical posture of bucolic ease: 'I shall sing thus reclining against a pine' (3.38; *cf.* 7.66, 89, 133). But bucolic calm is soon undercut by despair that brings incapacity for song at the end: 'I sing no longer, but shall fall down and lie there and wolves will eat me up. May this be as sweet to you as honey in your throat' (3.52-4). The rejection of song in the lover's exaggerated emotionality brings a hypothetical invasion of the bucolic world by dangerous predators (53). The sweetness of honey in the last line (with which we may compare the positive and songful sweetness of 1.1-8) becomes part of the disappointment and bitterness that stifle song. At the opposite extreme is the honey-fed 'divine' goatherd-singer of *Idyll* 7, Comatas, into whose mouth the bees brought honey from the meadows 'because the Muse poured sweet nectar into his mouth' (7.80-85). This goatherd inspires Lycidas/Tityrus with the wish for sweet song and easeful reclining (7.86-89):

> Would that you were numbered among the living in my day that I might have pastured the lovely goats on the mountains hearing your voice, and you would have reclined under oaks or pines, singing sweetly, divine Comatas.

This landscape, moreover, has the unique quality of sympathetic response to the two mythical herdsmen, Daphnis and Comatas. In a symmetrical balancing of life and death, the mountain and oaks lament the death of the one (7.74), while the bees and flowers preserve the life of the other (7.80-85).

The songfulness of the bucolic locus too reaches its highest point in this *Idyll*, where even every pebble sings as it strokes your sandals (7.20), 'larks sing' (141), and 'chirping cicadas have their toil' in song (139).[53] The word 'toil', *ponos*, earlier described the song of Lycidas (7.51), the sympathetic grief of the mountain for Daphnis (74), and the season of imprisonment which Comatas miraculously survives thanks to the bees (85). Hence its echo here in 139 sums up the favoring accord between man and nature which finds its ultimate expression in poetry itself. In *Idyll* 5, to be sure, nature is also songful, but it is grasshoppers (not cicadas) and birds in general (not larks) that sing (5.34 and 47); and there is, of course, none of the harmony between man and nature or between man and man that is so striking a part of *Idyll* 7. In *Idyll* 1 the death of the herdsman-singer Daphnis not only turns the bucolic locus upside down, but also disrupts the beauty of natural song: owls, lugubrious birds (*cf. Odyssey* 5.66), sing to nightingales (1.136).

These elements of a songful poetic landscape have their roots deep in the Greek poetic tradition. Hesiod is the earliest example, with his 'songful cicada' who 'sits on a tree and pours out shrill song . . . in the season of toilsome summer' (*Works and Days* 582-3). Here too are the motifs of shade (589, 593), goats and kids, a spring of flowing water. The copses of Aristophanes' *Birds* similarly resound with song, and the myth-filled shady grove of Plato's *Phaedrus* (230 B-D), symbol of philosophical *hêsychia* ('calm serenity'), 'echoes with the shrill summery music of the cicadas' chorus' (230 C). A pastoral epigram attributed to Plato gives 'voice' to the pine itself (*phônéessan*); and working with the shade, breezes and plashing streams bring the drowsy revery of poetic 'enchantment' or *thelxis* to those who hear the syrinx (*Anth. Plan.* 13).

This pastoral image of a songful locus soon becomes commonplace. In an epigram of Anyte the 'sweet song' of the breeze among the leaves adds to the travelers' rest (*Anth. Plan.* (A) 228 = Gow-Page 734-7). An epigram of Mnasalces is entirely based on the motif of the pleasure brought by the grasshopper's song as one 'reclines beneath the shady leaves' (*Anth. Pal.* 7.192 = Gow-Page 2647-50). In Virgil the motif is so familiar that the poet, speaking *in propria persona*, can assure a living contemporary, Varus, '. . . Our tamarisks and all our grove will sing of you' (*E.*6.10-11).[54] The pseudo-Theocritean Eighth *Idyll* varies the motif by asking the 'vales and rivers', 'springs and pasture' to feed and fatten the flock if the song reaches its usual excellence (8.33-40). The rhetoric here crystallizes what never needs to be said explicitly in the genuine *Idylls,* namely that the richness of the bucolic locus nurtures song as well as animals, the creativity of art as well as the fertility of earth. In the epigrammatic line that commemorates the archetypal herdsman-singer of the first *Idyll* Daphnis is dear not only to the Muses, but also to the Nymphs, to the goddesses of nature as well as to those of art (1.141; *cf.* 120-1).

This interpenetration of reality by myth and of myth by reality, the combination of the elusive with the particular, the tempering of the lyricism of the imagination by the irony of self-knowledge ('Now I know . . .', 3.15 and 28, 11.30) all give Theocritus' bucolic *Idylls* their multilayered meanings. They are refractory to easy generalization. Even on the level of verse graceful lilt and melodious resonance can change suddenly to harsher and more abrupt rhythms (*cf.* 4.38-57, 5.31-62, 11.45-53).

Beneath even the 'realistic' glimpses of butting goats and nibbled olive shoots, however, runs the mythic continuity of a landscape permeated by the songs of Pan, the Muses, Daphnis. The prominence of Daphnis, inventor of pastoral song (Diodorus 4.84.3), in the two most elaborate of the *Idylls* assures Theocritus' bucolic world of its mythic status. Daphnis and his happier, if even more evasive, counterpart, Lycidas, are still in touch with the incantatory magic or *thelxis* (*Epigram* 5.3) of early Greek poetry and the life-fostering function of fiction-making and myth-making (Bergson's *fonction fabulatrice*) in an ironic age when myth was losing or had lost its ancient role of comprehending and ordering reality.[55] Lycidas may smell of goats and rennet, but when he descends from his mountains to meet the city-dwellers on the plain, he brings with him not only the divine epiphanies of Homeric epic, but also the mythic world of a shepherd-singer some half-millenium in the past on whose mountain mortals could still consort with the goddesses of poetry.

École Pratique des Hautes Études, Paris
and Brown University, Providence.

NOTES

1. Quoted in Reuben Brower, *Alexander Pope, The Poetry of Allusion* (Oxford 1959) 15.

2. For the 'realistic' Theocritus see especially Bruno Snell, 'Arcadia: The Discovery of a Spiritual Landscape', in *The Discovery of the Mind*, tr. T. G. Rosenmeyer (Oxford 1953) 282-4, with some qualifications at 287f. For the complexities of the issue see Alfred Körte and Paul Händel, *Die hellenistische Dichtung*[2] (Stuttgart 1960) 218-9; Renato Poggioli, 'The Oaten Flute', *Harv. Lib. Bull.* 11 (1967) 167-8; Adolf Köhnken, *Gnomon* 44 (1972) 751-2; Ernst A. Schmidt, *Poetische Reflexion: Vergils Bukolik* (Munich 1972) 23-4.

3. E.g., Snell (preceding note) 282-4; M. C. J. Putnam, *Virgil's Pastoral Art* (Princeton 1970) 14.

4. See Thomas Rosenmeyer, *The Green Cabinet: Theocritus and the European Pastoral Lyric* (Berkeley and Los Angeles 1969) 278ff. On the differences between Virgilian and Theocritean symbolism which this feature of the *Idylls* implies, see Snell (above, note 2) 306-9 and C. Segal, 'Theocritean Criticism and the Interpretation of the Fourth *Idyll*', *Ramus* 1 (1972) 1-3, 20-2.

5. See Gilbert Lawall, *Theocritus' Coan Pastorals: A Poetry Book* (Cambridge, Mass. 1967) 5ff. and passim. R. Vischer, *Das einfache Leben* (Göttingen 1965) 135: Theocritus' poetry is 'im Grunde eine Poesie unwirklicher Liebe'. Francis Cairns, 'Theocritus Idyll 10', *Hermes* 98 (1970) 38-44, has recently shown how Theocritus has fused the sophisticated conventions of Hellenistic amatory poetry with the pastoral/Hesiodic frame.

6. See J. B. Van Sickle, 'The Fourth Pastoral Poems of Virgil and Theocritus', *Atti e Memorie dell' Arcadia*, Ser. 3, vol. 5, fasc. 1 (1969) 7ff.; Segal, 'Fourth Idyll' (above, note 4) 7-11. S. Lattimore, 'Battus in Theocritus' Fourth *Idyll*', *GRBS* 14 (1973) 319-24, stresses the literary side of Battus that would bring him even closer to concerns with poetics. A. Barigazzi, 'Per l'interpretazione e la datazione del carme IV di Teocrito', *RFIC* 102 (1974) 301-11, criticizes some symbolic interpretations without seeming to have grasped their implications (or indeed having read the authors he cites: *cf.* pp. 302-3, note 1). His own psychological interpretations of Battus and Corydon (p. 303) are as ill-founded as his disproportionate emphasis on line 32 and the historical interpretation he seeks to extract from it (p. 310). For other aspects of *Id.* 4 see G. Giangrande, 'Theocritus' Twelfth and Fourth Idylls', *QUCC* 12 (1971) 104ff.

7. On *hasychia* see the good remarks of G. Serrao, *Problemi di poesia alessandrina*, I, *Studi su Teocrito* (Rome 1971) 67f.

8. Helmut Kuhn, 'The True Tragedy', II, *HSCP* 53 (1942) 83. See also Ruskin's *Modern Painters*, vol. 3, part 4, chap. 14, sect. 7: '. . . Exactly in proportion as the idea of definite spiritual presence in material nature was lost, the mysterious sense of *unaccountable* life in the things themselves would be increased.'

9. For the metaphor see LSJ s.v. *têkô*, II.2; Pearson *ad* Sophocles, frag. 941.7.

10. See Ph. E. Legrand, *Etude sur Théocrite*, Bibl. des Ecoles françaises d'Athènes et de Rome 79 (Paris 1898) 197ff.; G. Soutar, *Nature in Greek Poetry* (London 1939) 223; Rosenmeyer (above, note 4) 186ff., esp. 204-5. Representative texts, though not very helpful discussion, will be found in K. Hartwell, 'Nature in Theocritus', *CJ* 17 (1921-22) 181-90.

11. See Adam Parry, 'Landscape in Greek Poetry', *YCS* 15 (1957) 14.

12. On the discordant loci of *Id.* 5 see Rosenmeyer (above, note 4) 188; E. A. Schmidt, 'Der göttliche Ziegenhirt', *Hermes* 102 (1974) 216-8.

13. Legrand (above, note 10) 201. For *ponos* see *infra*.

14. See U. v. Wilamowitz, *Die Textgeschichte der griechischen Bukoliker*, Philol. Untersuch. 18 (Berlin 1906) 180, who calls attention to the parallel with 4.39. The best discussion of the persona of *Id.* 12 is Giangrande (above, note 6) 101-5, 110-12; see also Francis Cairns, *Generic Composition in Greek and Roman Poetry* (Edinburgh 1972) 17-31, esp. 25f.

15. Compare also *Id*. 1.121 where Daphnis gives his cows drink, and Virgil, *E*.7.11. The search for drinking water occurs in the mythological *Idylls* as an epic motif, fraught with danger: see 13.36 and 22.62 and on the latter passage G. Roux, *RPh* 37 (1963) 80-1.

16. Eleanor Winsor Leach, *Vergil's Eclogues: Landscapes of Experience* (Ithaca and London 1974) 83 and *cf*. also 182ff. As I hope to show in another essay, however, the elements in this landscape are less static than Mrs Leach, following Rosenmeyer and E. R. Curtius, allows (pp. 81ff.).

17. On the sea mythology here see my remarks in 'Theocritus' Seventh Idyll and Lycidas', *WS* N.F. 8 (1974) 53ff. *Cf*. also the halcyon in ps.-Moschus, *Epitaph. Bionis* 40-2 and Moschus, *Europa* 115-24, with its imitation in Catull. 64.14-18. In the literary background may lie also Alcman frag. 26P= 94D.

18. I cannot agree, then, with Schmidt (above, note 2) 77, 'In Theocritus' *Idylls* landscape as space has not yet been discovered'. The passage in *Id*. 8 seems actually closer to the secure limits of Tibull. 1.5.45-8. On *Id*. 11.17f. and *E*.2.4f. see Marie Desport, *L'incantation virgilienne* (Bordeaux 1952) 42. On the Hellenistic predilection for the vast spaces of sea, sky, stars see Carl Schneider, *Kulturgeschichte des Hellenismus* I (Munich 1967) 155, citing Menander 416K = 481E.

19. With Gow, *Theocritus* (Cambridge 1950) *ad loc*. I take the *nin* of 6.11 to refer to the dog and not Galatea. U. Ott, *Die Kunst des Gegensatzes in Theokrits Hirtengedichten*, *Spudasmata* 22 (Heidelberg 1969) 77 nicely points out the contrast between the calm sea and the agitated dog, the tangible presence of the animal and the 'kapriziöse Unfassbarkeit und Unsichtbarkeit Galateias'.

20. Paul Alpers, 'The Eclogue Tradition and the Nature of Pastoral', *College English* 34 (1972) 353.

21. See Albert Cook, *The Classic Line* (Bloomington, Ind. 1966) 173; Segal, 'Fourth Idyll' (above, note 4) 2-3, 20-2.

22. Marvell, 'The Garden', 9-10. His 'Mower against Gardens' also plays on a contrast between a lost 'Nature most plain and pure' and a 'willing Nature' which 'does to all dispense / A wild and fragrant innocence'.

23. See Marvell, 'The Garden', 61-4 and R. Poggioli, 'The Pastoral of the Self', *Daedalus* 88 (1959) 694-8.

24. See Rosenmeyer (above, note 4) 119.

25. See my 'Simaetha and the Iynx', *QUCC* 15 (1973) 42-3.

26. Cited from W. S. Merwin's edition and translation, Pablo Neruda, *Twenty Love Poems and a Song of Despair* (London 1969) 24 and 22 respectively.

27. E. Panofsky, '*Et in Arcadia Ego*: Poussin and the Elegiac Tradition', in *Meaning in the Visual Arts* (New York 1955) 300.

28. Alpers (above, note 20) 355-6.

29. For the noon hour see Plato, *Phaedrus* 242A, 259A; Callim.,*Hymn* 5.72-4; Virg., *G*. 4.401-2; Sen., *Phaedra* 778ff. See in general Rosenmeyer (above, note 4) 76 and 88f.; W. H. Roscher, *Ausführliches Lexicon der griechischen u. römischen Mythologie* III.1 (1897-1909) 1395-1401, s.v. 'Pan'.

30. *Id*. 7.8 and 136 ～ *Od*. 5.64; *Id*. 7.8 ～ *h.Ven*. 20 and *cf*. Bion, frag. XIII Gow; *Id*. 7.135ff. ～ *Od*. 7.114-31; *Id*. 7.136-7 ～ *Od*. 13.103-12; *Id*. 7.149 ～ *Il*. 9.404, *Od*. 8.80, *h.Merc*. 401.

31. See Snell (above, note 2) 282, 286-7; Gordon Williams, *Tradition and Originality in Roman Poetry* (Oxford 1968) 274ff., 303ff., 316ff.

32. See Alpers (above, note 20) 368-70.

33. See R. Y. Hathorn, 'The Ritual Origin of Pastoral', *TAPA* 92 (1961) 228-38, esp. 233ff.; I. Trenscényi-Waldapfel, 'Werden und Wesen der bukolischen Poesie', *Acta Antiqua* 14 (1966) 1-31, esp. 21-31; William Berg, *Early Virgil* (London 1974) 15-22. For Stesichorus see Aelian, *Var. Hist*. 10.18 = frag. 279P.

34. See my ' "Since Daphnis Dies": The Meaning of Theocritus' First Idyll', *MH* 31 (1974) 1-22, esp. 13ff.

35. See my remarks in 'Seventh Idyll' (above, note 17) 31ff. with the references in notes 41-42 there, to which add Schmidt (above, note 2) 227-38; Berg (above,

note 33) 22-5; E. R. Schwinge, 'Theokrits "Dichterweihe" (Id. 7)', *Philologus* 118 (1974) 40-58, esp. 43ff.

36. Sea, of course, can also appear in the 'Hesiodic' vein as a place of the hard work of the fisherman in contrast to the secure and leisurely life of the herdsman: *Id.* 1.40-4, 3.26, frag. 3; Moschus, frag. 1; ps.-Theocr. *Id.* 21, although even in this realistic poem the sea can, for a moment, reflect a beckoning dream-world of mythical deities: 21.52-5.

37. For the relation between the frame and the songs of *Id.* 6 see Lawall (above, note 5) 70-3; Ott (above, note 19) 67-71; Cairns (above, note 14) 195.

38. 'Appear': 11, 19, 37, 38; 'see': 8, 9, 11, 22, 25, 28, 31, 35. Note also the emphasis on the eye in 22 and 36 and see Ott (above, note 19) 81-2.

39. See Anne Brooke, 'Theocritus 11: A Study in Pastoral', *Arethusa* 4 (1971) 73-81, esp. 74. See also E. Holtsmark, 'Poetry as Self-Enlightenment: Theocritus 11', *TAPA* 97 (1966) 256-7; Ott (above, note 19) 199ff. Cairns (above, note 14) 145 shows how the sea replaces the threshold of the house where the comast sings to his mistress.

40. See Plato, *Sympos.* 200A-201C.

41. See Gow *ad* 11.26 and Ott (above, note 19) 206 on the mother as a 'Katalysator zwischen Land und Meer'. For a possible psychological view see Holtsmark (above, note 39) p. 257, note 6.

42. For the correspondences see Ott (above, note 19) 204-5; Hartmut Erbse, 'Dichtkunst und Medizin in Theokrits 11. Idyll', *MH* 22 (1965) 233-4.

43. Other interpreters have taken a more positive view of Polyphemus' 'cure': see Erbse (preceding note) 233-4; Brooke (above, note 39) 79; R. Stark, 'Theocritea', *Maia* 15 (1963) 368. This ambiguity of the 'cure' is reflected in the ambiguous function of 'singing' as both part of the disease and the problem: *cf.* 11.13 and 18; Legrand (above, note 10) 408-10; Gow *ad* 11.13; Erbse, pp. 233-4 with note 1; E. W. Spofford, 'Theocritus and Polyphemus', *AJP* 90 (1969) p. 22 with note 1 and pp. 34-5; A. Barigazzi, 'Una presunta aporia nel c. 11 di Teocrito', *Hermes* 103 (1975) 179-88.

44. See Spofford (preceding note) 31-2; Kurt Lembach, *Die Pflanzen bei Theokrit* (Heidelberg 1970) 174-9.

45. The motif of 'on the mountains' is trivialized in the imitation in ps.-Theocr. 20.30, 'All the women on the mountains say I am handsome'.

46. Compare also the mountainous setting of Pindar, *Pyth.* 3.89-90 and *Nem.* 6.45-6; Soph. *Trach.* 436-7; Eur. *Bacch.* 714-27. See in general Soutar (above, note 10) chap. 3.

47. See Hesiod, *Theog.* 22-3, exploited, ironically, also by Philetas, frag. 10 Powell.

48. See my 'Death by Water: A Narrative Pattern in Theocritus', *Hermes* 102 (1974) 32-3, 37-8; 'First Idyll' (above, note 34) 13-15, 18-19.

49. J. B. Van Sickle, 'The Unity of the *Eclogues*: Arcadian Forest, Theocritean Trees', *TAPA* 98 (1967) 491-508, esp. 493f., 501ff. and in greater detail, 'The Bucolics of Virgil', in *Aufstieg und Niedergang der römischen Welt* (Festschrift J. Vogt), II, Prinzipat, Sprache und Literatur (Berlin 1975) section III B 4 and IV D 10.

50. See Schmidt (above, note 12) 216, 225, 235ff.

51. Schmidt, *Poetische Reflexion* (above, note 2) 31f. suggests a connection between this 'sweetness' and Callimachean *leptotês* or 'thinness', 'fine elegance'.

52. Note that in *Id.* 7.89 the same words, *hadu melisdomenos*, describe the 'sweet singing' not of the landscape, but of the inspired herdsman-poet, the 'divine Comatas'.

53. See Lawall (above, note 5) 104-5; my 'Seventh Idyll' (above, note 17) 62.

54. For the songful locus in the *Eclogues* see E.2.13, 5.62-4, 6.83-6. Virgil, however, adds a new element, the power of the singer over his bucolic world: see E.6.27-30 and 9.19-20. See in general Desport (above, note 18) 108-19; Phillip Damon, 'Modes of Analogy in Ancient and Medieval Verse', *UCPCP* 15 (1961) 281; Charles Fantazzi, 'Virgilian Pastoral and Roman Love Poetry', *AJP* 87 (1966) 185-6.

55. See my 'Ovid's *Metamorphoses*: Greek Myth in Augustan Rome', *Studies in*

Philology 68 (1971) 371-6; H. Dörrie, 'Der Mythos im Verständnis der Antike, II, Von Euripides bis Seneca', *Gymnasium* 73 (1966) 44-62, esp. 47-56. As Schneider (above, note 18) 155 points out, Hellenistic man, too long in city pent, seems to have felt a special need for the 'echte Religiöse des griechischen Naturgefühls' and 'die Nähe des Göttlichen in der Natur'.

VERGIL'S *CAELATUM OPUS*: AN INTERPRETATION
OF THE THIRD *ECLOGUE*.

I

The ancient critics objected that *Eclogues* 4, 6, and 10 were
not truly pastorals.[1] They were in a sense right, but failed to
draw from their observations the significant conclusion, namely
that Vergil intended to do more in the *Eclogues* than reproduce
perfect examples of the pastoral convention. His poems form
a kind of dialogue not only with the pastoral tradition, but
with the poetic tradition of the past as a whole. Recent studies
of the Sixth *Eclogue* have shown how expansively Vergil could
conceive of the pastoral framework;[2] and the suggestion has
been made that in some of the *Eclogues*, again the Sixth and
also the Seventh, Vergil is attempting to sketch his "poetics" of
pastoral or even his view of poetry in general.[3] This "poetics"
would also include an attempt to define the relation of poetry
to other areas of life. Thus Vergil often steps beyond the limits
of his pastoral frame to a vantage point which offers a larger
perspective on poetry and pastoral. In *Eclogues* 1 and 9 and
the proem to 8 he develops the contrast between poetry and
themes of war and empire; in *E.* 6 and (to a lesser degree) in
E. 10 he introduces larger mythological and traditionally high
poetical subjects; in *E.* 4 and 5 he is concerned with great
historical issues, the destiny of Rome and the happiness of the

[1] See Donatus, *Vita*, 302-4 (Brummer); Servius, *Proem. in Buc.*
(Thilo-Hagen, III, fasc. 1, p. 3, lines 20 ff.). Also J. P. Elder, "*Non
iniussa cano*—Virgil's Sixth Eclogue," *H. S. C. P.*, LXV (1961), pp.
116-17, with note 32, p. 124.

[2] See Zeph Stewart, "The Song of Silenus," *H. S. C. P.*, LXIV (1959),
pp. 179-205 and Elder (preceding note), *passim*.

[3] On *E.* 7 see E. E. Beyers, "Vergil: Eclogue 7—A Theory of Poetry,"
Acta Classica, V (1962), pp. 38-47, especially 41-3. On Vergil's expres-
sion of the relation between pastoral and historical realities in *E.* 1 and
9, see my essay, "*Tamen cantabitis, Arcades*—Exile and Arcadia in
Eclogues 1 and 9," in *Arion*, IV (1965), pp. 237-66. Also B. Otis,
Virgil (Oxford, 1963), pp. 128 ff.

human race, but still invokes the pastoral Muses to announce his broader themes:

> Sicelides Musae, paulo maiora canamus!
> non omnis arbusta iuvant humilesque myricae.

And throughout the *Eclogues* runs the theme of love, sometimes happy, more often sad, culminating in Gallus' lament, the *omnia vincit amor* (69), and the poet's own *amor* (73) for his friend in the Tenth *Eclogue*.

The Third *Eclogue* gives an initial impression of being a pastoral poem pure and simple, of belonging entirely to the world of *arbusta* and *humiles myricae*. I shall attempt to show, however, that even in this most "pastoral" of the *Eclogues* Vergil attempts to indicate his awareness of the limits of the pastoral form, that he is consciously seeking, through the poem, to establish his peculiar relation with the pastoral tradition. Vergil explicitly announces, in mock-epic language, that his subject is a matter of no small significance: *sensibus haec imis* (*res est non parva*) *reponas* (54). And, as I hope to show, the subject-matter, structure, and tone of the Third *Eclogue* point to the areas of art and poetry (and not, for instance, political allegory) as the field of this *res . . . non parva*.[4]

Recently, D. E. W. Wormell, approaching the poem from a very different angle, has stated the need for "a reassessment of the tone and purpose of ths Third *Eclogue* as a whole," and has rightly pointed to the poet's concern with larger themes than pastoral realism:

> Despite touches of Theocritean vividness and rustic coarseness it is not meant to be a realistic picture of country life—lines 84-87 should have put critics on their guard. What is here encountered is that characteristic blend of naturalism and artificiality, of ingenuousness and sophistication, which gives the Eclogues their peculiar flavour and special charm.[5]

In pointing to this sophistication, Wormell has placed special

---

[4] The political interpretation of *E.* 3 is offered by J. J. H. Savage, "The Art of the Third *Eclogue* of Vergil (55-111)," *T. A. P. A.*, LXXXIX (1958), pp. 142-58.

[5] D. E. W. Wormell, "The Riddle in Virgil's Third Eclogue," *C. Q.*, n. s. X (1960), p. 32.

stress upon the riddles (lines 104-7). These riddles, as will appear, do indeed play an essential part in the structure of the poem. They have not generally been considered in relation to the poem as a whole and will be so considered later in this essay.

Vergil could not have begun the Third *Eclogue* on a more conventionally pastoral note. In his first two lines he translates literally the first two lines of Theocritus' Fourth *Idyll*, a realistic genre-scene of shepherd life. He then moves quickly to Theocritus V, another poem of realistic rusticity, from which he imitates (much diluted) the erotic suggestion of 8-9 (see Theocr., V, 12 ff.).[6] As happens elsewhere on the *Eclogues*, notably in the Ninth, this close imitation of Theocritus serves a double purpose: it acknowledges a debt, but it also alerts the reader to possible differences and innovations to follow. It sets up the norm of pastoral convention against which can be read the significance of individual deviations and modifications.

Thus here, after the "lower" pastoral vein of the opening lines, the tone begins to change: it shifts gradually away from rustic crudity to the "higher" aspects of the pastoral tradition. The change is perhaps prepared for already in the *faciles Nymphae* of 9—a hasty glance into the mythological realm which Vergil will explore more fully in *Eclogues* 6 and 10. It is intimated also in the *veteres fagos* of 12, the familiar and reassuring scenery of calm, beautiful Arcadia (cf. *sub tegmine fagi, E.*, 1, 1; *inter densas, umbrosa cacumina, fagos, E.*, 2, 3).

A more significant change of mood comes in line 21, where Vergil introduces the theme of song (*an mihi cantando . . .*) which is taken up emphatically in Menalcas' reply in 25, *cantando tu illum. . . .* Vergil is still within the rustic limitations of Theocritus V, for lines 25-7 are closely modelled after lines 5-7 of the Fifth *Idyll*:

> τὰν ποίαν σύριγγα; τὺ γάρ ποκα, δῶλε Σιβύρτα,
> ἐκτάσω σύριγγα; τί δ' οὐκέτι σὺν Κορύδωνι
> ἀρκεῖ τοι καλάμας αὐλὸν ποππύσδεν ἔχοντι;

[6] For Vergil's borrowings from Theocritus in *E.* 3 see A. Cartault, *Études sur les Bucoliques de Virgile* (Paris, 1897), pp. 127 ff.; H. J. Rose, *The Eclogues of Vergil* (Berkeley and Los Angeles, 1942), pp. 40 ff. (unsatisfactory); K. Büchner, "P. Vergilius Maro," *R.-E.*, VIII A 1 (1955), cols. 1193-4.

Cantando tu illum? aut umquam tibi fistula cera
iuncta fuit? non tu in triviis, indocte, solebas
stridenti miserum stipula disperdere carmen?

But Vergil has here treated his original with a freedom and
poetic orginality which are far from the close translation of
his opening lines. He focuses on the theme of song (*cantando*)
rather than the pipe (*syrinx*). He also replaces Theocritus'
coarse taunt, δῶλε, with *indocte*, a word which at this time
invokes a realm of associations quite different from those of
Theocritean rusticity, namely the literary sophistication of the
docti poetae. With this adjective the poet opens the way to
further departures from his crude pastoral beginning.

The next exchange contains another noteworthy departure
from the Fifth *Idyll*, for now Vergil turns to another poem of
Theocritus, his First *Idyll*. As in his opening lines, Vergil
gives a fairly close imitation (29-31):

> ego hanc vitulam (ne forte recuses,
> bis venit ad mulctram, binos alit ubere fetus)
> depono. . . .
> αἰγά τέ τοι δωσῶ διδυματόκον ἐς τρὶς ἀμέλξαι,
> ἃ δύ' ἔχοισ' ἐρίφως ποταμέλγεται ἐς δύο πέλλας
>   (I, 25-6).

But there follows forthwith Vergil's most elaborate use of—and
departure from—Theocritus in this *Eclogue*, the motif of the
cup of *Idyll*, I, 27-61.

Theocritus' First *Idyll*, unlike his Fourth and Fifth, has little
rustic frivolity. It is, rather, a poem of much lyrical beauty
in the decriptions of the country and culminates in the *pièce
de résistance*, Thyrsis' beautiful song of lament for Daphnis.
Yet the structure of the First *Idyll* is very like that of the Fifth:
an introduction consisting of pastoral dialogue occupying nearly
half the poem, a song, and a final pronouncement. Vergil draws
more heavily for his structure on *Idyll* V, with the amoebean
contest and the umpire speaking the closing lines. But his fusion
of *Idylls* I and V within a single *Eclogue* indicates that he
perceived the similarities of structure between the two poems,
and he turns this connection to his own purposes.[7] He creates

---

[7] Vergil's ability to borrow at will from different Theocritean contexts
indicates in itself that he conceives of his pastoral settings differently

thus a gradual progression from the humbler themes of *Idylls* IV and V to the loftier and more elaborate subject of *Idyll* I. At the same time he effects a complex fusion of three different Theocritean poems: the kindly rustic conversation of IV, the more acrid banter and competitive spirit of V, and the peaceful elevated tone of I.

It is at this point, when his fusion of these different elements begins to take effect, that Vergil makes his most significant departure from Theocritus, his treatment of the shepherds' cups. Theocritus' cup gives a panoramic view of his pastoral world. It contains, on the outside, ivy and helichryse (I, 29-31), the floral luxuriance and beauty that are recurrent and fundamental elements in his pastoral settings (e. g. V, 45 ff.; VII, 7-9, 135 ff.; XI, 45 ff.). There follow scenes of rustic life, set down with a delicate and amusing realism and forming a kind of pastoral Shield of Achilles (there are in fact echoes both of Homer and of the Hesiodic Shield of Heracles).[8] First appears a handsome woman, coyly inattentive to two rival admirers (32-8); then a hearty old fisherman drawing his nets (39-44), and finally (45-54) a boy intent on weaving a cage and two foxes with designs on the boy's knapsack and the grapes he is supposed to be watching. Acanthus enframes the whole, making it an αἰπολικὸν θάημα (56), "a wonder for shepherds," or more plausibly, "a wonder from the world of shepherds."[9]

This phrase, αἰπολικὸν θάημα, perhaps indicates that Theocritus intended the scene to serve as a kind of general introduction to the poetic possibilities of his rustic world and as a foil to the loftier tone and sadder subject of the second half of the *Idyll*, the lament of Daphnis. Vergil, perceiving this possibility, uses the passage to set forth and clarify his own ideas about the

from Theocritus and has different notions about the unity of a poem. See Büchner's fine remarks (*loc. cit.*): ". . . bei Vergil hat alles Sinn und Funktion in der individuellen Ordnung eines Gedichtes, ist mithin unvertauschbar, bei Theokrit hat alles seine Ordnung in den objektiven Gegebenheit des Lebens der Hirten."

[8] Theocritus, I, 40-1 imitates the Hesiodic *Aspis*, 213-15. Cf. also Theocritus, I, 34 and 46 with *Iliad*, XVIII, 506 and 561 respectively.

[9] An inferior tradition gives at line 56 the reading, αιολικὸν θάημα," a brilliant sight" (confusing θάημα and θέαμα). See A. S. F. Gow, *Theocritus* (Cambridge, 1950), *ad loc.*, II, p. 13. Gow suggests as the meaning, "an object for a goatherd to marvel at."

range and limits of his pastoral world[10] (from the point of view of *Eclogue* 3, of course, Theocritus' actual intention is irrelevant: cf. Vergil's famous "mistranslation" from Theocritus I in *E.*, 8, 58).

In Theocritus' *Idyll* the cup is one of two gifts (the other being a goat) intended to persuade the talented poet-shepherd to sing. Theocritus has the single shepherd offer both cup and goat. The two gifts are of coordinate value. Together they are part of a unified pastoral framework which easily contains both high poetry and rustic realism. Hence after the Daphnis-song the shepherd can say of his cup,

$$\eta\nu\iota\delta\epsilon\ \tau o\iota\ \tau\grave{o}\ \delta\epsilon\pi\alpha s\cdot\ \theta\hat{\alpha}\sigma\alpha\iota,\ \phi\iota\lambda os,\ \dot\omega s\ \kappa\alpha\lambda\grave{o}\nu\ \ddot{o}\sigma\delta\epsilon\iota\cdot$$
$$\dot\Omega\rho\hat{\alpha}\nu\ \pi\epsilon\pi\lambda\dot\upsilon\sigma\theta\alpha\iota\ \nu\iota\nu\ \dot\epsilon\pi\grave{\iota}\ \kappa\rho\dot\alpha\nu\alpha\iota\sigma\iota\ \delta o\kappa\eta\sigma\epsilon\hat{\iota}s\ (149\text{-}50)\ ;$$

and then, after bestowing the goat, he can turn to his own goats, who at this moment are behaving in realistically caprine fashion (151-2). Theocritus' transition from the "high" poetic effect of line 150 to the realism of his last two lines is perfectly smooth; and even within line 150 the addition of δοκησεῖs, "you will think," makes it entirely clear that the poet is able to juxtapose his two levels without confusing them or feeling them in conflict.

For Vergil, on the other hand, there is a cleavage between the two realms. He creates quite a different balance between the rustic and the poetic by tempering Theocritus' realism with the total unreality of myth and imagination. This imaginative transformation of Theocritus (to stress an often-made, but important point) pervades the *Eclogues* and is essential to their suggestiveness and poetic concentration.[11]

Here Vergil's Damoetas makes the conventional gesture of staking a cow. Menalcas, however, declines competition on these

---

[10] It is, of course, highly characteristic of Vergil to define his own ideas of a poetic form and his own place in a poetic tradition by reference to and modification of that tradition. See Elder (above, note 1) and Stewart (above, note 2), *passim*: also W. F. J. Knight, *Roman Vergil* (London, 1945), p. 121.

[11] On this transformation of Theocritean realism see B. Snell, "Arcadia: The Discovery of a Spiritual Landscape," in *The Discovery of the Mind*, tr. T. Rosenmeyer (Cambridge, Mass., 1953), chap. 13. This subject is treated in connection with a single poem of Vergil, *E.* 2, by F. Klingner, *Gnomon*, III (1927), pp. 579-81.

terms and offers the cups instead: *de grege non ausim quicquam deponere tecum* (32). It is true that his reason is a practical one: the watchfulness of his father and his stepmother, who is a traditional *iniusta noverca* (33). But this dickering over the prize is more than another piece of rustic "realism." It introduces an unexpected " jog " in the progression of the action. It leads to the description of the cups and to the loftier tone which that description strikes. Thus it begins to create that division between " rustic " and " poetic " which is lacking in Theocritus. Menalcas makes a value-judgment which does not merely affect the present context, but soon ramifies to include the question of the nature of Vergilian pastoral and its relation to its predecessors.[12] His cups, Menalcas asserts, are of far greater significance than the cow (35-7) :

> verum, id quod multo tute ipse fatebere maius
> (insanire libet quoniam tibi), pocula ponam
> fagina, caelatum divini opus Alcimedontis.

The addition, *insanire libet quoniam tibi,* is a small, but important touch in establishing this more " poetic " atmosphere. The phrase suggests that these shepherds may look away from the practical realities of their flocks, away from questions of price and value. They may succumb to a " poetic " moment, a moment of excitement, rashness, passion, a moment when engraved cups appear as more valuable than a solid cow, the artistic object more valuable than the practical. It is noteworthy

---

[12] In his treatment of Theocritean rusticity in *Idylls* IV and V and of the cup of I, Vergil would probably have agreed with the youthful judgment of a later "Augustan," Pope, in his " Discourse on Pastoral Poetry ": " He [Theocritus] is apt to be too long in his descriptions, of which that of the Cup in the first pastoral is a remarkable instance. In·the manners he seems a little defective, for his swains are sometimes abusive and immodest, and perhaps too much inclining to rusticity; for instance, in his fourth and fifth Idyllia." Note too what Pope does with the cup-motif in his own pastoral: he makes the adornments even more elevated and grander than Vergil did (" Spring: The Pastoral, or Damon ") :

> And I this bowl, where wanton Ivy twines,
> And swelling clusters bend the curling vines:
> Four figures rising from the work appear,
> The various seasons of the rolling year;
> And what is that, which binds the radiant sky,
> Where twelve fair Signs in beauteous order lie?

that neither shepherd makes any claims for the *usefulness* of his cups; both stress the maker and the adornment. It is interesting too that *insanire* is the verb used of the passionate poet-lover of *Eclogue* 10, Gallus, who does not properly belong to the pastoral world and who, for the moment, is abandoning everything, even life itself, to the intensity of his passion: *Galle, quid insanis . . .* ? (*E.*, 10, 22).

This scene of bargaining, then, begins to open the dichotomy between practical and aesthetic, "rustic" and "poetic" (note the deprecating reference to the "rustic Muse" in the second half of the poem: *Pollio amat nostram, quamvis est rustica, Musam*, 84). The poem, however, does not yet commit itself fully to the "poetic" side. Damoetas retains his rustic hardheadedness and practical sense of values. "If you make any comparison with the cow," he says, "you'll have no grounds for praising the cups" (*si ad vitulam spectas, nihil est quod pocula laudes*, 48). But now Menalcas, in his turn, is carried away by his confidence in his skill. Thus he agrees to compete even on these terms and accedes to Damoetas' initial proposal of 29 ff., the cow: *numquam hodie effugies; veniam quocumque vocaris* (49).

The issue between them, then, cups or cow, aesthetic or practical, is still unresolved at the moment when Palaemon, the umpire-to-be, appears and brings an end to this first half of the poem. But the whole episode of the wager (29-49, nearly a fifth of the entire poem) gives the contest itself a significance which goes beyond a mere singing-match. Damoetas' *res est non parva* (54) may refer to more than the value of the cow. Both the cups and the contest of which they are the prize become meaningful at a level other than that of rustic realism: both are transformed into something symbolic.

It is this process which Vergil is engaged in throughout the *Eclogues*. It is a characteristic mode of his art, both here and in his later works, to find new possibilities in the traditions of the past and through original syntheses and transformations to reawaken them to a new and different life. Ernst Curtius, in an essay that deserves to be better known, has aptly described the process:

> Denn es ist eine Grundkraft und ein Grundwille Virgils, das Währende durch allen Wandel hindurch zu bewahren.

Wiederholung als Wiederbringung, Finden als Wiederfinden, Erneuung als Bestätigung und Erhohung des Besessenen,— das ist ein Herzensanliegen Virgils gewesen. . . . Das Verlorene und Vergangene auf fremden Boden, in neuem Stoff aufzuerbauen, das ist Wille und Weg virgilscher Weisheit.[13]

And Curtius, looking also to the *Aeneid*, seeks the deeper roots of this attitude in the Roman, and generally ancient concern with continuity, history, tradition:

Jenes Persönliche verbindet sich aber mit einem Überpersonlichen: mit der römischen Funktion der Kontinuität, ja vielleicht mit einem für die ganze Antike geltenden Lebensgesetz, wonach alles Neugeschaffene seine Bestätigung von einem Altüberlieferten hier erweisen und auf es verweisen muss: die Kolonie auf die Mutterstadt, die Satzung auf einen Gründer, der Sang auf die Musen, das Abbild auf das Urbild und die Kunstübung auf Muster.

Thus it is that Vergil's motif of the cups takes on meaning beyond the concrete situation, meanings which lead symbolically to the broader "continuities" of which Curtius speaks. Theocritus' cup in *Idyll*, I, 150, it is true, seems to approach having symbolical value: "You will think it was washed in the springs of the Seasons." But, as noted before, the addition, "you will think," subtly keeps real and symbolic clearly distinguished and holds fast to the particularity of the objects in their specific setting. The cups of Vergil's Menalcas, however, shade off inevitably into the realm of symbol:

36   pocula ponam
    fagina, caelatum divini opus Alcimedontis,
    lenta quibus torno facili superaddita vitis
    diffusos hedera vestit pallente corymbos.
40   In medio duo signa, Conon, et—quis fuit alter,
    descripsit radio totum qui gentibus orbem,
    tempora quae messor, quae curvus arator haberet?
43   Necdum illis labra admovi, sed condita servo.

The cups themselves are of beechwood (*fagina*, 37) and hence a part of the rustic world wherein beech trees are so familiar a part of the scenery (see line 12, and the passages cited above). Yet they are also the work of a highly skilled, indeed inspired

[13] This and the following quotation are from Ernst Curtius, "Virgil," in *Kritische Essays zur europäischen Literatur* (ed. 2, Bern, 1954), p. 14.

craftsman, *caelatum divini opus Alcimedontis* (and it is not surprising that this Alcimedon is totally unknown to us and is very likely Vergil's invention). They do not contain scenes of the simple events of daily rustic life, but allude to learned astronomical research. Though the actual carving on the cups presents only the figures of the two astronomers, presumably in medallion-like design, they comprehend by implication the wider terms of lines 41-2 (one thinks of the famous *caelique meatus/describent radio* of *Aeneid* VI). They present the *totum orbem*, the large suggestions of the astronomers' benefactions to all mankind (*gentibus*), and the rhythms of the natural world— the seasons of harvest and sowing—which astronomy helps indicate and measure.

Vergil thus incorporates themes of a broader nature than those of Theocritus—the *paulo maiora* of heavenly phenomena as they are to appear fleetingly in the *caelum altum* of *E.* 4 (cf. lines 5 and 50-1) and the stars of *E.* 5 (cf. 23, 43, 51, 56 ff., 62) and are to be more fully developed in *E.* 6 (33 ff., especially 37). The passage seems to foreshadow too the Iopas song of *Aeneid* I and especially the expansiveness of the *Georgics*, with their translations from Hellenistic astronomical poetry (see *G.*, I, 231-56, 351 ff.) and their praise of natural science, especially the knowledge of the movements of the heavens (*caelique vias et sidera* . . ., *defectus solis varios lunaeque labores*, II, 475-8). And it is interesting in this connection that the singing contest here in the Third *Eclogue* begins with an adaptation of the opening lines of Aratus' *Phaenomena*.[14]

Nor is Vergil troubled by his shepherd's knowledge of the name of an Hellenistic astronomer. Indeed, this fact, like the translation from Aratus, is part of his attempt to state the dignity and complexity of his pastoral art. This motif of the learned, or pseudo-learned, shepherd probably comes again from Theocritus' Fifth *Idyll* (104-5), where Comatas sings,

ἔστι δέ μοι γαύλος κυπαρίσσινος, ἔστι δὲ κρατήρ,
ἔργον Πραξιτέλευς· τᾷ παιδὶ δὲ ταῦτα φυλάσσω.

[14] Vergil may be referring to Theocritus, XVII, 1; but, as commentators have often pointed out, the second part of his line, *Iovis omnia plena*, confirms the connection with Aratus: see *Phaen.*, 2, μεσταὶ δὲ Διὸς πᾶσαι μὲν ἀγυιαί, κ. τ. λ.

But Theocritus, with his clear separation and balancing of rustic realism and "higher" themes, uses this reference to Praxiteles with deliberately humorous intent in order to add another fine stroke to his rustic character portrayal. The simple shepherd has only heard vaguely of Praxiteles and claims him boastfully as the author of his bowl, intending, doubtless, to profit from his companion's equal ignorance, though he himself thereby displays his own naive ignorance of Praxiteles' work.[15] At the same time Theocritus further limits any seriousness in the theme by having his shepherd keep the bowls as gifts for his girl-friend (τᾷ παιδὶ δὲ ταῦτα φυλάσσω, 105).

Vergil, on the other hand, treats the cups of *E.*, 3 with a seriousness which derives from the fact that they are not just rustic gifts, just as his pastorals are not just rustic songs or realistic genre-scenes. He emphasizes the *art*, the act of creation that has made the cups (note *caelatum, torno facili*, 37-8), just as he emphasizes the inspiration of the maker (*divini Alcimedontis*, 37). He is self-consciously aware that his cups are an *opus*, a work of art. Hence his addition of the epithet *divinus* may not be a mere rhetorical adornment, as Cartault had claimed,[16] but part of an intentional modification of his source.

So too Vergil has doubled the motif of the cups and put a second set of cups, also by Alcimedon, into the hands of the other shepherd, Damoetas (44-7):

> Et nobis idem Alcimedon duo pocula fecit,
> et molli circum est ansas amplexus acantho,
> Orpheaque in medio posuit silvasque sequentis.
> Necdum illis labra admovi, sed condita servo.

Damoetas' cups are surrounded by "soft acanthus," an obvious reference back to the enframing acanthus (ὑγρὸς ἄκανθος) that closes the description of the cup in Theocritus I. Yet these

---

[15] This interpretation of the Praxiteles-reference is supported by the scholia and maintained by Gow (above, note 9), II, p. 110: "He means that it is a very splendid piece, and therefore assigns it to the most eminent artist he has ever heard of." Gow cites as parallels Martial, IV, 39 and Phaedrus, 5 *prol.*

[16] Cartault (above, note 6), p. 133: "L'adjonction de l'épithète s'explique par un motif de rhétorique. . . ." It is perhaps possible too that the epithet *divinus* was suggested by Theocritus' τι θεῶν δαίδαλμα (I, 32). For *divinus* in connection with poetic inspiration in the *Eclogues* see *E.*, 6, 67 (*divino carmine*); *E.*, 5, 45; 10, 17 (*divine poeta*).

cups contain the image of Orpheus, the pastoral poet *par excellence*, the poet who can move the natural world in sympathetic response to his art: *Orpheaque in medio posuit silvasque sequentis* (46). Orpheus occurs throughout the *Eclogues* as the symbol of the poet, especially the divinely gifted poet who stands in intimate and mysterious relation to the world and brings a kind of order to its diversity through the beauty of his song, the poet who thus recreates a lost harmony between man and nature.[17]

In the juxtaposition of the two sets of cups, then, Vergil balances the ordering of the heavens (note *descripsit*, 41) for the good of man with a kind of ordering of the natural world (*silvasque sequentis*) by the inspired poet. Both are in profound contact with the rhythms of the cosmos and both are concerned with the establishment of an harmonious relation between the cosmos and man. And both are encompassed in the art-work of the inspired craftsman, the *caelatum opus*.

If Vergil is then using Theocritus' cup to suggest something of the scope of his own pastoral, there may be some significance in his alteration of the enframing designs. To the ivy of Theocritus, I, 29-31 he adds the vine: *superaddita vitis* (38); and the verb *superaddita* (perhaps the first occurrence of this rare compound in Latin) makes the addition stand out with special emphasis. There are, to be sure, grapes in Theocritus, but only as a separate scene, not as one of the framing devices. Vergil's addition is perhaps to be connected with his calling the creator of the cups *divinus*. Wine is traditionally associated with poetic inspiration and is perhaps especially appropriate since Orpheus is to follow (46). One recalls Silenus, a Dionysiac figure, in the Sixth *Eclogue, inflatum hesterno venas, ut semper, Iaccho* (15); and like Orpheus in *E.* 3, Silenus is a poet whose song evokes response and participation from the natural world (*E.*, 6, 27-8):

[17] For Orpheus and the power of inspired poetry *E.*, 6, 27-30 is the *locus classicus* in the *Eclogues*; see also *E.*, 6, 82 ff.; 4, 55; and for the sympathy between nature and the poet, 8, 2 ff.; 9, 19 f.; 10, 8; 10, 13 ff. For Orpheus' connection with other inspired poet-figures, see Elder (above, note 1), p. 115 and G. P. Sullivan's unpublished Harvard Honors Thesis, " Elements of Unity in the Sixth Eclogue: Some Notes on Vergil's Literary Method " (1953), in the Harvard College Library. Vergil will return to Orpheus in his associations with the creative forces of life

tum vero in numerum Faunosque ferasque videres
ludere, tum rigidas motare cacumina quercus.[18]

Indeed the following two lines of *E*. 6 (29-30) make an explicit
link between Silenus and Orpheus:

nec tantum Phoebo gaudet Parnasia rupes,
nec tantum Rhodope miratur et Ismarus *Orphea*.

And Phoebus Apollo will play an important role in *E*. 3 also
(see 62, 104, and *infra*).

The two sets of cups, then, set the stage for the contest to follow
and fix it within a larger perspective. They introduce material
deeply connected with the nature of poetry, but (in the case of
Menalcas' cups) extending beyond the conventional limits of
pastoral poetry. Vergil is not simply changing Theocritus'
subjects for the sake of *variatio*, nor is he necessarily inferior
to his model as Cartault maintained:

Il les a donc remplacés d'une part par les deux astronomes,
de l'autre par Orphée charmant les forêts; cette dernière
représentation est banale, la première est prétentieuse et
froide, bien que Virgile se soit appliqué à mettre ses savants
en relation avec l'agriculture. Quant à la distribution des
deux guirlandes entre deux coupes différentes elle témoigne
d'une véritable pauvreté d'invention.[19]

But rather than being impoverished in invention, Vergil is
creating a typical fusion of different elements into a new com-
plex and suggestive unity. His poet-shepherds, united through
a single creative impulse, the work of the " divine Alcimedon,"
are put in touch with the beauty both of cultivated (42) and
uncultivated (46) nature, with the obviously useful aspects of

more deeply at the end of the *Georgics*: see my article on *Georg*. IV in
A. J. P., LXXXVII (1966), pp. 307-25.

[18] For the Dionysiac aspects of Silenus and his associations with
inspiration see E. de Saint-Denis, "Le chant de Silène à la lumière
d'une découverte récente," *Rev. Phil.*, XXXVII (1963), pp. 23-40. Note
also *E.*, 10, 26 ff., where, shortly after the description of the sympathy
of pastoral nature for the poet, Pan himself appears, the embodiment of
Arcadian energy and the spirit of remote pastoral nature, *Pan deus
Arcadiae*; and he is *sanguineis ebuli bacis minioque rubentem*, very
much like the drunken Silenus in *E.*, 6, 22. The vine is added to the
ivy also in another imitation of Theocritus, I. 29 ff.: Nonnus, 19, 25.

[19] Cartault (above, note 6), p. 134.

creative effort (astronomy and agriculture) and its purely non-
utilitarian expression (poetry), with historical figures and real
human beings like Conon and with totally mythical and half-
divine figures, like Orpheus.   This scene, then, presents in
small that fusion of the real and the mythical which is charac-
teristic of the *Eclogues* and lies at the heart of their suggestive
power.

   With the larger themes adumbrated in the two sets of cups,
the way is fully open for a significant change of tone.   This
comes with the appearance of the umpire, Palaemon.   Vergil is
still following Theocritus V (see V, 62 ff.), but with a difference:
in Theocritus no real change in tone occurs, nothing analogous
to the broad, calming effect given by Palaemon's lines (55-7) :

   Dicite, quandoquidem in molli consedimus herba.
   Et nunc omnis ager, nunc omnis parturit arbos,
   nunc frondent silvae, nunc formosissimus annus.

The lines present an ideal of pastoral beauty and serenity:
nature at the height of gentleness and fruitfulness, inviting rest
and song.

   The lines recall several Theocritean contexts (see, e. g., *Idylls*,
I, 12 ff. and 21 ff.; V, 31 ff. and 45 ff.) ; but in Theocritus this
gentler pastoral atmosphere is diffused over the whole poem,
from its beginning on.   In Vergil, however, the poem begins on
a harsher, more acrid note and only gradually wins its way to
the peaceful breadth of view in which song is possible.   The
universal fertility is emphasized by the four-fold *nunc* and by
the heavy and dignified rhythm of the concluding *nunc formo-
sissimus annus* that sums up the preceding lines.   The verses
put a definitive end to petty quarreling and recall Damoetas and
Menalcas to their heritage and obligations as rustics who are
poets as well as shepherds.

   These lines come in the exact center of the poem.   Vergil
seems to have reserved for this late moment what he elsewhere
in the *Eclogues* sets forth at once.   *Eclogues* 5 and 7 are
especially close parallels:

   Cur, non, Mopse, boni quoniam convenimus ambo,
   tu calamos inflare levis, ego dicere versus,
   hic corylis mixtas inter consedimus ulmos? (*E.*, 5, 1-3).
   Forte sub arguta consederat ilice Daphnis (*E.*, 7, 1).

Eclogue 1 also begins by establishing the calm of the pastoral world (*Tityre, tu patulae recubans sub tegmine fagi* . . .). And in *E.* 9 a pastoral description, delayed, but still far earlier in the poem than that of *E.* 3, partially soothes the disturbance and restlessness with which the poem began and leads, eventually, to pastoral song (7-9):

> Certe equidem audieram, qua se subducere colles
> incipiunt mollique iugum demittere clivo,
> usque ad aquam et veteres, iam fracta cacumina, fagos. . . .

The Third *Eclogue*, however, is an exception to this familiar pattern, and the difference seems to underline the fact that the meditative peace necessary for song is not always easily obtainable or readily at hand. Sometimes it comes slowly or by a happy accident. *Eclogue* 9 perhaps comes closest to this delayed effect; but this feature in *E.* 3 is unique and perhaps bears on its relation to other poems in the collection (see part II, below).

As the representative of this larger pastoral setting, Palaemon has a dignity hitherto lacking in the rival shepherds. Hence he can bring order to their songs and direct their quarrelsome energies into poetry (*E.*, 3, 58-9):

> Incipe, Damoeta; tu deinde sequere, Menalca.
> Alternis dicetis; amant alterna Camenae.

Palaemon brings a reminder both of beauty and of order; and both are needed before the songs can begin. He awakens to life what was carved, static, and inanimate, on the cups: the vitality of the natural processes and the beauty that lies all around (55-7) and the presence of the creative energies in man: the Muses (*Camenae*, 59). His speech ends on *Camenae*, and the songs begin forthwith.

The shepherds begin, significantly, with an invocation to the gods of order in both nature and art: Jupiter, the Muses, Apollo (60-3):

> *Dam.* Ab Iove principium Musae: Iovis omnia plena;
> ille colit terras, illi mea carmina curae.
> *Men.* Et me Phoebus amat; Phoebo sua semper apud me
> munera sunt, lauri et suave rubens hyacinthus.

Damoetas' opening lines are especially interesting in that they link the pervasive presence of Jupiter with the Muse. The first

part of line 60 has two possible meanings (taking *Musae* as
genitive): [20] "From Jupiter is *my* Muse's beginning," and
"From Jupiter is the beginning—origin, foundation—of the
Muse (of poetry in general)." Vergil departs subtly but signifi-
cantly from his Greek models by substituting a more abstract
and suggestive noun, *principium*, for Aratus and Theocritus'
totally unambiguous verb, ἀρχώμεσθα. Even though in this
translation he is preceded by Cicero in his translation of Aratus
(*A Iove Musarum primordia, De Leg.*, II, 3, 7), his singular is
more general (and in his verse also more ambiguous) than
Cicero's plural. At any rate the change wrought by Palaemon's
presence is immense, for the first line spoken after his exhorta-
tion claims for poetry an intimate affinity with the divinity
who orders the world.

Damoetas' second line, reinforces this connection of poetry
with the divine ordering of the world: Jupiter looks after the
earth's fertility, and yet is concerned with the shepherd's
songs: *ille colit terras, illi mea carmina curae*. Jupiter literally
"cultivates the earth"—just as the human race itself does in
the description of the cups (41-2). Jupiter as god of the
heavens, as the "source" of the Muse, and as sponsor of agri-
culture thus looks back to the scene of the cups. The union of
cosmic and poetic order in Jupiter here is paralleled in that
scene too, possibly in the juxtaposition of artist (*divini Alci-
medontis*) and astronomers (*descripsit radio qui gentibus orbem*,
41) within the first set and certainly in the combination of
astronomers and Orpheus between the two sets.

Commentators on line 60 generally refer to the Aratus and
Theocritus passages cited above (note 14). But Vergil may
have in mind a yet more exalted source, one that would further
link humble pastoral with lofty themes and the highest poetic
inspiration, namely Hesiod (*Theog.*, 94-6):

[20] Editors are divided as to whether *Musae* in 60 is genitive or
vocative. See the discussion and passages cited in Conington, *ad loc.*
If *Musae* is understood as genitive (as I believe it should be), the
linking of poetic and cosmic order is especially close. The singular,
Musam, in 84 also helps confirm this interpretation. Cartault (above,
note 6), pp. 140-1 arbitrarily condemns Damoetas' invocation as inferior
to its immediate source, Theocritus, V, 80 ff.: "Au v. 60 sq. il invoque
Jupiter, ce qui lui donne un début plus magnifique mais plus banal que
celui de Théocrite."

ἐκ γάρ τοι Μουσέων καὶ ἐκηβόλου Ἀπόλλωνος
ἄνδρες ἀοιδοὶ ἔασιν ἐπὶ χθόνα καὶ κιθαρισταί,
ἐκ δὲ Διὸς βασιλῆες . . . .

Vergil's emphasis on Apollo in the next two lines helps support
this further reference; and in the Sixth *Eclogue,* adapting
another, and more famous, passage from the proem of the
Theogony (22 ff.), Vergil makes Hesiod his model of the inspired
poet: Silenus reports Linus' words, sung *divino carmine,* as he
presented his flute to Gallus (*E.,* 6, 69-71):

> Hos tibi dant calamos, en accipe, Musae,
> Ascraeo quos ante seni, quibus ille solebat
> cantando rigidas deducere montibus ornos.

The language has some obvious connections with the Third
Eclogue. Hesiod here is like Orpheus in *E.,* 3, 45; and he would
be relevant also as a poet whose works—both the *Theogony* and
the *Erga*—strongly assert the connection between poetic and
cosmic order.

Vergil seems to have intentionally given a rather grandiose
invocation to an amoebean singing match. He has here made a
distinct departure from his immediate source, for although
Theocritus' shepherds call upon the Muses and Apollo, they do
so still in a purely pastoral context of goats, rams, and rustic
festivals (V, 80-3):

> — ταὶ Μοῖσαί με φιλεῦντι πολὺ πλέον ἢ τὸν ἀοιδόν
> Δάφνιν· ἐγὼ δ' αὐταῖς χιμάρως δύο πρᾶν ποκ' ἔθυσα.
> — καὶ γὰρ ἔμ' Ὠπόλλων φιλέει μέγα, καὶ καλὸν αὐτῷ
> κριὸν ἐγὼ βόσκω· τὰ δὲ Κάρνεα καὶ δὴ ἐφέρπει.

But this divergence is only a part of a larger attempt at a
redefinition of pastoral in loftier terms. In the songs which
follow, the two shepherds can offer to the familiar pastoral loves,
Amyntas and Galatea, such poetically elaborate gifts as *aëriae
palumbes* (69) and *aurea mala* (71). Pollio can make a promi-
nent appearance (84-9), and the Muse again—*quamvis est
rustica* (84), precisely when, after 60-3, she is considerably less
"rustic." Or the simpler pastoral and the loftier, "poetical"
tones can be juxtaposed in contiguous couplets, as in 88-9 and
90-1:

> Qui te, Pollio, amat, veniat quo te quoque gaudet;
> mella fluant illi, ferat et rubus asper amomum.

Qui Bavium non odit, amet tua carmina, Maevi,
atque idem iungat vulpes et mulgeat hircos.

The first couplet has, of course, Hesiodic echoes again and intimations of the Fourth *Eclogue* (see *E.*, 4, 25, 30) ; but the answering couplet, though more "rustic," is still literary in its reference and rhetorical in its style. How different this juxtaposition is from Theocritus, where there is a much freer mixture of rusticity and lyricism and much less concern for maintaining a certain level of poetic decorum. In the Fifth *Idyll*, for instance, to round out a beautiful description of trees, cool springs, birds, and fleeces "softer than sleep" (a phrase borrowed by Vergil in *E.*, 7, 45), one goatherd tells the other, "Your goats smell worse than you do yourself" (45-52).

This interplay in the Third *Eclogue* between these two levels of poetry, the high and the low, is present most clearly in the differences between the two halves of the poem. But it operates in the second half also and here takes the form of an alternation between the themes of love and poetry in the songs of the two shepherds. Of the twenty-four couplets which they sing, only four deal wtih purely pastoral themes. Twelve couplets deal with love; six—just half that number—with poetry.[21] (I omit the two riddling couplets which have a special relation to the others and will be considered separately below.) This alternating pattern appears as follows:

60–63	Poetry (traditional: the Muses, Apollo)	2	couplets
64–83	Love (among shepherds)	10	"
84–91	Poetry (contemporary: Pollio)	4	"
92–99	Pastoral themes	4	"
100–3	Love (in animals)	2	"

This alternation of rustic love and poetry has its place in the first half of the poem too, for there the two shepherds gradually move from rustic themes of an erotic nature (see 7 ff., 12 ff.) to the subject of song (25 ff.). Indeed, this division between love and poetry is hinted at in the characters of the two contestants, for Menalcas (12-15) lost his temper over a gift of

---

[21] For a somewhat different division of the subjects see Büchner (above, note 6), col. 1192.

bow and arrows to Daphnis (love presumably being involved),[22] while Damoetas became similarly angry because of a singing-contest (21 ff.). At the end of the match this balance between love and poetry is still maintained, for it is again Damoetas who is on the side of poetry, offering as the prize for the solution of his riddle, *Et eris mihi magnus Apollo* (104), whereas Menalcas, true to his earlier propensity, states as his prize, *Et Phyllida solus habeto* (107).

We come now to the riddles themselves (104-7):

Dam. Dic quibus in terris—et eris mihi magnus Apollo—
tris pateat caeli spatium non amplius ulnas.

Men. Dic quibus in terris inscripti nomina regum
nascantur flores, et Phyllida solus habeto.

The riddles are puzzling, as riddles are meant to be. Whether or not we can believe the story about Caelius given in Servius, the riddles do serve a unifying function. As the last words of the two shepherds they take up several themes suggested earlier in the poem and provide a kind of summary of certain major motifs.

The riddles refer back, both directly and obliquely, to the description of Menalcas' cups and to the invocations in 60-3; and these references, especially the latter, make a kind of ring-composition, an ending that turns back to the beginning. The *caeli spatium* (whatever the truth of the Caelius story) recalls the astronomical subject of Menalcas' cups; and the paradox *in terris . . . caeli spatium* recalls also the fusion of earth and sky—the divisions of the sky for the sake of the cultivation of the earth—in 41-2. In the second riddle, though the subject is more terrestrial, the word *inscripti* is perhaps an echo of *descripsit* in 41. Astronomers "describe" figures which are of use to the generality of men—the "reaper and bent plowman"—for the continuation of life; but the figures "inscribed" by the gods involve kings (*regum*) long dead and, however beautiful, have no practical use.

The *magnus Apollo* in 104 recalls also Phoebus in Menalcas'

---

[22] For the probable erotic implications of the situation compare *E.*, 2, 29, where hunting is part of the love-relationship; and note too Menalcas' couplet on hunting with his beloved, Amyntas, later, *E.*, 3, 74-5.

invocation in 62. The connection with this passage is strongly emphasized by the second part of that invocation: *Phoebo sua semper apud me / munera sunt, lauri et suave rubens hyacinthus* (62-3). The flower of the riddle is, of course, the hyacinth. The answer to Menalcas' riddle is thus contained in his opening lines. This fact gives an important clue to the first riddle, for perhaps in Damoetas' *caeli spatium* there is some reference to his own invocation which dwelt upon the pervasive influence of Jupiter the sky-god (*Iovis omnia plena*, 60) and claimed that this Olympian deity took care of the earth (*ille colit terras*, 61).

Perhaps more interesting for the thematic significance of the riddles, however, is a recent suggestion of Wormell. Wormell has taken up and defended an old suggestion that the answer to the first riddle, "Where on the earth does the space of the sky extend not more than three cubits," is a celestial globe or sphere, perhaps to be connected with the orrery of Archimedes brought to Rome by Marcellus (see Cicero, *De Re Publ.*, I, 14, 21-2).[23] If this is so—and it is the most plausible solution that has been given—one answer to the first riddle, like that of the second, is clearly contained in the preceding portion of the poem. The *quis fuit alter* of 40 might even refer to Archimedes, whose name will not fit into hexameter verse.

If this solution is correct, the parallel between the two riddles is reinforced by the fact that both solutions are anticipated within the preceding text of the poem itself. This parallel is structurally and thematically significant too. Astronomy (the celestial sphere) in the first riddle would thus be juxtaposed with poetic myth (*nomina regum*) and love (*Phyllida* and the story of Hyacinthus) in the second. Vergil would then be resuming his earlier contrast between creative activity for utilitarian purposes (astronomy and agriculture) and the "pure" creativity of poetry (Orpheus).

The two riddles, then, concentrate a number of important contrasts presented throughout the poem: the astronomers and

---

[23] Wormell (above, note 5), pp. 29-32. This solution, notes Wormell, is as old as J. Martyn, 1749. Like the second riddle too the first has a double answer, it being possible to reply "at Rome" (where Archimedes' device presumably still was), or "at Rhodes," where there was a similar device made by Poseidonius. A new solution has recently been proposed by M. C. J. Putnam, *Mnemosyne*, ser. IV, XVIII (1965), pp. 150-4.

Orpheus, erudition and simplicity, useful scientific knowledge and poetic myth, sky and earth, large themes of cosmic significance (*caeli spatium, magnus Apollo*) and humbler pastoral song (*Phyllida*). There is also a tension between sadness and happiness, for the joyfulness in the prize offered for the solution of the riddles (*eris mihi magnus Apollo*; *Phyllida solus habeto*) is in contrast with the sadness of the content, at least in the second riddle with the allusion to Hyacinthus' unhappy love and Ajax' death, and possibly in the first riddle too, if there is any truth in the story about the tomb of Caelius (there is no reason, of course, why the riddles cannot have more than one answer).

This tension is maintained in the closing lines, Palaemon's speech (108-11) (the translation and interpretation presented here follow the manuscript-reading at the famous crux in 109-10):

> Non nostrum inter vos tantas componere lites.
> Et vitula tu dignus et hic, et quisquis amores
> aut metuet dulcis aut experietur amaros.
> Claudite iam rivos, pueri; sat prata biberunt.

> It lies not in us to resolve such great quarrels; both you and he are deserving of the cow, and (so is) whoever will either fear love-affairs when they are sweet or will have experience of them when bitter. Now close off the streams, my lads; enough have the meadows drunk.[24]

The wisdom of a serene and ideal figure like Palaemon includes both the joys and the sadnesses of life and love. He stands beyond the two shepherds' intense involvement in love, just as he stands outside the contest itself. Yet he knows more both of love and of pastoral beauty than they do. His role at the

---

[24] This interpretation of 109-10 seems to me satisfactorily defended by E. de Saint-Denis in his Budé edition, *Virgile, Bucoliques* (Paris, 1942), p. 38, n. 5, noting that both shepherds have sung of the happiness and of the misery of love (lines 64-83). Savage (above, note 4), p. 144 is not altogether convincing in emphasizing the different characters of the love-affairs of the two shepherds. Heyne remarked pessimistically (and with a characteristic acerbity) on these two lines, "Ut haec verba per se sensum satis obvium habeant, non tamen, quid ad reliquam sententiam faciant, ab ullo interprete monitum aut dictum est, neque umquam dici posse existimo. Referre interpretum commenta nil attinet; frigere enim ea cum ipso carmine necesse est."

end is exactly analogous to that at his first appearance: he introduces a sensitive and compassionate wisdom which puts the contestants in touch with the rhythm and balance in things which they have forgotten. He is perhaps to be compared also with the inspired craftsman of the cups, whose work can include both the exuberance of winding ivy and vine and the toil of reaper and "bent plowman."

The doubling of the subject of the second riddle, the reference to *two* princes, Hyacinthus and Ajax, is a detail that has puzzled scholars.[25] But it may also be part of this balancing of "sweet" and "bitter" of Palaemon's *aut—aut* formulation and the general opposition of rustic and lofty in the poem: Hyacinth's story is a pathetic love-tale involving a tender youth and full of vaguely pastoral elements; Ajax' is a high-tragic theme of a great hero, self-willed and intransigent; one death is accidental, the other sternly chosen and grimly executed.

We were told at the beginning that the contest involved issues of no small moment (*res est non parva,* 54); and Palaemon, at the end, confesses himself unable to decide "such great quarrels" (108). May not these "great issues" be none other than the fundamental opposites hinted at throughout the poem: the simplicity of pastoral poetry and the call to loftier themes of Apollo and Jupiter; the concrete goodness of the physical world, with its *aëriae palumbes* and *inscripti flores,* and the larger concern for the *totum orbem* and the *caeli spatium;* the carefree exuberance of amoebean song and the sad reminders of unhappy loves and premature, wasteful death? Or may they be understood as an opposition between pastoral and reality, between the fictions which poetry (or any art) uses and the "truth" which poetry conveys? Probably no single formulation is possible; none, certainly is totally adequate. Yet it is characteristically Vergilian not to resolve these conflicts, to see and present the heavy truth that they are unresolvable, exist only in tension: *Non nostrum inter vos tantas componere lites.*

So it is that neither poet is the winner. Though Menalcas

[25] Wormell (above, note 5), p. 29 refers the doubling of the hyacinth motif to Euphorion's *Hyacinthus* (frag. 40 in Powell's *Collect. Alex.*), where Euphorion's μία φῆμις implies that he also gave a second story. For an ingenious, but unconvincing attempt to account for the doubling, see Savage (above, note 4), pp. 148-9.

may be inclined more to love, Damoetas more to poetry (see above), yet the larger vision of the *caelatum opus* is made to belong to Menalcas. Conversely, though these astronomical themes are initially Menalcas' (40-2), Damoetas is the one to begin his song with Jupiter (60-1), and his is the riddle about the *caeli spatium*. It was Menalcas too who invoked Phoebus Apollo at the beginning of the contest (62-3), but it is Damoetas who respectfully recalls Apollo at the end (104). Both shepherds, then, are capable equally of singing of love and of dealing with larger themes. Hence both have cups carved by the "divine Alcimedon."

Structurally too the poem expresses this interplay of opposites. It falls evenly into two halves, the first (1-54) consisting of rustic banter, the second (55-111) of pastoral song. Yet within the first part the humble and lofty are juxtaposed in the contrast of the rusticity of the opening dialogue (1-31) and the cups of Alcimedon (32-54). In the second half, lofty invocation is conjoined with simple pastoral themes, culminating in the multiple contrasts of the riddles.

The riddles effect still another confrontation and fusion of opposites. The riddle as a form of speech is a folk-motif and belongs naturally to simple people, to the rustic world from which this complex poem gradually emerges (although curiously there are no comparable riddles in Theocritus).[26] The first riddle seems to be a version of an especially popular and widespread "folk-riddle." [27] But Vergil has taken this popular form and made it the vehicle for the learned themes of astronomy and mythology within the complex, allusive structure of his own poem. What he does with the riddles, therefore, is only another example of what he does with the whole of the Theocritean pas-

---

[26] W. Schultz, "Rätsel," *R.-E.*, I A 1 (1914), col. 117, says that Vergil in *E*. 3 "ahmt den Wettgesang theokritischer Hirten nach"; but I can find no Theocritean instance of riddles used in a rustic amoebean contest.

[27] On the folk-element in this riddle see K. Ohlert, "Zur antiken Räthselpoesie," *Philologus*, LVII (1898), p. 599: "Wir haben vielmehr ein echtes Volksräthsel vom Brunnen vor uns, dem der Dichter nur die schöne Form gegeben hat." He quotes an old German form of this riddle (*Strassburger Räthselbuch*, ed. Butsch, 1876):

In wölchem landt ist der hymmel nur drey eln langk?
In einer pfitzen oder lachen, in sollicher gröss wird er
also gesehen.

toral world: transform the rustic frame by infusing into it an elaborate poetic sophistication and a self-conscious sense of structure and symbol.

In view of what may be called the creative suspension in which Vergil has framed the antitheses of the poem, it may be significant that it is not one of the competing shepherds, but Palaemon, the arbiter and the bringer of pastoral calm, who ends the *Eclogue.* There is an interesing structural device here too, for while the exchange of songs (60-107) begins and ends with gods, Jupiter and Apollo, with celestial or regal themes, the poem as a whole begins and ends with pastoral subjects. A pastoral frame thus includes elements of greater significance, just as the ivy and vine on Alcimedon's cups enframe the learned astronomers.

Palaemon's closing speech brings the poem back to its rustic setting (108-9):

> non nostrum inter vos tantas componere lites.
> et vitula tu dignus et hic. . . .

The cups and the long debate on the relative value of cups and cow (29-49) are now forgotten. The poet returns to and reaffirms the simplicity of his original pastoral setting after he has intimated the larger possibilities which lie within it, possibilities symbolized by the *caelatum opus.* May there be here also a touch of the reputed modesty of Vergil (see *Vit. Donat.,* 11; *Vit. Serv.,* 8), an acknowledgment of the limitations of his form even though he has, within the poem itself, transcended these limitations?

Perhaps it is in terms of these possibilities that we are to understand Vergil's ending:

> claudite iam rivos, pueri; sat prata biberunt.

On the one hand this line seems to be a final return to the pastoral frame. It is a practical gesture belonging to the realities of goatherding and agriculture, to the world of the *curvus arator.* But these "streams" seem to be at least as metaphorical as they are real, and the line thus resumes the "dialogue" between practical activity and the "pure" creation of beauty. Yet now this opposition approaches being dissolved or transcended. The poem's striving to blend the lofty and the humble, the useful and the beautiful, and ultimately the real and the symbolic, is now completed in the pure and smooth fusion of metaphor which, gracefully and without violence, puts an end to the previous division. Such too was the graciousness of Palaemon's first appearance (55-9), heralding a deeper awareness of and connection with the beauty of the pastoral world. Now, with Palaemon's concluding four lines—the only return of continuous discourse in the poem since his first speech in 55 ff.—amoebean rivalry is over. Fusion through metaphor succeeds competitive juxtaposition.

Simultaneously the concrete realism of the pastoral setting gives way to a vagueness and indefinite mixture of reality and unreality. Here "streams" and "meadows" blend into the realm of metaphor and symbol (contrast the specific *hic ad veteres fagos,* 12). The opposition of trivial and serious ends with a pastoral motif which is *both* real and metaphorical, both rustic and "poetic." The poem has moved beyond even the pastoral ideality of the "soft grass" and the *formossisimus annus* of Palaemon's first description. Here the pastoral reality of streams and meadows is one with the universal and symbolic "streams of song" from which the pastoral rivulet flows.[28]

---

[28] E. Derenne, "Le jugement de Palémon," *L. E. C.,* XXI (1953), pp. 184-5, stresses the return to a Roman practicality in the last line: " S'étonnera-t-on que Palémon quitte immédiatement la poésie pour envisager la réalité? Il ne serait pas Romain s'il ne considérait pas la littérature comme une bagatelle, et s'il ne tirait pas de l'aventure qui l'a fait arbitre d'une joute poétique une sorte de conclusion morale qui, malgré sa forme plaisante et ironique. lui est inspirée par son bon sens d'homme pratique." And he goes on, " Propriétaire dont les pieds prennent solidement appui sur ses terres, Palémon ne se soucie guère de poésie." Yet this view greatly oversimplifies the situation, for Vergil's rustics are seldom unpoetic. It also neglects both the metaphorical implications of Palaemon's last lines and the highly " poetic " tone and function of his first speech (54-9). On the metaphor of the last line Conington (*ad loc.*) remarks, "If Palaemon says this to his slaves, it also alludes metaphorically to the streams of bucolic verse." The metaphor of the streams of song is, of course, an obvious and familiar one. See, *inter alia,* Callim., *Hymn,* 2, 108 ff.; Longin., *De Sublim.,* 35, 4; Hor., *Serm.,* I, 4, 11. Vergil himself elsewhere makes the comparison of poetry to a refreshing stream of water: *Tale tuum carmen nobis, divine poeta,* / *. . . quale per aestum* / *dulcis aquae saliente sitim restinguere rivo* (*E.,* 5, 45-7). There is also, of course, the familiar motif of the "fountains " of poetry: *Georg.,* II, 175; Lucret., I, 927; Propert., III, 1, 3 ff. See generally Sittig, " Hippokrene," *R.-E.,* VIII, 2 (1913), cols. 1853-6.

Thus by the end of the poem Vergil has transformed the pastoral world with which he began. Palaemon's closing lines complete the movement which he himself initiated. Pastoral setting and love are united, but on a higher plane and in a more inclusive statement than was possible for the simpler pastoral figures, the two contestants. Given Palaemon's importance in the poem, it is significant that Vergil has him appear only after the two competitors have established a "lower" pastoral atmosphere. By thus reserving until the center of the poem (55 ff.) the pastoral peace and beauty which he sets forth early in other *Eclogues*, Vergil perhaps suggests that this peace and ideality evolve, as it were, that they sometimes come into being only slowly, even fortuitously, when there appears a Palaemon to evoke them out of life's petty, surface disturbances, one who can see through to the beauty and promise that are easily forgotten even by those who live in the midst of them, the inhabitants of Arcadia themselves. Is not such a task, after all, the eternal vocation of the poet?

II

The harmony and resolution of opposites at the end of the Third *Eclogue* may also contribute to an understanding of its relation to the other poems in the collection. Though one must beware of imposing a rigid *schema* on these delicate and elusive poems, there is in the first half of the *Eclogues* a suggestion of a progression, almost poem by poem—though by no means a completely clear or even progression—into the peace of the pastoral world (it should be emphasized, of course, that this progression has to do only with the final carefully planned arrangement of the collection; it implies nothing about the order of composition).

In *E.* 1 this peace is troubled by political disturbance and the threat of exile; in *E.* 2, it is obscured by passion and uncertainty of the value of the pastoral realm (cf. *sordida rura / atque humiles habitare casas*, *E.*, 2, 28-9; *sordent tibi munera nostra*, *E.*, 2, 44). But finally in the Third *Eclogue* its beauty and tranquillity can be reached despite petty quarrels. Thus by the Fourth *Eclogue* the poet can hope that the whole world may be touched and permeated by this ideal of pastoral beauty and peace. In the Fifth *Eclogue*, the world of pastoral nature can then even console man for the losses that are part of his existence (see *E.*, 5, 20 ff., 58 ff.), until the grief of nature over his *crudeli funere* (20) is answered by a universal joy (*voluptas*) and a pervasive concord like that of the Fourth *Eclogue*:

> Ergo alacris silvas et cetera rura voluptas
> Panaque pastoresque tenet Dryadasque puellas.
> Nec lupus insidias pecori, nec retia cervis
> ulla dolum meditantur; amat bonus otia Daphnis.
>
> (*E.*, 5, 58-61)

This movement within *E.* 5 resembles that larger movement from the *discordia* of the First *Eclogue* (71) to the *concordes Parcae* of the Fourth (47).

The Third *Eclogue*, then, seems to articulate an important point in the movement of the collection, a point after the pastoral world has been entered in the first two *Eclogues*, but just before the larger, calmer atmosphere of *Eclogues* 4, 5, 6. If there is any validity to the triadic arrangement of the *Eclogues* (1-3, 4-6, 7-9, 10 by itself),[29] *Eclogue* 3, with its alternation of humbler and larger themes could be seen as intimating the expansive possibilities of the triad to follow and thus marking a transition to these "non-pastoral," or "supra-pastoral," poems. As noted earlier, the references to Pollio and line 89 (*mella fluant illi*) seem explicitly to anticipate the Fourth *Eclogue*; and the inclusion of Hellenistic learning and astronomy is perhaps a vague anticipation of *E.* 6.

The Third *Eclogue* is also obviously related to the Seventh, for both are amoebean contests involving a third shepherd; and their connection may be part of the often noted correspondence between poems in each of the two halves of the collection (i. e. 1 and 9, 2 and 8, etc.). In *E.* 7, also, the third person is the one to create the setting of pastoral calm; but, unlike *E.* 3, he appears at the very beginning of the poem. Thus the atmosphere of politeness, amity, rural tranquillity is established from the start. Yet here, though the setting is initially more harmonious, the two competing poets are judged unequal. These

---

[29] For the theory of the arrangement of the *Eclogues* by triads see E. A. Hahn, "The Characters in the *Eclogues*," *T. A. P. A.*, LXXV (1944), pp. 239-41. On the structural unity of the *Eclogues* see now Otis (above, note 3), pp. 128 ff.

two points of contrasts with *E.* 3, the setting and the judgment, are perhaps connected. The issues in *E.* 3 can be left unresolved, for the whole setting is less homogeneous, itself contains tensions and contraries, and is in a state of development and evolution. The uniformity of the setting in *E.* 7, part of an equilibrium and clarity of definition achieved after a much longer immersion in the pastoral world, makes possible a clear standard and consensus.

But there may be another reason more closely connected with the characters of the Third *Eclogue.* *E.* 3 contains no judgment because *both* shepherd-poets admit a connection with and indebtedness to a larger realm—Jupiter and the Muse, Apollo and Orpheus. Both express some sense of the unresolved contraries of existence, the interplay of beauty and death in the riddles, confirmed by Palaemon's epilogue on " sweet or bitter loves." But in *E.* 7, as a recent study has re-emphasized,[30] the two poets are not equal in their relation to nature and the gods. Corydon humbly invokes the Nymphs with a prayer and seeks divine inspiration (21-4), while Thyrsis begins with a command, asserts his victory in advance, and speaks of *invidia* (25-8).[31] The knowledge of sweetness and bitterness that is shared by both shepherds in *E.* 3 is divided between the two contestants of *E.* 7 (cf. *dulcior,* 37; *amarior,* 41). While Corydon is appreciative of seasonal change and open to its beauties (45-8), Thyrsis defies the powers of nature, confident in man-made comforts (49-52), and tends to put himself in the center of things (cf. 59: *Phyllidis adventu* nostrae *nemus omne virebit;* 67: *saepius at si* me, *Lycida formose, revisas . . .*). Thus what both poets latently possess

[30] For the differences between the two poets in *E.* 7 see Beyers (above, note 3), *passim,* especially pp. 44 ff. I find Beyers' explanation for the final judgment on the whole more convincing than that of F. H. Sandbach, *C. R.,* XLVII (1933), pp. 216-19 (followed by Rose, above, note 6, pp. 145-7), where great stress is put on minor metrical and other technical flaws. But surely a poet with the mastery to write a line like *muscosi fontes et somno mollior herba* (*E.,* 7, 45) does not need to make minor details of technique the focal point of an entire poem. On the inadequacy of the " technical " interpretation see now H. Dahlmann, " Zu Vergils siebentem Hirtengedicht," *Hermes,* XCIV (1966), pp. 218-32, especially 228-9.

[31] On the opposition of intellect and inspiration in *E.* 7 see Beyers (above, note 3), pp. 39 and 44 ff.

in *Eclogue* 3, a reverent sense of the larger powers of the world, a balance between joy and suffering, a feeling of the mystery of man's sharing in the beautiful through knowledge and art— these are fully realized in the Seventh *Eclogue* by one poet only, however clever and confident his rival seems to be.

The balance between these elements suggested in the Third *Eclogue* is perhaps even more fully developed in another pastoral singing match, *Eclogue* 5. Here, as in *E*. 7, the poem asserts from the beginning an atmosphere of gentleness and recon- ciliation. One shepherd defers to the other (4) and each offers his song freely as a gift, not in competition (indeed, this is the only *Eclogue* where this occurs, for in *E*. 8 also the two shep- herds are involved in a contest, *certantis*, 3). Each shepherd, in *E*. 5, even finds his companion's song beyond the value of any gift he can give (53, 81). Perhaps we are to feel that the vision of universal harmony in the Fourth *Eclogue* has made possible a partial resolution of elements which are still in opposi- tion in *E*. 3.

As in the Third *Eclogue*, the Fifth also draws upon Theocritus I (the lament for Daphnis), but Vergil transforms his model even more radically. In the gentler setting of *Eclogue* 5 the dead poet can be restored to a life of a higher sort, and a mortal can pass beyond the boundaries separating earth and heavens, and can thus unite remote Olympus and the humble rustic world in a joyous new vision (56-9) :

> Candidus insuetum miratur limen Olympi
> sub pedibusque videt nubes et sidera Daphnis.
> ergo alacris silvas et cetera rura voluptas
> Panaque pastoresque tenet Dryadasque puellas.

And just as *Eclogue* 3 contrasts elaborate cups with the lowly cow, so the end of *E*. 5 contrasts the " fragile pipe " offered by Menalcas (*E*., 5, 85-7) with the rough shepherd's crook offered by Mopsus (88-90). The former is a work connected with artistic creativity, like the *caelatum opus* of *E*. 3 ; the latter belongs fully to the realm of " realistic " pastoral utility, like Damoetas' cow. Yet in *E*. 5, with its hopeful reconciliation of contraries, not just one, but *both* gifts are presented. Here even the rough crook, shod with bronze, is still *formosum* (90), the epithet of pastoral beauty used of Corydon whom the " fragile pipe" sang (86; note also *formosissimus annus, E.*, 3, 57). The two gifts, so different, come together in an harmonious resolution of fragility and firmness, imagination and reality.

In *Eclogue* 3 that resolution is not yet achieved, for the poet is still struggling to penetrate the superficies of the pastoral world. The Nymphs who in *E*. 5 lament the death of Daphnis (20 ff.) appear in *E*. 3 only briefly (9), to laugh in carefree fashion at rustic antics. Yet the cups adorned with astronomers and with Orpheus, Palaemon with his evocation of pastoral peace and beauty, the invocations to Jupiter and Apollo—all suggest the larger potentials of the pastoral frame which are to be developed in *Eclogues* 4, 5, 6, and 10. Trivial and celestial, learning and inspiration, love and death are all present, but not yet fully ordered into a unified vision. The riddles at the end, not present in any of Vergil's Theocritean models, raise this lack of a unified focus to a new dimension, for the riddles may be there to suggest those primally unresolved—and unresolvable—elements that lie at the heart of perhaps all poetry and certainly of Vergil's.

CHARLES PAUL SEGAL.

CENTER FOR HELLENIC STUDIES.

PASTORAL REALISM AND THE GOLDEN AGE:
CORRESPONDENCE AND CONTRAST
BETWEEN VIRGIL'S THIRD AND FOURTH ECLOGUES

The ram's voluntary mutation of colors in E. 4.42—44 has been adjudged, with some justification, "grotesque", "tasteless", "facetious"[1]:

> nec varios discet mentiri lana colores,
> ipse sed in pratis aries iam suave rubenti
> murice, iam croceo mutabit vellera luto ...

---

[1] So respectively K. Büchner, P. Vergilius Maro, der Dichter der Römer, Stuttgart 1956, 180; G. Williams, Tradition and Originality in Latin Poetry, Oxford 1968, 279—280; M. C. J. Putnam, Virgil's Pastoral Art, Princeton 1970, 153. Putnam, on the other hand, stresses the overriding serious side (153—155). At the opposite extreme is H. C. Gotoff, On the Fourth Eclogue of Virgil, Philologus 111, 1967, 66—79, who emphasizes the "light, elegant, fantastic" quality in the poem as a whole (Horace's molle atque facetum, Serm. 1.10.44): see especially pp. 74—75.

This scene of the miracles of the Golden Age, however, assumes a different significance if we recall that the previous Eclogue also described a ram and his fleece (E. 3.94 to 95):

> parcite, oves, nimium procedere: non bene ripae
> creditur; ipse aries etiam nunc vellera siccat.

In the light of Virgil's composition of the "Eclogue Book", arranged with self-conscious attention to the relations of the separate poems to one another[2], the resemblances between the two scenes are more than fortuitous. *Aries* and *vellera* occur only in these two places in the Eclogues. *Ipse*, an important element in the characterization of the Golden Age (we shall return to it later), is also present in both passages[3].

Does Virgil, then, mean us to think back with amusement from the utopian fantasy of E. 4.44 to the Third Eclogue's realistic vignette of a real ram shaking off water, not dye, in a quite plausible scene of rustic life? This possibility is certainly not to be excluded. But the echo may also have a more important function, that is, to underline the deliberate progression from the most realistic of the Eclogues, the one that is closest to the rustic realism of its Theocritean models, Idylls 4 and 5, to the *maiora* of Four's ambitious vision of a happier age. The trivial detail of a river bank which could not be "trusted" (*non bene ... creditur*, E. 3.94—95) contrasts with the gradually created image of a new world where complete trust is possible: *inrita perpetua solvent formidine terras* (E. 4.14). From this realm are banished too the "fear" of lions (*nec ... metuent*, E. 4.22) and the dangerous deceptiveness of poisonous plants (*fallax herba veneni*, E. 4.24), as well as the "lying" (*mentiri*) craft of dyeing wool (E. 4.42). The very difference in the levels of trust between the two Eclogues points up the progression from the light and realistic tone of E. 3 to the cosmic themes of E. 4. If one were momentarily to leave aside the question of the internal unity of the Liber Bucolicorum, one might, in the spirit of a purely historicist criticism, view the progression diachronically, as a reflection of the mood before and after the peace of Brundisium. For the present discussion, however, I wish to stress the synchronic aspect of the progression as a manifestation of the internal structure and coherence, thematic and stylistic, of the Eclogue Book.

I noted above the resemblance between *ipse sed in pratis aries iam* ... in E. 4.43

---

[2] For bibliography and discussion see Büchner (above, note 1), 235—237; C. Becker, Vergils Eklogenbuch, Hermes 88 1955, 314—349, especially 323 ff.; Br. Otis, Virgil: A Study in Civilized Poetry, Oxford 1964, 128 ff.; J. Van Sickle, The Unity of the Eclogues, TAPA 98, 1967, 491—508, and also his forthcoming survey article, "The 'Bucolics' of Virgil", Aufstieg und Niedergang der römischen Welt (Festschrift J. Vogt), II, Principat. Sprache u. Literatur (forthcoming); E. W. Leach, Vergil's Eclogues: Landscapes of Experience, Ithaca and London 1974, 245 ff.

[3] On the *ipse* motif see, inter alios, Büchner (above, note 1), 180; Becker (above, note 2), 347—348; K. Barwick, Zur Interpretation und Chronologie der 4. Ecloge des Vergils und der 16. und 17. Epode des Horaz, Philologus 96, 1943—44, 30 ff.; Fr. Klingner, Virgil, Bucolica, Georgica, Aeneis, Zürich and Stuttgart 1967, 80—81.

and *ipse aries etiam nunc* ... in E. 3.95. With this parallel should be considered another instance of the motif of *ipse*, namely E. 4.21 f.:

> *ipsae lacte domum referent distenta capellae*
> *ubera* ...

Whereas *ipse* in E. 3.95 and E. 4.43 singles out the ram from the rest of the flock in an event which is alarming in the one case and surprising in the other (*even* the ram, leader of the flock, will be deceived by the treacherous bank; *even* the stalwart ram will undergo these changes), *ipsae* in E. 4.21 is unambiguously positive within the framework of the pastoral economy: "by themselves" these goats of the Golden Age will find their safe way home, untroubled by the dangers that faced the sheep of E. 3.94—95. In this latter passage *ipse* occurs within a context which itself exemplifies the herdsman's strenuous efforts to protect his flock (hence the note of urgency in the imperative, *parcite, oves*) and illustrates also that flock's need of his attention. But the *ipsae* of E. 4.21 points to the spontaneous bounty of nature, analogous to Hesiod's ἄρουρα ... αὐτομάτη (Erga 117 f.; cf. E. 4.23), a natural world which not merely cooperates with man, but even provides its rich gifts (*distenta* ... *ubera*) without requiring his labor.

This contrast within the Eclogue Book is analogous to a contrast between the Eclogues and the Idylls of Theocritus. E. 4.21 f. has generally been viewed in terms of its chronological relation to the similar detail of Horace, Epode 16.49 f.[4]. The Theocritean reminiscence, however, also suggests that Virgil is self-consciously juxtaposing different levels of bucolic style. The scene which it recalls, Theocritus, Idyll 11.12, stands at the opposite end of the poetic and emotional spectrum from Eclogue 4: it describes the neglected herd of the Cyclops who is wasting away for love of Galatea on the shore:

πολλάκι ταὶ ὄϊες ποτὶ τωὔλιον αὐταὶ ἀπῆνθον.

By recalling this verse in E. 4.21, Virgil, I suggest, is, in characteristic fashion, commenting on and modifying his Greek original. Whereas Theocritus' αὐταί implies the loneliness of the herd abandoned by its love-sick attendant, (a pathos-evoking motif developed in greater detail in Id. 4,20 and 26f.), Virgil's *ipsae* signifies not that the goatherd has forgotten his beasts, but rather that in this safe, happy, and fruitful world the herd needs no herdsman at all. The contrast between the Virgilian and the Theocritean motif is emblematic of a larger contrast between barrenness and fertility, personal love and historical achievement, self-centered fantasy and wide prophetic vision.

That E. 4.44 glances back at the "lower" pastoral world of the poem which precedes it in the collection receives further support from a number of other

---

[4] See Br. Snell, Die 16. Epode von Horaz und Vergils 4. Ekloge, Hermes 73, 1938, 237—42, especially 240f.; Becker (above, note 2), 348; Gotoff (above, note 1), 77—78, with the literature there cited. W. Wimmel, Vergils Eclogen und die Vorbilder der 16. Epode des Horaz, Hermes 89, 1961, 212f. also calls attention to the parallel with E. 3.29—31 and other passages in the Theocritean corpus.

correspondences between the two Eclogues[5]. In E. 4.21, cited above, the ewes, unattended, bring their full udders safely home, whereas in E. 3.98—99 the shepherd lads have to enclose the sheep lest the milk be lost, as it was in the recent past:

> cogite ovis, pueri: si lac praeceperit aestus,
> ut nuper, frustra pressabimus ubera palmis.

Here again labor contrasts with ease, danger with security, loss with abundance[6].

Just before the description of the ram in E. 3.94—95 there occurs a collocation of snake and flowers which parallels the collocation of rich flowers and a world free of snakes in the first period of the Golden Age:

> qui legitis flores et humi nascentia fraga,
> frigidus, o pueri, fugite hinc, latet anguis in herba
>
> (E. 3.92—93);
>
> ipsa tibi blandos fundent cunabula flores.
> occidet et serpens ...
>
> (E. 4.23—24).

Scholars have occasionally observed the parallel, but missed its significance. Becker, for example, remarks, ,,Aber solche Anklänge sind vage und geben wenig aus (was hat die Warnung vor der im Gras lauernden Schlange in ecl. 3 mit dem Aussterben dieser Tiere in ecl. 4 zu tun?)."[7] We can answer Becker's question on the basis of the previously noted parallels: here, as in the account of the ram, the danger and untrustworthiness of the "real" pastoral world are replaced by a new and miraculous safety.

In like manner the dangerous bull of E. 3.86—7,

> pascite taurum,
> iam cornu petat et pedibus qui spargat harenam,

contrasts with the bull freed from the yoke in E. 4.41:

> robustus quoque iam tauris iuga solvet arator;

and we may compare also the Theocritean motif of the emaciated bull perishing of love in E. 3.100—103 (cf. Theocr. Id. 4.20 and also 12—16). Possibly too the bucolic commonplace of the danger of wolves to the stables in E. 3.80, *triste lupus stabulis*, is answered by the herds' freedom from the fear of lions in E. 4.22,

---

[5] We may add here the parallel between the *suave rubens hyacinthus* of E. 3.63 and the *suave rubenti / murice* of E. 4.43f., pointed out by A. Forbiger, P. Vergili Maronis Opera, I⁴, Leipzig 1872, ad E. 3.63.

[6] Becker (above, note 2) points out a possible parallel between E. 4.21 and E. 3.30 without noticing the closer parallel of 3.98f. On the problem of identifying the *pueri* of E. 3.93 and 98 see G. Jachmann, Die dichterische Technik in Vergils Bukolika, NJbb 49, 1922, 107, who rightly resists any attempt to reorder the lines.

[7] Becker (above, note 2), 321.

nec magnos metuent armenta leones. Though similar themes occur in E. 5.60—61 and E. 8.27—28[8], the reader of E. 4 would have E. 3.80 fresh in his mind.

Especially interesting is the adynaton in the verses for Pollio, E. 3.88—89:

> *qui te, Pollio, amat, veniat quo te quoque gaudet;*
> *mella fluant illi, ferat et rubus asper amomum.*

We are reminded not only of the general abundance of the Golden Age (E. 4.18 to 20), but some of its specific manifestations in nard and honey:

> *... Assyrium vulgo nascetur amomum* (E. 4.25)[9].
> *... durae quercus sudabunt roscida mella* (E. 4.30).

This last set of parallels between the two Eclogues calls attention to the new role of Pollio[10]. The unexpected appearance of a contemporary, without any particular thematic emphasis, in the middle of a bucolic singing match in E. 3 contrasts strikingly with the significance of that contemporary's consulship as the starting point for the glorious new age and its *magni menses* in E. 4:

> *teque adeo decus hoc aevi, te consule, inibit,*
> *Pollio, et incipient magni procedere menses;*
> *te duce, si qua manent sceleris vestigia nostri,*
> *inrita perpetua solvent formidine terras*
>   (E. 4.11—14).

What was a gesture of personal affection for Pollio in E. 3 (*qui te, Pollio, amat* ...) now expands to a concern for the whole history of humanity. The momentary glimpse of a Golden Age in Damoetas' song (E. 3.88—89) now extends beyond personal intimacy and private fancy to the whole human race, beyond pastoral conceit to an historical vision reported in the poet's propria persona (note the first-person verbs and pronouns of E. 4.1—3 and 53—59) after an entreaty to his Muses for "grander song" (E. 4.1).

At the same time something of that cosmic consciousness of E. 4 is prepared for in the opening of the Third Eclogue's singing contest, where the Muses are linked with a Jupiter who providentially oversees the whole world (*ille colit terras* ..., E. 3.61), in the astronomical themes of the cups (E. 3.40—42), and in the *spatium caeli* of the first riddle (E. 3.104—105). In these passages, however, the large is contained in the small, whereas E. 4 allows the *grandia* to reach their widest limits[11].

These connections between the humblest and the loftiest of the Eclogues, the most rustic and the most explicitly historical, then, reflect a subtle humor in the

---

[8] On the repetitions of this adynaton see Gotoff (above, note 1), 74—75; Snell (above, note 4), 237—239.

[9] Fr. Dornseiff, Verschmähtes zu Vergil, Horaz und Properz, SB Leipzig 97, Heft 6, Berlin 1951, 46 remarks, „Das amomum von 3,89 soll der Leser unmittelbar vor ekl. 4 gelesen haben."

[10] See also E. 3.84 and Büchner (above, note 1), 175.

[11] On the relation of E. 3 to the *maiora* of E. 4, 5, 6 see Ch. Segal, Vergil's Caelatum Opus: An Interpretation of the Third Eclogue, AJP 88, 1967, 304ff.

exuberance of the Fourth Eclogue's vision of a Golden Age. But they also confirm the internal unity of the Book and express a self-conscious progression from small to great themes, from the rustic Muse loved by Pollio as a private citizen (*Pollio amat nostram, quamvis est rustica, Musam*, E. 3.84) to the *Sicelides Musae* who will help sing the *grandia* which will come to pass under Pollio as an important public figure (*decus hoc aevi, te consule, te duce*, E. 4.11—14)[12]. This progression is signalled by a subtly invited comparison of bucolic and utopian details, lowly pastoral realism and one of man's loftiest and most persistent myths.

Brown University
Department of Classics
Providence, R.I. 02912 / USA

---

[12] On a possible connection between E. 3.84 and E. 4.1—3 see Becker (above, note 2), 321. The possible humor in E. 4.1 suggested by Gotoff (above, note 1), 67 ff. does not alter the progression suggested here. For a criticism of Gotoff's view see E. A. Schmidt, Poetische Reflexion: Vergils Bukolik, Munich 1972, p. 156 with note 145. Schmidt, whose book I was able to consult only after I had completed this paper, has well appreciated the change in the significance of Pollio in the two Eclogues: à propos of E. 3.89 he remarks (p. 161), „Der Zusammenhang in ecl. III macht klar, daß diese Wunder Ausdruck der Schönheit der Dichtung des Pollios sind. Was dort der Poesie galt, wird in ecl. IV Zeichen verwandelter Realität. Nicht die Lieder des Dichters Pollio, sondern Ereignisse, die mit den Taten des Konsuls Pollio zusammenhängen, werden besungen." The interplay between pastoral and history which I have stressed here also reinforces Schmidt's critique of Snell's conception of the escapist, dreamy quality in Virgil's pastoral world: Schmidt, 172—185; Br. Snell, Arkadien. Die Entdeckung einer geistigen Landschaft, in: Die Entdeckung des Geistes[3], Hamburg 1955, 371—400, Engl. trans. in: The Discovery of the Mind, trans. T. G. Rosenmeyer, Oxford 1953, 281—309.

TAMEN CANTABITIS, ARCADES—
EXILE AND ARCADIA
IN *ECLOGUES ONE AND NINE*

Charles Paul Segal

O<small>NE OF THE DIFFICULTIES HAMPERING</small>
students of Vergil's *Eclogues* has been a certain loss of perspective about the relations between poetry and biography. While no one would deny that Vergil's writing of the *Eclogues* has some definite relation to certain political circumstances, that relation is one of a poet and not an historian. It is the ability to transform personal experience into larger, more intensely significant terms wherein lies the distinguishing quality of the poet's genius. The poet's experience of the "actuality" around him is, as other men's, rooted in the succession of historical events; but, if he chooses— or feels compelled—to make poetry of these events, it is because they supply him with profound insights into issues which often far transcend their historical source and may be (in fact, usually are) of a totally nonhistorical character.[1] The poet, then, transforms historical reality into poetic reality; and it is with this transformed reality that the study of poetry is properly concerned, however much it may be aided by historical or biographical information. This distinction, though fundamental, has often become obscured in recent decades of "scientific" scholarship, though it has been restated sporadically by scholars of a rather more humanistic outlook, as for example by Plessis half a century ago:

> (Les Bucoliques) sont des oeuvres d'actualité—ce qui ne veut pas dire de circonstance,—et d'une actualité sentie par une des âmes les plus anxieuses et les plus belles qui ait jamais été; ce sont les tristesses et les rêves d'un grand coeur et d'une grande intelligence.[2]

Increasing numbers of scholars in recent years have abjured the "biographical fallacy" and its limitations; but the biographical approach still weighs heavily on students of the *Eclogues* and perhaps most heavily on students of *Eclogues* 1 and 9.[3] Vergil's farm—its location, confiscation, restoration—the identification of Tityrus or Meliboeus or Menalcas with Vergil, the chronological relation between the two poems, the ambiguous praise of Octavian (if indeed he is the *iuvenis* in *E.* 1) by the young poet— *audax iuventa*, "bold in his youth," as he says looking back on his poem a decade or so later (*Georg.* 4.565–66)—these are questions which have been discussed with such energy and subtlety that they have often (though by no means always) distracted scholars from approaching the two works as poetry. Furthermore, though scholars have examined the poetic qualities of each poem individually, studies of the relation between the two poems have all too often limited themselves to the "biographical" issues.

In the following pages I shall offer some detailed literary analysis of each poem separately, but my major concern will be the relation between the two poems and some of the larger implications of this relation in the light of the poetic character of the *Eclogues* considered as a unified work. This unity is, to be sure, of a looser kind than that found within a single poem. Yet these ten poems, written within the space of three years (if we can believe the biographical tradition) with their cross-references and recurrent characters, real and imaginary, are cast in a single mood and style. Indeed, it has been suggested that they may be the first book of single poems in Latin literature to have been put together with a conscious sense of the design and artistic unity of the whole.[4]

I

Eclogues 1 and 9 are obviously intended as pendants one to the other. Both involve exile from a peaceful, familiar world; and both develop a contrast (stronger and more pathetic in *E.* 1) between a shepherd facing exile and one who is still at rest within the pastoral world. Both too (in this like *E.* 6 and 10) end on the theme of rest and the fall of evening. Some deliberate verbal echoes make the connection even more explicit (though again the parallels provide no certain evidence for the chronological relation of the two poems). Most obviously, *E.* 9.50,

> Insere, Daphni, piros: carpent tua poma nepotes

> (Graft your pear-trees, Daphnis; your descendants will pluck the fruit)

recalls *E.* 1.73,

> Insere nunc, Meliboee, piros, pone ordine vitis

> (Now, Meliboeus, graft your pear-trees; set your vines out in rows),

save that this latter sentence is bitterly ironical, while the former is more neutral in tone, though as will appear later, also not lacking in a certain pathos. Further, in *E.* 1.16–17 Meliboeus speaks of a foreboding of his disaster which he failed to recognize:

> Saepe malum hoc nobis, si mens non laeva fuisset,
> de caelo tactas memini praedicere quercus

(I remember, if my mind hadn't been turned awry, that oaks struck by lightning foretold this woe to us.)

In *E.* 9.14–16, at roughly the same point in the poem, Moeris too describes an omen, though one which he successfully recognized:

Quod nisi me quacumque novas incidere lites
ante sinistra cava monuisset ab ilice cornix,
nec tuus hic Moeris nec viveret ipse Menalcas.

(But had not a raven from the hollow oak on my left hand warned me in advance to cut short somehow my new proceedings, neither your Moeris here nor Menalcas himself would be among the living.)

The difference between these two passages is symptomatic of general differences between the two poems. Though the disaster intimated by the omen of *E.* 9 makes that of *E.* 1 seem trivial by comparison, still the omen served its purpose. The warning was heeded and the disaster averted. Bad as things are, then, there still seems to be, in *E.* 9, some kind of favoring order. Hence one can still hope and look forward to better times:

Carmina tum melius, cum venerit ipse, canemus

(We'll sing our songs better when he comes himself, *E.* 9.67.)

Eclogue 1, on the other hand, ends less positively. Meliboeus, the exiled shepherd, is left in far greater despair than his counterpart, Moeris, in *E.* 9. In *E.* 9 too the threat of dispossession by no means suppresses the shepherds' delight in song, whereas the situation hangs more oppressively over the characters of *E.* 1. In *E.* 9, in other words, the pastoral world, the remote and imaginative song-filled hills of Theocritus, can assert itself still. In *E.* 1 this world is clouded over far more by the intrusive realities of Roman politics.

Yet to whatever degree the two poems complement one another, both, taken individually and as a pair, present a leitmotif of the *Eclogues*, the interplay between the real and the imaginary, between the familiar, often troubled present and the distant, hope-filled future.

This mixture of contrasting elements is perhaps the major stylistic device of *E.* 1 and, as will be suggested more fully later, is in part responsible for its opening the collection. The first exchange at once sets the oppositions into motion: two speeches of five lines each, both beginning with a vocative (*Tityre*, 1; *O Meliboee*, 6). The first speech complains of exile; the second exults in good fortune. The contrast of exile and settledness, however, is developed even within the first speech:

Tityre, tu patulae recubans sub tegmine fagi
silvestrem tenui musam meditaris avena:

nos patriae finis et dulcia linquimus arva.
nos patriam fugimus: tu, Tityre, lentus in umbra
formosam resonare doces Amaryllida silvas.

(Tityrus, you, as you lie under the cover of a spreading
beech, practise your forest muse with light oaten flute: we
leave the borders of our country and our sweet fields. You,
Tityrus, easeful in the shade, teach the woods to echo the
fair Amaryllis, 1–5.)

Not only is there the pointed contrast, "You under a beech . . . ;
we in exile . . ." (lines 1 and 3), but also the carefully balanced
Tityre, tu (1) . . . *tu, Tityre* (4) frames the statement of exile in
the central portion, lines 3–4. With "Tityrus" in line 4, the last
line and a half moves back into the pastoral peace, now lost to the
speaker, of lines 1 and 2:

tu, Tityre, lentus in umbra
formosam resonare doces Amaryllida silvas.

This circular a-b-a movement in the first five lines is, in small,
the pattern of the whole poem.[5] Thus from the good fortune of
Tityrus (6–10) we move again to Meliboeus' misfortune (11–18),
then back once more to Tityrus' success at Rome (19–25), with
its ramifications both into the past (27–41) and the future (46–58,
59–63), then once more to Meliboeus' misfortune (64–78), and
finally to Tityrus' promise of rest (79–84). This movement can
be tabulated sketchily as follows:

1–5   a-b-a Meliboeus' introduction
6–10   a   Tityrus' good fortune
11–18 b   Meliboeus' misfortunes
19–63 a   Emphasis on Tityrus' success and its background:
               1) 19–45: his past life leading up to his visit to
                  Rome
               2) 46–58: Meliboeus' description of the good
                  things Tityrus is to enjoy in the coun-
                  try (*Fortunate senex*)
               3) 59–63: Tityrus refers again to his success at
                  Rome
64–78 b   Meliboeus' lament for his exile; *At nos hinc* (64)
               marks the contrast with what precedes
79–83 a   Tityrus' promise of rest. *Hic tamen* (79) answers
               At nos hinc (64).

The middle section is complex, and I make no attempt here at a
complete analysis. The fact that Tityrus' good fortune is described
by the dispossessed Meliboeus (*Fortunate senex*, "happy old that
you are," 46) in the most "pastoral" part of the poem is a dra-
matic device which adds considerably to the pathos, for we see a

future projection of Tityrus' pastoral life, with its untroubled continuities, through the eyes of one condemned to give up this life as he has known it in his own past.

Tityrus, on the contrary, has been deeply and favorably impressed by the city and tends to demean his rustic surroundings by comparison to it:

> Urbem quam dicunt Romam, Meliboee, putavi
> stultus ego huic nostrae similem. . . .
> sic canibus catulos similis sic matribus haedos
> noram, sic parvis componere magna solebam.
> verum haec tantum alias inter caput extulit urbes
> quantum lenta solent inter viburna cupressi.

> (The city which they call Rome, Meliboeus, I thought in my foolishness to be like ours . . . So did I know that puppies are like dogs and kids like mother goats, thus was I wont to compare great things with small. But this city lifts its head as far among other cities as cypresses are wont to do among the winding osiers, 19–24.)

There is a further pathetic irony here in that the terms of Tityrus' comparison, and especially his last line,

> quantum lenta solent inter viburna cupressi,

vaguely seem to recall Meliboeus' lament in the opening lines, and intensify in Meliboeus the awareness of the beauty of exactly that which Tityrus is depreciating; and thus his response is,

> Et quae tanta fuit Romam tibi causa videndi?
> (And what great reasond did you have for seeing Rome? 26.)

There is a characteristic Vergilian delicacy and sensitivity, and a touch of humor too, in the *tanta* which effectively distinguishes the two men and the two situations. Tityrus, while demeaning the rustic world, unconsciously praises it; and Meliboeus, whose mind responds far more readily to the praise than the depreciation, can conceive of leaving it only under the compulsion of the weightiest reasons (*quae* tanta . . . *causa*, "what *so great* reason").[6]

Tityrus too has a more prosaic attitude than Meliboeus toward his rustic world. For him it is a place of work and hard-earned savings (*peculi*, 32) and frustrations (*pinguis et* ingratae *premeretur caseus urbi*, "and the cheese is pressed out for the *ungrateful* city," 34). The exile is far more prone to idealize what he must leave, and he dwells lovingly on the familiar features of his beloved country with lush adjectives which he seems scarcely able to refrain from applying to every noun. The bees are "Hyblaean," sleep is "soft," the rock is "lofty," the doves "hoarse," and in a single line (52) the founts "sacred" and the coolness "shaded."

The last two lines of the poem are again deep in the peace of the pastoral world:

Et iam summa procul villarum culmina fumant .
maioresque cadunt altis de montibus umbrae

(And already from afar the tops of the houses send forth their smoke and longer shadows fall from the tall hills)

and thus mark a circular return, though with a heavier, more somber resonance, to the untroubled liquids of the first two lines.[7]

Within this large movement there are several related groups of contrasts. First, as already suggested, that between country and city. The city is, of course, Rome (19) and hence connotes all the threatening realities (*en quo discordia civis/ produxit miseros*, "To what a pass has discord brought the wretched citizens," 71–72) which are driving Meliboeus out of the pastoral world. *Civis* in 71, and *miles* in 70, are significant words in pointing up the realities which the *urbs* threatens; they would ordinarily have no place in a traditional pastoral setting.

The city-country antithesis carries with it another contrast of a somewhat more subtle nature, that is, a difference between simplicity and artificiality of language. All the descriptions of the country are put into the mouth of the exiled Meliboeus. His language, lavish of adjectives as it may be in 46–58, is nevertheless direct and straightforward, whereas Tityrus tends toward syntactical complexity (note the harsh and unnatural syntax of 27–30) and rhetorical exaggeration (see 7ff., *namque erit ille mihi semper deus* . . . ; 22ff., *sic canibus catulos similis* . . .) which reaches its peak (or should one say nadir) in the inflated commonplaces and periodic structure of 59–63 (*Ante levesergo* . . . *quam nostro* . . .). It is not that Vergil had not quite completed his farewells to the *inanes* . . . *rhetorum ampullae* ("the empty jars of the rhetors," *Catalepton* 5), nor that "this verse [62], with its fortissimo in the dynamic movement of the poem, completes the breakthrough to the sublime."[8] Rather, Vergil, with a typically subtle humor, is using style to enhance the dramatic movement and the characterization. Tityrus' language can be attributed to the fact that he is, naturally, exultant. Yet it is perhaps also as if he has brought back from the city some of its complexity and artificiality. So too what is rhetorical artifice for Tityrus in 62 is bitter reality for Meliboeus in 64–66. Meliboeus, who has never been to the city but, because of the city and its wars, is being driven from his "sweet fields" (*dulcia arva*, 3) speaks with a directness and nobility that enhance the pathos of his situation. Simplicity of expression such as his is the natural vehicle for interpreting the simple beauty of the country. Meliboeus is the true poet, the one to describe the beauties of the country; Tityrus, whose mind seems as prosaic as his language, talks of savings and cheese. Yet he who appreciates this beauty and can respond to it and give it expression in its proper terms, he who possesses the true "forest muse" (*silvestrem musam*) with its "light oaten flute" (*tenui avena*, 2) is the one to be exiled.[9]

Through the stylistic differences in the speech of the two rustics also, city and the powerful "god" it contains are made even more remote from Meliboeus' world. They belong not only to a different geographical area, but also to a different verbal area, a mode of speech that is unfamiliar and distant. They thus appear as spiritually as well as spatially removed.

There is yet another important set of contrasts running throughout the *Eclogue:* the interplay between past and future. Meliboeus sees all his happiness as belonging to the past. His flock is *quondam felix*, "happy once" (74), while for the future he sees only darkness: "Shall I ever, a long time after (*longo post tempore*) look with wonder upon my native country . . ." (67–69); "I shall not in time afterward (*posthac*) see you . . . , my goats; no songs shall I sing" (75–77). Conversely he uses the same future tenses of Tityrus (*ergo tua rura manebunt*, "Your fields, then, will remain," 46), but his companion's future Meliboeus sees as unblemished happiness since he will stay in the country. Tityrus himself can regard as assured the calm link between past and future, for he has been told, "Pasture your oxen *as before*, my children" (*pascite* ut ante *boves, pueri*, 45). But for Meliboeus this link is broken, and he leaves behind his past happiness with his *patria*.

Yet just as Vergil ends the poem with the settled, not the exiled rustic, so in the concluding lines he leaves the complex movement from happy past to uncertain future for the calm certainty of the present. For this one night, at least, Meliboeus is promised rest: *Hic tamen hanc mecum poteras requiescere noctem* (79); and the poem ends with the same present-tense timelessness with which it began (cf. *sunt, fumant, cadunt,* 80–83; *recubans, meditaris, doces*, 1–2, 5).

Tityrus can still occupy the timeless present which is the heritage of every pastoral shepherd: action free equally from bondage to a past and from responsibility for future consequences and hence removed both from regret and from guilt. Action for Tityrus, then, is static, without results or limits, as Meliboeus unhappily points out in his opening lines (*recubans, meditaris, lentus, doces*; and the languor reaches also to the tree, the *patula fagus*, 1). But the present tenses used by Meliboeus of himself—*linquimus, fugimus*—only carry him farther away from Tityrus' happy world. And so the last lines of the poem, with the verbs of pastoral nonaction-in-action, are indeed a final attempt to regain peace, to reaffirm Arcady. But peace and Arcady belong now only to Tityrus.

Thus despite the temporary effort toward calm and rest the

tensions between sadness and peace, settledness and disposession are unresolved. Rest is promised, it is true, but exile is no less pressing. The morrow still awaits. This atmosphere of suspension amid contraries, of rest amid disturbance, sets the tone for the *Eclogues*. The momentary pause of these last lines creates the silence in which the collection can be entered. Yet the *temporary* duration of the silence is not forgotten, nor with it the sense of the effort required to create a world of peace and beauty apart from the surrounding threats of disturbance and violence.[10]

In such a world—the world before Actium—the poet is indeed an exile. He can respond to and express the beauty he can find in the world; yet he cannot claim this beauty as a stable and permanent possession. It is a precarious holding from which he may be all too easily dislodged.

II

Like *Eclogue* 1, the Ninth *Eclogue* is a dialogue between two shepherds, one dispossessed, the other apparently unthreatened by the troubles in the region. Yet there is a crucial difference. Lycidas, the unthreatened shepherd, makes a genuine attempt to console his friend. Unlike the self-centered Tityrus, his counterpart in *E.* 1, he does not simply receive congratulations on his good luck. In fact, the poem contains no reference to the happier fortune of Lycidas. Thus the contrast that is so strongly developed in *E.* 1 never fully materializes here. There is still some dramatic movement in the attempts of the rather enthusiastic and cheerful Lycidas to brighten the mood of his more somber and stolid friend. Yet Lycidas, though he is more sympathetic than Tityrus, is also less vivid. This lack of full characterization should not necessarily be regarded as a weakness in the poem (there has indeed been a tendency, unjustified, as I hope to show, to disparage the literary merits of *E.* 9);[11] it is probably a deliberate attempt on Vergil's part to restrict the dramatic element.

By so doing, Vergil helps diminish the reality of the entire situation and hence the intensity of the sense of loss. Measured against *E.* 1, this reduction is significant. The setting especially is not so clearly localized as in *E.* 1, with its explicit reference to Rome. Even lines 7–9 of *E.* 9, despite the claims of commentators hunting for Vergil's farm, present a fairly generalized description: hills sloping down gently, water, old beech trees; and, to confuse further any precise identification, the sea is in sight (note *aspice*, "behold," 57).[12] Also the relation of Moeris to Menalcas is left rather vague. It is presumably a master-servant relation, but it is never made quite clear whether Moeris is slave or free (contrast the emphasis on Tityrus' acquisition of his freedom in *E.* 1.27ff.). Then the fact that the loss of the farm primarily concerns a third person, the absent Menalcas, contributes to this same effect of rendering more remote the sense of disaster.

This lessening of the immediacy of the misfortune allows the poem to assume a more "literary" character than *E.* 1. The shepherds can take time to exchange songs, and they are not so crushed that there is a sense of incongruity between their singing and the darker mood created by the news of dispossession. In the same way the large number of translations from Theocritus which the poem contains and rather obtrusively exhibits reduces the dramatic immediacy and calls attention to the artificial, "literary" framework of the poem itself. There is thus a degree of poetic self-consciousness, heightened by the references back to the Fifth *Eclogue* in lines 19–20 (cf. *E.* 5.20 and 40), which is almost totally absent in *E.* 1. While the First *Eclogue*, then, attempts to present the situation in direct, dramatic form, the Ninth deflects attention to the intervening frame.

Paradoxically, the very beginning of the Ninth *Eclogue* is characterized by a greater dramatic vividness than that of the First. While *E.* 1 begins with the regretful fluidity and drawn out, almost sensuous melancholy of Meliboeus' lament,

Tityre, tu patulae recubans sub tegmine fagi,

E. 9 begins abruptly with a question in an almost flippantly conversational style and in a short, choppy rhythm:

Quo te, Moeri, pedes? an, quo via ducit, in urbem?

(Where do your feet carry you, Moeris? Is it where the road leads, to the city?)

Vergil is translating almost literally from Theocritus' Seventh *Idyll*, after which the setting of the poem as a whole is modelled. But the verse of Theocritus occurs well along in his poem (VII.21); and Vergil has modified the tone considerably:

Σιμιχίδα, πᾷ δὴ τὺ μεσαμέριον πόδας ἕλκεις;

(Where are you heading on foot, Simichidas, at mid-day?)

Vergil's line is far more elliptical, and its rhythm more harsh (he has two spondees—excluding the final foot—to Theocritus' one, and has broken up the utter simplicity of the Theocritean movement by placing the vocative later in the line and by interrupting any easy balance between the two coordinate phrases with the parenthetical *quo via ducit*). There is nothing like the easy dactylic flow of Theocritus' final four feet or the limpid syntax of his whole line. The addition, *in urbem*, "to the city," never a good sign for a Vergilian rustic as we have seen from *E.* 1, also adds a certain suggestion of foreboding, or at least unpleasantness.

Vergil can translate Theocritus better than this when he chooses. Here he has deliberately roughened Theocritus' verse for his own purposes. Thus by announcing, as it were, in the first line both his source and his intention to differ from his source, he lays the foundation for a significant contrast between his poem and its Theocritean model.

The tone of this difference develops quickly in the following lines. Moeris' speech, like Lycidas' question, is excited, abrupt, not especially adorned by poetical felicities. The words seem to pour out without any order, as if he is too excited to organize his thoughts; and indeed his first words come about as close to suggesting incoherence as the formal hexameter permits:

> O Lycida, vivi pervenimus, advena nostri
> (quod numquam veriti sumus) ut possessor agelli
> diceret: 'haec mea sunt; veteres migrate coloni.'   (2–4).

A somewhat exaggerated, yet justifiable, translation would punctuate with dashes:

> O Lycidas, we have lived to see—a foreigner—our own—a thing we never feared—that he should take possession of our little plot and say, "This is mine; you old settlers, depart."[13]

Instructive again is the contrast with the formal, plaintive tone of Meliboeus in *E.* 1 with its circular movement and studied repetitions. Equally important is the contrast with the Theocritean original, for the questioner in Theocritus goes on to observe that it is no time to travel: even lizards and tree-frogs sleep (22–23); and his friend, he conjectures with a lyrical comment, is going to a banquet or a revel: "Ah, as you walk every stone sings as it strikes against your sandals" (. . . ὡς τοι ποσὶ νισσομένοιο/ πᾶσα λίθος πταίοισα ποτ' ἀρβυλίδεσσιν ἀείδει, 25–26). He receives the reply, preceded by a gracious compliment about his own poetic superiority, that the friend, Simichidas, is going to a harvest-festival, the *Thalysia,* from which the poem derives its title in the ancient editions. The tone of Vergil's Moeris, however, is but one of several related differences: his journey has a different character and a different destination.

This tone, however, now changes in the reply of Lycidas in lines 9–10. Here the peaceful description of the country, with the reference to the old rustic traditions and sense of continuity in the old beech trees, *veteres, iam fracta cacumina, fagos* (9), introduces a note of quiet and stability which the poem is not to lose again. Thus even the reality of the loss of the farm to the rude arms of the soldier in Moeris' reply is tempered by the "literary" language which Moeris uses:

> sed carmina tantum
> nostra valent, Lycida, tela inter Martia quantum
> Chaonias dicunt aquila veniente columbas.

> (But our songs, Lycidas, have as much power amid the arms of Mars as they say the Chaonian doves have when the eagle comes, 11–13.)

The poetic proper adjectives and the contrived word order of line 13 (matched by a similar arrangement in line 15) distance the experience and remind the reader again of the poetic frame.[14] This frame obtrudes again even more strongly in the references to *Eclogue* V in 19–20, in the symmetrical quotations from Menalcas' songs in 23–25 and 27–29, in the two following songs of the shepherds themselves (39–43, 46–50), and in the allusions to the contemporary poets, Varius and Cinna, in line 35.

There is, it is true, a certain alternation, somewhat analogous to the movement in *E.* 1, between the pressing realities of the present and the realm of pastoral song. Most immediately, in each pair of songs the first is purely pastoral (so 23–25, 39–43), the second concerned with the political situation (27–29, 46–50). Vergil thus shifts quickly from the depths of the timeless pastoral world to Mantua and Rome of the present. Yet the fact that the references are parts of songs makes the shift less abrupt than would otherwise be the case; the "dissonance" is thus softened. Even the reference back to *E.* 1.73 in line 50 (*insere, Daphni, piros*) can here hardly carry with it the bitterness and irony of disappointment of that context, but occurs in a joyful song celebrating the beneficent star of Caesar. Hence the poem does not carry through the a-b-a alternation of *E.* 1. Instead the threatening realities of the introductory lines, though not entirely obliterated, are attenuated as the poem spins about itself its own world of pastoral song.

In its own terms, however, and with its difference of emphasis *E.* 9 contains as subtle a movement between reality and pastoral as *E.* 1. Much of this movement comes from Vergil's use of Theocritus. Since Theocritus VII is the most directly autobiographical of the *Idylls*, Vergil, by using it, may mean to indicate that he too is writing an autobiographical poem. The quotations from the Fifth *Eclogue* and the explicit reference to Mantua in line 27 confirm this suggestion.

At the same time, as the first line implies, Vergil is signaling deep differences between himself and his model, and these differences are made more pointed as the poem develops. Vergil translates from Theocritus' Third *Idyll* in lines 23–25 and returns to *Idyll* VII in 32ff., lines 33–34 being a close translation of Theocritus VII. 37–38:

> me quoque dicunt
> vatem pastores; sed non ego credulus illis

(The shepherds say that I too am a poet, but I am not inclined to believe them.)

> κἠμὲ λέγοντι
> πάντες ἀοιδὸν ἄριστον· ἐγὼ δέ τις οὐ ταχυπειθής.

The next two lines (35–36) are a freer adaptation from Theocritus VII. 39–41. Yet in what directly precedes this five-line close imitation of his Greek model, Vergil marks a sharp contrast with Theocritus. Moeris in 27–29 has sung of the dangers of Mantua, "too near to poor Cremona," and then Lycidas utters a two-line blessing (30–31) as a prelude to further songs:

> Sic tua Cyrneas fugiant examina taxos,
> sic cytiso pastae distendant ubera vaccae,
>   incipe, si quid habes.

(So may your bee-swarms escape the Corsican yews, so may your cows, well-grazed, stretch full their udders: begin with what you have.)

The corresponding passage in Theocritus (VII. 31–34) is as follows:

> ἁ δ' ὁδὸς ἅδε θαλυσιάς· ἦ γὰρ ἑταῖροι
> ἀνέρες εὐπέπλῳ Δαμάτερι δαῖτα τελεῦντι
> ὄλβω ἀπαρχόμενοι· μάλα γάρ σφισι πίονι μέτρῳ
> ἁ δαίμων εὔκριθον ἀνεπλήρωσεν ἀλωάν.

(This is the road for the Harvest Fesival, for our companions are making an offering-feast in honor of Demeter as the first-fruits of their bounty. For the goddess in rich measure filled their threshing floor to the full with good grain.)

In Vergil blessing alternates with disaster, and the first half of the blessing is itself a warning about sinister yews from remote Corsica. Rather than the unambiguous richness and exuberant fertility of Theocritus, then, Vergil presents a complex intermingling of hopefulness and danger. Characteristically too what good fortune Vergil does envisage refers to a remote and uncertain future; Theocritus' bounty is a tangible and established fact in the present.

In the two songs that follow (39–43, 46–50), as already noted, close imitation of Theocritus contrasts with the star of Caesar. Yet it is interesting that it is the troubled Moeris who sings the mythological themes of Hellenistic pastoral. The exiled shepherd has been silently meditating (tacitus . . . mecum ipse voluto, 37) on pastoral fancies about Galatea and the Cyclops. Moeris, even in the midst of his misfortunes, has forgotten neither pastoral song nor pastoral manners. So he grants his friends request, and with this rather gallant touch Vergil seems to assert a minor triumph of the poetic-pastoral spirit over the harsh facts of discord and force.

But later Moeris does remark sadly that he has forgotten all his songs (though he attributes his forgetfulness to age rather than to his present troubles: see 51ff.); and he then utters one of the most beautiful verses in the Eclogues:

> saepe ego longos
> cantando puerum memini me condere soles

(I remember that as a boy I often laid long days to rest with singing, 51–52.)

The joy of poetry is looked on with the vague nostalgia of something past and lost. The phrase is Vergil's own, and is eminently suited to the complex tone of this *Eclogue*. But again Vergil may be intentionally drawing a contrast with Theocritean pastoral. The language seems to have been suggested by Theocritus XI, 39–40, that is from the same general context as Moeris' song in 39–43. In the Theocritus passage, the Cyclops boasts of his skill in song:

> τίν, τὸ φίλον γλυκύμαλον, ἁμᾷ κἠμαυτὸν ἀείδων
> πολλάκι νυκτὸς ἀωρί.

(singing of you, my dear honey-apple, and myself together often late into the night.)

Vergil has taken the mythical, comic singer from his untroubled erotic context and made him a mortal facing age and sorrow in a disordered, violent world.

In keeping with the tone of *E.* 9, however, Vergil does not let this somber trait of Moeris go too far or dominate too much of the poem. He only touches on it here with a single fine stroke, and then has Lycidas try to coax him into song again. Lycidas' speech, his last in the poem, again draws heavily on Theocritus:

> Causando nostros in longum ducis amores.
> et nunc omne tibi stratum silet aequor, et omnes,
> aspice, ventosi ceciderunt murmuris aurae.

(By your excuses you only put off our desires. And now all the sea lies flat and silent, and look, all the breezes with their murmuring gusts have fallen, 56–58.)

Vergil's model, however, is a song, not direct speech, and a song of love, newly written by one of the rustic poets:

> θερμὸς γὰρ ἔρως αὐτῶ με καταίθει·
> χάλκυόνες στορεσεῦντι τὰ κύματα τάν τε θάλασσαν
> τόν τε νότον τόν τ᾽ εὖρον, ὃς ἔσχατα φυκία κινεῖ,
> ἀλκυόνες, γλαυκαῖς Νηρηίσι ταί τε μάλιστα
> ὀρνίχων ἐφίληθεν, ὅσοις τὲ περ ἐξ ἁλὸς ἄγρα.

(Warm love of him burns me. And the halcyon-birds will lay to rest the waves and the sea and the south wind and the east wind which stirs up the bottom-most sea-weed— the halcyons who most of all birds are beloved by the grey-eyed Nereids and by all who have their prey from the sea. VII. 56–60.)

The original is not only a song of love, but passes quickly into the realm of myth and mythical beings like the Nereids. It comes too at about a third of the way through the poem. In Vergil the words are direct speech, have no mythological allusions, and come at the end of the poem. He thus again takes the graceful calm of Theocritus and overlays it with a suggestion of complexity and melancholy. He seems to be glancing too at another Theocritean context where the silence of the sea does carry somber, even tragic overtones, that is, Theocritus' Second *Idyll*, the *Pharmaceutria*:

ἠνίδε σιγῇ μὲν πόντος, σιγῶντι δ' ἀῆται
ἁ δ' ἐμὰ οὐ σιγῇ στέρνων ἔντοσθεν ἀνία, ...

(Behold, the sea grows silent, silent the winds; but silent not my pain within my breast. II. 38–39.)[15]

And Vergil may have learned something from the expansive view out into a calm, but remote and indifferent realm with which Theocritus ends this poem:

χαῖρε, Σελαναία λιπαρόθρονε, χαίρετε δ' ἄλλοι
ἀστέρες, εὐκάλοιο κατ' ἄντυγα Νυκτὸς ὀπαδοί.

(Farewell, Moon-goddess of the brilliant throne, farewell you other stars, attendants following the chariot of still Night. II. 165–66.)

Within the framework of Vergil's own poem, then, his lines on the sea and the winds create a broad, quiet, more somber atmosphere after the conventional exchange of pastoral song—a hint at something remote, a more than human silence that seems to anticipate some of the mysterious and awesome nightfalls of the *Aeneid*:

Et iam nox umida caelo
praecipitat suadentque cadentia sidera somnos.

(And now the damp night falls from the sky and the falling stars urge sleep, *Aen.* 2.8–9.)

or

Iamque fere mediam caeli nox umida metam
contigerat, placida laxabant membra quiete.

(And now damp night had attained the mid-point of its goal in the sky, and peaceful limbs were being loosed in rest, *Aen.* 5.835–36.)[16]

This suggestion of a larger and darker perspective is deepened in the next two lines:

hinc adeo media est nobis via; namque sepulcrum
incipit apparere Bianoris.

(This is the middle of our road; for the tomb of Bianor be-
gins to appear.)

Again a close translation of the Seventh *Idyll*:

κοὔπω τὰν μεσάταν ὁδὸν ἄνυμες, οὐδέ τὸ σᾶμα
ἁμῖν τὸ Βρασίλα κατεφαίνετο

(And we did not yet reach the middle of our road, nor did
the tomb of Brasilas appear to us, 10–11.)

Yet in Theocritus this passage comes at the very beginning of the
poem to help create the setting and perhaps refers to a real place.
Vergil uses it at the end of his poem in close conjunction with a
later passage from *Idyll* VII, and (despite the ancient com-
mentators) he probably has no real place in mind. He uses the
tomb, after the solemn lines about the sea, to create a deeper
mood of sadness, a reminder of death that is in keeping with the
suggestions of melancholy in the poem, the vicissitudes of fortune
(5) and the losses entailed by age (51). (Note too that Vergil's
sepulcrum is a more sinister reminder of death than Theocritus'
neutral σᾶμα.) He thus sounds a new, typically Vergilian note
that will influence later conceptions of pastoral: Death too in
Arcady, *Et in Arcadia ego*.[17]
Vergil closes his poem too on a note of suspension and vague
hope. Lycidas, after his reference to the tomb in 59, suggests that
they sing right where they are, amid the rich foliage of the
pastoral setting:

hic, ubi densas
agricolae stringunt frondes, hic, Moeri, canamus.

(Here, where the farmers trim the thick leaves, here, Moeris,
let us sing, 60–61.)

But the timeless moment of pastoral is not for those who have
such a journey as Moeris. Thus Lycidas—almost inadvertently, it
would seem—recalls Moeris' destination and the pressing reality
of the journey: *tamen veniemus in urbem* ("even so we shall come
to the city," 62). His words, with their echo of *in urbem* of the
first line, evoke again the awareness of exile and unrest. His next
line too contains a mildly ominous element, also associated with
travel: the fear of nightfall and rain:

aut si nox pluviam ne colligat ante veremur,
cantantes licet usque (minus via laedit) eamus.

(Or, if we fear that night may first gather rain, we may go
straight on singing—the road is less irksome thus, 63–64.)

The sinister, or at least unpleasant, suggestion—carried largely through the vivid *colligat*—appears even through the bright naiveté and hopeful playfulness of a Lycidas. Despite the generosity and cheeriness of Lycidas, whose touching simplicity in offering help and a song strikes a more genuine and pathetic note than Tityrus' offer in *E.* 1, his more experienced companion cannot accept: *Desine plura, puer* ("cease from further efforts, my boy," 66) Moeris replies. His *puer* brings out, sadly, the difference between the two shepherds, a bit like Meliboeus' closing *amaras*, "bitter," in *E.* 1.78: the youthful singer who will remain among the *densas frondes* of 60–61, and the older man, travelling reluctantly *in urbem*. Amid such contrasts songs must be put off, at least for the moment: *Carmina tum melius, cum venerit ipse, canemus* ("We'll sing our songs better when he comes himself," 67).

This uncertain, hesitant ending is again in the most marked contrast with Vergil's model, for Theocritus' poem ends with laughter (128, 156) and an elaborate and graceful enumeration of all the beauties that the pastoral world holds, including Nymphs and Polyphemus (128–57). Indeed Theocritus' final lines leave a picture of the benign fertility of the grain-goddess and a "mellow fruitfulness" that is almost Keatsian in its richness:

ἆς ἐπὶ σωρῷ
αὖτις ἐγὼ πάξαιμι μέγα πτύον, ἁ δὲ γελάσσαι
δράγματα καὶ μάκωνας ἐν ἀμφοτέραισιν ἔχοισα.

(I wish I might fix in her grain-heap a huge winnowing-shovel while she laughs holding in either hand sheaves and poppies. VII. 155–57.)

Vergil thus creates a different kind of pastoral world, one which he subtly, but inevitably contrasts with that of his Greek predecessor. Theocritus' shepherd world is peaceful, happy, in close touch with the realm of myth; Vergil's is precarious and disturbed. The Roman poet, writing in the closing decades of the "Age of Agony," (as Toynbee has termed the period from about 300 to 31 B.C.) must come to closer grips with the realities of violence and disorder about him. He cannot so freely indulge in the exuberant richness that characterizes large parts of Theocritus' Seventh *Idyll*, and indeed nearly all the *Idylls*. Or, if he does turn to a beautiful and untroubled Arcady, he must come back, back to war-torn Italy, to Rome or to Mantua "too close to poor Cremona."

There is thus a divided tendency in Vergilian pastoral. On the one hand the pressures of the realities lead the poet to transform Theocritus' Sicily or Cos into a totally imaginary Arcadia, an Arcadia such as never existed in Greece or anywhere else. On the other hand, the poet cannot enter too far into his Arcady. Neither his purpose nor the pressing nature of the realities themselves will allow him. Hence he must check his song, resist the attraction which such an Arcady exerts: *Desine plura, puer, et quod nunc instat agamus* ("Cease from more singing, my lad, and let's attend to what is now at hand," *E.* 9.66). He might, of course, not have resisted; but then the *Eclogues* would lack the complexity of tone, the delicate mixture of beauty and sorrow that mark their poetic maturity and comprise half their beauty.

What has not often enough been made clear by those who emphasize the "realism" of Theocritus over against the dreamy unreality of Vergil is that even the "realistic" parts of Theocritus involve no actual break with his pastoral world. There is little discontinuity for the Greek poet between the erotically tinged realm of myth and the realm of "realistic" rusticity (also, usually, erotically tinged). In Theocritus' First *Idyll*, for instance, it is an easy and smooth movement from the song of Daphnis, dying of love, to the frolicsome female and lusty male goats of the shepherd in the last two lines. There is a certain contrast for an effect of pathos, it is true; but the rustics still stand partly in the mythical world, or at least the rustic "realities" are not at variance with the myth and do not disturb the frame into which the myth is set. For Vergil, however, there is a harsh discrepancy between the remote peace of pastoral Arcadia and the realities of the present, for these realities actually *do* threaten the pastoral world in a way in which Theocritus' touches of realism never do. For Theocritus the contrast between myth and "realism" may be amusing or pathetic, but it is never ominous or destructive.

The realm of myth for Theocritus too is much more present, much more an autonomous world than it is for Vergil. However vague and "unreal" Vergil's pastoral setting is, he has nothing that corresponds to the Polyphemus-Galatea *Idylls* or the Hylas *Idyll*. In works like *Idylls* I or VI or XI, where the myth is especially strong, Theocritus' rustics stand in some indefinable ground between the real and the imaginary, whereas Vergil's shepherds, however idealized, are always to some extent real people with real problems or sufferings. Theocritus, on the other hand, can dispense with the pastoral element almost entirely, as in *Idylls* II or XIV or XV. Here, in his treatment of love in a Greek town or his portrayal of middle-class life, Theocritus can be totally "realistic"—but he is not simultaneously pastoral. He can write *Idylls* which, properly speaking, are not bucolic at all. His range is wider than Vergil's, and this has led to an incorrect estimate of Theocritean and Vergilian "realism."

Most recently Snell has exaggerated Vergil's "dreaminess," his need for a "far-away land overlaid with the golden haze of unreality"[18] and has made of him "a nostalgic refugee from sombre realities."[19] Though such statements have some validity, they oversimplify Vergil's complexity. Vergil certainly longs for peace;

yet he has a keen sense of the discrepancy, the "dissonance" (to use Snell's own term) between the longed-for serenity and the realities which prevent such hopes from being more than the shelter and rest offered for a single night, as in *E.* 1, or the hesitant glance toward the future, as at the end of *E.* 9. Not only is it *not* true of Vergil that "the tension between the real and literary world which Theocritus had exploited for its peculiar charms is brought to nought, and everything shifts back to the even plane of an undifferentiated majesty,"[20] but, on the contrary Vergil (at least in *E.* 9) actually uses Theocritus' pastoral settings as a foil for the disturbed and threatened world from which his shepherds are brusquely exiled.

It is, in fact, just because Vergil's pastoral world is totally an artificial creation that it is so threatened by the realities "outside." Vergil's Arcady, unlike Theocritus' Greek or Sicilian landscapes, comes into being by opposition to and removal from these realities, but Vergil does not forget that the realities are there. Thus, while another Vergilian scholar, Klingner, is justified in stressing that " for Vergil the world of Theocritus' shepherds has hardened into a pastoral art-world (Kunstwelt) enclosed within itself,"[21] it should be remembered that the price of the ideality of this artificial world is exactly its fragility:

Hac te nos *fragili* donabimus ante cicuta

(First we shall present you with this fragile pipe, *E.* 5.85)

Vergil himself says of the instrument which sang *Eclogues* 2 and 3, two of the least trouble and most purely "pastoral" of the *Eclogues.*

Vergil's use of Theocritus should not, then, be looked upon as a mere exercise in translation for a poet with abundant leisure. It is rather in the nature of a creative borrowing and transformation by a poet who delights in allusion. The ancients themselves were aware of the extent to which Vergil deliberately modified his models. So, for example, Aulus Gellius:

> Sicuti nuperrime aput mensam cum legerentur utraque simul Bucolica Theocriti et Vergilii, animadvertimus reliquisse Vergilium quod Graece quidem mire quam suave est, verti autem neque debuit neque potuit. Sed enim quod substituit pro eo quod omiserat, non abest quin iucundius lepidiusque sit.

> (For example when just recently the Bucolics of both Theocritus and Vergil were both read together at table, we noted that Vergil left out something that was marvellously delightful in the Greek, but which he should not and could not have translated. But yet what he put in its place succeeds in being even more pleasing and graceful. *Noct. Att.* 9.4.4–5.)

Of modern critics, W. F. J. Knight has suggested an analogy with Pound's use of Propertius.[22] And elsewhere Knight remarks,

> In the *Eclogues* Vergil used the particular past of the *Idylls* in order to vitalize and generalize his own particular experience. He is a good poet partly because he takes that method, the best and perhaps the only good method, to make experience artistic. Poets must, for some mysterious reason, place themselves in a true relation to world poetry, by fixing themselves where they belong in its stream.[23]

And Vergil's ability to use Theocritean passages in complex new ways is well illustrated by the Eighth *Eclogue,* where Vergil not only adapts several Theocritean *Idylls,* but within his first song deepens the seriousness and sadness of Damon's love-plaint by fusing the rustic banter of Theocritus III with the somberness and pathos of Theocritus I (the lament for Daphnis). This tendency to combine different elements into a new and rich synthesis has long been noted as a characteristic of Vergil's art and is already well pronounced in the *Eclogues,* perhaps most notably in the Sixth.[24] There is, as already suggested, a possible example of this technique in the Ninth *Eclogue* too in the lines on the sea (57–58) with the probable reminiscence of Theocritus II.

This tendency of Vergil suggests a further motive in his use of Theocritus VII. Theocritus' poem is not simply an autobiographical account, but is concerned primarily with poets and poetry. Hence in using it, Vergil may be suggesting that the farm and the dispossession, however vivid and distressing in themselves, are but parts of a larger issue, that is, the nature of pastoral poetry, and in a sense all poetry, in a time of violence and disruption. The conflict between Arcady and Rome (or Mantua) is not only a conflict between peaceful Theocritean pastoral and Vergilian lament, but also, and more generally, part of a larger and sempiternal tension between the creative independence of poetry and the demanding, often chaotic, realities of the external world. It is a conflict, then (and one that occurs throughout Augustan literature) between order and disorder, between man as creative agent and man as passive victim of circumstance, between the formative act of will and mind and the fortuitous succession of events that are meaningless in themselves and dissolve the meaning and coherence that still remain.

That Vergil in the *Eclogues* is aware of these tensions and often self-consciously aware of poetry in its autonomous, creative power is intimated in the Sixth *Eclogue* and perhaps to some extent in the Tenth also. The various quotations of the *Eclogues* from one another also point to this poetic self-consciousness. That poetry itself is a major concern in the Ninth *Eclogue* appears from the emphasis given to song and singing throughout. Yet "songs" are mentioned only after the *Eclogue* has been introduced by the non-poetic realities of expulsion and war. Lines 1–6 have the movement of prose (in so far as this is possible in Vergil) rather than of verse; and it is significantly only after Lycidas' beautiful description of the country in 7–10 that the theme of song and the power of song emerges: *omnia carminibus vestrum servasse Menalcan* ("I heard . . . that your Menalcas had saved all with his songs," 10). Moeris, however, knows, sadly, of the weakness of song against force, and corrects his friend:

> Audieras, et fama fuit; sed carmina tantum
> nostra valent, Lycida, tela inter Martia quantum
> Chaonias dicunt aquila veniente columbas.

> (So you heard, and such was the tale. But our songs, Lycidas, have as much strength against the weapons of Mars as they say Chaonian doves have at the approach of the eagle. 11–13.)

Even so, the poetical coloring of this statement suggests that there is yet hope for poetry; and the two friends proceed to quote from Menalcas' songs and discuss their own poetic abilities with abundant references to words for song and singing like *carmen, canere, cantare* (see, e.g. 19, 21, 26, 33, 38, 44).[25] Yet Moeris, with his sober knowledge of the limitations of song reflects nostalgically on the time when he sang songs till sunset (52) and complains that he has now forgotten all his songs (*nunc oblita mihi tot carmina*, 53) and even has lost his voice. Lycidas, however, urges that they continue singing as they travel (*canamus*, 59; *cantantes . . . cantantes*, 64–65), but Moeris persists in his refusal and closes the poem with hope for songs in the future (*carmina*, 66).

The theme of song thus dominates the poem, but with a difference between the two singers. Moeris, the elder, has been more exposed to the realities which exist "outside" the realm of pastoral song. He has a sense of cruel forces in the world, of vicissitude and old age (note the parallel forms of expression, *quoniam fors omnia versat*, "because chance turns all things about," line 5, and *omnia fert aetas . . .* , "age carries off all things . . . ," line 51). He knows too from experience how feeble song is against the violence of the world "outside" (11ff., and note the military image in *victi*, "conquered," line 5); and he knows how easily the capacity for song is lost (52f.). Indeed in his words and in his situation he is the reminder of that "fragility" of the Vergilian pastoral world.

There is a corresponding difference in the subjects chosen by two friends. Lycidas refers to Menalcas' song about Nymphs and flowers (19) and quotes a song of his about Theocritean shepherds at play (23–25). Moeris, on the contrary, quotes from Menalcas' song about the woes of Mantua (27–29). Then in the second pair of songs, Moeris quotes his own song about Galatea, while Lycidas quotes from Moeris' song in honor of the star of Caesar. Lycidas' songs (i.e those he chooses to quote from Menalcas and from Moeris, lines 23–25 and 39–43) are direct, simple, exuberant; they belong to the untroubled rustic world of Theocritus, from whom they are largely close translations. Moeris' song of 23–25, on the other hand, deals with harsh political realities. Vergil thus creates an opposition between two kinds of pastoral song, one belonging to the Hellenistic past, the other to the troubled present. It would be oversimple to identify Lycidas with Theocritus (or Theocritean pastoral) and Moeris with Vergil, for Moeris too, after all, does quote an old song of his own on Galatea, dimly remembered though it is (39–43). What Vergil is perhaps suggesting, however, is that pastoral in his age must embrace the experiences of a Moeris as well as the gay enthusiasm of a Lycidas. His shepherd can no longer be simply a carefree singer but will know the insults of force, will have a sense of change and age, will be aware of the precarious fragility and vulnerability of song and the realms song can create.

It is perhaps for these reasons that the full realization of the pastoral form in Latin had to await Vergil, a poet with the technical skill to adapt Theocritean diction and rhythms into Latin, yet also with the depth of feeling and power of allusive fusion to remake the Hellenistic form into something expressive of the Roman *gravitas* and *dignitas*. Such a poet has (figuratively speaking) to reconcile Moeris and Lycidas, and this means to create a pastoral framework which can include also Rome and Mantua, wars and confiscations, a form in which the Greek feeling for pure beauty, for the formal qualities of image, rhythm, and sound for their own sake, can be fused with the Roman concern with the practical realities of administration, war, and empire and the sufferings they entail. Thus the eagerness and sunny flippancy of Lycidas (line 1) ripen into the deeper, more comprehensive experience and more complex hesitation of Moeris (lines 66–67). Or, to put it differently, the poet begins the Ninth *Eclogue* as a tentative Theocritus and ends it definitely, though delicately, as Vergil.

It is, however, perhaps because the realities of Rome can be kept in the background that the *Eclogues* succeed, within the limits of their intention and their form, more fully and unambiguously than does the *Aeneid* (which is not to say, of course, that they are greater). The small and intimate scale of the *Eclogues*, their personal tone and "literary" character enable the poet to keep firm control on the amount of "reality" and *Romanitas* that he need absorb into his poetry. When he is to attempt to absorb the totality of the Roman ideal into poetry, the results could not but be aesthetically less uniform and more controversial. But, as the ancients too realized, perfect evenness and freedom from flaws are not a final criterion of poetic greatness.[26]

III

The relation between the First and Ninth *Eclogues,* then, may be more significant than the fact that both concern the loss and restitution of a farm. Both poems, as has been seen, deal with the confrontation between a peaceful, undisturbed pastoral world and the hard political realities of the Roman present. In larger terms their theme is the problem of the writing of poetry, indeed the creation of anything beautiful, in an atmosphere of disruption and disorder. Hence the singer's loss of his songs recurs as an important subject at the end of both poems: *Carmina nulla canam* ("No songs shall I sing," *E.* 1.77); *Nunc oblita mihi tot carmina* ("Now I have forgotten so many songs," *E.* 9.53).

Of the many attempts to establish the chronological relation between the two poems, none have been decisive (though a strong tendency favors the priority of *E.* 9); and it is perhaps more fruitful and more in accord with Vergil's poetic intention to regard the poems as parallel in theme rather than sequential in time. So too Vergil's change of the names of his characters in the two works need not indicate, as has been claimed, a desire to plead his cause afresh or to intercede for both slave and free alike,[27] but may merely signify that he is treating different aspects of the same general theme. *Eclogues* One and Nine would thus span the collection (of *E.* 10 something will be said presently), again not necessarily, as has been suggested, because Vergil is trying to separate his personal troubles as far as possible from the triad, *E.* 4, 5, 6, in the center of the collection,[28] but rather because he thus frames the other poems, and especially the more purely "pastoral" *Eclogues* Two and Three and Seven and Eight, with a sense of the precariousness and threatened circumstances out of which such poetry is achieved, the difficulties from which is it wrested.[29] In this way too he colors the rest of the collection with the poignancy of beauty amid loss and sadness, the quality that so strongly predominates in *E.* 1 and 9.

There are reasons too why Vergil would have chosen *E.* 1 to begin the collection. Its position cannot be wholly accounted for by the explanation that it serves to dedicate the book to Octavian, for, as a host of commentators have noted, it offers as much criticism as praise of the young ruler (see especially lines 70ff.). One explanation can perhaps be found in the relation of the theme and tone of the poem to the pastoral framework of the *Eclogues* as a whole. Thus while concerned with the interplay between the imaginary and the real, the First *Eclogue* modulates with greater pathos than the Ninth from the beauty of the pastoral world to the disturbances in the poet's Italy. This pastoral beauty is seen with a heightened intensity precisely because it has to be left behind. Because of the "distancing" effects in the Ninth *Eclogue* discussed above, the pain of this loss is mitigated there, whereas the confrontation between pastoral and reality is sharper in *E.* 1 than in any other of the *Eclogues*. Perhaps, then, Vergil intended to begin with an emotionally involving situation and to reserve his more "intellectual" and more aesthetically self-conscious treatment of the same theme for the later place in the collection.

Yet at the same time the gentle note on which *E.* 1 begins and the circular, a-b-a movement of the introductory passage serve not only to present a microcosm of a characteristic movement in the *Eclogues*, but also to lead slowly and gradually into the pastoral world being opened, while lightly suggesting some of the complexities involved in the existence of that world.

The Ninth *Eclogue*, on the other hand, while beginning more harshly than the First, does not develop the threats of loss and exile so vividly. There is still a *scelus* (17), a sense of evil and disaster, but they remain further in the background than the *impius miles* of *E.* 1.70. The movement of *E.* 9 too, as befits a journey poem, is linear rather than circular; and the concluding lines make only a muted reference back to the disturbances at the beginning. This less pessimistic mood is again in keeping with the place of *E.* 9 in the collection, for it comes after the large con-statements of order in the three central poems, *E.* 4, 5, and 6. Indeed not only does it quote from the Fifth *Eclogue*, but in the song about Caesar's star (46–50) expresses hope for a more beneficent order of things. The attitude toward Octavian seems more optimistic too; but regardless of any chronological development, Vergil seems to have created a deliberate counterpoise between the First and Ninth *Eclogues*. He thus introduces an element of movement into the collection, a movement from the temporary rest of a single night to a more assured and stable, if still indefinite order, possible now after the vision of the *magnus saeculorum ordo* in *E.* 4 and the larger themes, the *paulo maiora* (*E.* 4.1) of *Eclogues* Five and Six. In the Ninth *Eclogue*, though we return again to the "mixed" atmosphere of violence in pastoral Arcadia, something can be envisaged, if only in song and poetic vision (cf. *ecce Dionaei processit Caesaris astrum*, "Lo, the star of Caesar, descendant of Dione, has come forth," 47), that seemed impossibly remote in the despairing atmosphere of the first poem of the collection.

Eclogue Nine too has a certain calm, lacking in *E.* 1, which is fitting at the point where the collection draws to a close. It is less dramatically intense than that poem, but has a wider scope, as in the expansive lines on the sea (57–58). The characters, though less vivid, convey a larger sense of the general condition of human life (see lines 5 and 51). Since the threat of exile is less explicitly visualized, the two shepherds, threatened and unthreatened alike, can still communicate through the medium of pastoral song. Vergil thus creates a sense of aesthetic completeness, characteristic of the individual poems, in ending his collection in an atmosphere of greater calmness and breadth of view.

The calmer and larger tone of the Ninth *Eclogue* also helps prepare for the Tenth. This poem, like *E.* 1 and 9, is concerned with exile; but, as in *E.* 9, the experience is at a certain remove, indeed far less serious than in either of these two poems. The spontaneous sympathy which Lycidas feels for Moeris in *E.* 9—rather more than Meliboeus is able to evoke from Tityrus in *E.* 1—also leads into the sympathy that the poet and the whole of Arcadia feel for the deserted lover in *E.* 10. The development is a natural one within the collection, for after poems like *E.* 2, 6, or 8 the pastoral world appears as colored with a certain gentleness and tenderness. By *Eclogue* Ten it is clearly as Snell called it, "a spiritual landscape." Hence the poet can confidently claim, *Non canimus surdis, respondent omnia silvae* ("We sing not to things deaf; the forests echo back all," *E.* 10.8). Hence too the lament of the pastoral world over the fading lover (13ff.). There is a similar passage in the First *Eclogue* (38–39), but the contrast is instructive, for there the description is shorter (only one-and-one-half lines), and only trees and fountains are involved. In the Tenth *Eclogue* all of Arcadian nature, trees, two major mountains, the rustic folk, even the sheep (*stant et oves circum*, 16) weep for Gallus (note too that in *E.* 1 the pines and fountains do not weep for Tityrus; they simply call him back: *vocabant*, 39). Thus what is a pretty conceit in the First *Eclogue* becomes expanded in the Tenth to suggest an element of feeling deeply pervading the pastoral world.

This pastoral world of *E.* 10, then, gains a reality and autonomy of its own. It is an imaginative creation of the individual poet, but it has something of the large independence that tradition conferred on the myths of Theocritus. This world, then, is no longer threatened by the reality outside, but can in fact attract these "real" figures into its own framework and even console them in their griefs.[30] Gallus would himself become an Arcadian shepherd (50ff.), though there is a slightly humorous suggestion that he sticks a bit at the reality of the transformation (cf. *iam mihi per rupes videor*, 58).

Yet there is seriousness amid the humor too, for the welcoming of the exiled poet in a gentle Arcadia is the inverse of the theme of *E.* 1 where the restored shepherd has himself been affected by the artificiality of the city while the "authentic" poet-shepherd, the one whose language and sensibilities fit and enrich the pastoral world, is exiled. Recompense is thus made for the violence done to the pastoral folk of *E.* 1. The Gallus-episode serves to reinstate the worth both of the poet and of the Arcadian landscape in which he lives after the losses and indignities of *E.* 1 and 9. Sympathy replaces insensitivity, war yields to love (*omnia vincit amor*, *E.* 10.69; contrast *E.* 9.5, *nunc victi, tristes, quoniam fors omnia versat*, "Now defeated, saddened, because chance turns all things about"). The victory of love for Lycoris, with the poetic consequences it inspires, over "the mad love for war" (*insanus amor duri me Martis in armis/ tela inter media, E.* 10.44–45)[31] is a validation of poetry in a troubled world and cancels the ineffectuality of the poet against force and brutality in the Ninth *Eclogue* (cf. *tela inter Martia*, 9.12. The arms which once unjustly drove the poet-shepherd out of his peaceful haunts are now to be cast away by a warrior who would abandon Mars for a poetic Arcadia.

The end of *Eclogue* X provides another, and final, statement of reassurance to the threats of exile in *E*. 1 and 9. Gallus' exile is described in deliberately exaggerated rhetoric that recalls the tone of Tityrus in *E*. 1 (*E*. 10.56–58; cf. *E*. 1.59–63). But, as in the First *Eclogue* too, the wanderings to distant places are followed by the calm of nightfall and the placid regularity of shepherd life:

> Surgamus: solet esse gravis cantantibus umbra,
> iuniperi gravis umbra; nocent et frugibus umbrae.
> Ite domum saturae, venit Hesperus, ite capellae.

> (Let us rise; shade is wont to be harmful to singers, harmful the shade of the juniper; growing crops too are harmed by shadows. Go on homeward, full-fed, the Evening Star comes, go on my goats, *E*. 10.75–77.)

The echo of *E*. 1 is obvious and intentional. Yet here the "heavy shadow" follows directly upon a description of new growth in the spring:

> Gallo, cuius amor tantum mihi crescit in horas
> quantum vere novo viridis se subicit alnus

> (. . . Gallus for whom my love grows hour by hour as fast as a green alder shoots up when spring is fresh, *E*. 10.73–74);

and the goats are full-fed and are being driven *home*. The shepherd still has his goats and his *domus* to which to drive them. This shepherd-poet is far from the cry of Meliboeus in *E*. 1.74,

> Ite meae, quondam felix pecus, ite capellae.

> (Go on, my goats, once happy flock, go on.)

The prayer of *E*. 9.31,

> Sic cytiso pastae distendant ubera vaccae

> (Let the cows, grazed on clover, stretch full their udders)

is thus fulfilled, though in the most imaginary and least real setting of the *Eclogues*. And yet perhaps the poet who promises a time of better song (*E*. 9.67) has come.[32]

It is characteristic of the *Eclogues,* as should now be clear, that they should end with this mixture of spring and shadow, exile and home, unfaithful and faithful love (see *E.* 10.73). Yet the assurance of settledness and fullness in the last line of the collection, spoken by the poet *in propria persona* and thus bridging the gap between pastoral framework and reality, seems to answer the tentative note on which the Ninth *Eclogue* ended. In the Tenth *Eclogue,* not only the theme of song and exile, but also that of fertility and growth are given a final positive turn. Its conclusion, with the *saturae capellae,* is far closer to the richness and bounty of Demeter at the end of Theocritus VII, Vergil's model for *E.* 9. The assurance of settledness and fertility which could not be given there is given (though not unambiguously: there is still the *gravis umbra*) at the end of the whole collection. It is as if the Ninth *Eclogue* ends on a suspended cadence to which the Tenth finally gives a resolution, but still in a minor key.

On the whole, then, the last two poems are positive, optimistic, expansive; but they, and *Eclogue* 1 too, partake of the "mixed" quality characteristic of the *Eclogues* as a whole, the sense of joy amid sadness, beauty amid loss. The counterpoise between *Eclogues* 1 and 9 articulates this quality in terms of the movement and symmetry of the collection, spanning the whole with a suggestion of the tension between pastoral and reality and the larger conditions under which and in the midst of which this poetic world comes into being. That tension is given no easy or oversimplified resolution. The poet seems to wish, in *E.* 10, to make the final impression hopeful and positive. Yet exile still has a central place in the poem, and with it a sense of deliberate unreality, an element of wishfulness; and these themes, in their close relation to the contrasts and uncertainties of *E.* 1 and 9, evoke at the very end of the collection a quality of suspension, though hopeful and fruitful suspension, between fundamental contraries of human life.

Vergil's problem in adapting the untroubled limpidity of Theocritean pastoral for the Roman scene is analogous to that faced by other Roman poets trying to create things of beauty in times of war and disturbance. Lucretius prays to Venus to bring peace to Rome:

> Nam neque nos agere hoc patriai tempore iniquo
> possumus aequo animo
>
> (For we cannot work with calm spirit at a time of woe for our country, *De Rer. Nat.* 1.41–42.)

Horace too looks with admiration on a poet of the Greek past who, though "fierce in war," could yet sing, amid battles and dangers, of wine, song, and love (*Odes* 1.32.6ff.).

But Vergil, in balancing *E.* 1 by *E.* 9 and partially resolving the uncertainties of *E.* 9 in *E.* 10, affirms a hope and belief in order and beauty. Moeris' *carmina tum melius,* tentative as it is, is nevertheless a positive statement in the face of a negative world. Despite exile and disorder, still joy, beauty, and song predominate in the *Eclogues;* and in ending with *E.* 9 and 10 Vergil affirms a regenerative sense of life's continuities and possibilities, something of what Yeats, in another poem written in troubled times, spoke of as "gaiety transfiguring all that dread."[33] Vergil's "gaiety," however, is of a very mixed and complex nature; and it should be recalled that the *Aeneid* too, like *Eclogues* 1 and 9 a poem of exile and dispossession, ends with mixed triumph and shadows, but shadows of a far more sinister kind than those of the *Eclogues* (*vitaque cum gemitu fugit indignata sub umbras,* "with a groan his life fled in anger to the shadows [or, "to the shades"] below").[34] This sense of the sadness and losses of life, the Vergilian *lacrimae rerum,* already permeates the *Eclogues,* richly interwoven though they are with bucolic landscape and song. The presence of these "shadowy" elements, even in Arcady, is part of the complex greatness of Vergil's art. They are, indeed, essential to his, as to all, poetry, for they comprise that in the face of which poetry is almost always written, yet that which great poetry never forgets.[35]

NOTES

[1] Vergil's characteristic fusion of personal elements with larger themes in the *Eclogues* is stressed by F. Klingner, *Gnomon* 3 (1927) 581.

[2] F. Plessis, in Plessis et Lejay, *Oeuvres de Virgile* (Paris 1913) xvii.

[3] Biographical problems in *E.* 1 and 9 still receive a large share of the energy of Vergilian scholars, as can be seen from G. Duckworth's survey, "Recent Work on Vergil (1957–63)," *CW* 57 (1963–64) 198 and 200; see also the earlier survey (1940–56) in *CW* 51 (1958) 124. C. Vandersleyen, *LEC* 31 (1963) 266 has well protested, "Cette désolante explication autobiographique est répandue dans la majorité des éditions, scolaires ou autres." The most recent study of the Ninth *Eclogue* also focuses largely (though not exclusively) on biographical and historical matters: G. Cipolla, "Political Audacity and Esotericism in the Ninth *Eclogue,*" *Acta Classica* 5 (1962) 48–57.

[4] On the unity of the *Eclogues* see Klingner, *Gnomon* 3 (1927) 582, and, most recently, Brooks Otis, *Virgil* (Oxford, 1963) 128–43.

[5] For a similar circular movement in the introductory portion of the poem, compare also the Eighth *Eclogue,* where the introduction, also of five lines, begins, *Pastorum Musam Damonis et Alphesiboei,* and ends (line 5), *Damonis Musam dicemus et Alphesiboei.*

[6] The point of the *tanta* seems to be missed by G. Stégen in his discussion of the passage, "L'unité de la première Bucolique," *LEC* 12 (1943–44) 13–14. He refers the "so great reason" to Tityrus' leaving of Amaryllis who is mentioned twenty lines before(!) and again (by Meliboeus) some ten lines later. For the opposition of city and country, in favor of the country, see also *E*.2.60ff, esp., *Pallas quas condidit*

arces / ipsa colat; nobis placeant ante omnia silvae ("Let Pallas Athene herself inhabit the citadels she has founded; but let woodlands please us before all else").

[7] For a similar use of a circular movement compare also *E*.2, which both begins and ends with "shadows" (lines 3 and 67) and with the heat of passion (*ardebat*, 1; *urit*, 68) set against the peace and steadiness of nature and farm work (cf. 8–9, 10–11 with 63–65, 66–67, 70–72; also *at mecum raucis*, etc., 12–13, with *me tamen urit amor*, 68). Here, however, the circular form has its own special function, i.e., to suggest the hopeless continuity of Corydon's passion despite his rather vacillating efforts to cast it off. Compare too the theme of the disconsolate heifer in *E*.8: *immemor herbarum . . . iuvenca*, vs.2; *cum fessa iuvencum / . . . quaerendo bucula*, vss. 85ff.

[8] F. Klingner, "Das erste Hirtengedicht Virgils," in *Römische Geisteswelt*, ed. 3 (Munich 1956) 307.

[9] The contrast between the two shepherds, by far in favor of Meliboeus, has been stated by René Waltz in an essay which deserves more attention than it has received, "La Ire et la IXe Bucolique," *Rev. Belge de Philologie et d'Histoire* 6 (1927) 31–58. The contrast has recently been stressed again by L. A. MacKay, *Phoenix* 15 (1961) 157.

[10] The tension between peace and disorder is brought out (though with some overstatement) by Vandersleyen (above, note 3) 270: "Ainsi par la confrontation entre les deux hommes, entre ce bonheur et malheur, le poème se charge progressivement d'une douleur qui éclate à la fin en chagrin, colère, ironie amère. Est-ce là l'esprit d'une bergerie? Ou un remerciement, alors que le privilégié est ridicule et honteux de lui-même?" With Vandersleyen, I cannot agree with interpretations that make *E*.1 into a laudation of Octavian, as does Hanslik *WS* 68 (1955) 18–19.

[11] E.g. Waltz (above, note 9) 51; Stégen, *LEC* 21 (1953) 334. *Contra*: Sellar, *Vergil* (Oxford 1897) 142.

[12] A glance at Duckworth's survey, *CW* 57 (1963–64) 200, shows that the search for the country described in *E*.9 goes on apace.

[13] On Moeris' incoherence see Waltz (above, note 9) 45.

[14] Conington's view, in the introduction of his edition (ed. 3, London 1872, I 6–8), that Vergil's "literary" epithets like *Chaonias* are the result of his youthful bookishness and lack of experience of the world, thus needs strong qualification. Vergil uses such epithets often with dramatic intention (as in *E*.1) or with a touch of humor (as in *E*.2. 24, *Amphion Dircaeus in Actaeo Aracyntho*), or for the "distancing" effect conveyed here.

[15] Vergil's adaptation of Theocritus II in *E*.8 helps support the possibility that he has that poem in mind here; at least he knew it well and admired it. The closing lines of Theocritus II seem to have impressed another of Vergil's contemporaries: see Tibullus 2.1.87–88.

[16] For Vergil's early sensitivity to scenes of nightfall, the transitional, penumbral states he is to depict so often in the *Aeneid*, compare *E*.8.14, *Frigida vix caelo noctis decesserat umbra*.

[17] On later treatments of this theme of death in Arcady see E. Panofsky, "*Et in Arcadia Ego*: Poussin and the Elegiac Tradition," in *Meaning in the Visual Arts* (New York, 1955) 297ff.

[18] Bruno Snell, "Arcadia: The Discovery of a Spiritual Landscape,"

in *The Discovery of the Mind,* tr. T. Rosenmeyer (Cambridge, Mass. 1953) 282.

[19] *Ibid.* 293.

[20] *Ibid.,* 286–86. A different, and on the whole more satisfactory, view has been expressed recently by J. Heurgon, "Virgile, la poésie et la vérité," *L'Information littéraire* 10 (1958) 68–72 and esp. p. 69: "Les guerres civiles l'injustice des spoliations, l'angoisse générale s'imposent de plus en plus à lui. C'est ce progressif et irrésistible envahissement de son art par l'actualité, sous le voile de l'allégorie d'abord, mais parfois aussi directement exprimée, qui me paraît merveilleusement lisible dans la diversité des *Bucoliques.*" In fairness to Snell, however, it should be granted that he does, at one point (p. 292), qualify his position and speak of the "genuine political reality" which the *Eclogues* reflect and the "important political and historical function" they exercised (on this latter point not all would agree). But Snell's overwhelming emphasis is in the opposite direction. Vergil's relation to historical realities in the *Eclogues* has been sensitively treated by Otis (above, note 4) 128ff, though his conclusions on E.1 and 9 differ from those reached here.

[21] Klingner, *Gnomon* 3 (1927) 582.

[22] W. F. Jackson Knight, *Roman Vergil* (London, 1945) 79.

[23] *Ibid.,* 121.

[24] For Vergil's synthesis of diverse elements in *E.6* see the recent study by Zeph Stewart, "The Song of Silenus," *HSCP* 64 (1959) 170–205. For a good example of the ways in which Vergil can use different Theocritean contexts to modify the tone of an *Eclogue* see Klingner on *E.2, Gnomon* 3 (1927) 579–81.

[25] Hanslik (above, note 10) 10–11 argues that the two songs, 39–43 and 46–50, are both songs of Menalcas and not of the two shepherds. But his argument is unconvincing, resting as it does on the assumption that whatever is translated from Theocritus (including lines 32–36) must belong to Menalcas (=Vergil); and he must give a forced and unnatural interpretation to line 55. Some scholars, however, while not going so far as Hanslik, have taken lines 31–36 as a quotation from a song of Menalcas and not part of Lycidas' own words: so H. J. Rose, *Mnemosyne* 7 (1954) 58–59. I find this assumption awkward for the movement of the dialogue (esp. in lines 32–33) and disturbing to the symmetry created by the balance of 21–23 and 27–29.

[26] See, for instance, Ps.—Longinus, *De Sublimitate* 33–34, 36.

[27] For these suggestions see Hahn, *TAPA* 75 (1944) 224–26.

[28] *Ibid.,* 239–41.

[29] Heurgon (above, note 20) 70 has suggested that *E.9,* at the end of the collection, serves as a farewell to older poetic forms and an invocation to the new ones to come. And he notes that Vergil's "farewells" are never abrupt and final, as *Catalepton* 5 shows.

[30] L. Alfonsi, "Dalla II alla X Ecloga," *Aevum* 35 (1961) 193–98, has also pointed out some interesting parallels between the Second and Tenth *Eclogues,* suggesting that the Arcady that is tenuous and hesitant in *E.2* is clear and strong in *E.10.* Thus in *E.2.* 28–30 the lover tentatively invites his beloved to the *sordida rura* and *humilis casas* of a rather lustreless pastoral life, whereas in *E.10* the lover himself is eager to enter Arcadia and finds there not "lowly huts," but brightly colored flowers, cool springs, soft meadows (*E.10.* 35–43).

31 Whether *Martis* should go with *amor* or with *armis* is a little uncertain. Conington argues persuasively for the connection with *amor*, and this seems to me the more natural reading, both for the word order and the sense. In either case the attitude toward war is not favorable, and it certainly comes out inferior to love, as line 69 makes unambiguously clear: *omnia vincit Amor.*

32 With *E.9.31* compare *E.10.30: nec cytiso saturantur apes nec fronde capellae* ("nor are the bees sated on clover nor the goats on leaves"). But in *E.10* it is love, not exile, which creates this effect, and this love is to be consoled and answered within the framework of the poem (lines 73–74):

> Gallo, cuius amor tantum mihi crescit in horas
> quantum vere novo viridis se subicit alnus

(. . . Gallus, for whom my love grows hour by hour as fast as a green alder shoots up when spring is fresh.)

33 Yeats, "Lapis Lazuli," in *Last Poems* (1936–39). Indeed, the structure of Yeats' poem might be compared to that of the *Eclogues* as a whole. It begins with a sense of uncertainty and dissolution amid the threats of war ("I have heard that hysterical women say / They are sick of the palette and fiddle-bow, . . ."); and it ends with the reaffirmation of "gaiety," though with a complex mixture of sadness, age, decay in the "discoloration of the stone," the wrinkles in the Chinamen's eyes, the expectation of "mournful melodies":

> One asks for mournful melodies;
> Accomplished fingers begin to play.
> Their eyes mid many wrinkles, their eyes,
> Their ancient, glittering eyes, are gay.

(*The Collected Poems of W. B. Yeats*, New York, 1956, 293). The Yeatsian, and modern, restlessness, however, knows not the suspended bucolic peace that ends the *Eclogues*.

34 On a larger meaning in the "shadows" at the conclusion of *E.1* (and, one should add, of *E.10* too) see Elder's fine remarks in *HSCP* 65 (1961), unfortunately relegated to a footnote (p. 124, note 36):

> Consider the first Eclogue. Here Vergil probes, as he will in the *Aeneid*, the absorbing contemporary problem of the individual and social upheaval. The Eclogue offers no pragmatic answer; Tityrus is safe but Meliboeus is ruined. Yet the poem finally breathes out a peace and a harmony, not economic but emotional, and that is owing to the bucolic closing. The shadows of the oncoming evening and the mountains are regular and constant, and against them transitory man and his ephemeral problems are dwarfed.

Peace and order are there, to be sure, and the regular cyclical movements of nature; but also the touch of sadness and uncertainty that goes with all things that end. Hence the melodious, but somber intimation at the conclusion of *E.10, gravis cantantibus umbra, / iuniperi gravis umbra.* Panofsky (above, note 17) 300, speaks of this "vespertinal mixture of sadness and tranquillity" as "perhaps Virgil's most personal contribution to poetry."

35 I am indebted to Professor Charles Babcock, my colleague at the University of Pennsylvania, for a number of helpful criticisms and suggestions.

VERGIL'S SIXTH *ECLOGUE* AND THE PROBLEM OF EVIL

CHARLES SEGAL

Brown University

I

Eclogue 6 is one of Vergil's most ambitious and most difficult short poems.[1]   Grand themes are its concern: passion, violence, cosmic and poetic creation, the relation between man and nature.   No one formulation of the many subtle and complex relationships between these themes is likely to prove definitive, just as no one principle of unity for its bewildering exuberance of narrative material has emerged as

[1] I shall refer to the following by author's name only: Carl **Becker**, "Virgils Eklogenbuch," *Hermes* 83 (1955) 314–49; Karl **Büchner**, "P. Vergilius Maro," *RE* 8A1 (1955) 1219–24 (on *E.*6): John **Conington and** Henry **Nettleship,** edd., *P. Vergili Maronis Opera*, I⁴ (London 1881); J. P. **Elder,** "*Non Iniussa Cano:* Virgil's Sixth Eclogue," *HSCP* 65 (1961) 109–25; Charles **Fantazzi,** "Virgilian Pastoral and Roman Love Poetry," *AJP* 87 (1966) 171–91; G. Karl **Galinsky,** "Vergil's Second *Eclogue:* Its Theme and Relation to the *Eclogue* Book," *C & M* 26 (1965) 161–91; A. **Hartmann,** "Silenos und Satyros," *RE* 3A1 (1927) 35–53; Herbert **Holtorf,** *P. Vergilius Maro, Die grösseren Gedichten, I, Einleitung, Bucolica* (Freiburg/Munich 1959); Günther **Jachmann,** "Vergils sechste Ekloge," *Hermes* 58 (1923) 288–304; Friedrich **Klingner,** *Virgil, Bucolica, Georgica, Aeneis* (Zürich/Stuttgart 1967); Eleanor Winsor **Leach,** "The Unity of *Eclogue* 6," *Latomus* 27 (1968) 13–32; Brooks **Otis,** *Virgil* (Oxford 1963); Jacques **Perret,** *Virgile* (Paris 1959); H. J. **Rose,** *The Eclogues of Vergil* = "Sather Classical Lectures" 16 (Berkeley and Los Angeles 1942); E. de **Saint-Denis,** "Le chant de Silène à la lumière d'une découverte récente," *RPh* 37 (1963) 23–40; Otto **Skutsch,** "Zu Vergils Eklogen," *RhM* 99 (1959) 193–201; Bruno **Snell,** "Arcadia: The Discovery of a Spiritual Landscape," in *The Discovery of the Mind,* tr. T. G. Rosenmeyer (Cambridge, Mass. 1953) 281–309; Zeph **Stewart,** "The Song of Silenus," *HSCP* 64 (1959) 179–205; John B. **Van Sickle,** "The Unity of the *Eclogues:* Arcadian Forest, Theocritean Trees," *TAPA* 98 (1967) 491–508; Gordon **Williams,** *Tradition and Originality in Roman Poetry* (Oxford 1968); K. **Witte,** "Vergils sechste Ekloge und die Ciris," *Hermes* 57 (1922) 561–87. I wish to acknowledge a special debt of gratitude to my friend Professor John Van Sickle, whose detailed comments on this paper and scrupulous resistance to simplistic approaches to the *Eclogues* have been both a help and an example.   I am especially indebted to his concept of dialectics in the poems, though I have not always interpreted the dialectical movement along lines with which he would agree.

entirely satisfactory. "No one can feel confident of exhausting all
the possibilities of this poem or of understanding all that Virgil intended:
it is the original creation of a fertile poetic imagination."[2]

There has been a growing dissatisfaction with attempts to interpret
the *Eclogue* in terms of external criteria: the work of Gallus, Vergil's
relations to Callimachean poetics or to Alexandrian themes or to
contemporary literary genres or works.[3] Recent interpreters like
Otis, Klingner, and Mrs. Leach have concentrated more fully upon
the moral and aesthetic attitudes which the poem implies,[4] have
allowed a more flexible, less mechanical unity to the whole and especi-
ally to Silenus' song, and have recognized that the poem may be far
more than a "document of Virgilian literary autobiography."[5] I
propose to follow this line of approach, laying perhaps more stress than
the above-mentioned scholars on the moral outlook implied in the
poem, yet acknowledging that the poem's moral and aesthetic positions
—the emphasis upon the creative power of poetry[6]—are inseparable.
Not only does my interpretation posit a firm unity for the *Eclogue*,
but it seeks to give the proem (1–12) a more integral part in that
unity than most previous interpreters have done.

The entire corpus of Vergil's work involves a profound knowledge
of and struggle with the reality of evil in the human psyche. Asking
why history contains such suffering, the *Aeneid* finds a partial answer,
at least, in the passions within man. From the *Eclogues* to the *Aeneid*,
outward events and settings have a symbolical correspondence with
the inner world of human emotional life; and the inner world is as
much the subject of Vergil's poetry as the outer.[7] Juno, obstructress

[2] Williams 249; it is worth repeating his quotation (246) from F. Leo, *Hermes* 37
(1902) 22: "Man wagt kaum mehr es laut zu sagen, aber ich glaube immer noch, wenn
ich Vergil tractire, dass ich es mit einem Dichter zu thun habe."

[3] For discussion and bibliography of the various views and especially those of Franz
Skutsch, see Jachmann 288–89, Rose 97 ff., Saint-Denis 20–35, Stewart 181–83.

[4] Otis 137–39, Leach *passim*, Klingner 106–11. See also Williams 243–49, who takes
"strange and tragic love" as "a unifying thread" (248), yet hedges on the question of
whether one should look for any unity at all (245).

[5] The phrase is Elder's (121), though his own approach goes beyond the biographical
interpretation in a narrow sense.

[6] See Büchner 1219 and 1223–24, Elder 111, Klingner 110, Saint-Denis 40, Van Sickle
504.

[7] *Aen.* 1.92–101 and 198–209 are the familiar examples: see Victor Pöschl, *The Art
of Vergil*, tr. Gerda Seligson (Ann Arbor 1962) 48–53 and *passim*.

of a tranquil and stable order, is symbolically identified with these internal disorders and makes use of figures (like Allecto) who are as much symbols of the life of the soul as powerful agents in the external world.[8]   The *Eclogues*, as Bruno Snell has argued,[9] go even further than the *Aeneid* in using the forms of the external world to create a symbolical landscape of the emotional life, a "spiritual landscape," in Snell's phrase.   The emotions dealt with in the *Eclogues*, however, are not always so tender as Snell maintains.   The sixth *Eclogue* especially casts into the terms of pastoral something of that correlation between disorder in the universe and evil within man which is so richly developed in the *Aeneid*.

One of Vergil's achievements in the sixth *Eclogue* is precisely the incorporation of these basic moral issues into his poetics and *vice versa*. Through his concern with the scope and character of creativity in pastoral (and by extension in all poetry), he seeks, as Mrs. Leach observes, "to present a satisfactory symbolic discourse encompassing all nature."[10]

II

The problem of evil is not foreign to the *Eclogues*.   The idea of a *scelus*, a moral impurity infecting the whole Roman people, was much in the air (see G. 1.501–14, Horace, *Epod.* 7 and 16).[11]   The political disorders of *E.* 1, the callous soldier of *E.* 9, death (*E.* 5), and above all the passion of love, are all tokens of the disturbing realities against and amid which the poet weaves his fragile symbolic refuge of art and love (see *E.* 10.71, *E.* 5.85).[12]   The fourth *Eclogue* desiderates a

---

[8] For the symbolical fusion of inner and outer realms, soul and action, see Pöschl (above, note 7) 17–18; Otis 230–33, 276–77, 322–28; Francis A. Sullivan, S. J., "Virgil and the Mystery of Suffering," *AJP* 90 (1969) 168–71.

[9] Snell, *passim*, especially 301–2, emphasizing Vergil's union of "poetic reverie, unifying love, and sensitive suffering" (301) and the Vergilian idea of the special sensitivity of the poet who "receives the sympathy of nature . . . because his feelings are more profound than those of other men, and because therefore he suffers more grievously under the cruelties of the world" (302).

[10] Leach 31; Klingner 109 also points out the *Eclogue*'s concern with "etwas Allumfassendes."

[11] See Otis 139: "The dark *amores* and *metamorphoses* of 6 are . . . symbolic of the moral decline (scelus) of the 'iron age' through which Rome had just passed."

[12] Perret 64 speaks of "la fragilité de l'univers arcadien."   See also my essay, "*Tamen*

visionary peace which will obliterate "the traces of our sin (*sceleris vestigia nostri*, 13) and free the world of fear (14). Yet even here, amid the bounty of the pacified nature of the *aurea aetas*, some traces of human sinfulness remain (*pauca tamen suberunt priscae vestigia fraudis*, 31).[13] Thus even in this hopeful mood Vergil qualifies any total optimism about human destiny. *Scelus* recurs in the ninth *Eclogue*, as the shocked pastoral singer recognizes that invaders from the world of war and politics will dispossess and even kill the helpless Arcadian: *heu cadit in quemquam tantum scelus?* (17). War, at the end of the first *Georgic*, reveals the *multae scelerum facies* (G. 1.506).

Like the *Aeneid*, the sixth *Eclogue* correlates internal and external disorder and fixes the source of evil within man. He can, like the poet-shepherd, Tityrus, or like the poet Gallus on Helicon, follow the "orders" (*non iniussa cano*, 9) of Apollo and receive homage from "Apollo's band" (*Phoebi chorus*, 66). Or, like Pasiphae, Scylla, Tereus, he can sink into bestial degradation which finds its external ratification in bestial metamorphosis.

While *Eclogue* 4, like the end of the first *Georgic*, projects the problem of evil upon the history and traditions of man or the Romans generally, *Eclogue* 6, like *Eclogue* 10, examines it within the framework of the private, individual life as writ large in mythical paradigms (Pasiphae, Scylla, Tereus). Yet the sixth *Eclogue* also raises the question of a fundamental flaw in human nature. The myths of lines 41–42 involve a constellation of ideas centering upon human perversity and the loss of a happy state because of human evil:

> hinc lapides Pyrrhae iactos, Saturnia regna,
> Caucasiasque refert volucris furtumque Promethei.

In the story of Pyrrha and her husband, Deucalion, Jupiter destroys the human race with a flood because he cannot endure man's evil ways. The stones (*lapides . . . iactos*) out of which the new race of men

---

Cantabitis, Arcades—Exile and Arcadia in *Eclogues* One and Nine," *Arion* 4 (1965) 254–56; Van Sickle 505, note 30.

[13] Otis 139 stresses "the inverse relation of *Eclogues* 4 and 6," though I think he oversimplifies the relation for the sake of his schematic symmetry: *scelus* by no means dominates *E*. 6; and the Pasiphae episode, though important, should not be exaggerated out of all proportion to the rest of the poem (see below, Section III). We should not forget the presence of Apollo along with the Dionysian Silenus: see Van Sickle 502–5 and below, note 40.

is created are, according to Ovid, a fitting aetiology for the hardness
of his lot (*Met.* 1.414–15):

> inde genus durum sumus experiensque laborum
> et documenta damus qua simus origine nati.

The *Saturnia regna* of 41 are obviously connected with a happy time
of innocence and purity lost in the harshness of a later time.[14] Pro-
metheus in 41, though not necessarily connected with an evil inherent
in man, is yet a reminder of an anthropomorphic cunning and pride
refractory toward the divine order; and his tale is also connected with
the bad character of the female half of the species (see Hesiod, *Erga*
59–82; *Theog.* 570–602). Even more important, Prometheus is asso-
ciated with the development of technology; and technology, as *Eclogue*
4 makes clear (see *E.* 4.18 and generally 18–45), accompanies the loss
of the simple innocence of the Golden Age.[15] The three myths of
41–42, then, all form a cluster of ideas focusing on that antinomy
between innocence and sinfulness which is part of the Golden-Age
theme. Vergil has perhaps deliberately jumbled the chronology of
the three episodes in order to make the reader think about the element
they have in common: the flawed character of human existence and
man's removal from any absolute purity of life or spirit.

These very concise allusions should not be pressed too hard. Yet
combined with the amount of space devoted to Pasiphae and with the
eschatological frame of the preceding two *Eclogues* (in *E.* 5 see especially
57–64), they indicate a recurrent concern with the moral problem of
human nature. By including the myths of Hylas, Phaethon, and
Tereus along with those of Pasiphae and Scylla, incidentally, Vergil

[14] For the theme of the *Saturnia regna* see Becker 321, Klingner 107, Leach 19, and
Otis 138–39. One should recall in this context *Aen.* 6.791–94, 7.45–49, 8.324–27,
and 11.252–54. On the first three of these passages see my remarks in *Arion* 5 (1966)
49–50, and most recently R. J. Rowland, *Latomus* 27 (1968) 832–42 with the bibliog-
raphy cited in note 2, p. 832.

[15] See Jachmann 293; Aeschyl. *PV* 436–506. Many of the arts of civilization listed
in *E.* 4.18–45 belong, of course, in the culture-histories with which Prometheus is
associated, notably sailing (*PV* 467–68) and the domestication of animals (*PV* 462–66).
Agriculture and the city, though not specifically attributed to Prometheus, usually
have a place in such lists; Soph. *Antig.* 335–60; Pl. *Protag.* 322 AD. For possible influence
of the Aeschylean Prometheus figure on the *Eclogues* (somewhat straining the evidence)
see William Berg, "Daphnis and Prometheus," *TAPA* 96 (1965) 15–20.

goes beyond Hesiod's localization of evil in the woman: Vergil distributes it more equitably between both sexes.[16]

The first two poems of the *Eclogue Book* pair war (*E.* 1) and love (*E.* 2) as both manifestations and causes of evil and disorder. War plays a relatively minor part in *Eclogue* 6, but it is not entirely negligible. The Apolline warning against *reges et proelia* (3) may be more than a literary program,[17] if, as we have suggested, the moral and the aesthetic spheres are closely joined. War and love, kept separate in *Eclogues* 1 and 2, are first brought together, though haltingly, in *Eclogue* 6. *Eclogue* 10 will establish a still firmer connection, until, in the *Aeneid*, with its symbolical interplay between the political and psychological, external and internal realms, war and love are coordinate destroyers both of inward and outward order.

For a people destined *paci(s) imponere morem*, war represents the victory of chaos and unreason. *Bella, horrida bella* carry an especially ominous ring in the *Aeneid* (see 6.86, 7.41). Juno, exultant in the triumph of irrationality that she has engineered, bursts open the *geminae belli portae* (7.607–22) and lets in a mood of murderous violence that is not stilled even in the final outcome of the battles (12.945–52). Juno's minister, Allecto, with all her dark associations of the Underworld, is both the inspirer of inward *furor* and the inciter to war (7.324–26):

> luctificam Allecto dirarum ab sede dearum
> infernisque ciet tenebris, cui tristia bella
> iraeque insidiaeque et crimina noxia cordi.

Allecto's sister, Tisiphone, rages amid the futile slaughter and "empty wrath" of the poem's most tragic battle (10.755–61); but she also punishes the guilty souls in Tartarus' *durissima regna* (6.555, 571–72). In the fourth *Eclogue* the disappearance of war accompanies a confidence in the regeneration of human nature, in man's capacity for order and

---

[16] See Witte 571–72, who compares Theocr. *Id.* 13.64–71 and *E.* 6.47 and 52.

[17] Skutsch 193; Wendell Clausen, "Callimachus and Latin Poetry," *GRBS* 5 (1964 193–95. See the valuable reservations of Leach 26–27, with notes 1 and 3, p. 26. Clausen, however, also observes that Vergil's refusal to write about war "was not merely esthetic, it was also (as the reminiscence of the first Eclogue intimates) moral" (194).

happiness. Universal peace is a distinguishing trait of the new moral order and a sign of the conquest of evil. The *puer* will reign over a world made peaceful by the virtues of his father (17).

The sixth *Eclogue*, in introducing war, sets it against two related opposites: the pastoral world and pastoral-poetic *amor*. *Tristia bella* in line 7 may later become something of a cliché, but here it still has considerable force. *Tristis* itself is a strong word in the *Eclogues*.[18] It is used again in connection with the horrors of war in *E*. 9.5: *nunc victi, tristes, quoniam fors omnia versat.*

Vergil places these *tristia bella* immediately against a line in which the language and careful word-order stress the delicacy, fragility, and contemplative peace of his poetic Arcadia (8):

> agrestem tenui meditabor harundine Musam.

The echo of the opening lines of the collection (*E*. 1.1–2) suggests that Vergil is thinking of the *Eclogue Book* and his pastoral world as a whole. It also reminds us of the threats to Arcadian peace presented in that initial poem: *tu ... silvestrem tenui musam meditaris avena: nos patriae finis et dulcia linquimus arva.* Yet in *E*. 6 Arcady is to win out over war. The Tityrus who in *E*. 1 escaped being exiled from Arcadia by making an unbucolic visit to the *urbs*, is here chosen to reject warlike themes. No urban *iuvenis* (*E*. 1.42), but Apollo himself will keep him within the realm of his *pinguis ovis*.

War and Arcadia, epic and pastoral, stand against one another in terms of content as well as style. Having framed their antithetical relation in lines 1–8, Vergil goes on to widen that antithesis by introducing poetic *amor*. If the reader, "caught by love" (*captus amore*), reads this poem, then "our tamarisks and every grove, Varus, will sing of you" (9–11). The *amor* of poetry serves both to create another opposition to war and to establish an antithesis with a different kind of *amor* later in the poem. Yet this *amor*, though it excludes the violence of war, does not necessarily exclude totally the violence of erotic passion (cf. Corydon in *E*. 2 and Gallus in *E*. 10). It thus hints at a dialectical union of the two poles of art which is to be explored more deeply in the interplay between Silenus and Apollo (see 13–30, 82–83, and below, sections III and V).

[18] In addition to *E*. 9.5 see *E*. 2.14 (*irae*), *E*. 3.80 (*lupus*), *E*. 10.31 (the suffering Gallus).

Poetry turns the tables on war in two ways. First, the language of *captus amore* uses a military metaphor (*captus*) for a most unmartial experience.[19]   Second, pastoral incorporates the warrior. The pastoral world threatened by the warrior in *E.* 1 can now enclose the warrior Varus, metaphorically, amid its groves and make his name one of those songful echoes which the exiled Meliboeus of the first *Eclogue* finds such pain in leaving (*E.* 1.5).

At the same time Vergil recognizes that love and desire do not always lead to peaceful themes. Despite Tityrus' own Apolline call to the *deductum carmen*, there will be more than enough (*super*) of others who "desire" (*cupiant*) to sing of war (6–7). Presumably the reader who is *captus amore* in Vergil's sense will not feel such "desires." Here too the poem intimates the divergent paths which love and desire may take.

Deepening and sharpening the opposition between pastoral and epic, Arcadia and Varus, enters the figure of Silenus (13). Mythical, grotesque, fantastic, he stands as far as possible from the flesh-and-blood, responsible Varus.[20]   Not only is he an Alexandrian symbol of poetry, as O. Skutsch has pointed out;[21] he is also a drunken, amorous reveler, a sensualist and a follower of Dionysus.[22]   As part of this opposition, the line which introduces him (13),

> pergite, Pierides.   Chromis et Mnasyllus in antro
> Silenum . . . videre,

belongs fully to poetry (*Pierides*) and to bucolic levity. As a nature-

---

[19] Elder 112 calls attention to *amor* in a similar context in Lucret. 1.924–25, *amorem / Musarum quo nunc instinctus.*   Cf. also *G.* 2.476 and 3.291–92. If Vergil had this passage in mind, the change from *instinctus* to *captus* is a typically Vergilian toning down of Lucretian violence.   Snell 302 stresses the peculiarly Vergilian (and un-Callimachean) emotionality implied in the phrase: "This sympathetic affection is the mark of the poet, and the poet seeks to transmit his compassion to his reader."   Van Sickle 505 notes the possible ambiguity of the *amor* of *E.* 6.10.   In the light of the attitude toward war through the *Eclogues* one may wonder if *tristia condere bella* does not play on the double sense of *condere*, viz. "compose" and "put away": cf. *E.* 9.52 and Holtorf *ad loc.*

[20] See Büchner 1220: "Übermutiger Scherz . . . und laszive Andeutung . . . spielen in diesem Stück, das aus dem Vollen schöpft, wie sonst nirgends in den Eklogen eine Rolle."

[21] Skutsch 194.

[22] For Silenus' connections with Dionysus see Hartmann 39 and 43; James A. Notopoulos, "Silenus the Scientist," *CJ* 62 (1966–67) 308–9.

god, Silenus' sphere is totally removed from the urban atmosphere where war and politics have their seat. His audience, Chromis, Mnasyllus, and Aegle, are doubly removed from Roman political realities by their associations with a mythicized nature and by their suggestive Greek names.[23]

If the ambiguous possibilities of love and poetry are hinted at in lines 6–10, they are fully developed in Silenus. He is an embodiment of the opposites which Vergilian poetry seeks to span.[24] Hence his song will embrace that array of diverse myths which has puzzled interpreters. Here too we should not try to reduce to a bare schematic simplicity what Vergil intended to stand as deliberate multiplicity.

Silenus is central to the poem's fusion of the aesthetic and moral realms. He is a poet whose song moves all nature in rhythmic harmony (27–28). Yet he is also a mythical figure who brings into focus the problematical quality of human nature. He is, according to tradition, part animal himself; yet he is possessed of supernatural powers and mysterious wisdom about life and death.[25] Pindar makes of him a sort of impassioned dancer.[26] His veins are full of Dionysiac spirit, in more than one sense (cf. *Iaccho*, 15; *gravis attrita . . . cantharus ansa*, 17).[27] Yet at the end his song is identified with that of Dionysus' opposite, Apollo (82–84).[28] He has obvious affinities with the natural world and its earthy appetites: witness his offer to Aegle (26) and his

[23] Klingner 106 observes the mythical and unreal quality of the setting. On the effect of such names in the *Eclogues* see also Snell 306.

[24] See my essay, "Vergil's *Caelatum Opus*: An Interpretation of the Third *Eclogue*," *AJP* 88 (1967) 300–4, 307–8.

[25] E.g. Cic. *Tusc. Disp.* 1.48.114; [Plut.] *Cons. ad Apoll.* 27 (115B). For the complexity of Silenus see Hartmann 40 ff., esp. 43: "Weit entfernt von der rohen und lächerlichen Figur, die man später ihn gern machen lässt, ist er ein sehr ernst genommener Gott, dem tiefste Weisheit und Erfahrung eignet, der Musik und Tanz liebt" (43). Also Servius on *E.* 6.13 and Conington's introductory note; Klingner 111, Saint-Denis 37–39, Stewart 197, Holtorf on *E.* 6.14 (p. 190), and Notopoulos (above, note 22) 308–9. The name of Tityrus also has something in common with satyrs, as appears in the lexicographical equation, *satyroi–tityroi–tragoi*: see Hartmann 52.

[26] Pindar, frag. 156 Snell³ = 142 Bowra (Pausan. 3.25.2) ὁ ζαμενὴς δ' ὁ χοροιτύπος. See also Lucret. 4.580–89.

[27] Servius on line 17 notes *attrita ansa, frequenti scilicet potu*. See also the Berne scholia *ad loc.*

[28] It is now generally agreed that 82–84 mark the identification of Silenus' song with Apollo's, not another item in Silenus' song as F. Skutsch and Leo had held: see Witte 572 and Stewart 196.

effect on the Fauns and wild beasts (27). Yet the subject of his first
song is philosophical (31–40); and serious themes of both philosophical
and historical import continue in the stories of Pyrrha, the *Saturnia
regna*, and Prometheus (41–42), with their implications of didactic and
theological poetry.[29]

The scene between Silenus and his captors forms a little drama
illustrating his special relation to the energies of nature and his easy
participation in its mythical life of rustic demigods. Chromis and
Mnasyllus, as Servius (followed by Heyne) suggests, are Fauns or
satyrs;[30] and hence they are plausible acquaintances of the Naiad,
Aegle. *Pueri* (14) and *saepe* (19) emphasize the familiar terms on which
they and Silenus stand. Aegle, "the shining one," is, as her name
might suggest, "the most beautiful of the Naiads" (21). The young
Fauns would bind, though hesitantly (*timidis*, 20), this mysterious
figure; but they are warned off by the somewhat ominous reminder
of his strange power: *satis est potuisse videri* (24): "It is enough to have
seemed able (to bind me)."[31] The allusion to Silenus' sensual appetite
in 26 clearly marks him as one of the gay crew of nature-spirits,
figures close to the earth and fully endowed with spontaneous animal

---

[29] See Stewart 186–88.

[30] Most modern scholars seem to assume that Chromis and Mnasyllus are human
shepherds. Yet their long-continued familiarity (cf. *saepe*, 18) with Silenus, their easy
association with a Naiad, the liberties they take with Silenus himself tell against this
view. It is true that in Theopompus' *Thaumasia* it is shepherds who capture Silenus
(cf. Servius on line 13 and 26 and Aelian, *VH* 3.18). But that tale is only a loose parallel
to Vergil's, and Vergil's freedom in transforming his originals is well known. The
presence of sheep in 85 is also inconclusive. Mortals ran a risk from *seeing* figures
like Silenus, and with the present question is therefore connected the interpretation
of line 24, for which see the next note. For fuller discussion see my forthcoming
paper, "Two Fauns and a Naiad? (Virgil, *Ecl.* VI, 13–26)," *AJP* 92 (1971).

[31] The two possibilities are given by Servius *ad loc.*: (1) "It is enough for me to have
been able to be seen," and (2) "It is enough for you to have seemed able (to bind me)."
Servius also notes that (1) implies that the attackers must be men to whom Silenus
would usually be invisible. This interpretation involves a contradiction (of which
Servius seems unaware) with his previous identification (on 13 and 14) of the *pueri*
as Satyrs. Conington arrives at no solution, though he points to *videre* in 14 as favoring
(1). This point, however, is not necessarily valid, for the specialness of "seeing"
Silenus would seem to contradict the frequent association between Silenus and his
attackers. Further, if the emphasis in 14 and 24 were on seeing, one would expect
the active voice in 24. *Potuisse* could also be taken absolutely (as in *Aen.* 5.231), but
this would not substantially change the meaning of (2).

energies. Yet he is not merely a participant in nature's life. He also stands apart from nature and exerts a creative power over it, as the next lines (27–28) show. We have here a dichotomy particularly suggestive for the nature of poetry, but relevant equally to the nature of man.

Silenus gives an amusing twist to the rejection of *tristia bella* in the proem. Martial language figures in the attack upon him: *adgressi* (18), the chains (*vincula*), and the "bloody" (*sanguineis*, 22) mulberries with which the *pueri* paint his face. But naturally these warlike gestures are all play. Play is the appropriate way to approach such a figure, who is himself playful (*luserat*, 17). Playfulness of a sort also characterizes the Apolline *deductum carmen* of pastoral (*ludere versu*, 1). The language used of Silenus in 18–19 and 22 dramatically heightens the rejection of Varus' *tristia bella*: the attack on Silenus transforms war into its opposite, a bit of light horseplay appropriate to Arcady and its mythical characters. *Grandia* are stood on their heads. Yet there is an underlying seriousness, "Ernst im Spiel," as Klingner remarks of the entire Silenus-scene.[32] By neutralizing war (and the language of war, line 3) through play, poetry offers a restorative perspective in which it can survive the threats posed to it by the unplayful reality which appears in *Eclogues* 1 and 9.

Silenus will sing at length of the terrible passion of Pasiphae (45–60). Yet in his own person he handles love with a healthful frolicsomeness and an open naturalness far from any morbidity (cf. 26).[33] Like Vergil himself in the proem, he answers war (or mock-war) with song and love. The balanced phrasing of lines 25–26 presents song and love as equal, coordinate elements: *carmina vobis, | huic aliud mercedis erit.* Taken together, Silenus'.two gifts stand in a balance of appetite and intellect, sense and spirit, which is, once again, both aesthetic and moral in its implications: it applies both to poetry and to the question of human nature.

The binding of Silenus and the extortion of a song, therefore, are on the one hand poetry's attempt to encompass that mysterious, magical realm where Silenus dwells, to fix its forms in song, to "capture" the essence of nature's movements, and ultimately to relate

---

[32] Klingner 111.
[33] In Pindar, frag. 156 (above, note 26), he is "the Naiad's husband" (ἀκοίτας).

nature's vitality to art's.   On the other hand, it is an attempt to confront and grasp intuitively the duality of human nature and seize through imagination and myth the basic forms of experience.[34]   Silenus may be compared with Proteus in the fourth *Georgic*, also a deity to be bound, also located between man and nature and encompassing all experience (G. 4.387–414).[35]

As in the case of Proteus, approaching Silenus has its dangers: *solvite me pueri; satis est potuisse videri* (24): Behind the laughing face (23) lies the demonic otherness of nature, a realm to which men dare not abandon themselves fully.   But Silenus, through his song, belongs both to humanity and to nature.   He is, in a sense, the subject of his song as well as the singer, or, in Yeats' terms, both "the dancer" and "the dance."

Like his counterpart, Proteus, Silenus points to the elusiveness of the creative energies in ourselves, the Dionysiac in the midst of the Apollonian (cf. 82–84)—imagination, playful spontaneity, love—and to the shifting, iridescent quality in the experiences in which these energies are present.   To touch these Dionysian energies and the sources in ourselves from which they spring, Vergil has, of necessity, recourse to a symbol: the mythical magic of a charmed *locus* removed from time and space (the only indications are *in antro* and *hesterno*), where Satyrs, Fauns, and Naiads drink wine, play, sing, make love.[36] This concern with the shifting quality of our experience and the duality in our nature upon which it is in part founded is perhaps another reason for the poem's emphasis upon metamorphosis.   Silenus' realm, no more than Silenus himself, is not easily held firm; its essence is a kaleidoscopic intensity.

Not only human experience, but the natural world envisaged by the poem is full of movement and instability.   The first part of Silenus' song (31–40) stresses the changes of state in nature.   The soft becomes hard, the liquid elements become firm (33–36), and nothingness (cf. *magnum per inane*, 31) gives way to the solid matter of the

[34] For a different interpretation of the binding-motif see Leach 24–25.

[35] See Klingner 106.

[36] One might compare Hermann Hesse's use of the Dionysian figure of Pablo (a mysterious jazz-player) and his "magisches Theater" ("Eintritt nur für Verrückte, kostet den Verstand") to explore (far more morbidly) this area of experience in *Der Steppenwolf*.

present world. The effect of Silenus' singing is to change the clear, fixed relation between the animate and inanimate in favor of more fluid relationships: he makes the "stiff (*rigidas*) oaks move their tops" (28). He knows how things find their forms (*et rerum paulatim sumere formas*, 36). This mastery of the *rerum formas* applies to the elements of experience as well as to the elements of the physical world. Singing of the creation of the natural world both illustrates poetry creating a world and is a symbol of the encompassing power of poetic creativity. Poetry, like cosmogonic processes, gives form to reality. Silenus, standing between human and animal impulses, a playful dealer in love and war as well as in song, a singer both of nature and of myth, philosophy and love, is the archetype of the poet reaching out to give shape to all of reality. His active power over nature is continued in the active verbs which describe his song (*solatur*, 46; *erigit*, 63; and see note 47, below). Yet his art does not just order nature: it also invites nature to participation and shared joyous fusion (27–30).

The poem provides an analogue to the binding of Silenus which puts that action into perspective, namely the attempt of Pasiphae's Nymphs to close in the bull (55–56):

> claudite, Nymphae,
> Dictaeae Nymphae, nemorum iam claudite saltus.[37]

In the bull, symbol of nature's animal energies from Minoan times on, Pasiphae seeks to possess something of that power with which Silenus is in touch. The Dictaean Nymphs on whom she calls are kindred to Silenus' Fauns and Naiads. But, of course, she fails. Passion *per se* cannot make up for the spontaneous animal life of these nature spirits, nor does it give her a controlling intellectual order through which she could hold such energies within the frame of human life.[38] Instead her passion distorts her grasp on reality, on the relation between man and nature. Her Dictaean Nymphs thus become a part of her delusion rather than an indication of reconciling man and nature. She is too

---

[37] For the attribution of the lines to Pasiphae see Servius *ad loc.* On the scene see Leach 20–21.

[38] It is interesting that where Pasiphae returns in the *Aeneid* there is a not dissimilar contrast between the creative, encompassing order of the artist, his pity, and his mastery of darkness and the maze on the one hand (*Aen.* 6.28–30), and the queen's bestial *crudelis amor*, the *Veneris monimenta nefandae* (*Aen.* 6.23–26) on the other.

willing to abandon the human form.   In this, she stands at the oppo-
site extreme from the daughters of Proetus with whom she is unfavor-
ably compared (48–51), for in one version of their myth they become
mad because of their resistance to Dionysian rites.[39]

Silenus in a sense stands between Pasiphae and Apollo, comprehend-
ing both in his many-faceted nature.   Thus his song is in touch with
the earthiness of Fauns, wild beasts, trees; yet he is compared to Apollo
and Orpheus (29–30).   His *vincula* and the laughter at the *dolum* of
his captors (23) contrast with the serious bondage and *furtum* of Pro-
metheus (42), as his playful sexual proclivities are the lighter side of
what emerges later in Pasiphae, Scylla, Tereus.   Everything about him,
as we first see him, is formless, slack, dissipated (14–17, where note
delapsa and *pendebat*); yet his concern is with a creative ordering of
experience.   The contrast between his outward appearance and his
power of song is itself an attempt to confront the Dionysian-Apollonian
duality of his nature and to resolve what a recent critic has called
"the pure dialectics of passion and form."[40]   The rhythmic play
(*in numerum ludere*) to which he moves the Fauns and beasts (27–28)
expresses just this transcendence of the dichotomy between passion
and form, animal energies and spirit.   *Ludere* is a word which applies
both to poetry and love.[41]   Its poetic meaning occurs in the first line
of the *Eclogue*, and both meanings are perhaps present in the allusive
description of Silenus' past relation with his rustic attackers: *nam saepe
senex spe carminis ambo luserat* (18–19).   Such a being can elicit spirit
from matter (27–28), but also knows of the violence in nature's processes
(cf. *discludere*, 35; *stupeant*, 37).   Communicative (albeit reluctantly,
13–26) of Apolline order, he is also a Dionysian participant in those
experiences which efface the barriers between man and nature: wine
(15–17) and love (26).

Later in the *Eclogue* a mortal poet is also given the power to move

[39] Apollodorus 2.2.2; but this version of the myth has been doubted: see G. Radke,
"Proitides," *RE* 23.1 (1957) 118–19, 123.

[40] Van Sickle 504, who also goes on to assert (505) that *E*. 6 is "the most Dionysian"
of the *Eclogues*.   From another point of view (cf. the proem and Gallus' "Dichterweihe")
it is also the most Apollonian: this too is part of the "dialectic."   For the importance
of Apollo in the poem see Becker 317–18, Elder 115–16, Williams 249.

[41] For *ludere* see Leach 27 with note 1.   For its combination of erotic and literary
meaning cf. Catull. 2.2, 2.9 and 50.2, 50.5.   Poem 50 probably exploits the double
sense.

nature. Linus presents Hesiod's reed-pipe to Gallus with the explana-
tion that Hesiod too could "by singing lead the stiff ash trees down
the mountains": *cantando rigidas deducere montibus ornos* (71). *Rigidas
... ornos* is a verbal and metrical echo of the *rigidas ... quercus* of line
28. Yet there is a subtle difference. There is no mention here of the
playing (*ludere*) of Fauns and wild beasts (27–28). *Deducere* too implies
an element of direction and constraint absent from the simple *motare
cacumina* of 28. Indeed *deducere* can even have the connotation of
leading the trees *away* or *down from* their mountains, removing them
from their natural setting.[42] The Dionysian poet thus seems able
to allow nature a greater measure of its inherent spontaneity, a greater
freedom on its own terms, than the purely Apolline band on stately
Helicon.

III

Love is an important motif in the *Eclogue*, extending from the proem
(10) through the meeting with Silenus (26) to the song he sings and
finally by implication to Apollo at the end (82–83). In love, as in
Silenus himself, Vergil reveals contrasting possibilities and thus poses
from a different point of view that complexity of experience which
the poem seeks to confront.

The two extremes are the poetic *amor* of line 10 and the passion
of Pasiphae (45–60). Pasiphae's tale receives both more space and a
more dramatic coloring than any other single episode (e.g. the second-
person address of 47, 52, 55–60).[43] This emphasis confers a special
importance upon her. She is the fullest embodiment of the problem-
atical side of human nature. Although Vergil's generalizing diction
and the lyrical call to the Nymphs enable him to keep the tale within
the distanced, imaginary frame of Silenus' song, her desire for union
with the bull is the poem's most disturbing instance of the potential
bestiality in man.

The word *amor* occurs only in line 10 and line 46. Art and animal

---

[42] Holtorf *ad loc.* (p. 197), however, explains *deducere* as leading "zum Tanz nach
dem Takt des Flötenspiels," but offers no evidence. For a different interpretation
see Leach 28–29.

[43] See Stewart 179, 189–90.

passion, both forms of *amor*, are thus made to contrast. The one subordinates nature to human imagination, filling the groves with song; the other leads the human imagination to run riot in a lustful and deranged union with nature. Silenus unites the best of both realms. He joins song and love (25–26); and his healthy, playful love (cf. also *luserat*, 19) keeps an exquisite balance between the two extremes.

Amor is usually a negative force in the *Eclogues*.[44] In *Eclogue* 6, however, though the negative side preponderates, Vergil also lets us glimpse other possibilities, obviously in the *amor* of line 10, but also within the myths of Silenus' song.

The story of Hylas (43–44) alludes to a passion which balances Pasiphae's,[45] though neither Theocritus nor Vergil would regard the homosexual attachment, unlike Pasiphae's bestiality, as "unnatural." But through its connection with the Argonauts' expedition, it is also connected with the positive side of close male companionship, wherein, of course, erotic ties may play a part. If Vergil has intensified the emotional and lyrical side of the tale in using the repeated, melodious *Hyla, Hyla*, instead of Theocritus' more formal anaphora, τρὶς μὲν ῞Υλαν ἄϋσεν, . . . / τρὶς δ᾽ ἄρ᾽ ὁ παῖς ὑπάκουσεν . . . (*Idyll* 13.59–60), he has also laid greater stress on the human community by having the cry come from the sailors (*nautae*, 43). In Theocritus it is Heracles, alone in the woods, who shouts (13.58); and there is in fact a sharp and somewhat hostile division between the rest of the expedition and Heracles (cf. 13.69–75). The *nautae* of 43–44 are also to be connected with another group of marine adventurers, the *timidi nautae*, victims of Scylla, with whom the singer commiserates in 77. In both cases we have a hint of the human bonds of fear and cooperation—not just erotic love—which may exist among men involved in a common enterprise and subject to the dangers of supernatural forces. In the Hylas episode, however, this humane companionship is left unfulfilled and helpless as the sailors' cries echo along the empty shore.[46] There is a strong contrast with the controlled and friendly aspect of nature which appears in the songful echoes of pastoral woods in lines 10–11 and 84.

[44] E.g. (in addition to *E.* 10) *E.* 2.68, 3.101, 8.18 and 47.
[45] See Witte, cited above, note 16.
[46] See Leach 20.

The sisters of Phaethon are another partial corrective to Pasiphae's subhuman passion. They exemplify a sisterly rather than an erotic love, a strength of affection which makes them worthy of pity rather than reproach. Hence their love unites them with nature in a more positive way than Pasiphae's. The expression *solo proceras erigit alnos* (63) suggests life and creation.[47] There is even a sad, vague beauty in their metamorphosis: not only is the bark "bitter," but it is "the *moss* of bitter bark," *musco amarae corticis*. This expression is a lovely synecdoche. *Musco* is chosen not only for the sound and the association with water (cf. *muscosi fontes*, E. 7.45), but also for the suggestiveness of the genitival construction which appears to make the bark less real, stranger, even gentler. One is again reminded of that shifting between different tactile senses in 31–40. The metamorphosis is very different from the shocking transformation which Pasiphae desires, and it has a beauty to which Vergil, like Euripides before him (*Hipp.* 737–40), was highly sensitive, as his fine lines in the *Aeneid* show (10.189–90). Though the girls are surrounded by "bitter" bark, that "bitterness" also has associations with poetic creation and enduring life: the shepherd Linus, "of divine song," is crowned with "bitter parsley" only six lines later (68, where *amarus* also stands emphatically at the end of the verse).[48]

After the account of Gallus on Helicon, Silenus returns to the passionate and disastrous type of love in the Scylla and Tereus narratives (74–81). But the last tale of love to which the poem alludes is the story of Hyacinthus in 82–84:

> omnia quae Phoebo quondam meditante beatus
> audiit Eurotas iussitque ediscere lauros,
> ille canit (pulsae referunt ad sidera valles) . . . .

Here Apollo himself is the lover, and his love for a mortal leads to a song which once more fruitfully bridges the gap between man and

[47] Stewart 191–92 tries (implausibly) to find a connection with "the *activity* created uniquely by the dramatist" (192). To Leach 22, "*Erigit*, a word usually associated with some form of mental stimulation or renewal, even with cheering and consolation, seems ironic in this context." I agree about the "renewal" or "cheering," but not about the irony.

[48] On the repetition see Leach 22. For the suggestive connotations of *amarus* see E. 1.77, 3.110, 7.41 and Segal (above, note 24) 306. Perhaps *Doris amara* in E. 10.5 anticipates the tone of sadness and defeat in that poem.

nature and repeats nature's response to Silenus in 27–28. Here too, as in line 10, love and poetry are joined to create an order which overlaps the dualities (man-nature, sense-spirit)of our world.[49] The fusion of Silenus' song with Apollo's in 82–84 is the ultimate statement of confidence in the power of art to unify experience. This confidence is affirmed by the active participation of nature: the valleys carry this plaint of death-tainted love to the remote stars. Celestial rhythms end the poem, but all the gods (not just Apollo) have been involved: *invito processit Vesper Olympo* (86).

In another way too poetry bridges dualities here at the end, for the ending joins the lofty personifications, Vesper and Olympus, with the humble pastoral task of driving home and tallying the sheep (85). *Numerumque referre* (85) recalls the songful echo, *referunt*, in the previous line (84), and also the *numerum* (= "rhythm") with which the Fauns and beasts danced to Silenus' song in 27. Through these verbal parallels the prosaic terms of pastoral life are made to overlap with the wide-reaching metaphors of echoing nature and divine singers. Rather unexpectedly, the "sheep-pasturing" and the "slight song" of line 5 attain the full measure of dignity which the opening lines claimed for them. Even more, the earthy side of pastoral life seen in 5 and 85–86 has been transfigured through the Silenus episode of 13–30 and the scenes of 64–73 and 82–84. The shepherd's humble pastoral realm in the proem has been touched by the power of mythical singers and encounters with hallowed poets on sacred mountains. The rustic Muse whom the poet meditates in 8 gains both in dignity and solidity as we hear of Gallus being ushered into the Muses' presence (cf. 65, 69). As the poem goes on, the groves and tamarisks of lines 10–11 become increasingly a magical realm of Fauns, Naiads, and mountain Nymphs.

IV

Giving form to the formless, reconciling passion and order involve not only poetry and love, but also nature. Throughout the sixth *Eclogue* it is the natural world which stands in antithesis to man as the substance and the symbol of recalcitrant matter. The recurrent

---

[49] For a fuller discussion of the ending see below, Section v.

exclamations of compassion and the adjectives expressing or implying moral evaluation in Silenus' song define the distinctively human qualities of feeling and judging and thereby set into sharper relief the differences between man and nature. We may list here *fortunatam*, *a virgo infelix*, and *tam turpis* of Pasiphae (45, 47, 49), the richly connotative *amarae* of 62, the exclamatory *a timidos nautas* in 77, *infelix* again of Philomela in 81, and *beatus* in 82.

Vergil is careful to keep before us the concreteness and the multiplicity of the natural world. He attains this effect through the presentation of the power of the elements and the diversity of earth, sea, sun, forests in 31–39, through the sounds and suggestive phrasing of some of his descriptions of natural phenomena, like *summotis nubibus imbres* in 38 or *musco . . . amarae corticis* in 62–63, or the carefully juxtaposed adjectives of 53–54. He gives scrupulous attention to different kinds of trees, all enumerated in concrete detail (see 10, 22, 28, 54, 63, 71, 83).[50] Although nature, like almost everything else in the poem, becomes symbolical of the ramifying struggle between passion and order, Vergil also allows it to stand in its own right as the physical setting of our experiences.

He skilfully uses the "pathetic fallacy" to break through the reductive dichotomizing of man and nature. The trees move in response to song (27, 71), the mountains feel joy and wonder (*gaudet, miratur, 29–30*),[51] the river Eurotas is "happy" as it hears Apollo's song (82) and teaches the laurels (83). Yet the artificiality and conventionality of the device keep us aware that this deliberate humanization of nature is only a metaphor, a way of expressing the power of art. Vergil retains the complexity and the truth of our relation to the world in two ways. First, he keeps in the background the ungentled violence of nature which cannot be absorbed into the pathetic fallacy: the deserted shore of Hylas, Pasiphae's bull, Scylla's dangerous sea. Second, by his descriptions of the actual processes of nature (31–40) and the concrete particularity of its phenomena, he allows nature to resist total symbolification and enables it to keep its autonomy and its mystery.[52]

---

[50] See Elder 118. Cf. also the contest of trees in *E.* 7.61–68.

[51] See *E.* 8.3, where the lynxes are *stupefactae* at the shepherds' song.

[52] For a similar point on the bees of *G.* 4 see R. D. Williams, "Virgil," *G & R, New Surveys in the Classics* 1 (1967) 22.

Like Silenus and *amor*, nature is also a focal point of fundamental antinomies. It has both negative and positive aspects. The forests (*silvae*) of line 2 form a place of Arcadian peace where the Muse does not blush to dwell. Related to this image of nature, which is really a metaphor for pastoral poetry and the atmosphere it both needs and creates, are the *agrestis Musa* of line 8 and the tamarisks (significantly "*our*" tamarisks) and the echoing grove of lines 10–11.

Yet forests can also reflect the elemental power of nature's processes and a realm less immediately amenable to the gentle Muse. The earth, when it "gapes in amaze" at the new sunlight (37), and the forests, when they "first begin to rise forth" (39), show a vital potency in nature which contrasts with the gentler landscape, the tamarisks and groves of 10–11 and the *deductum carmen* to which it belongs. So we have the *agrestis Musa* of 8 and the Grynean grove of Apolline song (73–74), yet also the *agri* which the maddened daughters of Proetus fill with their lowing (48) and the grove of Pasiphae's bull (55–56). The shore which resounds to Hylas' cry (43–44), the ominous "deep sea" (76) where Scylla preys on "frightened sailors" (contrast Mopsus' joy in the power of the sea in the preceding *Eclogue*, 5.82–84),[53] the "deserted places" traversed by the transformed Philomela (80), are all reminders of nature's vast and threatening power. The beginning of Silenus' song describes a *mundus* which is *tener* (34), "new" or "fresh." The adjective also connotes the delicacy and gentle beauty of the pastoral landscape where the down of apples, myrtle, rushes, grass, thickets, and trees may be *tener* (*E*. 2.51, 7.6, 7.12, 8.15, 10.7, 10.53). But this *tener mundus* comes into being with a force that awakens overpowering wonder (cf. *stupeant*, 37).

These glimpses of a non-pastoral nature are nevertheless incorporated into a pastoral song. Thus the modest self-limitation and self-deprecation in the proem prove to be a bit of playful, ironic understatement. Vergil here follows an amusing device common in the *recusatio* (e.g. Horace, *C*. 1.6). His *agrestis Musa* shows herself able, after all, to reach beyond her *deductum carmen* with its groves and tamarisks. Indeed not only the didactic verses of 31–40, but the

---

[53] Cf. also the quiet beauty of the calm sea (if that is the meaning of *aequor*) in *E*. 9.57–58, though there too the dangerous violence of sea is in the background: *insani feriant sine litora fluctus* (43).

entire *Eclogue* anticipates the *Georgics* in commanding a broad range of natural phenomena and appreciating nature's violence beside her pastoral charm.

In Silenus' song, as elsewhere in Latin poetry, contact with nature's mysterious power often takes the form of wandering.[54]   Wandering in the mountains can be a sign of disorder, passion, potential violence.[55] The *rara animalia* wandering through *ignaros montis* in 40 belong to a world still in the process of being created and hence in some sense imperfect.   It is "in the mountains" that the luckless Pasiphae "wanders" (52), while her bull's wandering tracks (*errabunda vestigia*) are to be found in the meadows (55–58).   On the other hand, Gallus, "wandering to the streams of Permessus" (64), is led to the Muses' mountain, symbolical center of Apolline order and beauty.   Why should the poet too be a "wanderer"?   Perhaps Vergil means to suggest that poetry is akin to erotic passion in confronting (but overcoming) the threat of disorder and formlessness.   Inspired poetry too, as the figure of Silenus implies, is in touch with nature's vital energies and animal force, but ultimately, unlike Pasiphae, contains the potential for bending them to its will (see 27–28, 71).   Against the nameless mountains of the *rara animalia* (40) and Pasiphae (52) stand the mythical mountains connected with Orpheus, Apollo, the Muses: Parnassus, Rhodope, Ismarus in 29–30; the "Aonian mountains" (Helicon) in 65.

Though nature yields to the Apolline order of poetic form (27–28, 71, 82–84), it also has its own lessons to teach.   It is not simply the utter negation of order.   In this respect it shares the complexity of its poet, Silenus.   The human Pasiphae is inflamed by a shameful and unnatural passion, while the bull's quiescence on the "pale grass" (53–54) stands almost as nature's reproach to her wild search (52).   The bull is not even *captus amore* (10), but *herba captus viridi* (59).   The effect of this animal's ruminatory peace is analogous to the contrast between the regular work on the land and Corydon's *dementia* at the

---

[54] See Lucret. 1.926; Verg. G. 3.291–93. For the theme of wandering generally in *E.* 6 see Elder 118–19, Leach 28–29.

[55] Cf. *E.* 8.41, *me malus abstulit error.* The story of Hylas too suggests wandering: cf. Theocr. *Id.* 13.66–71. Note too the dangerous wandering in remote places in Ovid's *Metamorphoses*: 1.479, 3.25, 3.175, 3.370, 4.292–95.

end of the second *Eclogue* (67–72), a passage which, in fact, Vergil has in mind here (*quae te dementia cepit? E.* 2.69 and *E.* 6.47).[56]   Nature's peace here reads a lesson to human passion, as poetic *amor* and the pastoral echoes do to man's delight in war and warlike poetry in the proem (6–11).

From Homer and Hesiod on, a bounteous and harmonious order of nature is a symbol and a proof of a larger moral order.[57]   This symbolical significance of nature still has validity for Vergil.   At a time when the civil wars—the symptom and expression of moral disorder—have interrupted work on the land, order, peace, and the regular cultivation of nature's goods are easily felt to go together.   *E.* 4.18–45 makes just this correlation between moral, political, and natural order. To that set of analogies *Eclogue* 6 adds order brought through art, while Silenus' cosmogonic song (31–40) and Pasiphae's love expand and intensify the themes of natural and moral order to include nature's remoter processes and man's inner being.

                                    V

It is significant that it should be Vesper, the personification of one of nature's rhythms, that ends the poem.   He commanded (*iussit*, 86) the bringing in of the sheep and then "strode forth" (*processit*), though the gods were still held by the song: *invito processit Vesper Olympo* (86).   *Processit*, like the "rising up" (*surgere*, 39) of the primal forests, is a reminder of nature's autonomous energies.   The Olympians, the gods of light and the day, must give way, and a new power enters to lead in the realm of darkness which does not belong to them. Earlier Apollo had given his commands to the poet (*non iniussa cano*, 9), and the poet has commanded nature (27–28, 70–71).   Now it is nature which commands man.

The poet stands in both an active and a passive relation to the world. He may move trees and animals to his rhythms; yet, as the double nature of Silenus and Gallus' wandering imply, he may also participate in her animal energies.   The end of *Eclogue* 6, like the natural frame

56 See Büchner 1221, Galinsky 178.
57 Homer, *Od.* 19.109–14; Hesiod, *Erga* 225–47.

at the end of *Eclogues* 1 and 2, extends to him the possibility of receiving the boon of her beauty and regularity. The sheep here at the end evoke (as in *E.* 2) the fruitful bond which must exist between man and nature if man is to survive, both physically and spiritually.[58] At the same time the closing in of the sheep (*cogere . . . ovis stabulis*, 85) points back to the Nymphs' attempt to close in the bull (55–56). That effort, within the frame of Silenus' song and thus in the realm of art and imagination, belongs to a love which violates nature's laws. The shepherd's safe enclosure of his sheep, however, reflects an obedience to those laws in the tranquil round of daily labor and implies an objective reality to which imagination and art are ultimately subject.

Love, however, continues to be present at the end in the figure of Eurotas. He is chosen because the river Eurotas is the setting for the tale of Hyacinthus, and Apollo presumably sang this song to assuage his grief.[59] Like Vesper, Eurotas belongs to nature. Yet he also reflects that bridging of the dichotomy between human personality and the impersonality of nature with which the poem has been struggling. He too gave "commands" (*iussit*, 83). Yet his commands resemble not just those of Vesper, but those of the poets, Silenus, Orpheus, Hesiod: he bids the laurels to learn Apollo's song and proves again the harmony between art and nature, between human feeling and the material world.

As the poem's last two lines reflect a return to a harmonious relation to nature's laws, so the Eurotas reminds us of a kind of love that breaks through the antinomy of passion *versus* order. The Eurotas, scene of unhappy love, can be *beatus*. There is an obvious contrast with the *infelix* of Pasiphae and Philomela (47, 52, 81), which in turn measures the difference between Apolline and Pasiphaean love. The latter leaves only an infamous name; the former, though also tragic in its outcome, leaves the "soft hyacinth" (cf. 54 and Linus' flowers in 68)[60] and the beautiful song which makes the Eurotas "happy."

[58] For the "overarching frame" of "bucolic elements" in *E.* 6 see Elder 117–18, with note 36 on p. 124; also Fantazzi 190–91. On the ending of *E.* 2 see Eleanor Winsor Leach, "Nature and Art in Vergil's Second *Eclogue*," *AJP* 87 (1966) 442–45.

[59] See Williams 247.

[60] It may be that the hyacinth in 54 is meant to help prepare for the allusion to the Hyacinthus myth at the end. *E.* 3 seems to use this kind of anticipation (lines 63 and 106–7): see Segal (above, note 24) 297–98.

But the "happy Eurotas" also implies some unresolved antitheses.
Nature (here the personification of a landscape) can be "happy" as
the lover (god or man) cannot; the echoing song brings joy, though
it is the outpouring of grief. *Pulsae referunt ad sidera valles* (84) may
suggest the indifference of nature's vast spaces as well as possible
sympathy. We may note once again the ambiguity of the "pathetic
fallacy" in the poem pointed out above (p. 425).[61]

The rather abrupt and arbitrary allusion to the Eurotas and the
story of Hyacinthus implies that Apollo, the symbol of poetic order,
restraint (3–5), and beauty throughout the *Eclogue*, can also experience
love and pain. Even the Apolline realm can be affected by *amor*.
Poetry and love are thus once more associated in a positive sense as
they were in the proem (10, *captus amore*). The order imposed by
art is not stark and rigid, not out of touch with suffering.

The allusion to Apollo's love confirms in another way the identifica-
tion of Silenus' song with Apollo's. The Dionysian satyr and the
god of the orderly, intellectual aspect of art are identified, not opposed.
Both have a common ground in a susceptibility to love (cf. 26). So
the Apolline poet's "wandering in the mountains" (64–65) and the
"bitter" parsley which crowns Linus (68) have affinities with the pre-
ceding tales of passion and suffering (52, 62), realities which the poet
incorporates but holds in tension with his commanding power of
form.[62]

It is Silenus, as we have seen, who is the chief representative of this
freer, more flexible, more encompassing view of the order under
which art and passion meet and grapple with one another. Hence
it is appropriate that the song, with all its intensity and diversity of
experience, should be his. But by fusing Silenus' song with Apollo's

[61] *Beatus* occurs only here in the *Eclogues* and only twice in the *Aeneid*, both in emphatic
emotional contexts stressing an impossible happiness or a tension between suffering
and happiness: *o terque quaterque beati*, 1.94; *sedesque beatos* of the Elysian fields, 6.639.
Both in this latter passage and in Horace's *beata arva* (*Epod.* 16.41–42) the word carries
associations of an innocent joy far from the world's trouble or the ordinary state of
human existence, but a joy quite remote from present reality. On *E*. 6.82–83 Galinsky
178 remarks, "But the desire for *beatitudo* clashes strongly with the actual subjects of
Apollo's and Silenus' songs, i.e. the *infelices* and *indigni amores* which are described in
gruesome detail."

[62] "Wonder" (*mirari*) may be inspired in the realms of both art (30, Orpheus) and
love (61, Atalanta).

and by hinting at Apollo's experience of love, Vergil deepens these responsive connections between art and passion, the ordering human mind and nature's unbound, wayward energies.

VI

In the light of the poem's confrontation of opposites we may look again at the puzzling appearance of Gallus. Gallus, writer of love-elegies, is potentially a representative of passion in its disordered aspect. It is in this function that he appears in *Eclogue* 10, and we must now briefly consider that poem's connection with *Eclogue* 6.

In *Eclogue* 10 love, in its violent invincibility, defeats the pastoral tranquillity for which Gallus longs (see *E.* 10.36–43). *Nunc insanus amor* of the next line (44) sets Arcadian peace sharply against the reality of passion. With this *insanus amor* are to be compared the other statements of love's power throughout the poem: *sollicitos amores* (6); *indigno . . . Gallus amore peribat* (10); *crudelis Amor* (29); *deus ille malis hominum mitescere discat* (61). Apollo, Pan, and Silvanus all appear, but to no avail. They recall the fanciful mythology of the Silenus scene of *Eclogue* 6, and Pan is painted by the "bloody berries" (*E.* 10.27), like Silenus (*E.* 6.22). The helplessness of Pan and Silvanus only underlines the defeat of the creative power of imagination and art which triumphed so exuberantly through Silenus in *Eclogue* 6.

Though Gallus imagines pastoral amours with a Phyllis or an Amyntas (38–41), his language is that of the disruptive passion of the Pasiphaean type (note *furor, E.* 10.38). Even the quiet he thinks of has an erotic tinge in the first two words of *molliter ossa quiescant*, 33. His thoughts of a serene natural setting (*gelidi fontes, mollia prata, nemus*, 42–43) are vitiated by the vehemence of his emotional vocabulary in these same lines: *consumerer* (43) and *insanus amor* (44).[63]

The potential wildness of nature which appeared in Hylas' shore or Pasiphae's mountains or Philomela's *deserta* in *E.* 6 becomes much more tangible and ominous in *E.* 10. Now it engulfs not just remote

[63] See Fantazzi 183–84 and Perret 64–65, who see in Gallus' defeat the "décomposition de l'univers arcadien" (64): "Mais l'amour est le plus fort, Gallus s'en va, la poésie n'a pu sauver l'un des meilleurs de ses fidèles et pour lui l'Arcadie désormais n'est plus qu'un rêve" (65). Snell 296 underestimates the irony and bitterness in the passage when he speaks of its "sentimental sensuality."

mythical characters, but the "real," living Gallus (see *E.* 10.47–52, 55–56). Gallus will wander on the mountains hunting savage (*acris*) boars (56–57), and he will surround the peaceful Arcadian meadows with hunting dogs (*E.* 10.57; contrast the meadows of *E.* 6.53–56).

In using the violent pursuit of hunting to solace his love, Gallus reveals how far his restlessness stands from the peacefulness of an Arcadian romance. Hunting and love can go together, at least in imagination, for the regular figures of pastoral too (see *E.* 2.29, *E.* 3.75). But Gallus will hunt with a "Parthian bow" (*E.* 10.59). The epithet is more than just decoration. It marks another abrupt intrusion of an un-Arcadian reality, the presence of a foreign and brutal world with which Gallus is in closer touch than the shepherds. The Parthian bow is also a small example of the other threat, besides passionate love, to pastoral serenity: that is, war and politics. War and love, as we have seen, both have their place in *Eclogue* 6. But *Eclogue* 10 expands the negative power of both. Gallus, both a warrior and a lover, is doubly removed from the Heliconian poet led to Apollo's band in *E.* 6.63–73. Gallus' initiation into that Apolline realm in *E.* 6 is both an expression of confidence in the encompassing power of art in that poem and a measure of Gallus' defeat through *furor* in *E.* 10.

Yet Vergil does not end *Eclogue* 10 on an entirely negative note. After Gallus' capitulation (*omnia vincit Amor: et nos cedamus Amori*, *E.* 10.69), Vergil, with a rare intrusion of the first person (*mihi*, 73), declares his own *amor* for his friend.[64] The growing (*crescit*, 73) of this love answers the growing of the trees into which the desperate Gallus carved the tale of his stubborn passion (*crescent illae, crescetis, amores*, *E.* 10.54; contrast the *crescentem poetam*, to be adorned with ivy, in *E.* 7.25).[65] *Amor* in 73, unlike the disruptive, dispersive *amor* of Pasiphae or Gallus' *insanus amor*, has a creative, unifying force, like the *amor* of *E.* 6.10.

As in *Eclogue* 6, Vergil ends the tenth *Eclogue* with evening and with the humble pastoral task of driving home the flock (*E.* 10.76–77). Here, however, the remote mythical figures in the sixth *Eclogue*—

---

[64] The interpretation of *E.* 10.73–74 as referring to "Gallus' love for Lycoris" recently suggested by R. R. Dyer, *CP* 64 (1969) 233–34, seems to me unconvincing, though his remarks on Vergil's rejection of escapism are valuable and interesting.

[65] On *E.* 7.25 see Van Sickle 502–3.

Apollo, Eurotas, Olympus—are subordinated to the small, intimate details of personal life and personal affection. The little basket woven of the slender hibiscus (*gracili fiscellam texit hibisco*) suggests the creative efforts of poetry and recalls the *deductum carmen* of *E.* 6,[66] as the humble goats at the end of *E.* 10 also recall Apollo's command about the sheep in *E.* 6.4–5. The *Pierides* are here too (*E.* 10.72), as in the other poem (*E.* 6.13). But the basket, symbol of poetry, makes creation a much humbler, yet also a more personal, more human, more accessible activity. The power lies not with mythical figures on Greek mountains, but in the hands of the "I" who speaks of his friend and "sits" (*sedet*) quietly at his work.

Here Vergil retreats from the lofty claims of *Eclogue* 6. But he holds to at least one part of the achievement of that poem, the bridging over of the gap between emotional intensity and artistic order. The woven basket, a sign of order and artistic "making," not only answers the violent *amor* which drives Gallus from Arcadia; it is followed by an offer of personal *amor* which grows with the alder in the new springtime (*E.* 10.73–74). This love, growing in the spring, brings together the poet's participation both in emotional life and in the rhythms of nature. One kind of *amor* can cut Gallus off from the peace of pastoral glades and founts; another *amor* can join the poet with his friend and with the freshly burgeoning green of vernal growth.

These alders recall another attempt to connect human emotion and nature. The alders of *Eclogue* 6 are the trees into which Phaethon's sisters are transformed (62–63). In this episode growth and movement are also present, though more faintly than in *E.* 10, as an answer to death: *solo proceras erigit alnos, E.* 6.63; *viridis se subicit alnus, E.* 10.74. In both passages a non-passionate, fraternal, or sisterly love is associated with a union with nature. The fact that Phaethon's sisters are usually transformed into poplars, not alders, enhances the possibility of a deliberate connection between the two passages.

Yet in the calmer, less Dionysian atmosphere of the end of *E.* 10 the poet will retain his poetic and human self-consciousness (cf. *poetam*, 70; *mihi*, 73), while still sharing in the warmth of affection associated

---

[66] On the *fiscella* Fantazzi 184 remarks, "The key word is *gracili*, symbolic of his *carmen deductum*."

with those trees in *E.* 6. But both the *amor* and the identification with nature's rhythms in *E.* 10.73–74 mark a greater concession to the realm of nature, feeling, matter. It is as if the lesson of Gallus' disruptive *amor* has brought the poet closer to a Silenus-like participation in nature than to Apolline-Orphic control over it.

At the same time this very openness of participation in nature raises the possibility that the poet may be more exposed to its dangers and to the mystery of its unfathomed power. The darkness which comes with the regular close of day can be harmful to singer and crops alike: *gravis cantantibus umbra, . . . nocent et frugibus umbrae* (75–76). At the close of *E.* 6, Olympus was unwilling to see the night descend, but there was no sense of a potential danger. Here nature, not art, has the upper hand.

Silenus' play with the Fauns and Naiad of *E.* 6 implied that *amor*, poetry, and participation in nature's life go together. But *E.* 10 is much less sanguine about the power of art to hold passion or nature at a safe distance. Both realities are much less amenable to enclosure in the frame of a Silenus' song, and the "singers" have a healthy appreciation of their subjection to nature (75). Yet the poet's little basket—to which nature, the hibiscus, contributes the material—marks a modest yet courageous gesture of artistic independence. Nature's forbidding desolation and the waves of human passion do not submerge the poet's capacity to realize beauty and love, albeit in little things. The poet of this *Eclogue*, nevertheless, less innocent and less hopeful about nature's power, knows that he dare not expose himself to night's *gravis umbra.*[67]

VII

To return to our starting point, *Eclogue* 6, like *Eclogues* 4 and 10, is concerned with the *sceleris vestigia nostri*, man's capacity for destructive passion in love and incidentally in war (*E.* 6.7). It knows of tragic passion, but incorporates it into the playful, controlling framework of a song sung by a grotesque character immersed in the fanciful

[67] It is part of the deliberate tension at the end of the *Eclogue Book*, however, that these goats are *saturae* and have a *domus* (i.e. unlike *E.* 1). For this positive aspect of the passage see Segal (above, note 12) 261–62, which should now be balanced by the interpretation offered in the present essay.

world of Fauns and Naiads. In *E.* 10 the destructive forces within man, war and love, are in the ascendant; and Apollo—along with Silenus' mythical kindred, Silvanus and Pan—are helpless bystanders of passion's triumph (*E.* 10.21–27).

Eclogue 6 suggests an answer to the tension between order and passion in man by fusing them in the process of artistic creation and symbolically in the figure of Silenus. In *Eclogue* 10, however, the fusion fails. War and passion win out. Gallus, carried to Helicon in *E.* 6, falls a victim to *crudelis Amor* in 10.

This somber end to the *Eclogue Book* is a typically Vergilian acknowledgment of the complexities of existence and of the need for a "dialectical" response to them. Moving from the liberating buoyancy of Silenus' joyful spanning of sense and spirit to the irresistible harshness of *crudelis Amor*, Vergil refuses to dwell entirely in the world of the imagination. The refusal is already implicit in the presence of war and history in *Eclogues* 1, 4, 9, and passion in *Eclogues* 2, 6, 8.

This movement from *E.* 6 to *E.* 10 is itself, in small, a foreshadowing of the poet's development to the stern, tragic realities of the *Georgics* and the *Aeneid*. Yet the *amor* and the green alder at the end of *E.* 10, like the *captus amore* and the rising alders of *E.* 6.10 and 63, imply an ability to face the chaos of human existence without losing sight of the positive potential of human nature and human creativity. Not all emotion need be destructive, not all love selfish and unnatural.

If the defeat of Gallus foreshadows the disastrous *furor* of Orpheus in the fourth *Georgic* or Dido's passion and Aeneas' all too human violence in slaughtering Turnus; if the ominous *gravis umbra*, dangerous to singers, anticipates in its hint of nature's foreignness to man the savage Ciconian matrons who tear the poet apart to vindicate the claims of nature, nevertheless the poet's personal declaration of love for his lost friend anticipates those redeeming moments of melancholy tenderness that illumine the dark sufferings of the *Aeneid*: Creusa at the end of II, Anchises and Marcellus in VI, Nisus and Euryalus in IX, Pallas and Lausus in X.

TWO FAUNS AND A NAIAD? (VIRGIL, *ECL.* 6, 13-26).

In one of the most charming passages in the *Eclogues* Chromis and Mnasyllus, otherwise unidentified, see the drunken Silenus asleep in his cave; with the help of a naiad, Aegle, they bind him with his own wreaths and thus extort the song which occupies the remainder of the poem. Are Chromis and Mnasyllus shepherds, or are they satyrs or fauns? Servius first affirms the latter (*ad vv.* 13 and 14), but then a few lines later (*ad v.* 24) contradicts himself and reverses that judgment. Editors have been divided. Heyne, for example, favored fauns, Conington shepherds.[1] Most modern scholars tend either to ignore the problem or assume (without discussion) that Silenus' captors are shepherds.[2] The question is in need of reexamination. As we shall show, it has some importance for grasping the nature of Virgil's settings and the quality of the Virgilian imagination.

In a poet like Virgil, who deliberately blurs details and is more concerned with atmospheric effect than prosaic exactitude in every detail, absolute certainty in such a matter is perhaps impossible. Yet the evidence of the poem inclines heavily, I believe, in favor of fauns or satyrs.

First, Chromis and Mnasyllus have a degree of familiarity with Silenus which would be unusual for shepherds (18-19):

> nam *saepe* senex spe carminis ambo
> luserat . . . .

Conington cites Voss' observation "that the wood-gods did not commonly appear to shepherds, who were believed to be struck

---

[1] C. G. Heyne, *Publius Virgilius Maro*, ed. G. P. E. Wagner, I⁴ (Leipzig, 1830), *ad loc.* and Excursus II; John Conington and Henry Nettleship, *P. Vergili Maronis Opera*, I⁴ (London, 1881), *ad loc.* Heyne is followed by Albertus Forbiger, *P. Vergili Maronis Opera*, I (Leipzig, 1836), *ad loc.* and T. Ladewig and Carl Schaper, *Vergils Gedichte*, I⁶ (Berlin, 1876), *ad loc.*

[2] For instance, H. J. Rose, *The Eclogues of Vergil*, " Sather Classical Lectures," XVI (Berkeley and Los Angeles, 1942), p. 94; Gordon Williams, *Tradition and Originality in Latin Poetry* (Oxford, 1968), p. 243; K. Büchner, " P. Vergilius Maro," *R.-E.*, VIII A 1 (1955), col. 1220.

with madness by the sight of them." He retorts by stressing, with Martyn, the word *timidis* (20), which "shows the adventurers to have had a sense of their danger. . . ." But surely *timidis* is a playful hint first of Silenus' power and mystery and second of Aegle's forwardness. If there were any real "danger" in seeing Silenus, they could not "often" (*saepe*) have been playfully cozened (*luserat*) out of a promised song. The parallels which Conington cites (*E.*, 10, 24 ff., *G.*, II, 493-4) are not really to the point, since these passages imply no such close association of satyrs and rustic folk as that of the Sixth *Eclogue*.[3]

A second point favoring fauns or satyrs is the presence of Aegle: *addit se sociam timidisque supervenit Aegle* (20). She is a naiad, indeed *Naiadum pulcherrima* (21). Thus she too belongs among the nature deities. The ease with which she attaches herself to her "fearful" companions suggests that Chromis and Mnasyllus stand on an equality with her, i. e. are also forest demigods. It is natural, of course, that they should not share her daring: this lovely creature can be fairly certain of her ability to manage Silenus (cf. 26), as her companions cannot.

So much on the positive side. It remains to answer objections raised against interpreting Chromis and Mnasyllus as fauns or satyrs. Some of these can be easily dismissed. That they are called *pueri* (14) is completely indecisive, as Servius saw.[4] Nor should we be tempted to identify these *pueri* with the small figures on the third-century mosaic found at Tunis and discussed at length by Saint-Denis.[5] That scene does not correspond closely enough to the Sixth *Eclogue* to aid its interpretation substantially. It has, for example, three *pueri*, not two, and a female

---

[3] For the air of mystery and remoteness surrounding these figures cf. Lucretius' lovely "bucolic" digression on echoes (IV, 580-9), where there is a strong (if benign) division between the satyrs and fauns on the one hand and the *genus agricolum* on the other.

[4] *Ad v.* 14: *Nonnulli 'pueri' non absurde putant dictum, quia Sileni priusquam senescant satyri sunt. utrum ergo aetate pueros, an ut ministros et familiares solemus communiter pueros vocare?*

[5] E. de Saint-Denis "Le chant de Silène à la lumière d'une découverte récente," *R. Ph.*, XXXVII (1963), pp. 23-40. Heyne, on the other hand (Excursus II, p. 256), cites a carved gem showing Silenus seated in a cave with a nymph and two satyrs who seem to be listening to him ("Satyris duobus auscultantium similibus").

figure larger than the rest. In any case its plump cherubs have none of the attributes of either shepherds or satyrs and thus help neither interpretation.

It is true that in the *Thaumasia* of Theopompus, which (according to Servius) Virgil is following, the captors of Silenus are shepherds: *regis pastores,* says Servius. Yet shepherds seem not to have been an essential part of the tale. Ovid (*Met.,* XI, 91) has Silenus caught by *ruricolae Phryges,* who could be shepherds. But Ps.-Plutarch (*Cons. ad Apoll.,* 27, 115B, quoting Aristotle), Aelian (*V. H.,* III, 18), and Athenaeus (II, 45 C), all of whom use this story, make no mention of shepherds or country folk. Herodotus, who also alludes to a capture of Silenus by Midas says nothing about the captors (VIII, 138, 3). Even if Theopompus made a point of stressing the shepherds (which does not seem inherently likely in the light of the later treatments of the tale), Virgil's tendency to transform his sources is well known.

There are, in fact, important differences between Virgil's account and that of Theopompus. In the latter the shepherds are only the intermediaries. They lead Silenus to the court of the king, where he reveals his wisdom; and their mission involves considerable risk. The parallel with Virgil is very loose. In Virgil there is no removal of Silenus to a palace and only a minimal sense of danger. Even more important, the captors themselves, not their king, enjoy the privilege of hearing Silenus.

Virgil himself offers a possible parallel to a *pastor* capturing a mysterious and wise nature-deity: the tale of Aristaeus, *pastor Aristaeus* (*G.,* IV, 317), and Proteus in the fourth *Georgic.* Yet Aristaeus is no ordinary *pastor.* His mother Clymene is a sea-goddess, and he is himself a kind of agricultural deity (Pindar, *P.,* 9, 65 and frag. 266 Bowra = Servius *ad G.,* I, 14).

One could perhaps argue that if Apollo can pluck shepherd Tityrus' ear (1-5), then shepherds can bind the mysterious Silenus. But the two narratives belong on different planes. Tityrus' encounter with Apollo is obviously not to be taken literally, and especially because it is an intentional echo of the proem to Callimachus' *Aitia* (I, 21-4).[6] The Silenus episode, on the other hand, is a full-scale narrative which demands to be

---

[6] See most recently Wendell Clausen, " Callimachus and Latin Poetry," *G. R. B. S.,* V (1964), pp. 182-96, especially pp. 193-4.

read as a story, not a pure metaphor or a literary convention.

In still another respect Chromis and Mnasyllus differ from the shepherds mentioned in the poem, *pastor Tityrus* (4) and *pastor Linus* (67). The two *pastores* (who are, incidentally, explicitly defined as such) are singers. Chromis and Mnasyllus, though eager to *hear* a song, are not necessarily creators themselves.

The reference to driving home the sheep at the end (*cogere . . . ovis stabulis . . .* , 85) has been taken as "an incidental proof that Chromis and Mnasyllos were shepherds, as no others are represented as listening to the song" (Conington, *ad loc.*). Yet Virgil does not explicitly say that these are the sheep of Chromis and Mnasyllus. It is perhaps significant that *cogere* has no expressed subject. Virgil does not want us to think too precisely of who the shepherds here at the end are. The tallying of the sheep at the close of day is a conventional and symbolic gesture which is not necessarily to be referred back to the racy narrative of Chromis and Mnasyllus. It is instead a convenient way of closing a pastoral poem, of balancing the sheep at the beginning (*pascere oportet ovis*, 5), and thus of creating "an overarching frame" of "bucolic elements."[7] It is true that the bucolic frame would be more consistent if the audience were the owners of the sheep at the end. Yet we may note that within Silenus' song Virgil is very much aware of the artificiality of the frame and often intrudes the summarizing, editorial comments of the narrator: *namque canebat*, 31; *his adiungit*, 43; *tum canit*, 62 and 64; *quid loquar*, 74; *ille canit*, 84. These phrases serve as indications that the vivid setting of 13-26 is allowed to fade somewhat as Silenus' song goes on, until Silenus himself is only the *ille* of 84 and is fused with the figure of Apollo in 82-6.

Finally, there is the question of line 24: *solvite me, pueri; satis est potuisse videri*. Servius gives both of the possible interpretations:

> sufficit enim, quia potui a vobis, *qui estis homines*, videri: quod ideo dicit, quia hemithei cum volunt tantum videntur, ut fauni, nymphae, Silenus. potest et aliter intellegi: solvite me; sufficit enim, quod talis vobis visus sum, ut etiam ligari possim.

[7] So J. P. Elder, "*Non Iniussa Cano*: Virgil's Sixth Eclogue," *H. S. C. P.*, LXV (1961), p. 117.

If Chromis and Mnasyllus are fauns or satyrs, however, Servius' first interpretation, which requires that they be *homines,* must be wrong. Both the syntax and the context of the line also tell against Servius' first interpretation.

In line 14 Virgil states that Chromis and Mnasyllus " saw " (*videre*) Silenus in the cave. This verb receives no special emphasis (note also *videnti,* in a different sense, of Silenus' awakening, in 21 and *videres,* again unemphatic, in 27). Silenus' emphasis in line 24 is clearly upon the *binding,* not the seeing, as the first word *solvite,* indicates. The sentence should be translated, " Loose me, lads ; it is enough for you to have seemed able (to bind me)." Even for fauns or satyrs there is a limit to the liberties that can be taken with this mysterious figure. If the emphasis were upon *seeing* Silenus, we should expect the active verb, *videre,* i. e., *satis est potuisse (me) videre.* The parallel which Conington cites, *omnis de colle videri / iam poterat legio* (*Aen.,* VIII, 604-5) is again not to the point, for *poterat videri* has an expressed subject (*legio*), which is just what is lacking in our impersonal construction, *satis est.*

With the preceding *solvite me, pueri,* it is probably easier to continue with the same second-person plural subject (" it suffices *for you* . . .") than to supply *me* as the subject of *vider*i (" it is enough for me to have been able to be seen "). The latter is, of course, not impossible. But in so polished and graceful a poem as this it is awkward. Favoring our (or Servius' second) interpretation of the line is also the point made above : if *seeing* Silenus is singled out for special emphasis in 24, there is a discrepancy with the previous ease of intercourse implied in *saepe . . . luserat* of 18-19.

Having established the extreme likelihood that the characters confronting Silenus are fauns or satyrs, we must ask about the significance of this detail.

By introducing fauns or satyrs into his little drama, Virgil strengthens the mythical, unreal quality of the setting in which Silenus sings. The element of unreality deepens our sense of the magic of his song and indeed of the magic of all poetry, which is one of the themes of the poem (see 27-30, 70-1, 82-4). A magical singer who moves fauns, animals, and trees with his song will naturally consort with similar nature sprites. We may recall Lucretius' vivid account of how satyrs, nymphs, and

fauns make music with one another (IV, 580-9). Virgil's
Silenus and his crew suggest that we have penetrated beyond the
ordinary limits of reality and reached that realm of the imagina-
tion in which nature and art are in perfect accord. The highly
fanciful setting of 13-26 is also in keeping with the mythical
material of much of the song itself and with the appearance,
figurative though it is, of Apollo in the proem. It also follows
naturally upon the defiance of reality in the apotheosis of
Daphnis in the second half of the preceding *Eclogue.*

At the same time Virgil has handled his narrative with con-
summate tact. He does not insist upon the exact identity of
Chromis and Mnasyllus, just as he does not actually mention
shepherds in his closing lines. We may be tempted to connect
them with the dancing fauns of 27 (*in numerum Faunosque
ferasque videres / ludere*), but Virgil leaves the details deliber-
ately undefined. It is enough that his two characters carry
with them the magical aura of a charmed world in which trees,
beasts, and mountains can respond to song. This atmosphere of
suspended reality is enhanced by the mellifluous, exotic quality
of the names themselves [8] and by the abruptness of their en-
trance, as if they were part of an intimate circle of which we, by
a special privilege, are allowed a glimpse.[9]

One of the achievements of the Virgilian imagination is the
blending of "the currents of myth and empirical reality." [10]
Thus we can move from the historical Varus to a song sung in
a totally fantastic setting amid fantastic creatures. In the proem
Virgil promised that the groves of his pastoral world will re-
sound with the name of Varus (9-12). It is a characteristically
Virgilian proof of his power to fulfil his promise that another
"real" Roman, Gallus, can be included in a song sung by a
Silenus and heard by two fauns and a naiad.

CHARLES SEGAL.

BROWN UNIVERSITY.
    INTERCOLLEGIATE CENTER FOR
        CLASSICAL STUDIES IN ROME.

[8] See Bruno Snell, "Arcadia: The Discovery of a Spiritual Land-
scape," in *The Discovery of the Mind*, tr. T. G. Rosenmeyer (Cam-
bridge, Mass., 1953), p. 306.

[9] For the significance of the unintroduced character in pastoral see
T. G. Rosenmeyer, *The Green Cabinet: Theocritus and the European
Pastoral Lyric* (Berkeley and Los Angeles, 1969), p. 107.

[10] Snell (above, note 8), p. 283.

CAVES, PAN, AND SILENUS: THEOCRITUS' PASTORAL EPIGRAMS AND VIRGIL'S SIXTH *ECLOGUE*

According to Servius Virgil borrowed from Theopompus the motif of the captured Silenus as the narrator of philosophical or cosmic subjects (Serv. *ad Ecl.* 6.13; see Aelian, *Var. Hist.* 3.18).[1] There are, however, a number of similarities between the scene of Silenus' capture in *Eclogue* 6. 13—26 and the Third and Fifth pastoral *Epigrams* of Theocritus which indicate that these poems, certainly as likely to be familiar to Virgil as Theopompus, may have suggested to Virgil some of the details of his setting.

The Sixth *Eclogue* above all is the place where one may expect a fusion of different sources.[2] The name Chromis in line 13, as commentators note, certainly points back to Theocritus (*Id.* 1.24). Although the transmission of the text of these epigrams is obscure (there is no certain evidence for their inclusion in a collection of *Boukolika* prior to the first century A.D.[3]) and although there is no absolute certainty that they are by Theocritus himself,[4] it is not unlikely that a poet as learned and as interested in Hellenistic pastoral as Virgil would have access to these works. His familiarity with and use of the Hellenistic epigram for the *Eclogues* is proven by his adaptation of Callimachus, *Epigram* 2 Pfeiffer =34 (1203ff.) Gow-Page, to the bucolic setting of *Ecl.* 9. 51—2.

---

[1] See in general F. Skutsch, *Aus Vergils Frühzeit* (Leipzig 1901) 29f.

[2] See especially O. Skutsch, „Zu Vergils Eklogen", *RhM* 99 (1959) 193—201; Z. Stewart, „The Song of Silenus", *HSCP* 64 (1959) 179—205; C. Segal, „Vergil's Sixth *Eclogue* and the Problem of Evil", *TAPA* 100 (1969) 407—35 with the bibliography cited in note 1, p. 407; E. A. Schmidt, *Poetische Reflexion: Vergils Bukolik* (Munich 1972) 261ff.

[3] See R. J. Smutny, „The Text History of the Epigrams of Theocritus", *UCPCP* 15.2 (1955) 75ff.; A. S. F. Gow, *Theocritus* (Cambridge 1950) I. lxix — lxii; U. v. Wilamowitz, *Die Textgeschichte der griechischen Bukoliker*, Philologische Untersuchungen 18 (Berlin 1906) 113ff. Wilamowitz would date a collection in the first half of the first century B. C., which Gow allows as possible, but unprovable, while Smutny stresses the lack of evidence for a collection prior to the latter half of the first century A. D.

[4] Gow (previous note) II.527 inclines toward accepting these epigrams as Theocritean.

The generation of Catullus, Cinna, Calvus had made the Hellenistic epigram the literary property of subsequent Roman writers.

The Third *Epigram* of Theocritus reads as follows (Gow's text, OCT 1952):

Εὕδεις φυλλοστρῶτι πέδῳ, Δάφνι, σῶμα κεκμακός
   ἀμπαύων, στάλικες δ'ἀρτιπαγεῖς ἀν' ὄρη·
ἀγρεύει δέ τυ Πὰν καὶ ὁ τὸν κροκόεντα Πρίηπος
   κισσὸν ἐφ' ἱμερτῷ κρατὶ καθαπτόμενος,
5 ἄντρον ἔσω στείχοντϛς ὁμόρροθοι. ἀλλὰ τὺ φεῦγε,
   φεῦγε μεθεὶς ὕπνου κῶμα † καταγρόμενον.

Pan and Priapus, the latter's head crowned with crocus and ivy, are „hunting" Daphnis as he rests, tired from setting out his hunting nets, on the leaf-strewn earth. In the fifth line we learn that the setting of this „leaf-strewn ground" is a cave. The little poem ends with an exhortation to Daphnis to throw off sleep and flee.

The rapidity of the vignette in sketching the situation and creating an evocative mood of pastoral myth colored by a rustic and unreal eroticism has been justly admired.[5] It is just this mood of myth and imagination which Virgil has created at the beginning of the Sixth *Eclogue*.[6] To enhance his mythical atmosphere he combines the cave setting with the mythical Silenus and the possibly mythical Chromis and Mnasyllus, whom I take to be fauns, not ordinary shepherds.[7]

As in Theocritus' third *Epigram*, there are two figures who approach a sleeping third figure in a cave *(in antro, Ecl.* 6.13). Although Aegle in 19—20 changes the composition of the group from two intruders to three, Virgil makes it clear that she is a special addition, a kind of afterthought (20):

addit se sociam timidisque supervenit Aegle.

As „the most beautiful of the Naiads" *(Aegle Naiadum pulcherrima,* 21) however, she also has the function of reinforcing the mythical element and of adding the erotic note which in Theocritus is carried by Pan and Priapus themselves (cf. *huic aliud mercedis erit.* 26).

Virgil's choice of a setting in a cave is natural enough; but the cave plays no part in the capture of Silenus in any

---

[5] See Wilamowitz (above, note 3) 120—1.

[6] See Segal (above, note 2) 414ff.; Schmidt (above, note 2) 258: „Der Leser ist auf Erhebendes und Geheimnissvolles, auf wunderbare tiefsinnige Enthüllungen gerichtet".

[7] C. Segal, „Two Fauns and a Naiad? (Virgil, *Ecl.* 6, 13—26)", *AJP* 82 (1971) 56—61.

of his Greek sources of this tale[8], nor does it seem to figure in the Silenus mosaic which Saint-Denis adduced as a close visual representation of Virgil's scene.[9] One of the earliest versions of a capture of Silenus, Herodotus 8.138, locates the event in the gardens of Midas.

Silenus' garland, like Priapus' wreath, receives special emphasis *(Ecl.* 6.16):

serta procul tantum capiti delapsa iacebant: cf. lines 3—4 of the Third *Epigram, supra.* Both wreaths also have associations with Dionysus, for ivy is the usual plant of the Dionysiac garland[10], and Virgil specifically mentions Iacchus in the line just before the garland *(Ecl.* 6.15):

inflatum hesterno venas, ut semper, Iaccho.

If Theocritus' Third *Epigram* suggested to Virgil some of the details for the attack of two rustic demigods (assuming Chromis and Mnasyllus to be fauns) upon a sleeping pastoral figure in a cave, the Fifth *Epigram* may have suggested the connection of that cave setting with the theme of song. In a scene possibly imitated from the beginning of the First *Idyll (Id.* 1ff. and 15ff.) the speaker imagines a small group of herdsmen, including the cowherd Daphnis, who will sing and play their instruments, a gathering which also resembles *Idyll* 7.71ff. The setting is „a shaggy oak behind a cave" where they will „deprive the goat-mounting Pan of sleep":

Λῆς ποτὶ τᾶν Νυμφᾶν διδύμοις αὐλοῖσιν ἀεῖσαι
ἁδύ τί μοι; κἠγώ πακτίδ' ἀειράμενος
ἀρξεῦμαί τι κρέκειν, ὁ δὲ βουκόλος ἄμμιγα θέλξει
Δάφνις κηροδέτῳ πνεύματι μελπόμενος.
5 ἐγγὺς δὲ στάντες λασίας δρυὸς ἄντρου ὄπισθεν
Πᾶνα τὸν αἰγιβάταν ὀρφανίσωμες ὕπνου.

The exact relation of the singers to the cave remains rather vague[11], but the blend of a rustic setting with pastoral mythology, the awakening of a rustic god from sleep, and the

---

[8] See Aelian, *Var. Hist.* 3.18; Xen., *Anab.* 1.2.13; Cic., *Tusc. Disp.* 1.114 (Crantor); Plut., *Consol. ad Apoll.* 27, 115Bff. (Aristotle and Crantor); Paus. 1.4.5; Ovid, *Met.* 11.90ff. For further references see Frazer *ad* Paus. 1.4.5 and E. Rohde, *Der griechische Roman und seine Vorläufer*[3] (Leipzig 1914) pp. 219—20 with notes 3—4.

[9] E. de Saint-Denis, „Le chant de Silène à la lumière d'une découverte récente", *RPh* 37 (1963) 23—40, esp. 35ff.

[10] E. g. Pratinas 708.15 Page; *h. Hom.* 21.1; Aristoph., *Thesm.* 987 and 999f.; Eurip., *Bacch.* 81 with the note of E. R. Dodds. *Euripides, Bacchae*[2] (Oxford 1960) *ad loc.*; Kurt Lembach, *Die Pflanzen bei Theokrit,* Bibl. d. klass. Altertumswiss., N. F., 2 Reihe, 37 (Heidelberg 1970) 119—20.

[11] Gow (above, note 3) *ad Epigram* 5.5.

presence of a cave all suggest affinities with the Silenus scene of the Sixth *Eclogue*. The magical „charm" (θέλξει, 3) of Daphnis' song reminds us that Daphnis, like Silenus, is a famous singer whose music creates a special sympathy between man and nature (cf. *Ecl.* 6.27—30 and *Id.* 1.71ff., 115ff., *Id.* 7.75—7).

Virgil, of course, has individual touches not to be found in the Theocritean epigrams: the amusing drunkenness of Silenus, the painting of his face with mulberry juice, the subtle mixture of humor and dangerous mythic power in his reaction to the garlands which bind him *(Ecl.* 6.23—4). But even if we cannot definitively prove that these two Epigrams influenced Virgil's conception of the capture of Silenus, the comparison shows how much of this kind of playful mythological-pastoral poetry there was in the literary tradition for Virgil to draw upon and how fully he was able to incorporate the fanciful mythology and light eroticism of such poetry into the large and complex dimensions of his own bucolic poetry, with its more serious and more comprehensive concern with myth, art, and love.*

Brown University.   *C. Segal.*

---

* Since the submission of this paper there has appeared a valuable re-examination of Virgil's use of Silenus in the Sixth *Eclogue:* M. Hubbard, „The Capture of Silenus", *PCPhS* 201 (N. S. 21) (1975) 53—62. Mrs. Hubbard's doubts about Virgil's possible use of Theopompus (pp. 56—57) seem to me to rest on subjective and uncertain grounds. Her arguments in favor of the influence of Cicero's philosophical works are plausible, but in any case do not change the conclusions reached in my essay.

Index

Acheron, 25, 51

Achilles, 85-86, 91; and *Idyll 1*, 43; and *Idyll 11*, 217

Actium, 278

Adonis, and *Idyll 1*, 28, 39, 42; and *Idyll 3*, 66-72; and *Idyll 15*, 33, 50; and iynx, 75

Aegle, and *Eclogue 6*, 330-35; significance of name, 309-10

Aelian, and iynx, 76; *V.H.* and *Eclogue 6*, 332, 336

Aeneas, 85; and *Eclogue 6*, 329

Aeschylus, 44; nature in, 211; on truth and *plattein*, 170-71

Agamemnon, sceptor of, 162

Ajax, and riddles in *Eclogue 3*, 256; and Theocritean Daphnis, 211

Alexandrian Erotic Fragment, and *Idyll 2*, 79n23

Allecto, in *Aeneid*, 306

Alpers, P., on pastoral, 6, 10, 13, 15, 19

amor, 307-308, 315-16, 319-20, 325ff.; *see also eros*

Anchises, and *Idyll 1*, 202, 207; *Homeric Hymn to Aphrodite* and *Idyll 7*, 131

Anyte, and *locus amoenus*, 229-30

Aphrodite, 64; and herdsman, 131; and *Idyll 1*, 27-30, 34-35, 38-40, 42, 52-53, 171, 180, 202, 207, 214, 218-19; and *Idyll 2*, 80, and *Idyll 3*, 66-72; and iynx, 75

Apollo, 23, 86; and *Eclogue 3*, 247, 249, 251-53, 255-58, 262, 264; and *Eclogue 6*, 304, 307, 309, 312, 314-15, 317-19, 321-25, 327-29, 332-33, 335; and *Idyll 7*, 122

Apollodorus, and myth of Adonis, 69

Apollonius of Rhodes, and *Idyll 1*, 51; and *Idyll 7*, 168; and *Idyll 13*, 56-58; *Argonautica*, 50, 56-58

Aratus, 157, 178; *Phaenomena* and *Eclogue 3*, 244, 250

Arcadia, 14, 22, 24, 144, 179, 216, 220, 227, 237, 260, 285-89, 298nn17-18, 307-308, 319, 327; and *Idyll 1*, 30, 34, 40

archaic elements, and Theocritus, 50

Archimedes, orrery of, and riddles in *Eclogue 3*, 254

Arethusa, in *Idyll 1*, 29

Argonauts, and *Idyll 13*, 60, 61

Aristaeus, and *Eclogue 6*, 332

Aristophanes, 6, 72; *Birds* and poetic landscape, 229; symposia in, and *Idyll 7*, 141

Artemis, *Hymn to*, of Callimachus, 226

Asclepiades, 178; and *Idyll 7*, 167-68, 173

Astarte, 68

Athena (*Odyssey*), and *Idyll 7*, 121

Athenaeus, 204; and *Eclogue 6*, 332

Aulus Gellius, on Virgil, 288

Bardon, H., on pastoral, 120

Becker, C., on *Eclogue 4*, 268

Bellerophon (*Iliad VI*), and *Idyll 1*, 43

Berg, W., on Virgil, 12

Bergson, Henri, 230

Bignone, E., on *Idyll 4*, 94-95, 97

biographical fallacy, 271

Bion, 9; *Epitaphios Adonidos*, 70, 226

Boileau, 3, 5

boukolos, 8; and *Idyll 1*, 40, 42

bricolage, 7

Brundisium, peace of, 266

bucolic, 8, 172

bucolic masquerade, and literary criticism, 111-14

bucolicize, 135-36, 157, 171, 173, 186-87

Byblis, and *Idyll 7*, 145

Caesar, Julius, and *Eclogue 9*, 293

Callimachus, 86, 115, 121, 123; *Aitia*, 70, 112; *Aitia* and *Eclogue 6*, 332; and *Idyll 1*, 49; and *Idyll 4*, 88; and *Idyll 7*, 112, 168; and Muses, 163; and Virgil, 302; *Epigram 22*, 61, 226; *Epigrams*, 336; *Hymn to Artemis*, 226

Calvus, and Hellenistic epigram, 337

Calypso, 158-59, 206; and *Idyll 7*, 220

Cameron, A., on *Idyll 7*, 112, 121-22

Cartault, A., on *Eclogue 3*, 245, 247

Library of Congress Cataloging in Publication Data

Segal, Charles, 1936-
  Poetry and myth in ancient pastoral.

  (Princeton series of collected essays)
  Bibliography: p.
  Includes index.
  1. Pastoral poetry, Classical—History and
criticism.   2. Theocritus—Criticism and inter-
pretation.   3. Virgil—Criticism and interpretation.
I. Title.
PA3022.P3S4   884'.01   81-47155
ISBN 0-691-06475-X   AACR2
ISBN 0-691-01383-7 (pbk.)

                                        Rev.